Palgrave Studies in Sustainable Business In Association with Future Earth

Series Editors
Paul Shrivastava
Pennsylvania State University
University Park, PA, USA

László Zsolnai
Corvinus University of Budapest
Budapest, Hungary

Sustainability in Business is increasingly becoming the forefront issue for researchers, practitioners and companies the world over. Engaging with this immense challenge, Future Earth is a major international research platform from a range of disciplines, with a common goal to support and achieve global sustainability. This series will define a clear space for the work of Future Earth Finance and Economics Knowledge-Action Network. Publishing key research with a holistic and trans-disciplinary approach, it intends to help reinvent business and economic models for the Anthropocene, geared towards engendering sustainability and creating ecologically conscious organizations.

More information about this series at
http://www.palgrave.com/gp/series/15667

Thomas Walker • Dieter Gramlich
Mohammad Bitar • Pedram Fardnia
Editors

# Ecological, Societal, and Technological Risks and the Financial Sector

palgrave
macmillan

*Editors*
Thomas Walker
Department of Finance
John Molson School of Business
Concordia University
Montreal, Canada

Dieter Gramlich
Department of Banking
Baden-Wuerttemberg Cooperative
State University
Heidenheim, Germany

Mohammad Bitar
Nottingham University
Business School
University of Nottingham
Nottingham, UK

Pedram Fardnia
John Molson School of Business
Concordia University
Montreal, QC, Canada

ISSN 2662-1320 ISSN 2662-1339 (electronic)
Palgrave Studies in Sustainable Business In Association with Future Earth
ISBN 978-3-030-38857-7 ISBN 978-3-030-38858-4 (eBook)
https://doi.org/10.1007/978-3-030-38858-4



This Palgrave Macmillan imprint is published by the registered company Springer Nature Switzerland AG.
The registered company address is: Gewerbestrasse 11, 6330 Cham, Switzerland

# Preface

The world is facing various new challenges stemming from ecology, society, and technology. Climate change and cyber-attacks (among others) undoubtedly affect the financial sector as well as unresolved problems within the financial system itself. However, the identification, measurement, and management of these emerging risks among academics, financial practitioners, and regulators are still at a developmental stage. Our edited book will shed light on this topic by examining the unique measurement and modeling challenges associated with each of these risks, the connectivity of emerging risks, and their interaction with finance. Specifically, it will (1) identify and classify evolving risks from outside (and inside) the financial system, (2) explore approaches to assess and operationalize emerging risks in finance, and (3) show how they affect the financial system (thereby exploring the vulnerability of financial institutions and financial markets).

A comprehensive analysis of emerging risks in finance should—as an extension—provide the basis for the development of appropriate risk management techniques. Approaches may include both actions to protect against the threats from emerging risks and measures to benefit from opportunities arising from upcoming changes. We address this topic from the perspective of institutional investors who engage in the risk and return management of financial firms as well as from the perspective for whom emerging risks create new challenges. Additionally, every risk factor discussed in this book creates unique challenges for individuals and institutions as well as for our society as a whole, and traditional risk management approaches are typically inadequate in addressing them.

The book takes account of a recent paradigm shift regarding financial systems. In recent years, new ways of thinking and doing business have emerged among academics, practitioners, and policymakers, many of who no longer consider the financial system a closed and isolated system. Rather, these parties often argue that the financial system has (or should) evolve into a larger socio-ecological system where finance, social wellbeing, natural resources, and planetary health are highly interlinked. Whereas the financial system has traditionally been considered as a responsive system that is exposed to and reacts to external challenges, financial institutions and markets are increasingly considered as primary actors who affect and influence the surrounding natural and social system by means of their actions and/or inactions. Under this theory, the world cannot move toward an overall balance (sustainability), address climate change, reverse environmental degradation, and improve human wellbeing without aligning the financial system with sustainable development goals.

Academics, policymakers, and practitioners are currently developing new tools and methods to include geopolitical, socio-political, and economic factors in the way they evaluate and make business decisions. However, these concepts are still in their infancy, and many of the proposed ideas and approaches have been highly controversial. Our book fills a gap in the literature, provides important insights from experts in both academia and industry, takes a transdisciplinary approach, and explores a wide range of topics in the field.

| | |
|---|---|
| Montreal, QC, Canada | Thomas Walker |
| Heidenheim, Germany | Dieter Gramlich |
| Nottingham, UK | Mohammad Bitar |
| Montreal, QC, Canada | Pedram Fardnia |

# Acknowledgments

We acknowledge the financial support provided through the Autorité des marchés financiers and the David O'Brien Centre for Sustainable Enterprise at Concordia University. In addition, we greatly appreciate the research and administrative assistance provided by Kalima Vico and Tyler Schwartz as well as the excellent copy-editing and editorial assistance we received from Adele Dumont-Bergeron and Julie Elizabeth Brown. Finally, we feel greatly indebted to Arlene Segal, Joseph Capano, Stephane Brutus, Anne-Marie Croteau, and Norma Paradis (all at Concordia University) who in various ways supported this project.

# Contents

# Notes on Contributors

**Amr Addas** is an adjunct professor and director of the Van Berkom Investment Management Program at the John Molson School of Business at Concordia University, Montreal, and a member of the faculty for the Sustainable Investment Professional Certificate (SIPC) program. He has taught at McGill University and Sherbrooke University. Together with his partners at the Sustainable & Impact Finance Institute (SAIFI), he offers ESG investment integration training to corporates and financial institutions. He obtained his MBA degree from the University of Michigan at Ann Arbor. He is an active member of the CFA Institute.

**Mohd Hafdzuan Bin Adzmi** is in the Ph.D. program at the Graduate School of Global Environmental Studies at Sophia University, Japan. He has ten years of experience in governmental departments focusing on the promotion of sustainable sources including the Biofuel Group at the Primary Industries and Sustainable Energy Division at the Ministry of Energy, Science, Technology, Environment, and Climate Change in Malaysia. He holds a Master's degree in climate change from the University of East Anglia, UK. His research interests lie in institutions, organizations, stakeholders, and their responses to climate change policies in the energy sector.

**Sureyya Burcu Avci** holds a Ph.D. degree in business administration from Ozyegin University, Istanbul, Turkey. She has been teaching and conducting financial research at several academic institutions. She is teaching finance at Sabanci University. Her research focuses on corporate finance, corporate ethics, insider trading, and sustainability. Her research activities are interdisciplinary and connect finance, economics, law, and business.

**Sandra Batten** is a senior economist at the Bank of England. Her research focuses on productivity growth, and in particular the role of technological innovation and international trade. She is also interested in the implications of climate change for the macroeconomy. She holds both a Ph.D. and an M.Sc. degree in econometrics from the London School of Economics (LSE).

**Mohammad Bitar** is Assistant Professor of Finance at Nottingham University Business School, UK, where he teaches banking and FinTech courses. Previously, he taught at the John Molson School of Business at Concordia University, Canada, and studied Finance at Grenoble Alps University, France.

**Robert E. Bopp** is the director of Business Development Financial Services at Ernst & Young, Germany. He holds an M.S. degree in multinational commerce from Boston University, and an M.A. in international relations and diplomacy from AGS in Paris, France. In his day-to-day business activities, he focuses on regulatory required governance, risk, and compliance management. He collaborates with the German Hub for Sustainable Finance and the Green Finance Initiative Frankfurt, among others. He contributes regularly to journals and newspapers such as the *German Börsen-Zeitung*, *Handelsblatt*, and *FAZ* on climate change and sustainability issues as well as on reputation and the impact of a carbon sensitive industry transformation.

**Martin Boyer** holds the Power Corporation of Canada Research Chair in Insurance and Pension Plans at HEC Montréal. He serves as associate editor of the *Journal of Risk and Insurance.* Boyer holds a Ph.D. degree in insurance and risk management from the University of Pennsylvania. He is a current member of the Risk Theory Society. He has published numerous articles on a large variety of insurance topics and has co-authored many case studies in finance and financial economics.

**Michèle Breton** holds a BSc.A. (industrial engineering), an M.Ing. (operations research), and a Ph.D. degree (computer science). She is presently Professor of Management Science at HEC Montréal. Her research interests include dynamic game theory applied to the energy, environment, and finance sectors, about which she has published more than 100 scientific papers. She is a member of the Royal Society of Canada.

**Huiying Cai** is in the Ph.D. program at the Graduate School of Global Environmental Studies at Sophia University in Japan. Cai obtained her Bachelor's degree in finance from Sichuan International Studies University (China), and her Master's degree in Finance from the University of St. Andrews (UK). She is presently a research assistant at the United Nations University Institute for the Advanced Study of Sustainability (UNU-IAS). Her research in the Ph.D. program is related to the evaluation of stranded assets in the coal power industry in China, the transition to a low carbon economy, and ESG.

**Bradly J. Condon** is the WTO Chair Professor of International Trade Law and a founding director of the Centre for International Economic Law at the Instituto Tecnológico Autónomo de México (ITAM), Mexico City, where he teaches international economic law. He also serves as a senior fellow at the Tim Fischer Centre for Trade and Global Finance at Bond University, Australia. He has published numerous academic articles in international journals and eight books. He has served as a peer reviewer for leading academic publishers and journals, including Cambridge University Press, Oxford University Press, and the *World Trade Review*.

**Shaen Corbet** is Associate Professor of Finance at Dublin City University Business School in Dublin, Ireland, previously working as a commodities trader and economist with the Central Bank of Ireland. He has published numerous research papers in top-quality internationally recognized journals and is a member of multiple interdisciplinary working groups. He is actively involved in the fields of financial economics, financial technology (FinTech), financial markets, banking, crisis and financial stress measurement, crisis management, and the effects of crises on the financial markets.

**Carmela Cucuzzella** is an associate professor in the Design and Computation Arts Department and is holder of the Concordia University Research Chair in Integrated Design, Ecology, and Sustainability for the Built Environment. Her research work is framed within the broad domain of design studies where she investigates questions of sustainable design for urban living. She has expertise in environmental and social life cycle analysis, in green building rating systems, and in design and architecture.

**Adele Dumont-Bergeron** is an MA student in English literature and creative writing at Concordia University, Montréal. She serves as a research assistant for Concordia's Finance Department. She recently completed a research project about plastic taxes and has co-authored an article, soon to be published, on the topic. In her department, she has won the Compton-Lamb Memorial Scholarship and has been awarded a fellowship to pursue her work in literature. She has presented and published her work at several literary conferences. Her interests include sustainability, feminism, and modernity.

**Allan Dwyer** is a CFA charterholder and a professor of finance at Mount Royal University in Calgary, Canada. He is interested in sovereign debt, alternative measures of credit quality, financialization, and financial crises in history.

**Pedram Fardnia** is a Ph.D. candidate and staff researcher at the John Molson School of Business at Concordia University, Canada. Among other things, his research focuses on corporate governance issues within the finance sector, with a specific focus on the aviation industry.

**Pascal François** is Professor of Finance at HEC Montréal, Director of the Canadian Derivatives Institute, and co-editor of the journal *Finance*. His research focuses on contingent claims analysis applied to corporate finance. Among others, his work has been published in the *Journal of Business*, the *Journal of Financial and Quantitative Analysis*, and the *Journal of Banking and Finance*. He is the author of three finance textbooks and holds a joint Ph.D. degree from Sorbonne University and ESSEC Business School.

**Dieter Gramlich** is Professor of Banking & Finance at DHBW—Baden-Wuerttemberg Cooperative State University in Heidenheim, Germany, where he serves as Head of the Banking Department. He previously studied at the University of Mannheim and was an interim professor and Chair of Banking and Finance at the University of Halle in Germany.

**Constantin Gurdgiev** is Associate Professor of Finance with the Middlebury Institute of International Studies (USA) and an adjunct professor with Trinity College Dublin (Ireland). His professional experience and research are concentrated in the fields of investments, and geopolitical and macroeconomic risk and uncertainty analysis. He is a co-founder of two European charities, and advises a number of FinTech start-ups in Europe and the US.

**Karsten Haustein** works as a postdoctoral researcher at the School of Geography and Environment at the University of Oxford. He received his Ph.D. degree in geosciences from the Polytechnical University of Catalonia in Barcelona, Spain, and holds an M.Sc. degree in meteorology from the University of Leipzig, Germany. Haustein's research interests are in the field of climate modelling and atmospheric aerosols including their direct and indirect effects on clouds and radiation.

**Matthias Horn** is a research and teaching assistant in the Department of Finance at Bamberg University, Germany, where he received his Ph.D. degree in 2018. His fields of interest include empirical and behavioral finance, risk management, asset pricing, household finance, and FinTech.

**Tashfeen Hussain** is Assistant Professor of Finance at Mount Royal University in Calgary, Canada. He received his Ph.D. degree in finance from Queen's University in Kingston, Ontario. His research interests include the interactions between firms and debt markets, creditor monitoring, and corporate fraud, as well as emerging issues such as the increased emphasis on corporate social responsibility, the ubiquity of fake news, and terrorism.

**Stéfanie D. Kibsey** specializes in advancing sustainability research, education, and industry best practices. She holds a bachelor's degree from McGill University and an interdisciplinary Master of environmental studies from the University of Waterloo, Canada. Previously at Concordia University, she coordinated the programs, activities, and research projects of the David O'Brien Centre for Sustainable Enterprise and helped shape the curriculum for the Sustainable Investment Professional Certification program offered by the University. Her interests include environmental change, water issues, and the science-practice-policy interface.

**Stephen Kibsey** has over 30 years of experience as an investment professional. Now retired, he worked for 21 years at the Caisse de Dépôt et Placement du Québec, most recently as a vice-president in the Investment Stewardship Group. He has for many years been at the forefront of responsible investment through his involvement with the creation of the Sustainable Investment Professional Certificate at Concordia

University. He lectures at Concordia University and at McGill University. He has a seat on the Investment Committee and Risk Sub-committee of the McConnell Foundation in Montréal.

**Cary Krosinsky** is an independent author, educator, and advisor on sustainability and investing as a positive driver of change for the benefit of shareholders and society. He teaches two seminars at Yale University, as well as an MBA class at the University of Maryland. He has taught at Columbia University and has been an advisor for Cambridge University's Investment Leaders Group. He is the editor of the *Journal of Environmental Investing*. Krosinsky serves on the board of the Carbon Tracker Initiative and is a director of the Network for Sustainable Financial Markets.

**James Leaton** is vice-president at Moody's Investor Services in London. He is leading the global development of a framework for assessing carbon transition risk at the credit rating agency. He is the lead author of the Unburnable Carbon series of research published by Carbon Tracker. He has experience in partnering with a number of energy institutes, including the International Energy Agency and the Grantham Institute at Imperial College, London. He has worked with PricewaterhouseCoopers as a climate and sustainability consultant and the World Wildlife Fund as a senior policy advisor. He has an M.Sc. in environmental technology from Imperial College, London.

**Andreas Oehler** holds the chair of finance at Bamberg University, Germany, since 1994. He received his Ph.D. degree at the University of Mannheim and his Habilitation degree at the University of Hagen. He has published widely, in particular in the area of credit risk management, banking, behavioral and empirical finance, as well as investor protection. Since 2012 he is director of the Research Center "Household Finance & Financial Literacy." He is a member of various expert committees such as chairman of the board, Stiftung Warentest, Germany's leading product-testing institute.

**Jordan Owen** graduated from McGill University in 2016, earning a Bachelor of Commerce (with honors) in investment management. Upon graduation, he joined Mondev Construction, managing four projects with a cumulative construction budget of over US$80 million. He is pursuing a dual Master's degree in real estate development and city planning at the Massachusetts Institute of Technology (MIT), with the intention to research geospatial targeting of real estate opportunities and quantifying the value of design in real estate.

**Peter Pfleiderer** studied physics at the Free University in Berlin, Germany. After writing his Master's thesis about persistent weather conditions at the Potsdam Institute for Climate Impact Research, he commenced working as a research analyst at Climate Analytics. He is a Ph.D. candidate at Humboldt University, Berlin, where he conducts research on extreme weather events and their attribution to climate change.

**Quintin Rayer** holds a Ph.D. degree in physics from the University of Oxford, is a fellow of the Institute of Physics, a chartered fellow of the Chartered Institute for Securities & Investment (CISI), a chartered wealth manager, and a graduate of the Sustainable Investment Professional Certification (SIPC) program at Concordia University. With experience in actuarial consultancy and wealth management, he founded P1's ethical investment proposition in January 2017.

**Tapen Sinha** is the ING Commercial America Chair Professor at the Instituto Tecnológico Autónomo de México (ITAM) in Mexico City. He is also a special professor at the School of Business, University of Nottingham, UK. He holds a Ph.D. in economics from the University of Minnesota. He is the founder-director of the International Center for Pension Research, ITAM, and an associate of the Centre for Risk and Insurance Studies at the University of Nottingham. Sinha has published over one hundred papers and five books. He has been a consultant for a number of multinational companies and governments on different continents.

**Carla Santos Skandier** is a Brazilian attorney who holds an LLM in energy law from Vermont Law School. She has experience in environmental protection enforcement and community renewable projects. In 2015, she joined The Democracy Collaborative's Next System Project, where her work focuses on mitigating climate change through systemic solutions.

**Rhiannon Sowerbutts** is a senior economist in the Macroprudential Strategy and Support Division of the Bank of England. She received her Ph.D. degree in economics from Universitat Pompeu Fabra in Barcelona, Spain. During her Ph.D. studies, she was an intern at the Bank of England and at the International Monetary Fund (IMF). Her research interests include macroprudential policy, regulatory arbitrage, international banking flows, banking, and banking crises.

**Masachika Suzuki,** Ph.D., is a professor at the Graduate School of Global Environmental Studies at Sophia University, Japan, and a senior research fellow at the United Nations University Institute for the Advanced Study of Sustainability. He received his Ph.D. degree from Erasmus Universiteit Rotterdam in the Netherlands and holds Master's degrees from both Columbia University (USA) and Keio University (Japan). His previous work engagements include a senior analyst position at Mitsubishi Securities as well as consultant positions at the Department of Economic and Social Affairs (DESA) at the United Nations in New York and at the United Nations Framework Convention on Climate Change in Bonn, Germany.

**Misa Tanaka** is the head of research at the Bank of England. She holds a D.Phil. in economics from Nuffield College, University of Oxford. She has previously published articles on international policy spillovers, bonus regulations, and sovereign debt finance in the *Journal of Money, Credit and Banking*, the *Journal of Financial Intermediation*, and the *Economic Journal*, among others. Tanaka's current research interests include macroprudential policy, microprudential policy, and the impact of climate change on the financial system.

**Kalima Vico** is a research associate at the John Molson School of Business at Concordia University, Montréal. She has served with Concordia's David O'Brien Centre for Sustainable Enterprise and is part of Sustainable Concordia. She is finishing her Bachelor of Commerce in finance with a concentration in economics at Concordia. She has participated in and worked on well over 25 research papers and projects within the Finance Department. She has organized the Emerging Risks in Finance conference that is related to this book. Her research interests include diverse topics in economics, psychology, organizational behavior, finance and sustainability.

**Thomas Walker** is Professor of Finance at Concordia University, Canada, and previously studied at Washington State University, USA. Prior to academia, he worked for several years in the German consulting and industrial sector at Mercedes Benz, Utility Consultants International, Lahmeyer International, Telenet, and KPMG Peat Marwick.

**Stefan Wendt** is Associate Professor of Finance at the Department of Business Administration of Reykjavik University, Iceland. From March 2005 until March 2015, he was a research and teaching assistant at the Department of Finance at Bamberg University, Germany, where he received his Ph.D. degree in 2010. His fields of interest include financial markets and asset pricing, risk management, corporate finance and governance, small and medium-sized enterprises, behavioral finance, and financial intermediation.

**Gio Wiederhold** is Professor Emeritus of Computer Science, Electrical Engineering, and General Internal Medicine at Stanford University. He was educated in Germany and the Netherlands and emigrated to the US in 1958. He obtained a Ph.D. degree in medical information science in 1976. He consulted for many organizations, both locally and internationally, including the United States Agency for International Development (US AID) from 1964 to 1965, the United Nations Development Programme (UNDP) from 1966 to 1975, and since 2002 consults for an international branch of the US Treasury. He has published several books including *Valuing Intellectual Capital*, *Multinationals*, and *Taxhavens* (2014).

**Melanie Windirsch** graduated from the Duale Hochschule Baden-Wuerttemberg as an M.A. in business management/finance in 2018. She has a background in business administration and finance, and in particular in insurance. She has been working at Allianz Global Corporate & Specialty SE, the industrial insurance arm of Allianz, since 2011, where her current areas of responsibility focus on underwriting-related topics. Her research interests include, but are not limited to, risk management in insurance, risk modeling, and actuarial analysis.

# List of Figures

# List of Tables

CHAPTER 1

# Emerging Risks: An Overview

*Thomas Walker, Dieter Gramlich, Kalima Vico, and Adele Dumont-Bergeron*

One of the core functions of financial institutions is risk management. Until recently, most institutions have focused on concepts such as cyclical variations in their business and the economy, their exposure to low and even negative interest rates, and the consequences of various other macroeconomic developments and internal decisions on their profit margins, solvency, and efficiency, among others. Our world is changing, and individuals and businesses are increasingly affected by factors that arise from outside the economy and the financial markets, yet display multiple interactions with the eco-financial system. Today—arguably more than ever—financial

T. Walker (✉)
Department of Finance, John Molson School of Business, Concordia University, Montreal, Canada
e-mail: thomas.walker@concordia.ca

D. Gramlich
Department of Banking, Baden-Wuerttemberg Cooperative State University, Heidenheim, Germany
e-mail: dieter.gramlich@dhbw-heidenheim.de

K. Vico • A. Dumont-Bergeron
John Molson School of Business, Concordia University, Montréal, QC, Canada



T. Walker et al. (eds.), *Ecological, Societal, and Technological Risks and the Financial Sector*, Palgrave Studies in Sustainable Business In Association with Future Earth,
https://doi.org/10.1007/978-3-030-38858-4_1

institutions face a variety of new challenges that require them to seriously rethink their risk management and investment practices. Climate change, mass migration, political extremism, trade wars, terrorism, cybersecurity threats, and the current evolution of financial technology (FinTech) are just some examples of ecological, societal, and technological factors that affect and interact with our financial markets. This book aims to highlight not only the threats but also the opportunities associated with these emerging risks, thereby providing an inspiration for academics, practitioners, and regulators who already work in or are interested in this field.

Our environment is rapidly changing: natural disasters, heat waves, and rising sea levels affect our personal lives as well as businesses and the overall economy; new technologies continuously reshape the way we communicate, entertain ourselves, and make purchase decisions; and globalization requires companies—many of which are increasingly spread out across continents—to rely on ever more complicated supply chains, transportation systems, and tax management. As a result, the public perception of sustainability is shifting and is paving the way for new business, investment, and regulatory approaches to address today's ecological, societal, and technological challenges.

Almost all of the emerging risks discussed in this book come with their own unique opportunities and threats. For instance, Internet-based technologies facilitate the way we carry out business and conduct financial transactions. Yet, cybersecurity vulnerabilities and the hackers who exploit them can be highly detrimental to consumers as their personal and financial information can be compromised and potentially sold around the globe. Mobility is facilitated by ever faster land, air, and sea transportation; however, the consequences of energy consumption and carbon dioxide ($CO_2$) emissions have to be considered as well. With such a variety of new developments, firms and investors must adjust their behaviors and regulators must reconsider existing laws to better mitigate and adapt to the arising challenges. The adoption of a less carbon-intensive economy and the consideration of environmental, social, and governance (ESG) factors in business and investment decisions are two possible ways of reacting to these challenges from a risk management perspective.

Our financial, banking, and governmental systems are also changing. They are far from immune from technological developments, emerging risks, and the social uprising around them. Climate change affects the way central banks manage their inflation controls, and FinTech is changing the way transactions are made. Thus, the social, environmental, and technological developments discussed in this book have strong repercussions for the financial system and the way it operates.

As global citizens, we need to be informed about these possible risks, the ways they affect us, and the solutions to counter—and abate—them. We need to change how we invest and how we strategize our businesses. The roles of analysts and managers must be redefined, and the sooner we implement these changes, the better equipped we will be to face the transition risks and any other emerging risks that may still be coming.

Social, environmental, and technological risks are relatively new topics, but they have gained momentum recently as different books and researchers have addressed similar themes. Ackerman (2017) addresses extreme cases of climate risk and financial crises in institutions and the financial system. Aldridge (2017) describes the market microstructure and modern risks with a focus on FinTech. Taplin (2016) focuses on cyber risks in the financial sector. Tadokoro et al. (2018) discuss emerging risks from a social perspective taking the heterogeneity among different countries into consideration. Finally, the World Economic Forum (WEF 2019) provides a basic overview of today's economic, environmental, geopolitical, societal, and technological risks. There are many other works on the topic of emerging risks, but these are arguably the most comprehensive and significant contributions related to our book.

Unlike many of the works mentioned above, our book draws on both the academic and practical worlds. The views and research exhibited in this book stem from academics and practitioners with a vast diversity of experiences. We offer a transdisciplinary approach, linking the social and natural sciences, with a specialized focus on the emerging risks affecting finance (see Fig. 1.1). We consider businesses, financial products, the stock and bond markets, as well as the global economy to offer a comprehensive and connected approach to assess new risk categories that affect each of them.

**Fig. 1.1** Emerging risks and the financial system

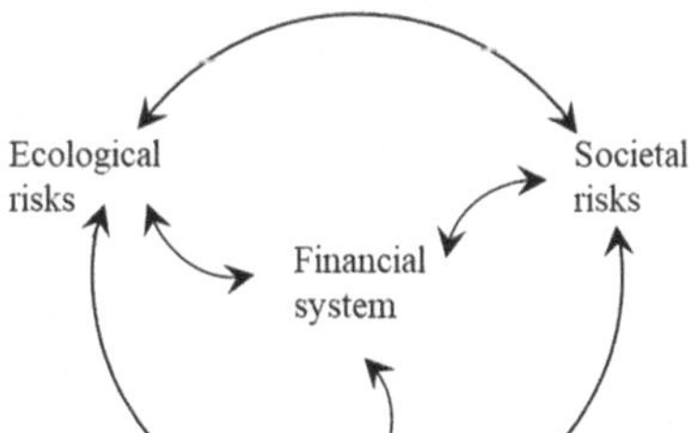

Finally, we feature different countries, from Pakistan to the United States, England, and Canada, to show how emerging risks affect different societies with different ecosystems. In the end, these specific examples demonstrate that the emerging risks discussed in this book unify us on a global level.

Our book is divided into three parts, each examining a different type of emerging risk and its associated opportunities for the financial markets.

## Part I: Ecological Risks

The first part of this book contains chapters related to ecological risks and finance. In "Climate Change: Macroeconomic Impact and Implications for Monetary Policy", Sandra Batten, Rhiannon Sowerbutts, and Misa Tanaka, from the Bank of England, address climate change–related challenges from the perspective of a central bank. Specifically, the authors highlight how climate change increases the difficulty of managing certain monetary policy objectives such as maintaining a low and stable inflation rate. They describe climate change risks as being both physical and transitional in nature, given that climate change imposes not only direct risks on various entities but also the risk associated with the current economy transitioning toward a greener one. These risks are not only felt by central banks but also by the labor market and thereby the overall economy and the financial markets.

The following chapter, "Global Warming and Extreme Weather Investment Risks" by Quintin Rayer, Peter Pfleiderer, and Karsten Haustein, explains the ways in which extreme weather events affect the financial markets. They review historical meteorological data and show that global warming has decreased the frequency but increased the intensity of hurricanes. The increased intensity causes higher disaster-related damages and liabilities for companies that operate in disaster-prone areas and ultimately affects their share price. In order to address the perceived inaction by some players, they explore why there are climate change deniers and whether these deniers may have economic incentives that drive their stance on the climate change question. They conclude that change (and the pressure to change) needs to come not only from carbon-intensive companies but also from the legal, academic, scientific, and financial community, as well as the general public.

James Leaton, a senior credit officer at Moody's, examines climate risks from a lender's and an investor's perspective in his chapter "Mapping Out

When and Where Climate Risk Becomes a Credit Risk". He discusses different climate change–related risks and highlights the physical and transitional risks for various industry sectors using examples from the coal mining industry, the European utility sector, and car manufacturing. The author examines the different transmission channels that make the transitional risks felt in these industries and discusses a variety of techniques that can be used to determine the financial impact of these risks.

Martin Boyer, Michèle Breton, and Pascal François analyze the ways in which climate change, as embodied through more severe hurricanes, affects the insurance market in their chapter "Designing Insurance Against Extreme Weather Risk: The Case of HuRLOs". Their work focuses on Hurricane Risk Landfall Options (abbreviated as HuRLOs in their title)—an investment tool that has been designed as a result of the market's increased concern about hurricanes. These options allow investors to take positions on hurricane landfalls, thereby providing a hedging instrument against catastrophic losses. In their chapter, the authors evaluate the effectiveness of this unique hedging instrument in a realistic setting.

Chapter 6, "The Evolving Risk Management Opportunity and Thinking Sustainability First", by Stephen Kibsey, Stéfanie D. Kibsey, Amr Addas, and Cary Krosinsky, addresses the need of defining investors' and corporations' fiduciary duties in the context of sustainability-oriented management and investing in order to reduce any ambiguity in their decisions. The chapter highlights the importance and necessity of ESG themes in the decision making and risk management process. It uses certain examples such as increasing talent diversity, implementing stronger cybersecurity, and transitioning to a lower-carbon economy to highlight how incorporating ESG considerations can lead to opportunities and benefits for both companies and investors.

## Part II: Societal Risks

The second part and the six chapters therein relate to societal risks and how they affect our financial system. In the chapter entitled "Terrorism and Trading: Differential Equity and Bond Market Responses During Violent Elections", Allan Dwyer and Tashfeen Hussain examine how the efficient market hypothesis applies to the emerging countries market. They use data on electoral violence in Pakistan and analyze the stock and bond market's response to news about related terrorism events. In doing so, they also investigate country risk and the credit rating process in an emerging market such as Pakistan and how it responds to political violence.

Chapter 8, "The Effect of Corporate Tax Avoidance on Society", by Gio Wiederhold, discusses how tax avoidance, on both corporate and individual levels, affects global welfare. In this context the chapter highlights the difficulties of taxing intangible goods, such as intellectual property and related patents, and the services offered by Internet information providers. Wiederhold canvasses how multinational corporations and wealthy individuals avoid taxation using various intermediaries and complex corporate and investment structures. He offers suggestions for several actions governments can take to help mitigate the effects of tax avoidance.

In her chapter "Planning for the Carbon Bubble", Carla Santos Skandier discusses the problem of stranded assets for fossil fuel companies. She compares the current carbon bubble to the recent subprime mortgage crisis, which has the potential to burst and become a new financial crisis as it did in 2008. She promotes the Federal Reserve as the institution with the best means for addressing and mitigating the carbon bubble which she argues looms over the financial markets. She proposes several unique ideas such as a re-envisioned financial system and public banks, as well as green banks.

Carmela Cucuzzella and Jordan Owen review a recent policy change that attempted to increase social housing and the related benefits in the Montreal real estate market. In their chapter "Economic Risks from Policy Pressures in Montreal's Real Estate Market", they examine the factors behind the increased demand for social housing as well as the recent policies that affect it. Supporting their research with a case study, they demonstrate the effects of the newly passed policies on new real estate projects. They conclude their study with an analysis of both the costs and the social and economic effects of the recent policy changes.

In the next chapter, entitled "Climate Change and Reputation in the Financial Services Sector", Robert Bopp, from Ernst & Young, focuses on climate change–related reputational risks for financial institutions. He first defines firm's reputation, differentiating it from an image or a brand. He argues that reputation is a major concern for stakeholders and that the way companies conduct their business in relation to climate change influences both their profitability and social responsiveness. The chapter examines how financial institutions respond to stakeholders' experiences and expectations. The author concludes by highlighting the need to integrate climate change to remain relevant and outlines a variety of new business implications and strategic considerations that come with it.

The last chapter of this part, "Financial Risk Management in the Anthropocene Age", is written by Bradly Condon and Tapen Sinha. They take a global perspective and discuss various channels through which climate risk can lead to societal risks. Specifically, they address the issue of mass migration and the associated growth in climate refugees, while supplying an estimate of the related costs of climate change per country. They review past market successes and failures surrounding sulfur dioxide ($SO_2$) related air pollution. Based on the experiences obtained from $SO_2$, they suggest a series of voluntary and compulsory steps to help reduce current $CO_2$ emissions. Specifically, they focus on the role of insurance companies in mitigating some of these effects.

## Part III: Technological Risks

The last part of this book addresses technological risks and their impact on the financial world. The first chapter of this part, entitled "An Incentives-Based Mechanism for Corporate Cyber Governance Enforcement and Regulation", by Constantin Gurdgiev and Shaen Corbet empirically examines how institutional structures can help propagate risk contagion effects and how cyber threats pose a potential systemic risk to financial stability. The authors highlight the vulnerabilities of private sector companies, central banks, and regulators in the face of a major cyberattack. They discuss the use of white knights and incentives to help reduce this threat and provide an implementation guideline to do so.

Next, Matthias Horn, Andreas Oehler, and Stefan Wendt examine the opportunities and threats associated with FinTech in their chapter "FinTech for Consumers and Retail Investors: Opportunities and Risks of Digital Payment and Investment Services". They take on both a consumer's and retailer's viewpoint, provide a series of recent examples of technical innovations in the payment and investment realm, and analyze the benefits and threats of new technologies. Specifically, they discuss the societal and ecological risks of mobile payments, cryptocurrencies, and crowdfunding, as well as newly emerging investment methods such as social trading, robo advisors, and crowd investing.

The chapter "Empirical Modelling of Man-Made Disaster Scenarios" by Melanie Windirsch from Allianz Global uses historical data to model man-made disaster scenarios. She concentrates on fire- and explosion-related events that have occurred recently and describes the inherent difficulties in modeling man-made disaster scenarios. She argues that—contrary to natural catastrophes—man-made disasters are more challenging to model due to their wider variety of loss triggers and their low frequency of occurrence. She further argues that if their risk is not properly managed, man-made disasters can trigger market shocks and subsequent economic downturns.

Mohd Hafdzuan Bin Adzmi, Huiying Cai, and Masachika Suzuki examine the effect of policy changes and climate change mitigation strategies in the coal industry. In their chapter "Changing Dynamics of Financial Risk Related to Investments in Low Carbon Technologies", they look at the effects of divesting from fossil fuels and the problem of stranded assets. To do so, they review recent measures taken around the globe to encourage a low-carbon shift, honing in on their impact on the coal industry and the potential actions by companies to address these risks.

The final chapter in this part, "A New Era in the Risk Management of Financial Firms", by Sureyya Burcu Avci, analyzes the effect of emerging technologies and their associated risks on the risk management of financial institutions. The chapter defines and reviews traditional risks and risk management principles and argues that these remain relevant for emerging risks, yet have to be adjusted. She reviews the business continuity principles for financial companies and proposes a set of new principles for the financial industry. Avci details the different processes within a business in order to better understand the challenges imposed by new technological risks. She concludes with a proposed series of new business principles that firms should follow in order to better manage and mitigate technological risks.

## Summary

In summary, the chapters presented in this book aim to provide detailed insights and introduce ground-breaking new approaches for the management of newly emerging risks that affect today's financial system. Our world is marked by an ever-changing ecological, societal, and technological environment as well as changing business models, customer preferences, and market regulations that have a profound effect on the financial markets. In striving to make our markets more resilient and sustainable, these developments must be addressed as soon as possible to limit the risks that affect not only our central banks, but also businesses, the real estate market, and our financial and economic system per se.

The second chapter in our book quotes Carney (2018) who noted that "… the longer the implementation of these policies and the transition to a low-carbon economy are delayed, the sharper the future reduction in carbon emission to meet the climate goal will need to be, and the higher the transition risks". The alarm has been sounded and a sense of urgency is associated with emerging risks. As demonstrated and discussed throughout the chapters, adaptation is as necessary as it could be profitable, while inaction may lead to missed opportunities and even financial distress. There is more pressure to be sustainable, not only from regulators but also from investors and consumers. A company's reputation could also be at stake if it fails to be ecologically/socially sustainable or if it suffers from a cybersecurity breach.

What appears clear and consistent, however, is that there are plenty of solutions to address the emerging risks we face today: sustainable strategies as well as diversity can help a company's reputation and their competitive advantage as they mitigate risks and employ stronger talent to implement change; intangible assets such as corporate responsibility and social stewardship can ultimately increase a firm's profitability; investment gains can be achieved (or losses can be avoided) by trading on hurricanes and social unrest; and money can be saved by using ESG principles to manage business risks. In addition, new jobs can be created, for example, by employing white knights to mitigate private and public cybersecurity risks.

New regulations and policies can support this transition: greener banks and public banks can be implemented, taxation can be improved to reduce tax-havens, and the insurance system can create incentives to deter us from producing more emissions. Moreover, through stricter regulations, the government can help increase the cybersecurity of consumers, thereby protecting their personal and financial information. Indeed, in almost all areas reflected upon in this book, financial market regulators can help by implementing modified regulations and better frameworks to address the risks discussed.

Ultimately, we need to implement a variety of changes at the personal, business, investor, and regulatory levels and be transparent about them. Transparency is needed, both to address the environmental, social, and governmental risks companies and other entities face and to identify the risks for the associated stakeholders.

The chapters featured in this book should be of interest to anyone who owns or works at a financial institution, who uses a bank or FinTech service, or who seeks to minimize their risks and increase their profitability (which ultimately encompasses every investor who actively or passively invests in the market). The chapters not only provide ample food for thought but also offer detailed suggestions for changes by highlighting, for example, the risk management strategies in dealing with cybersecurity and climate change risks. Our world is changing and the need to adapt is now. We hope this book inspires our readers to become more educated and to be better corporate citizens, not only for the good of the planet but also for more profitable and safer business and investment strategies.

## References

Ackerman, F. (2017). *Worst-case economics: Extreme events in climate and finance.* London: Anthem Press.

Aldridge, I. (2017). *Real-time risk: What investors should know about FinTech, high-frequency trading, and flash crashes.* Hoboken, NJ: John Wiley & Sons, Inc.

Carney, M. (2018, November 21). *Remarks at the accounting for sustainability summit 2018 accounting for sustainability forum*, London.

Tadokoro, M., Egashira, S., & Yamamoto, K. (Eds.). (2018). *Emerging risks in a world of heterogeneity: Interactions among countries with different sizes, polities and societies* (Vol. 10). Berlin: Springer.

Taplin, R. (2016). *Managing cyber risk in the financial sector: Lessons from Asia, Europe and the USA.* Abingdon: Routledge.

WEF—World Economic Forum (2019). The global risks report, 14th edition, Geneva.

PART I

# Ecological Risks

CHAPTER 2

# Climate Change: Macroeconomic Impact and Implications for Monetary Policy

*Sandra Batten, Rhiannon Sowerbutts, and Misa Tanaka*

## Introduction: Why Central Banks Care About Climate Change

Central banks across the world have been increasingly paying attention to climate change, having to acknowledge that it could affect their ability to meet their monetary and financial stability objectives. Climate change also poses economy-wide and societal challenges, which inevitably require the financial system to take a central role in managing climate risks and financing the carbon transition.

The views expressed in this chapter are those of the authors and not necessarily those of the Bank of England or its committees. We are grateful to Jenny Lam and Andre Moreira for help and to Ryan Barrett, Theresa Lober, Warwick McKibbin and participants at the Economics of Climate Change conference at the Federal Reserve Bank of San Francisco on 8 November 2019 for helpful suggestions. All remaining errors are solely the authors'.

S. Batten (✉) • R. Sowerbutts • M. Tanaka
Bank of England, London, UK
e-mail: Sandra.Batten@bankofengland.co.uk;
Rhiannon.Sowerbutts@bankofengland.co.uk;
Misa.Tanaka@bankofengland.co.uk



T. Walker et al. (eds.), *Ecological, Societal, and Technological Risks and the Financial Sector*, Palgrave Studies in Sustainable Business In Association with Future Earth, https://doi.org/10.1007/978-3-030-38858-4_2

The Bank of England was the pioneer among central banks in the assessment of the climate risks for central banks: from understanding the impact of climate change on the insurance industry (Bank of England 2015), the banking sector (Bank of England 2018) and the wider central bank objectives (Carney 2015; Batten et al. 2016, 2018) to devising a response to these challenges (Scott et al. 2017).

Many other central banks and financial supervisors are now involved in climate change initiatives. For example, central banks and financial regulators and supervisors have supported the initiative by the Financial Stability Board to establish a Task Force for Climate-related Financial Disclosures (TCFD), in order to help improve disclosure of climate-related risks by firms (TCFD 2018).

In 2017, central banks and supervisors have also established the Network for Greening the Financial System (NGFS) to "help strengthening the global response required to meet the goals of the Paris Agreement and to enhance the role of the financial system to manage risks and to mobilize capital for green and low-carbon investments" (NGFS 2019). As of March 2020, the Network included 42 members and eight observers across five continents.[1]

And in early 2019, a group of US senators have written to the Chairman of the Federal Reserve (Fed) Powell, urging him to ensure that the US financial system "is prepared for the risks associated with climate change" and requesting information on the steps the Fed has taken to identify and manage climate-related risks in the US financial system (US Senate 2019). Soon after that, Rudebusch (2019) published an article examining the implications of climate change for the Federal Reserve.

This chapter focuses on the impact of climate change on central banks' monetary policy objective of maintaining low and stable inflation. For most central banks, price stability is usually the primary monetary policy objective, while some have output stability as an additional or a secondary objective. For example, the Bank of England's monetary policy objective is to maintain price stability within the United Kingdom and, subject to that, to support the economic policy of Her Majesty's Government, including its objectives for growth and employment. The US Federal Reserve's mandate includes three goals of equal priority: maximum employment, stable prices and moderate long-term interest rates in the US economy. The single monetary policy objective of the euro

[1] The NGFS's first comprehensive report was published in April 2019 (NGFS 2019).

system—that is, the European Central Bank (ECB) and the national central banks of the euro area countries—is to maintain price stability.

The chapter is organised as follows. Section "Climate Change Risks" introduces the risks arising from climate change. Section "Climate Change and the Macroeconomy: The Transmission Channels" discusses the channels of transmission of those risks to the macroeconomy, and section "Implications of Climate Change for Monetary Policy: A Summary" introduces the implications of climate change for monetary policy. Sections "Physical Risks, Macroeconomic Impacts and Implications for Monetary Policy" and "Transition Risks, Macroeconomic Impacts and Monetary Policy" discuss the implications of physical and transition risks in more detail, while section "Implications for the Analytical Framework of Monetary Policy Authorities" discusses the implications for the modelling framework of central banks and section "Interactions Between Macroeconomic and Financial Climate Shocks" describes the interaction between financial and macroeconomic aspects of climate change.

## Climate Change Risks

This section sets out the risks from climate change that could affect the macroeconomy and price stability, and therefore affect the core objectives of monetary policy, following the established taxonomy that distinguishes physical and transition risks of climate change (Carney 2015; Bank of England 2015).

***Physical risks*** can be defined as "those risks that arise from the interaction of climate-related hazards (including hazardous events and trends) with the vulnerability of exposure of human and natural systems, including their ability to adapt" (Batten et al. 2016, p. 5). There are two main sources of physical risks: (1) ***gradual global warming*** and the associated physical changes, for instance, in total seasonal rainfall and sea level; and (2) increased frequency, severity and correlation of certain types of ***extreme weather events***. The effects of these two types of risks on the macroeconomy are likely to differ in terms of timing and severity, and therefore their implications for monetary policy.

***Transition risks***, on the other hand, are defined as those risks that might arise from the transition to a low-carbon economy, which will be required to limit the cumulative emission of greenhouse gases (GHGs), particularly carbon dioxide, to achieve the Paris Agreement of limiting the global warming to well below 2 °C above pre-industrial levels.

While the definition of physical and transition risks is well established, it is important to stress that these risks are dynamic, in the sense that they evolve over time and are not independent from each other but tend to interact. For example, the physical risks of climate change are likely to intensify in the future, even under the benign scenario of limiting global temperature increase to 1.5 °C (IPCC 2018). Moreover, the increasing frequency and severity of extreme weather events have been linked to global warming (see e.g. Stott 2016; Stott et al. 2016). In particular, evidence shows that climate change has already led to an increase in the frequency and intensity of daily temperature extremes (Bindoff et al. 2013) and contributed to the intensification of daily precipitation extremes (Zhang et al. 2013) in certain countries.

The extent to which climate change influenced the likelihood and severity of specific weather-related events is the focus of a relatively new but active area of scientific research called 'event attribution'. One of the vehicles for the ***dissemination*** of the results of such attribution studies is the annual reports in the Bulletin of the American Meteorological Society, which seek to explain extreme events of the previous year. For example, the 2018 report (AMS 2018) showed that, in 2017, the droughts in the US Northern Plains and East Africa, the floods in South America, China and Bangladesh, and the heatwaves in China and the Mediterranean were made more likely by human-induced climate change.

To deliver on the international commitment to limit temperature increases to less than 2 °C, carbon emission will have to be reduced significantly relative to the 'business-as-usual' scenario. Climate policies to achieve a reduction in carbon emissions need to be implemented swiftly and extensively to limit the physical risks from climate change. The longer the implementation of these policies is delayed, the sharper the future reduction in carbon emission to meet the climate goal will need to be, and the higher the transition risks (Carney 2018). A late and sudden transition ("hard landing") will also exacerbate the physical risks of climate change (ESRB 2016).

## Climate Change and the Macroeconomy: The Transmission Channels

Climate change risks manifest themselves as economic shocks—defined as unpredictable events that produce a significant change within an economy. ***Supply-side*** shocks affect the productive capacity of the economy:

examples of shocks that can arise from physical climate risks are the price volatility caused by shortages of commodities such as food and energy, and the damage to the capital stock and infrastructure due to extreme weather events. The supply-side risk from the transition to a low-carbon economy is represented by the *trade-off* between the need to limit the future damage from global temperature increases and the present cost of reducing emissions, which reduces the resources available for economic growth in the near term.

Representing the physical and transition risks from climate change as purely supply-side type shocks (McKibbin et al. 2017; Cœuré 2018), however, is too simplistic. Losses deriving from extreme climate events such as floods and storms also lead to ***demand-side*** shocks, for example by reducing household wealth and thus private consumption. While reconstruction activities could lead to an increase in investment, business investment could also be affected negatively by uncertainty and financial losses following climate disasters. Batten et al. (2016) noted that weather-related natural disasters are more likely to lead to a negative demand shock if losses are largely uninsured. Moreover, the impact of natural disasters on bilateral trade is well established (Gassebner et al. 2010; Oh and Reuveny 2010; Felbermayr and Gröschl 2013; El Hadri et al. 2017). Finally, demand-side shocks can also be caused by the transition to a low-carbon economy. Tighter climate policy could cause dislocations in high-carbon sectors, including a large and sudden reduction in investment. Moreover, like all forms of public investment, government investment in low-carbon technologies could result in 'crowding-out' of private investment in those technologies. Some examples of the macroeconomic risks deriving from climate change are presented in Table 2.1.

## Implications of Climate Change for Monetary Policy: A Summary

Climate change can affect monetary policy in different ways. First, the physical and transition risks from climate change can affect the macroeconomy and the prospects for inflation. Second, climate change can also affect monetary policy indirectly, through its impact on households and firms' expectations about future economic outcomes (Lane 2019).

The impact of climate change on the economy is subject to profound uncertainty, in particular over the magnitude of the effects and on the horizon over which they will play out. While central bankers might believe

**Table 2.1** Macroeconomic risks from climate change

| *Type of shock/impact* | | *Physical risks* | | *Transition risks* |
|---|---|---|---|---|
| | | *From extreme weather events* | *From gradual global warming* | |
| Demand | Investment | Uncertainty about climate events | | 'Crowding out' from climate policies |
| | Consumption | Increased risk of flooding to residential property | | 'Crowding out' from climate policies |
| | Trade | Disruption to import/export flows due to natural disasters | | Distortions from asymmetric climate policies |
| Supply | Labour supply | Loss of hours worked due to natural disasters | Loss of hours worked due to extreme heat | |
| | Energy, food and other inputs | Food and other input shortages | | Risks to energy supply |
| | Capital stock | Damage due to extreme weather | Diversion of resources from productive investment to adaptation capital | Diversion of resources from productive investment to mitigation activities |
| | Technology | Diversion of resources from innovation to reconstruction and replacement | Diversion of resources from innovation to adaptation capital | Uncertainty about the rate of innovation and adoption of clean energy technologies |

Source: Batten (2018)

the horizon of climate change impacts might be beyond the horizon relevant for monetary policy, climate change is likely to affect monetary policy whether it is addressed in the present—through the economic cost of reducing carbon emissions (transition risk)—or whether it is left unchecked, through the impact of increased extreme climate events (physical risk) (Cœuré 2018). Indeed, these two scenarios are likely to coexist for the foreseeable future. A summary of the economic impacts of climate change and their timing is presented in Table 2.2.

**Table 2.2** Economic impacts relevant for monetary policy and time horizon for the materialisation of climate risks

| *Type of risk* | | *Economic outcome* | *Timing of effects* |
|---|---|---|---|
| Physical risks from: | Extreme climate events | Unanticipated shocks to components of demand and supply | Short to medium run |
| | Global warming | Impact on potential productive capacity and economic growth | Medium to long run |
| Transition risks | | Demand/supply shocks or economic growth effects | Short to medium run |

The next two sections examine the implications of physical and transition risks for monetary policy in more detail.

## Physical Risks, Macroeconomic Impacts and Implications for Monetary Policy

The existing climate-economy literature points to a number of channels via which ***gradual global warming*** could reduce the potential growth rate of the economy: first, global warming could lead to a reduction in the effective labour supply in the economy, due to the reduction in labour productivity caused by diminished physical and cognitive performance of human capital.[2] Extreme heat could also reduce effective labour supply by increasing the mortality and morbidity of the population, for example, due to the increased incidence of diseases such as malaria (Fankhauser and Tol 2005). Deryugina and Hsiang (2014), for example, found that productivity declines roughly by 1.7% for each 1 °C increase in daily average temperature above 15 °C, using variations across counties within the United States over a 40-year period, while Acevedo et al. (2018) found that higher temperatures also have a negative effect on a broader indicator of human well-being as measured by the Human Development Index, a weighted average of per capita income, educational achievement and life expectancy.

A second effect of global warming could be a reduction in the rate of productive capital accumulation, through permanent or long-term

[2] A survey of experimental studies reported by Dell et al. (2014) concluded that there is a productivity loss in various cognitive tasks of about 2% per 1 °C for temperatures over 25 °C.

damage to capital and land (Stern 2013) or an increase in the rate of capital depreciation (Fankhauser and Tol 2005).

Finally, global warming could lead to a reduction in the growth rate of total factor productivity, because adaptation to rising temperatures will divert the resources available from research and development. Moreover, if adaptation requires more investment to be directed to repair and replacement, there may be less productivity gains through 'learning by doing' than if more investment is directed towards innovation (Pindyck 2013; Stern 2013).

While economists are still debating whether global warming affects the level or the growth rate of the economy, ignoring these effects could potentially lead central banks to misjudge the evolution of the output gap and inflationary pressure. The impact of climate change on productivity in the first half of the twenty-first century could be modest in most advanced economies if the increase in local temperatures itself is limited during this period. Monetary policy authorities may still need to take these effects into account in the coming decades if global temperature increases lead to international inflationary pressures on food and other commodities.[3]

Over a shorter time horizon, on the other hand, some ***extreme weather-related events*** could have a significant impact on the aggregate economy and inflation, requiring the monetary policy authorities to react appropriately, depending on the response of output and inflation to these events. Three competing hypotheses that describe the impact of environmental catastrophes on output in the short and long run are illustrated in Fig. 2.1. In the aftermath of a natural disaster, a loss of gross domestic product (GDP) is very likely. In the medium and long run, however, different scenarios might occur (see e.g. Hsiang and Jina 2014):

1. The 'creative destruction' hypothesis argues that, following a natural disaster, there might be a period of faster growth that puts the economy on a higher GDP path than before the event, due, for example, to an increase in demand for goods and services as lost capital is replaced, to growth-promoting international aid following the disaster or to innovation stimulated by the environmental disruption.
2. The 'recovery to trend' hypothesis argues that, after growth slows following the natural disaster, income levels should eventually return

[3] Batten (2018) provides a more detailed discussion of the literature.

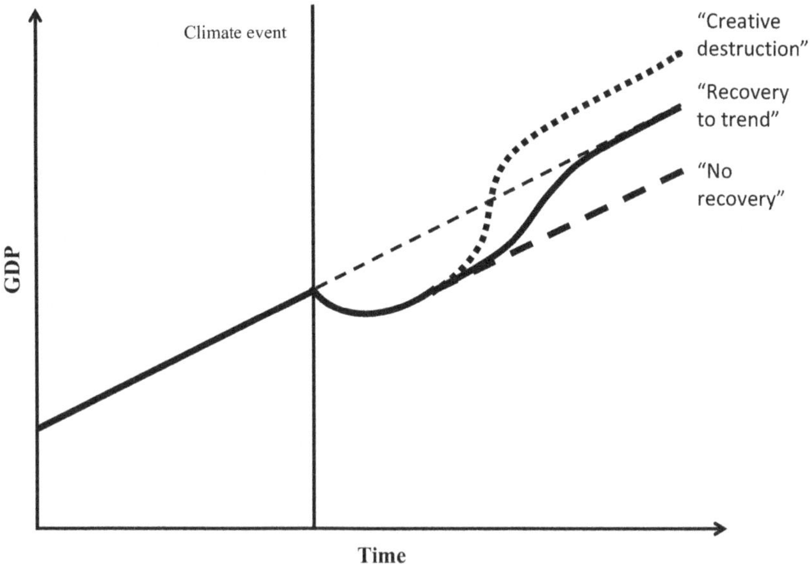


**Fig. 2.1** Possible effects of natural disasters on GDP. (Source: This figure is taken from Batten (2018) and is a modified version of Figure 1 in Hsiang and Jina (2014))

to their pre-disaster trend through a catch-up period of faster than average growth. This rebound should occur because the marginal product of capital will rise when capital is destroyed by a natural disaster and becomes relatively scarce, causing resource reallocation into devastated locations.

3. The 'no recovery' hypothesis argues that disasters slow down growth by either destroying productive capital directly or by destroying durable consumption goods (e.g. homes) that are replaced using funds that would otherwise be allocated to productive investments. In this case, no rebound occurs because the reallocation of resources fails to compensate for the negative effect of a natural disaster on productivity. While post-disaster output may continue to grow in the long run, it remains permanently lower than its pre-disaster trajectory.

The literature surveyed by Cavallo and Noy (2010) concluded that, on average, natural disasters had a negative impact on short-term economic growth. The literature on the long-run effects of natural disasters is relatively scarce and the results are mixed, in part reflecting the difficulty associated with constructing the appropriate counterfactual research. Some studies found that natural disasters tend to have contractionary effects on growth due to the cumulative output losses associated with indirect damages, while others found expansionary effects due to 'creative destruction' processes, especially in developed countries. In a recent cross-country study of the economic impact of tropical cyclones during 1950–2008, Hsiang and Jina (2014) found a small but persistent suppression of annual growth rates over the 15-year period following the disaster.

Because any tightening monetary policy reaction might worsen the impact of the weather disaster on economic activity, flexible inflation targeting would allow a central bank to use discretion to avoid exacerbating any real effects of weather shocks. Central banks would need to assess the size and persistence of the impact on supply relative to demand, and hence the output gap: unpredictable shocks such as climate-related events would, however, increase the difficulty of forecasting potential output.

The destruction of capital stock due to natural disasters tends to reduce aggregate supply, while reconstruction efforts could increase aggregate demand. If a natural disaster generates a positive output gap and an upward pressure on inflation, then a central bank might consider tightening monetary policy (Keen and Pakko 2010). But a natural disaster could also have a large and persistent negative effect on demand—and thus generate a negative output gap—if it severely damages household and corporate balance sheets in affected areas and reduces their consumption and investment. A natural disaster could also undermine business confidence and trigger a sharp sell-off in financial markets, which in turn could increase the cost of funding new investments and thus reduce investment demand.

In practice, central banks have responded differently to natural disasters depending on their magnitude and their estimated impact on the output gap. For example, the Federal Reserve had increased the interest rate in its first meeting after Hurricane Katrina in August 2005—which caused a total loss of US$125 billion (1.0% of US GDP in 2005)—as had been expected before the disaster, characterising the macroeconomic effects of the hurricane as significant but "essentially temporary".[4] By contrast, the Bank of Japan (BoJ) eased monetary policy following the Great East Japan

[4] See the minutes of the Federal Open Market Committee Meeting on 20 September 2005.

Earthquake in March 2011—which caused a total loss of US$210 billion (3.6% of Japan's GDP in 2011)—by expanding its asset purchase programme "with a view to pre-empting a deterioration in business sentiment and an increase in risk aversion in financial markets from adversely affecting economic activity".[5] The G7 also issued a statement to express their "readiness to provide any needed cooperation", while the Federal Reserve, Bank of England, Bank of Canada and European Central Bank joined the BoJ in intervening in the foreign exchange market to stabilise the yen exchange rates.[6] The Bank of Thailand also cut policy rates after the 2011 flood, which generated total losses of US$43 billion, or 11.6% of Thai GDP in 2011.

Extreme weather events are likely to have the most significant impact on the agricultural sector. Dell et al. (2012) report that, for developing countries at least, panel models typically found consistently negative impacts of bad weather shocks on agricultural output. A more recent cross-country panel study covering the 1964–2007 period by Lesk et al. (2016) also found that droughts and extreme heat significantly reduced national cereal production by 9–10%.

Extreme weather events affecting the global food production could temporarily increase food price inflation in countries that rely on imported food, and this impact could be exacerbated if the exporting countries resort to protectionist measures to keep domestic food prices down. For example, Russia banned grain exports following the 2010 drought and heatwave, thereby pushing up international prices for grains (Fig. 2.2). This was a factor that contributed positively to food price inflation in other countries (Fig. 2.3).

Heinen et al. (2016) find a large inflationary impact of extreme weather events in developing countries: a result confirmed by Parker (2018), who also finds effects are heterogeneous across disaster types. These inflationary effects in developing countries could also spread through international commodity trade: Peersman (2018) finds that exogenous international food commodity price shocks have a strong impact on consumer prices in the euro area, and these shocks can explain on average 25–30% of inflation volatility.

Thus, climate change could lead to greater volatility of headline inflation rates via increased volatility of food price inflation rates. While

[5] See the minutes of the BoJ Monetary Policy Meeting on 14 March 2011.

[6] See the statement of the G7 Finance Ministers and Central Bank Governors released on 18 March 2011, and Bank of Japan (2011).

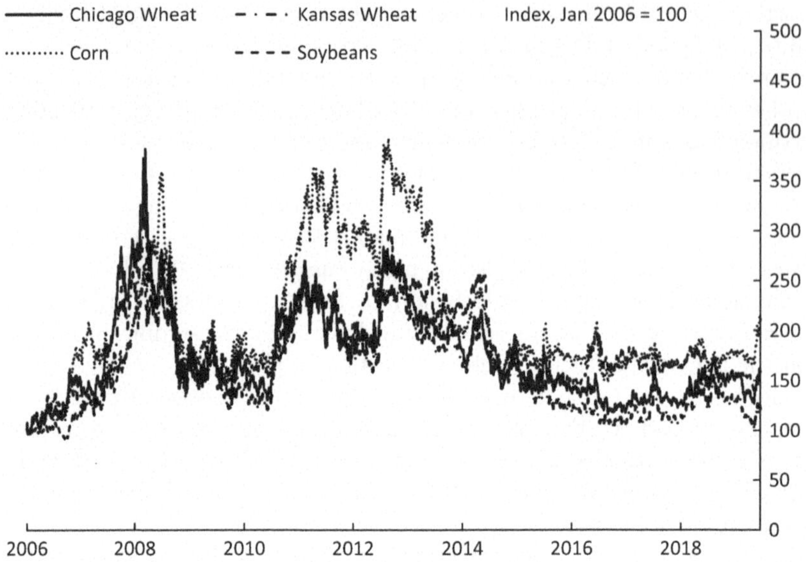


**Fig. 2.2** Selected food commodity prices, 2006–2019. (Source: Thomson Reuters Datastream)

sectoral price shocks could have a temporary effect on the headline inflation in the short run, central banks do not necessarily need to react to them if the sectoral price shocks do not affect inflation expectations and thus their effect on inflation is short-lived. As a result, central banks in countries with a credible monetary policy framework and well-anchored inflation expectations are less likely to face the need to react to sectoral price shocks, although such volatility could complicate the communication of their monetary policy strategy at times. But the increased volatility of inflation rates represents a bigger challenge for those central banks with less well-established credibility, where sectoral price shocks risk de-anchoring inflation expectations and triggering a second-round effect that increases inflationary pressure in the medium-term.

If, as discussed in section "Climate Change Risks", climate change leads to more severe or frequent extreme weather events in the future, monetary policy makers will be faced with larger and more frequent negative supply shocks. It will also become more important for central banks to be able to disentangle the impact of climate-related weather events from

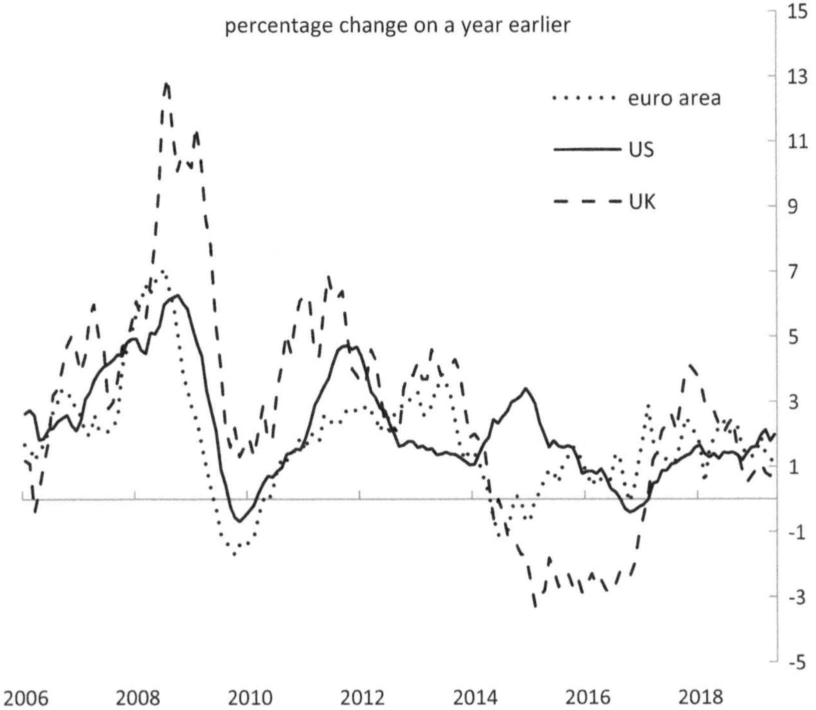


**Fig. 2.3** Food price inflation, 2006–2019. (Source: Thomson Reuters Datastream)

other inflation drivers and to be able to model the impact of these events on macroeconomic variables (modelling issues are discussed in more detail in section "Implications for the Analytical Framework of Monetary Policy Authorities").

## Transition Risks, Macroeconomic Impacts and Monetary Policy

The risks to the macroeconomy from the transition to a low—and ultimately zero—carbon economy can be understood in terms of the Kaya identity (Kaya 1990), which provides a framework for analysing emission drivers by decomposing overall changes in GHG emissions into underlying factors:

$$CO_2\,\text{emissions} = \text{population} \times \frac{\text{GDP}}{\text{population}} \times \frac{\text{Energy}}{\text{GDP}} \times \frac{CO_2\,\text{emissions}}{\text{Energy}}$$

In the Kaya identity, $CO_2$ emissions are expressed as a product of four underlying factors: (1) population, (2) per capita GDP (GDP/population), (3) energy intensity of GDP (Energy/GDP) and (4) $CO_2$ intensity of energy ($CO_2$ emissions/energy).

This formulation implies that the reduction in GDP growth needed to achieve a given reduction in carbon emissions will rely on the decrease in energy intensity (a reduction in energy used/GDP), which can be achieved through lower or more efficient energy consumption, and the reduction in carbon intensity of energy (a reduction in carbon/energy used), through the adoption of cleaner sources of energy. If a reduction in carbon emissions is to be achieved entirely via a reduction in energy intensity, then the resulting reduction in output could be substantial: for example, using a simple growth accounting framework, Smulders et al. (2014) report that a 10% reduction in energy use reduces output by around 1%.[7]

By contrast, if the reduction in carbon emissions can be achieved through shifts to cost-effective low- and zero-carbon energy supply, and greater energy efficiency, then the growth impact of a tightening of policy on carbon emissions can be expected to be smaller. This implies that the transition to a low-carbon economy could be achieved without causing a large negative supply shock if sufficient investment takes place in low-carbon energy sources at an early stage.

If the transition leads to an increasing share of bioenergy, the volatility of inflation rates could also increase as both energy and food prices could be affected by the same weather-related shocks.[8] Although this effect could be mitigated by a gradual reduction in the share of food and energy in the consumption basket (and hence the consumer price index) as

[7] Growth accounting assumes that the output elasticity of energy equals the cost share of energy in production in a competitive economy.

[8] The share of bioenergy is assumed to increase in the Representative Concentration Pathway (RCP) 2.6 which is likely to keep the warming below 2 °C (van Vuuren et al. 2011). IEA (2013) also projects that in order to achieve a 50% reduction in energy-related $CO_2$ emissions by 2050 (from 2005 levels), biofuels would need to provide 27% of the total global transport fuel, up from 3% currently. But there is a question over the sustainability of large-scale bioenergy production, given the competition with other land and biomass needs, such as food security and biodiversity conservation (Fuss et al. 2014).

countries become richer, it could be exacerbated by climate change which can make weather patterns more volatile.

The major source of transition risk from climate change to the macroeconomy is represented by climate policy: some of these policies—in particular price-based interventions (e.g. carbon pricing) or regulations—impose a burden to economic activity, at least in the short to medium term, as compliance with environmental regulation forces companies to curb production or to devote some of their resources to emission abatement, and thus are expected to negatively affect firms' profitability, productivity, employment and ultimately GDP.[9]

From a monetary policy perspective, price-based climate policy can be considered a negative supply-side shock.[10] By putting a price on carbon, regulatory authorities aim to discourage the production and consumption of high emission goods. A price for carbon can be established through a carbon tax or through a cap-and-trade system such as the European Union (EU) Emission Trading Scheme (ETS). Under a carbon tax, the price of carbon is set directly by the regulatory authority. Under a cap-and-trade system, the price of carbon or $CO_2$ emissions is established indirectly: the regulatory authority stipulates the allowable overall quantity of emissions and the price of carbon is then established through the market for allowances.

A one-off increase in carbon price would normally only have a temporary effect on the inflation rate, provided agents recognise it is a one-off change. The policy would result in higher price level, while the inflation rate would quickly return to its original level. The relative price of carbon-intensive goods would be permanently higher.

[9] Climate policy can also have a range of benefits in addition to the gains from reducing future climate change damage: these are often referred to as *co-benefits*. For example, policies that encourage innovation in low-carbon technologies can *spill over* to other industries and stimulate economic growth. Moreover, climate policy might result in productivity growth if they improve the allocation of resources or increase their degree of utilisation. Mitigation actions targeting clean energy technologies or energy efficiency are found to induce improvements in air quality by reducing local air pollution such as particulate matter, sulphur dioxide and nitrogen oxides, which are damaging for human health. Co-benefits can be expected to cover a significant part of climate change mitigation costs (see e.g. Bollen et al. 2009; Groosman et al. 2011). An attractive feature of co-benefits is that they occur in the medium run, while the direct benefits of GHG mitigation policies in terms of reduction of the impact of climate change are likely to occur only in the longer run.

[10] Other types of climate policies, such as incentives to innovation and investment in low-carbon technologies, can instead lead to an increase in potential supply.

The price level effect would generally depend on the carbon pass-through, defined as the incidence of a fixed carbon price or tradable carbon permit, that is, the proportion of carbon price that is passed into wholesale electricity spot prices.

Recent studies find evidence of a high degree of pass-through. Fabra and Reguant (2014) measure the pass-through of emissions costs to electricity prices using data from the Spanish wholesale electricity market covering the period in which the ETS was introduced and find that emissions costs are almost fully passed through to wholesale electricity prices. Hintermann (2016) finds similar results in a study of cost pass-through to hourly wholesale electricity prices in Germany. Lise et al. (2010) analyse the impact of the ETS on wholesale electricity prices in 20 European countries and find that a significant part of the costs of (freely allocated) $CO_2$ emission allowances is passed through to power prices, resulting in higher electricity prices for consumers. De Bruyn et al. (2015) find that the pass-through rates of the ETS were particularly high in carbon-intensive industries such as the utilities and metals industries, which are characterised by relatively large actors and limited competition.

Since the introduction of carbon pricing has a one-off, transitory effect on inflation, the monetary policy authorities will generally 'look through' this effect to avoid rising interest rates and depressing the economy. This was the case, for example, of the Bank of Canada's reaction following the introduction of a carbon price in some of Canada's provinces (Lane 2017).

## Implications for the Analytical Framework of Monetary Policy Authorities

Both the physical aspects of climate change and the transition to a low-carbon economy represent major structural changes: they will require system transition and innovation in many sectors of the economy. Many of these changes would be difficult to incorporate directly into existing economic models used by central banks, and the degree of precision around them might be limited: these might nonetheless be helpful "for characterizing the forces at work and capturing their interactions" (Lane 2017).

As discussed above, both the physical risks and transition risks arising from climate change could potentially affect long-run growth. The calibration of the long-run growth rate in forecasting models used by major central banks could have an important impact on short-term forecasts of inflation and output. Thus, if climate change can have permanent effects on the trend growth rate, it is potentially important to consider this in the forecasting process.

Future impacts of climate change on GDP—more specifically, the effects of gradual global warming—are often modelled using 'Integrated Assessment Models (IAMs)', which seek to capture the complex interactions between the physical and economic dimensions of climate change. Such models are, for example, used to estimate the 'social cost of carbon' in order to derive the optimal dynamic path of carbon price. The IAMs typically model the economic impact of global warming using a 'damage function', which links the increase in average global temperature from its pre-industrial level to a reduction in GDP in a given year. But as these damage functions are often arbitrary, these models are unlikely to provide reliable quantitative information needed for monetary policy.

By contrast, disaggregated quantitative analysis could potentially be more informative for monetary policy makers. For example, Houser et al. (2015) assess how climate change might affect five key sectors (agriculture, energy, coastal property, health and labour) in the US economy by building on both climate science and econometric research. Their study models climate impacts at a very high level of granularity, highlighting the regional variation of climate impacts. Further quantitative studies based on such granular data and climate science could potentially enable monetary policy makers to better estimate the long-term physical impacts of climate change.[11]

While the long-term impact of global warming on trend GDP growth is important, the medium-term impact of climate change—namely the effects of extreme weather events and the transition risks—are likely to be more relevant for the conduit of monetary policy.

Central banks are—to some extent—already accustomed to assessing the short-run impact of unusual weather conditions on economic activities. Examples include the Bank of England's assessment of unusual snow conditions on the retail, construction and hospitality sectors (Bank of England 2018), and the Fed's quarterly assessment of winter weather economic impacts (Gourio 2015; Bloesch and Gourio 2015). As a striking example of the kind of economic impact extreme weather can have on economic variables, JP Morgan estimated that the low level of the Rhine and other important German rivers caused by extreme heat in 2018 reduced economic growth by 0.7 percentage points (Bloomberg 2019). And the deviation of weather from the seasonal norms has been shown to

[11] Another example is OECD (2015).

significantly affect macroeconomic series such as monthly payrolls in the United States (Boldin and Wright 2015). As extreme weather events become more severe and frequent in the future, it might become necessary to routinely incorporate these effects in standard macroeconomic now-casting or forecasting models in central banks.

Short-term, dynamic stochastic general equilibrium (DSGE) models, of the type used for forecasting output and inflation within the time horizon of monetary policy (2–3 years) can be augmented with climate-related natural disasters. For example, in Keen and Pakko (2011), a natural disaster destroys a significant share of the economy's productive capital stock, as well as temporarily disrupting production, which is modelled as a transitory negative technology shock. There are, however, only a few examples of these types of models, and there is scope for improving the modelling channels to include, for example, the impact of domestic natural disasters on labour supply or the impact of natural disasters in partner countries on international trade and the exchange rate.

Transition risks associated with announced climate policies can be incorporated in macroeconomic forecasting models, while those associated with unannounced future policies and future technical changes are much harder to incorporate. The main transition risks are changes in climate policy, which are included in the broader fiscal policy variables, and energy supply risks, which can be modelled as technology shocks in a DSGE-type model.

There could also be macroeconomic risks from the materialisation of transition risks into large and permanent financial losses in asset values. The resulting loss of wealth and collateral might reduce household consumption and firms' business investment plans. These interactions between macroeconomic and financial impact of climate change are discussed in section "Interactions Between Macroeconomic and Financial Climate Shocks".

It is possible that conventional DSGE models might not be suited to analysing the complex system-wide transition to a low-carbon economy. Such models typically include a 'representative' consumer or firm and are built on the assumption that individual decisions by these agents can be scaled up to the aggregate economy level.

An example of an alternative modelling approach is agent-based modelling (ABM), which is more suitable for studying the emergent properties of complex systems, because it allows for interactions amongst heterogeneous agents, and the global system properties that result from those interactions (Patt and Siebenhüner 2005).

ABMs are commonly applied in climate change modelling, for example to analyse: climate change adaptation (Patt and Siebenhüner 2005); consumer energy choices (Rai and Henry 2016) and climate-related migration (Thober et al. 2018). ABMs have also found use in macroeconomics, including the analysis of business cycles (Gualdi et al. 2015) and monetary policy (Gatti and Desiderio 2015) that are of particular interest for central bank policy makers.[12] That said, ABMs often incorporate behavioural rules that are arbitrary, and the transmission mechanisms in such models are difficult to identify, such that caution is needed in drawing policy conclusions based on results emerging from these models.

## Interactions Between Macroeconomic and Financial Climate Shocks

It is widely recognised that macroeconomic and financial shocks can interact and amplify: in the past, price instability has been shown to contribute to financial crises.[13] Conversely, financial crises can generate large falls in output.

The interaction between macroeconomic shocks from climate change and financial stability shocks—and vice versa—has not, however, been explored in any detail, and this is a particularly important gap in the current literature. One example is the potential realisation of transition risks as 'stranded assets' and their impact on the real economy. Another example is the possibility of natural disasters reducing collateral values of the housing stock and weakening households' balance sheets, in turn reducing household consumption. Insured losses from natural disasters can lead to financial losses for both insurers and banks, reducing the latter's ability to lend to households and corporates and thus reducing the financing available for reconstruction of physical capital in affected areas. Increased uncertainty from more frequent climate-related weather events could also increase uncertainty for investors, causing falls in asset prices, losses for banks and reduced availability of lending for productive investment to corporates (Batten et al. 2018). Some of the linkages between macro and financial aspects of transition risks are depicted in Fig. 2.4.[14]

[12] See Turrell (2016) for a further discussion of ABMs application to macroeconomics.

[13] See, for example, Bordo et al. (2001).

[14] For a similar diagram for extreme weather events, see Figure 10.1 in Batten et al. (2018).

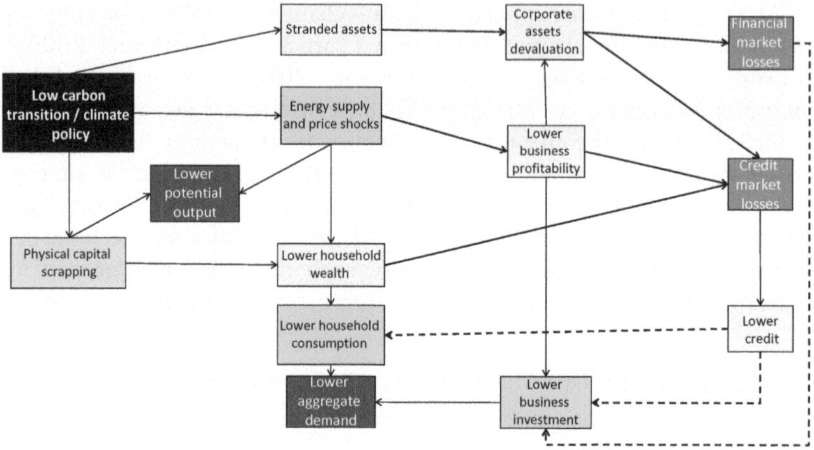


**Fig. 2.4** Transition risks, macroeconomic impacts and transmission to the financial system

## Conclusion

This chapter examined the impact of climate change on the monetary policy objectives of central banks. We have identified four main ways in which climate change and policies on carbon emissions could affect central banks' monetary policy objectives.

First, a weather-related natural disaster could trigger a macroeconomic downturn if it causes severe damage to the balance sheets of households, corporates, banks and insurers (*physical risks*). The economic impact of a given natural disaster is likely to be less severe if the relevant risks are priced in financial contracts ex ante, and the financial system has distributed them efficiently, for example, via insurance and reinsurance. Ex post, a central bank will need to react appropriately to a disaster to meet its monetary stability objectives. This requires assessing the impact of the disaster on the output gap and inflationary pressure, and adjusting monetary policy if needed.

Second, gradual warming could also affect an economy's potential growth rate. More reliable quantitative estimates based on detailed sector-level impact analysis would be needed before central banks can incorporate this effect in their monetary policy analysis.

Third, a sudden, unexpected tightening of carbon emission policies could generate a negative supply shock (*transition risks*). While the introduction or increase of a carbon price would have only a temporary effect on inflation, the short- and medium-term macroeconomic consequences could be severe if the increase is both sharp and sudden. Achieving an orderly transition requires governments to pre-announce a clear and predictable path for future tightening of carbon emission policies.

Finally, both the changes in weather patterns and the increased reliance on bioenergy could increase the volatility of food and energy prices, and hence the volatility of headline inflation rates. This could make it more challenging for central banks to gauge underlying inflationary pressures and maintain inflation close to the target.

Central banks will increasingly need to incorporate climate variables in their macroeconomic models (Campiglio et al. 2018; Mersch 2018; Debelle 2019). Specifically, to assess the impact of short-term extreme weather on economic variables such as GDP and inflation, now-casting and forecasting models could be expanded to include weather effects. Longer-term effects of gradual global warming on the growth rate of potential output might also need to be included in the monetary policy modelling toolkit. Finally, the interactions between financial and macroeconomic climate shocks could become an important source of risk for the future conduct of monetary policy.

## References


Acevedo, S., Mrkaic, M., Novta, N., Pugacheva, E., & Petia, T. (2018). *The effects of weather shocks on economic activity: What are the channels of impact?* IMF Research Department Working Paper, No. 18/144). Washington, DC: International Monetary Fund.

AMS—American Meteorological Society. (2018). Explaining extreme events in 2017 from a climate perspective. *Bulletin of the American Meteorological Society, 99*(12), 1359–1376.

Bank of England. (2015). *The impact of climate change on the UK insurance sector: A climate change adaptation report by the Prudential Regulation Authority.* London: Bank of England.

Bank of England. (2018). The impact of adverse weather. *Inflation report*, Q1, 12.

Bank of Japan. (2011). *Responses to the Great East Japan earthquake by payment and settlement systems and financial institutions in Japan.* Payment and Settlement Systems Department.

Batten, S. (2018). *Climate change and the macroeconomy: A critical review*. Bank of England Staff Working Paper, No. 706. London: Bank of England.

Batten, S., Sowerbutts, R., & Tanaka, M. (2016). *Let's talk about the weather: The impact of climate change on central banks*. Bank of England Staff Working Paper, No. 603. London: Bank of England.

Batten, S., Sowerbutts, R., & Tanaka, M. (2018). Climate change: What implications for central banks and financial regulators? In B. Caldecott (Ed.), *Stranded assets and the environment*. London: Routledge.

Bindoff, N. L., Stott, P. A., Achuta Rao, K. M., Allen, M. R., Gillett, N., Gutzler, D., Hansingo, K., Hegerl, G., Hu, Y., Jain, S., Mokhov, I. I., Overland, J., Perlwitz, J., Sebbari, R., & Zhang, X. (2013). Detection and attribution of climate change: From global to regional. In T. F. Stocker, D. Qin, G.-K. Plattner, M. Tignor, S. K. Allen, J. Boschung, A. Nauels, Y. Xia, V. Bex, & P. M. Midgley (Eds.), *Climate change 2013: The physical science basis. Contribution of Working Group I to the fifth assessment report of the intergovernmental panel on climate change*. Cambridge, UK and New York, NY: Cambridge University Press.

Bloesch, J., & Gourio, F. (2015). The effect of winter weather on U.S. economic activity. *Economic Perspectives, 39*(1), 1–20.

Bloomberg. (2019). *Is climate change drying up German rivers – and growth?* Retrieved from https://www.bloomberg.com/opinion/articles/2019-01-25/climate-change-is-probably-bringing-down-germany-s-growth.

Boldin, M., & Wright, J. H. (2015). Weather adjusting economic data. *Brookings Papers on Economic Activity, 2015*(Fall), 227–274.

Bollen, J., Guay, B., Jamet, S., & Corfee-Morlot, J. (2009). *Co-benefits of climate change mitigation policies: Literature review and new results*. OECD Economics Department Working Paper, No. 693. Paris: OECD.

Bordo, M. D., Dueker, M. J., & Wheelock, D. C. (2001). *Aggregate price shocks and financial stability: The United Kingdom 1796–1999*. Federal Reserve Bank of St. Louis Working Paper, No. 2001-018). St. Louis: Federal Reserve Bank of St. Louis.

Campiglio, E., Dafermos, Y., Monnin, P., Ryan-Collins, J., Schotten, G., & Tanaka, M. (2018). Climate change challenges for central banks and financial regulators. *Nature Climate Change, 8*(6), 462–468.

Carney, M. (2015). *Breaking the tragedy of the horizon – climate change and financial stability*. Speech at Lloyd's of London, London, 29 September 2015. London.

Carney, M. (2018). *Remarks at the accounting for sustainability summit 2018 accounting for sustainability forum*, London, 21 November 2018.

Cavallo, E. A., & Noy, I. (2010). *The economics of natural disasters: A survey*. IDB Working Paper Series, No. 124. Washington, DC: IDB.

Cœuré, B. (2018). *Monetary policy and climate change*. Speech given at the conference on Scaling up Green Finance: The Role of Central Banks. Berlin, 8 November 2018.

De Bruyn, S. M., Vergeer, R., Shep, E., Hoen, M. T., Korteland, M., Cludius, J., Schumacher, K., Zell-Ziegler, C., & Healy, S. (2015). Ex-post investigation of cost pass-through in the EU ETS. An analysis for six sectors, European Union Commission, November 2015.

Debelle, G. (2019). *Climate change and the economy.* Speech given at the Public Forum hosted by the Centre for Policy Development. Sydney, 12 March 2019.

Dell, M., Jones, B. F., & Olken, B. A. (2012). Temperature shocks and economic growth: Evidence from the last half century. *American Economic Journal: Macroeconomics, 4*(3), 66–95.

Dell, M., Jones, B. F., & Olken, B. A. (2014). What do we learn from the weather? The new climate–economy literature. *Journal of Economic Literature, 52*(3), 740–798.

Deryugina, T., & Hsiang, S. M. (2014). *Does the environment still matter? Daily temperature and income in the United States.* NBER Working Paper No. 20750. Cambridge, MA: National Bureau of Economic Research.

El Hadri, H., Mirza, D., & Rabaud, I. (2017). *Natural disasters and countries' exports: New insights from a new (and an old) database.* Document de Recherche du Laboratoire d'Économie d'Orléans, No. 2017-10.

ESRB—European Systemic Risk Board. (2016). *Too late, too sudden: Transition to a low-carbon economy and systemic risk.* Report of the Advisory Scientific Committee No. 6. Frankfurt am Main: European Systemic Risk Board.

Fabra, N., & Reguant, M. (2014). Pass-through of emission costs in electricity markets. *American Economic Review, 104*(9), 2872–2899.

Fankhauser, S., & Tol, R. S. J. (2005). On climate change and economic growth. *Resource and Energy Economics, 27,* 1–17.

Felbermayr, G., & Gröschl, J. (2013). Natural disasters and the effect of trade on income: A new panel IV approach. *European Economic Review, 58*(1), 18–30.

Fuss, S., Canadell, J. G., Peters, G. P., Tavoni, M., Andrew, R. M., Ciais, P., Jackson, R. B., Jones, C. D., Kraxner, F., Nakicenovic, N., & Le Quéré, C. (2014). Betting on negative emissions. *Nature Climate Change, 4*(10), 850–853.

Gassebner, M., Keck, A., & Teh, R. (2010). Shaken, not stirred: The impact of disasters on international trade. *Review of International Economics, 18*(2), 351–368.

Gatti, D., & Desiderio, S. (2015). Monetary policy experiments in an agent-based model with financial frictions. *Journal of Economic Interaction and Coordination, 10*(2), 265–286.

Gourio, F. (2015). The effect of weather on first-quarter GDP. *Chicago Fed Letter,* No. 341.

Groosman, B., Muller, N. Z., & O'Neill-Toy, E. (2011). The ancillary benefits from climate policy in the United States. *Environmental and Resource Economics, 50*(4), 585–603.

Gualdi, S., Tarzia, M., Zamponi, F., & Bouchaud, J. P. (2015). Tipping points in macroeconomic agent-based models. *Journal of Economic Dynamics and Control, 50, 29–61.*

Heinen, A., Khadan, J., & Strobl, E. (2016). *The inflationary costs of extreme weather in developing countries.* Mimeo.

Hintermann, B. (2016). Pass-through of $CO_2$ emission costs to hourly electricity prices in Germany. *Journal of the Association of Environmental and Resource Economists, 3*(4), 857–891.

Houser, T., Hsiang, S., Kopp, R., & Larsen, K. (2015). *Economic risks of climate change: An American Prospectus.* New York: Columbia University Press.

Hsiang, S. M., & Jina, A. S. (2014). *The causal effect of environmental catastrophe on long-run economic growth: evidence from 6,700 cyclones.* NBER Working Paper No. 20352. Cambridge, MA: National Bureau of Economic Research.

IEA—International Energy Agency. (2013). *Technology road map: Biofuels for transport.* Paris.

IPCC—Intergovernmental Panel on Climate Change. (2018). Global Warming of 1.5°C. An IPCC Special Report on the impacts of global warming of 1.5°C above pre-industrial levels and related global greenhouse gas emission pathways, in the context of strengthening the global response to the threat of climate change, sustainable development, and efforts to eradicate poverty. In Masson-Delmotte, V., P. Zhai, H.-O. Pörtner, D. Roberts, J. Skea, P.R. Shukla, A. Pirani, Moufouma-Okia, C. Péan, R. Pidcock, S. Connors, J.B.R. Matthews, Y. Chen, X. Zhou, M.I. Gomis, E. Lonnoy, Maycock, M. Tignor, and T. Waterfield (eds.). *World meteorological organization, Geneva, Switzerland.*

Kaya, Y. (1990). *Impact of carbon dioxide emission control on GNP growth: Interpretation of proposed scenarios.* Paper presented to the IPCC Energy and Industry Subgroup, Response Strategies Working Group. Paris.

Keen, B. D., & Pakko, M. R. (2010). *Monetary policy and natural disasters in a DSGE model.* Federal Reserve Bank of St. Louis Research Division Working Paper, no. 2007-025D. St. Louis: Federal Reserve Bank of St. Louis.

Keen, B. D., & Pakko, M. R. (2011). Monetary policy and natural disasters in a DSGE model. *Southern Economic Journal, 77*(4), 973–990.

Lane, T. (2017). *Thermometer rising – Climate change and Canada's economic future.* Remarks for the Finance and Sustainability Initiative. Montréal, 2 March 2017.

Lane, P. R. (2019). Climate change and the Irish financial system. *Economic Letters,* 01/EL/19.

Lesk, C., Rowhani, P., & Ramankutty, N. (2016). Influence of extreme weather disasters on global crop production. *Nature, 529,* 84–87.

Lise, W., Sijm, J., & Hobbs, B. F. (2010). The impact of the EU ETS on prices, profits and emissions in the power sector: Simulation results with the COMPETES EU20 model. *Environmental and Resource Economics, 47,* 23–44.

McKibbin, W. J., Morris, A., Wilcoxen, P. J., & Panton, S. J. (2017). Climate change and monetary policy: Dealing with disruption. *Brookings Climate and Energy Discussion Paper.*

Mersch, Y. (2018). *Climate change and central banking.* Speech at the Workshop discussion Sustainability is becoming mainstream. Frankfurt am Main, 27 November 2018.

NGFS—Network for Greening the Financial System. (2019). *A call for action: Climate change as a source of financial risk.* Retrieved from https://www.banque-france.fr/en/financial-stability/international-role/network-greening-financial-system.

OECD—Organisation for Economic Co-operation and Development. (2015). *The economic consequences of climate change.* Paris: OECD Publishing.

Oh, C., & Reuveny, R. (2010). Climatic natural disasters, political risk, and international trade. *Global Environmental Change, 20*(2), 243–254.

Parker, M. (2018). The impact of disasters on inflation. *Economics of Disasters and Climate Change, 2*(1), 21–48.

Patt, A., & Siebenhüner, B. (2005). Agent based modeling and adaptation to climate change. *Vierteljahrshefte zur Wirtschaftsforschung, 74*(2), 310–320.

Peersman, G. (2018). *International food commodity prices and missing (dis)inflation in the euro area.* CESifo Working Paper, No. 7338. Munich: CESifo.

Pindyck, R. S. (2013). Climate change policy: What do the models tell us? *Journal of Economic Literature, 51*(3), 860–872.

Rai, V., & Henry, A. D. (2016). Agent-based modelling of consumer energy choices. *Nature Climate Change, 6*, 556–562.

Rudebusch, G. D. (2019). Climate change and the Federal Reserve. *FRBSF Economic Letters*, No. 2019-09.

Scott, M., van Huizen, J., & Jung, C. (2017). The Bank of England's response to climate change. *Bank of England Quarterly Bulletin, Q2*, 98–109.

Smulders, S., Toman, M., & Withagen, C. (2014). Growth theory and 'green growth. *Oxford Review of Economic Policy, 30*(3), 423–446.

Stern, N. (2013). The structure of economic modeling of the potential impacts of climate change: Grafting gross underestimation of risk onto already narrow science models. *Journal of Economic Literature, 51*(3), 838–859.

Stott, P. A. (2016). How climate change affects extreme weather events. *Science, 352*(6293), 1517–1518.

Stott, P. A., Christidis, N., Otto, F. E. L., Sun, Y., Vanderlinden, J. P., van Oldenborgh, G. J., Vautard, R., von Storch, H., Walton, P., Yiou, P., & Zwiers, F. W. (2016). Attribution of extreme weather and climate-related events. *WIREs Climate Change, 7*, 23–41.

TCFD—Task Force for Climate-Related Financial Disclosure. (2018). *2018 Status report.*

Thober, J., Schwarz, N., & Hermans, K. (2018). Agent-based modeling of environment-migration linkages: A review. *Ecology and Society, 23*(2), 41.

Turrell, A. (2016). Agent-based models: Understanding the economy from the bottom up. *Bank of England Quarterly Bulletin Series, Q4*, 173–188.

US (United States) Senate. (2019). Letter to the Honorable Jerome H. Powell, Chairman of the Board of Governors, Federal Reserve System, 25 January. Retrieved from https://www.schatz.senate.gov/imo/media/doc/Letter%20to%20Federal%20Reserve,%20OCC,%20FDIC%20re%20Climate%20Change.pdf?mod=article_inline.

Van Vuuren, D. P., Edmonds, J., Kainuma, M., Riahi, K., Thomson, A., Hibbard, K., Hurtt, G. C., Kram, T., Krey, V., Lamarque, J. F., & Masui, T. (2011). The representative concentration pathways: An overview. *Climatic Change, 109*, 5–31.

Zhang, X., Wan, H., Zwiers, F. W., Hegerl, G. C., & Min, S.-K. (2013). Attributing intensification of precipitation extremes to human influence. *Geophysical Research Letters, 40*, 5252–5257.

CHAPTER 3

# Global Warming and Extreme Weather Investment Risks

*Quintin Rayer, Peter Pfleiderer, and Karsten Haustein*

## Introduction

Environmentally focused investors often consider climate risks (Porritt 2001; Stern 2006). However, emissions from carbon-intensive sectors create extreme weather events and, with them, potential liabilities for damages—that present risks that may not yet be reflected in current share prices (Krosinsky et al. 2012). Given the devastation of the 2017 Atlantic hurricane season, it is worth asking: how close are we to companies or sectors being held liable, at least partially, for their activities around

Q. Rayer (✉)
P1 Investment Management Limited, Exeter, UK
e-mail: quintinrayer@p1-im.co.uk

P. Pfleiderer
Humboldt University, Berlin, Germany
e-mail: peter.pfleiderer@climateanalytics.org

K. Haustein
School of Geography and Environment at the University of Oxford, Oxford, UK
e-mail: karsten.haustein@ouce.ox.ac.uk



T. Walker et al. (eds.), *Ecological, Societal, and Technological Risks and the Financial Sector*, Palgrave Studies in Sustainable Business In Association with Future Earth, https://doi.org/10.1007/978-3-030-38858-4_3

emissions? We may be closer than many might expect. The evolving field of extreme weather event attribution serves as a good example of how new science can raise important thought-provoking questions regarding the appropriate actions of both investors and companies under a changing climate. Science can also answer them with increasing confidence. For financial professionals seeking background on global warming, an excellent introduction can be found in HRH The Prince of Wales, Juniper, and Shuckburgh (2017).

Although the economic impact of extreme weather damages is beginning to be incorporated into some risk assessments (Dietz et al. 2016), the financial liability of carbon-intensive industries for these damages is a climate-related risk that may not be reflected in these companies' market valuations (Krosinsky et al. 2012). In recent articles, Rayer and Millar (2018a, b, c) estimated that the top seven carbon-emitting publicly listed companies, under a hypothetical climate liability regime, might increasingly see around 1–2% losses on their market capitalisations (or share prices) from North Atlantic hurricane seasons. This chapter gives a comprehensive exposition of how that estimate was arrived at, as well as clarifying how it was quantified. Related aspects from a physical point of view are provided, with an associated general overview of the current state of the related science of climate change, alongside a focus on extreme weather events.

Despite these already substantial and potential financial implications to date, future changes are projected to be even more significant. Recent research (National Academies of Sciences, Engineering, and Medicine 2016) implies that possible share-price impacts for high-emitting firms could be greater.

## Global Warming and Hurricane Damage

In September 2017, *TIME* magazine reported $200 billion damages over that year's Atlantic hurricane season, comprising hurricanes Harvey, Irma, Jose and Maria—possibly making that season the costliest for the US mainland to date (Johnson 2017). More recent estimates are even higher at $265 billion (all damage estimates are inflation-adjusted to 2017 US dollars) (National Hurricane Center 2018). This compares to damages of $211 billion in 2005 when Hurricane Katrina devastated New Orleans (Johnson 2017; National Hurricane Center 2018). Earlier articles outlining the share price implications of the 2017 hurricane season (Rayer and

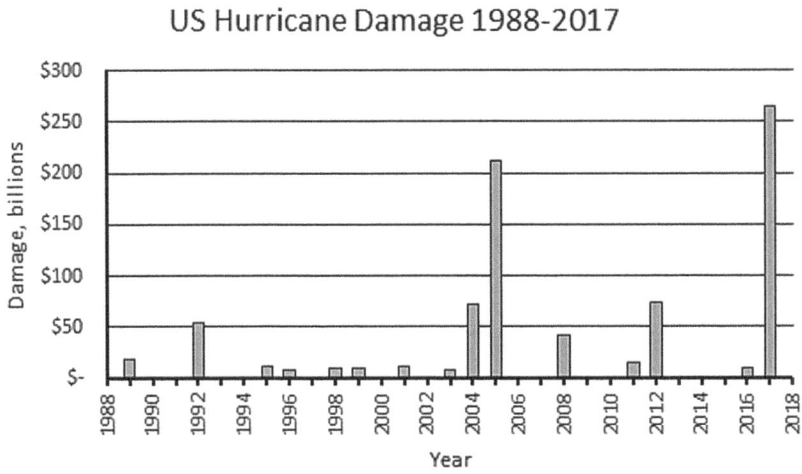


**Fig. 3.1** US hurricane damage estimates by year from 1988 to 2017 (National Hurricane Center 2018). Values are adjusted for inflation to 2017 US dollars

Millar 2018a, b, c) were based on the preliminary (lower) $200 billion damage figures reported in *TIME* magazine (Johnson 2017), rather than the more recent, higher $265 billion (National Hurricane Center 2018; Blake and Gibney 2011); therefore, the current analysis will differ in that respect. Damage estimates for the US over the period 1988–2017 are shown in Fig. 3.1. These statistics from the US National Hurricane Center ignore the severe hurricane damages that occurred in the Caribbean (National Hurricane Center 2018).

Hurricanes are rated by category, with a major hurricane being category 3, 4 or 5 (Simpson 1974). Hurricane categories are related to the maximum wind speeds on the Saffir/Simpson scale (Table 3.1).

In general terms, one might expect damage to be related to wind strength, although not necessarily in a straightforward way due to details such as geographical features, population centres and locations of economic assets. This is illustrated in Fig. 3.2, which shows the annual hurricane damage data of Fig. 3.1 against the maximum category. The highest category of hurricane has been taken each year as an indicator of the maximum wind speed potential to cause damage. Clearly the amount of damage that a hurricane can cause will depend on its path, areas of

**Table 3.1** Hurricane categories according to the Saffir/Simpson Hurricane Wind Scale, modified from (Simpson 1974)

| *Scale number (category)* | *Winds maximum 1-min (mph)* |
|---|---|
| 1 | 74–95 |
| 2 | 96–110 |
| 3 | 111–130 |
| 4 | 131–155 |
| 5 | >155 |

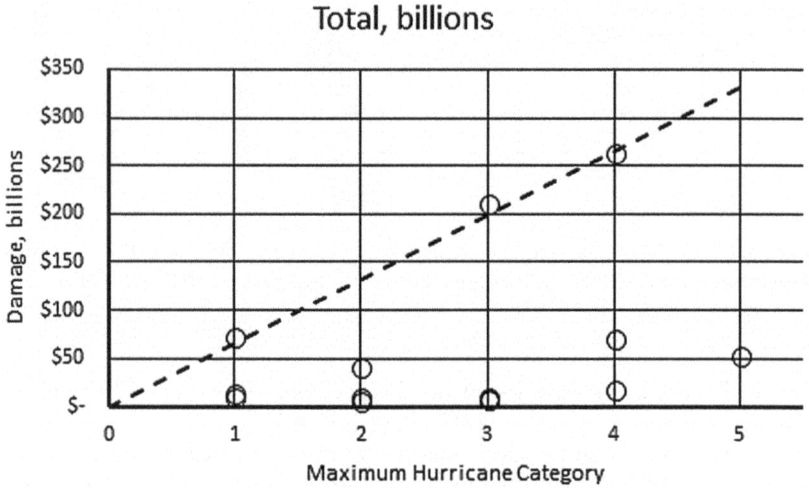


**Fig. 3.2** US hurricane damage estimates by year from 1988 to 2017 (National Hurricane Center 2018) (values adjusted for inflation to 2017 US dollars) against maximum hurricane category. The dashed line has intercept zero and gradient \$265 billion/4

population and valuable infrastructure it may cross. In this respect, the category (or wind speed) can only offer the potential to indicate the maximum damage that may occur. Although based on only three data points, the maximum damage estimates (based on inflation-adjusted figures to 2017 US dollars) appear to obey a simple function that can be approximated as follows (Fig. 3.2):

$$\$0 \leq \text{damage} \leq \frac{\$265\text{billion}}{4} \times \text{category}$$

If this relationship holds, an increasing frequency of stronger hurricanes will inevitably increase the risk for unprecedented total damage.

## The State of the Climate Sciences

The science showing how extreme weather events can be attributed to human-induced global warming is developing rapidly (National Academies of Sciences, Engineering, and Medicine 2016). On average, global warming is currently increasing at a rate of about 0.2 °C per decade from today's level of approximately 1 °C, and may be accelerating (Haustein et al. 2017). This is the amount the earth's climate has already warmed above pre-industrial levels. If we follow the current emissions' trajectory, the 1.5 °C threshold could be exceeded between the years 2030 and 2050. Given that humanity has to curb emissions by >5% per year from now on until net carbon-zero conditions are achieved (which would take ~45 years) to reach the 1.5 °C temperature target, it is extremely unlikely that this goal can be met without the implementation of major carbon removal mechanisms (Leach et al. 2018).

The UN Framework Convention on Climate Change's (UNFCCC) Paris Agreement acknowledges that even in the case of stabilising global temperatures below the target of 1.5 °C and well below 2.0 °C above pre-industrial levels, the impacts will continue to be felt, such as more frequent extreme weather events (UN FCCC 2015). In holistic terms, this is unsurprising. If the atmosphere-ocean system is considered a global-scale heat engine, the greater temperatures arising from global warming mean that the "global heat engine" is likely to run "faster" or with greater intensity, with potential for stronger storms (Peixoto and Oort 1992; Laliberté et al. 2015; Zielinski 2015). This analogy is also true from a global water cycle point of view, as more latent heat is released into the atmosphere. Yet, dynamical aspects often lead to counter-intuitive and regionally heterogeneous results. For example, latitudinal temperature gradients are reduced due to Arctic (temperature) amplification, potentially slowing the jet stream down and causing more severe winter weather in the mid-latitudes (Cohen et al. 2018).

The above gives an overview as to why global warming might be expected to generate stronger winds and heavier rainfall (i.e., more extreme weather events). The more detailed arguments as to how wind speeds and precipitation are being affected, and how these are likely to develop as global warming intensifies, are discussed below.

### *Intensity and Frequency of Tropical Cyclones*

An increase in hurricane intensities and frequencies in the Atlantic basin has been observed since the 1970s, and intensities are projected to increase further by state-of-the-art climate models (Hartmann et al. 2013; Walsh et al. 2016; Knutson et al. 2010). Due to a lull in Atlantic hurricane activity after 2005 and lack of observations before the satellite era, it is still debated whether the underlying increasing trend is robust, including for longer time periods before 1970 (Walsh et al. 2016).

For the intensification of tropical cyclones (TCs), relatively warm sea surface temperatures (SST) are required. TCs draw their energy from convection (as warm air rises) associated with latent heat transport from the lower to the upper troposphere. SSTs are rising globally in response to enhanced concentrations of greenhouse gases in the atmosphere. Therefore, an increase in TC intensity is expected to occur, because of thermodynamic feedback processes linked to warmer ocean waters (Ballinger et al. 2015; Emanuel and Sobel 2013).

Yet, while warm SSTs are a prerequisite for the intensification of tropical cyclones, they do not necessarily lead to the formation of hurricanes. Besides warmer SSTs, large-scale circulation patterns and the moisture content of the atmosphere influence the potential for formation of tropical cyclones. For instance, strong vertical or horizontal wind shear and the presence of large patches of dry air hamper TC formation or their strengthening. In addition, hurricanes are relatively rare events; each year, on average, ten tropical storms develop over the Atlantic Ocean, of which six become hurricanes (United States Search and Rescue Task Force 2018), and their number varies widely from year to year.

Together with the fact that a warmer atmosphere has an increased capacity to hold moisture (due to the Clausius-Clapeyron relationship), the rise in ocean temperature due to human-induced climate change is unambiguous, as is the role of these thermodynamic effects on hurricane intensification (Hartmann et al. 2013; Knutson et al. 2010). There is lower confidence in changes in specific atmospheric circulation features, which are also referred to as dynamic changes, although this has been helped by improved data sets (Hartmann et al. 2013). For example, increased freshwater input from melting Greenland ice sheets has slowed the Atlantic Meridional Overturning Circulation (associated with the so-called Gulf Stream). This has the potential to alter the wind shear over the North and tropical Atlantic Ocean, which would reduce the hurricane risk and hence counterbalance the increased risk from thermodynamic changes (Rahmstorf et al. 2015).

Despite advances in the field, forecasting the next hurricane season's activity remains a major challenge. While predictions of the path and intensity of individual TCs are good enough a few days in advance so that action can be taken, seasonal predictions are of more use for pricing risk and insurance. Approaches have been developed to predict seasonal TC activity averaged over an entire basin, such as the North Atlantic or Northwest Pacific. There has been a degree of success over longer periods, including from year to year. For example, North Atlantic predictions successfully warned of the very active 2010 season, but failed for the very inactive 2013 season (Vecchi and Villarini 2014). Clearly this is an area where further work will be required. This low confidence concerning modifications in TC formation under climate change is reflected by models projecting a slightly negative—yet insignificant—trend in overall TC counts for the North Atlantic basin (Christensen et al. 2013). Since the fifth Intergovernmental Panel on Climate Change (IPCC) assessment report (AR5 (IPCC 2013)), studies challenging the decrease in TC frequency have appeared (Emanuel 2013, 2017a; Bhatia et al. 2018) and, with the emergence of high-resolution climate models, more reliable projections are expected in coming years. Yet, there is an emerging consensus (> 50% chance) that the frequency of the most intense TCs will increase substantially in some ocean basins (AR5 Summary for Policy Makers (IPCC 2013)) (Walsh et al. 2016). In other words, there will be fewer storms, but those that eventually form are becoming stronger than in the past. So much so that category 5 hurricanes are expected to occur more often. It is only because of their rarity that an attribution statement with respect to frequency changes cannot currently be made with confidence.

As shown above, hurricane damages appear to substantially increase with their intensity. Thus, irrespective of the uncertainties in frequency of tropical cyclone formation, the increased risk of hurricanes intensifying to category 4 or 5 is alarming. On top of this risk, impacts can be expected to become more severe due to sea level rise and the increasingly dynamic water cycle of the atmosphere (Hartmann et al. 2013). Of course, many other factors contribute to the economic damages associated with hurricane-induced extreme rainfall, including population growth, city planning and water management policies, which will affect the resilience or vulnerability of areas hurricanes pass over. However, these trends point to increased hazards from extreme hurricane-induced rainfall and the possibility of higher future hurricane-induced damages, even if humanity succeeds in limiting global warming to the most ambitious threshold of the Paris Agreement.

### *Precipitation*

The science is clear: a hotter atmosphere has a more energetic water cycle and warmer air can hold more moisture (Clausius-Clapeyron scaling), both associated with an increased likelihood of more intense downpours (Durack et al. 2012). Under the RCP4.5 set of scenarios, which cover the years 2081–2100 (i.e., late twenty-first century) (Taylor et al. 2012), rainfall rates are likely to increase by 14% in the 100 km around a storm centre compared with 2001–2020 (i.e., present day) (Knutson et al. 2015).

Hurricane Harvey produced the largest rainfall of any US hurricane on record. Much of the rain fell in the low-lying greater Houston metropolitan area (Emanuel 2017b). The resulting natural disaster killed at least 70 people, displaced many thousands and caused damages expected to be above $150 billion (Emanuel 2017b). Projections suggest that the frequency of Harvey-like precipitation intensities have increased from 1-in-100-year events since the late twentieth century to around 1-in-16-year events in 2017, a sixfold increase in frequency (Emanuel 2017b). Between 1880 and 2017, it has been estimated that global warming increased the rainfall intensity by about 15% (in agreement with model projections), making such an event around three times more likely (van Oldenborgh et al. 2017). These same projections indicate that as global warming continues, further increases in rates of occurrence of such storms would be expected (Emanuel 2017b). Extrapolating to a world 1.5 °C warmer than the pre-industrial period, we might expect another 7–8% increase in possible hurricane-induced rainfall intensity, although understanding exactly how storm intensities will change in the future is currently a very active subject of research.

### *Storm Surge Risk*

Besides the high wind speeds and excessive amounts of precipitation, storm surges associated with tropical cyclones can lead to substantial damages. In 2012, Hurricane Sandy led to an exceptional storm surge in New York City, making it one of the costliest hurricanes in US history, costing the city $65 billion (National Hurricane Center 2018). The frequencies of floods comparable to Hurricane Sandy will increase with anticipated sea level rises (Lin et al. 2016).

In regions regularly affected by tropical cyclones, most annual sea level maxima can be attributed to storm surges related to tropical cyclones (Khouakhi and Villarini 2017). An intensification of tropical cyclones thus increases the risk of highly impacting flooding events in coastal regions of both the tropics and the subtropics.

Additionally, the risk of such storm surges increases with global sea level rise (Woodruff et al. 2013). Due to the melting of ice and glaciers and the thermal expansion of the oceans, the average sea level rises (HRH The Prince of Wales, Juniper, and Shuckburgh 2017; Hartmann et al. 2013). On a more local level, highly populated areas tend to be exposed to even higher sea level rise due to land subsidence, further increasing the risk of high economic damages.

### *Floods, Droughts and Heat Waves*

So far, we have focused on the effect global warming has on tropical cyclones, which is a rather complex research topic, as it includes thermodynamic as well as dynamic changes. For other extreme events, the influence of global warming is more direct. For instance, a rise in global mean surface temperatures (GMSTs) increases the risk of daily extreme temperatures as well as the risk of extended warm spells.

As explained above, the atmosphere's higher water-holding capacity intensifies precipitation extremes, and thereby increases the risks of river flooding and flash floods across the globe. At the same time, in a warmer atmosphere, evapotranspiration is enhanced, which can result in the drying of already arid areas. Hence for some regions, such as western Europe, it is a plausible scenario to have simultaneously increased floods and drought occurrences, while average rainfall amounts may suggest no change overall. In fact, flash flood events during an extended dry spell are one of the worst-case scenarios in terms of economic damage. This is a highly likely outcome of climate change, with evidence that it is already occurring (Lehmann et al. 2018). On top of these thermodynamic effects, changes in atmospheric circulation patterns can alter the intensity of extreme events regionally. However, whether Arctic sea ice loss plays a role is currently under debate (Francis et al. 2017).

In essence, there are a multitude of detrimental impacts, all of which will become increasingly difficult to adapt to if society fails to introduce effective mitigation measures as soon as possible. In the very long term, climate change could lead to a "hothouse earth" scenario if we do not act in time (Steffen et al. 2018).

## Climate Change Denial

Human activity is well established as the main cause of global warming (Stern 2006; HRH The Prince of Wales, Juniper, and Shuckburgh 2017; Oreskes 2007). Cumulative carbon dioxide emissions are the primary driver of global warming. In fact, approximately 100% of the observed warming since pre-industrial times is indeed human-induced (Haustein et al. 2017); that is, the natural warming contribution since 1850 is approximately zero.

From a scientific perspective there is no debate questioning whether global warming is genuinely occurring and that it is primarily caused by human activities (anthropogenic global warming or AGW), with over 97% of peer-reviewed scientific papers on AGW supporting this consensus (Cook et al. 2013). However, there is a significant gap between public perception and the reality of AGW, with 55% of the US public disagreeing or unaware that scientists overwhelmingly agree that the earth is warming due to human activity (Pew 2012). This situation is exacerbated by the way media frames the climate change issue, where a tendency to provide opposing sides with equal attention (a superficial or "false" balance) generates an informational bias which allows a vocal minority to have their views greatly amplified (Boykoff and Boykoff 2004). For example, in a BBC Radio 4 Today programme interview in August 2017, leading global warming sceptic Lord Lawson was not even challenged on claims that were later shown to be false (BBC 2017a). The BBC admitted that it broke its own guidelines and said that Lawson should have been challenged more robustly (BBC 2017b).

In fact, the aggregates of climate studies across disciplines with differences on the questions asked, timing and sampling methodologies demonstrate a very strong scientific consensus, as between 90% and 100% of published climate scientists say that humans are the primary cause for recent global warming (Cook et al. 2016). It is perhaps worth noting that in almost any other sphere of activity with such a high level of consensus, the matter in question would be regarded as settled. For example, the media would not feel it necessary to give equal time to proponents of a flat earth.

There is a strong consensus among scientists that global warming is occurring, and the evidence that humans are modifying the climate is compelling (Oreskes 2004). Today, all but a tiny handful of climate scientists are convinced that the earth's climate is heating up and that human activities are a significant cause (Oreskes 2007). An overview of the arguments supporting the view that the current scientific consensus is correct is provided in Oreskes (2007). It is worth noting that the vast majority of written materials denying the reality of global warming do not pass the most basic test to be considered scientific—namely, being published in a peer-reviewed journal (Oreskes 2007). Further details illustrating the pressure exerted on scientists by deniers are given in Lewandowsky et al. (2015). While Supran and Oreskes (2017) suggest that although ExxonMobil contributed to advancing science by its scientists' academic publications, it also promoted doubt in advertorials by emphasising uncertainties. The authors concluded that the oil company misled the public, a conclusion which ExxonMobil rejects. For an extensive discussion on the interaction between business, politics and climate science, interested readers are referred to Oreskes and Conway, "Merchants of Doubt" (Oreskes and Conway 2010).

Finally, it appears that the term "climate change" instead of the more accurate "global warming" was advocated for political reasons by the US Republican strategist Frank Luntz. "Climate change" was deemed to be less frightening (Lakoff 2010). The term has fallen into widespread use as scientists seek to be professional and non-alarmist in their terminology. By adopting this term, a subtle frame shift is achieved, which can de-emphasise certain aspects of a debate and instead promote one particular viewpoint. Using the term "climate change" instead of "global warming" shapes the way that people conceptualise and discuss the damage being done to the earth's delicate climate balance. This conceptualisation is done in a "hidden" manner by changing emotional associations; it is not done consciously (Lewandowsky et al. 2015; Lakoff 2010). In this respect, climate scientists may be falling into a trap by underplaying the crucial importance of their findings. This is now changing with scientists, politicians and UN officials starting to use stronger language, such as "climate emergency", "climate crisis", "global heating" or "climate breakdown" as better reflecting the reality of the emerging catastrophe (Carrington 2019).

Careful framing of information is something that many investors with insight into "behavioural finance" are aware of. The Financial Conduct

Authority (FCA) has published occasional papers on aspects of behavioural finance (Erta et al. 2013; Iscenko et al. 2014; Lukacs et al. 2016; Adams et al. 2016), seeking to understand the nature of mistakes made by consumers and how financial providers respond to these errors of judgement. One concern is that financial product design and sales processes may accentuate rather than ameliorate the effects of biases. In summary, perhaps climate scientists need to be more upfront about the implications of their findings, which are all too often hidden behind the cautious scientific language of uncertainty.

One such example is the seepage of the "hiatus" framing, referring to the alleged slowdown in GMSTs post 1998 and coinciding with the strongest El Niño event of the past century. Moving from the "denialosphere" into the realm of the climate sciences (Lewandowsky et al. 2015), this event resulted in over 200 peer-reviewed publications (Medhaug et al. 2017), all the while no such "hiatus" existed in the first place (Risbey et al. 2018). While rigorous discussions are necessary standard practice in science (for good reason), detailed technical debates can be detrimental to successful communication to the public. This is particularly true if the subject in question has been settled to the point it does not merit further scientific debate. In addition, when confronted with strongly crafted statements from outside sources with vested economic or ideological interests, scientists are often hesitant to speak up and defend their field or their views in equally strong terms. The framing and underplaying of climate change and the reluctance of scientists to defend their claims are pervasive reasons why the public is still confused about the reality of climate change.

Consequently, political and social scientists should continue to explore ways to avoid such detrimental messaging while at the same time providing tools for more effective communication in an ideologically-driven environment. Journalists may also need to be challenged in clearer terms if their narrative becomes victim to false balance too frequently. As suggested below, the discussion needs to shift more towards legal responsibilities given that physical causality and economic liability have been proven beyond doubt.

## Who Are the Emitters?

Analyses have begun to quantify the contributions to global warming considering the historical contributions from individual nations (Skeie et al. 2017) and companies (Ekwurzel et al. 2017), including changes in extreme event frequencies (Otto et al. 2017). However, from a stockholder perspective, investments are made into specific companies rather than into countries, thus sidestepping some national (and political) considerations.

Atmospheric $CO_2$ rose by about 98 ppm (parts per million) from 1880 (290 ppm) to 2010 (388 ppm) (IPCC 2013; Keeling et al. 2001), reaching 410 ppm in 2018 (Scripps Institution of Oceanography 2019). Climate modelling has been used at the industrial level (Ekwurzel et al. 2017), linking emissions from 90 major carbon producers showing that their emissions produced about 57% of the observed rise in atmospheric $CO_2$, approximately 42–50% of the rise in global mean surface temperatures and around 26–32% of global sea level rise over the 1880–2010 period (Ekwurzel et al. 2017). More recent figures for the 90 major producers indicate about 43% of atmospheric $CO_2$ rise, approximately 29–35% of global mean surface temperature rise and around 11–14% of global sea level rise since 1980 (Ekwurzel et al. 2017). Thus, around three-quarters (43/57) of the increase in atmospheric $CO_2$ is of recent origin, with analysis indicating that around two-thirds (29/42 or 35/50) of the rise in global mean surface temperatures can be traced to the more recent emissions (post 1980) (Ekwurzel et al. 2017). We can conclude that global mean temperature rises are around two-thirds attributable to accumulated $CO_2$ emissions between 1980 and 2010. Similar arguments could be explored in terms of global sea level rise, although this is not discussed here.

There is a great deal of complexity involved in estimating global warming from a range of different greenhouse gases, including $CO_2$, $CH_4$ and $N_2O$ (Skeie et al. 2017). Useful progress can be made by focusing primarily on $CO_2$ emissions, as cumulative $CO_2$ emissions are the primary cause of global climate system changes (Allen 2016), and historical responsibility can be allocated relatively simply. Our first estimate below neglects the question of the starting date for emissions and baseline hurricane levels, though this is discussed in the "Critique" section below.

The fossil fuel industry and its products accounted for 91% of global industrial greenhouse gas emissions in 2015 and about 70% of all anthropogenic emissions. If the trend in fossil fuel extraction continues over the next 28 years, as it has over the previous 28, global average temperatures would be on course to rise by around 4 °C (Griffin 2017). Since 1988 only 25 entities (both companies and state producers) accounted for 51% of global industrial emissions. Seven of these top 25 emitters were publicly

**Table 3.2** Cumulative 1988–2015 industrial greenhouse gas emissions from Scopes 1 + 3, % (Griffin 2017)

| *Producer* | | *Cumulative 1988–2015 emissions from Scopes 1 + 3 (%)* |
|---|---|---|
| 1 | ExxonMobil Corp | 2.0 |
| 2 | Royal Dutch Shell PLC | 1.7 |
| 3 | BP PLC | 1.5 |
| 4 | Chevron Corp | 1.3 |
| 5 | Peabody Energy Corp | 1.2 |
| 6 | Total SA | 0.9 |
| 7 | BHP Billiton Ltd | 0.9 |
| Total | | 9.5 |

owned companies (see Table 3.2), collectively accounting for 9.5% of Scope 1 and 3 emissions between 1988 and 2015[1] (Griffin 2017).

## What Would the Financial Damage Be?

The seven companies in Table 3.2 have a combined market capitalisation of around $1303 billion (August 2018) (Google 2018) [Previous articles used the combined market capitalisation for November 2017 of $1230 billion]. Consider the 9.5% figure from Table 3.2 and the $265 billion damages estimate for the 2017 Atlantic hurricane season, as an order of magnitude estimate. If, hypothetically, the seven firms contributed 9.5% of the hurricane damage from 2017, this would equal $25 billion [= $265bn × 9.5%]. An amount that would represent a 1.9% detriment to their market capitalisations (or share price), a significant sum, particularly considering that similar contributions might be requested in respect of other past and future extreme weather events.

The data in Fig. 3.1 includes the period 1988–2015, the same period as the emissions in Table 3.2. If the same logic is applied to the cumulative

[1] Scope 1 emissions are direct emissions that originate from sources that are owned and controlled by a company, for example, fuel used in company vehicles. Scope 2 emissions are indirect, resulting from energy used by a company, including electricity, steam, heating and cooling. This could include, for example, electricity purchased by a company from an external supplier. Scope 3 emissions cover all indirect emissions arising due to company activities. Scope 3 emissions include upstream and downstream value chain emissions. Scope 3 emissions include those of suppliers and customers using companies' products.

figures to 2017, the total inflation adjusted hurricane damages in 2017 US dollars are $816 billion. Under the same hypothetical calculation, if 9.5%[2] of this were to be contributed, this would amount to $77 billion [= $815.6bn × 9.5%], or 5.9% of share price. While this figure would cover historical emissions over the period 1988–2017, it omits other extreme weather events and consequences, such as sea level rise.

In a world where global warming causes more intense hurricanes which result in greater financial losses, if a hypothetical climate liability regime were to develop, damage contributions of around 1–2% of these high-emitting companies' market capitalisations (and share prices) might be anticipated increasingly frequently with each annual hurricane season. Furthermore, this figure ignores other global warming impacts, such as sea level rise, and could easily reach much larger sums if they were also included. It also neglects the likelihood of increasingly powerful climate responses as global warming intensifies.

### *Critique*

The current analysis is an initial exploration of how global-warming-induced extreme weather events may be attributed to specific companies. Estimates of the costs of those events have been expressed in terms of the decrease in the share price for the firms affected. At this stage, the arguments are incomplete, even though in broad terms the outline would appear scientifically robust. As such, although the scale of the quantitative estimates are uncertain, the potential for consequences for the share prices of individual companies are clear. The results presented here only relate to 2017 hurricane damages, and many other climate-related extreme weather events could result in additional damages, meaning that the risks are only partially quantified for investors in those companies.

A major question would be: what are the appropriate baseline levels to use? Hurricanes occurred before the onset of human-made global warming, so only the costs linked to additional frequency or intensity of hurricanes should be considered. While it may be difficult to estimate what the pre-global warming hurricane baseline should be, it would be a mistake to assume that the frequency or intensity of such events would be linearly dependent on atmospheric $CO_2$ concentrations or on global mean surface

[2] This assumes that the 9.5% contribution for the period 1988–2015 remains representative for the slightly longer 1988–2017 period.

temperature rise; there could easily be cliff-edge or non-linear effects. A small increase in $CO_2$ or global mean surface temperature could generate a disproportionately large extreme weather response. As highlighted recently, in the very long run, the earth may be nearing a regime where global warming becomes self-reinforcing (Steffen et al. 2018). For example, thawing of the Arctic could result in massive releases of methane, a powerful greenhouse gas, which would lead to further global warming (HRH The Prince of Wales, Juniper, and Shuckburgh 2017).

To estimate the pre-global warming hurricane baseline we consider precipitation levels. While precipitation is just one factor in TC damages, Hurricane Harvey may give an indication of baseline levels, with frequencies of such events increasing sixfold between the period 1981–2000 and 2017 (Emanuel 2017b). In this respect one estimate might be that as precipitation frequencies increased from 1 unit to 6 units over the interval, at least five-sixths of damage might be attributable to global warming since the late twentieth century. Of course, a larger portion would be attributable based on warming since earlier than 1981. The five-sixths factor based on the Hurricane Harvey precipitation increase since 1981 suggests that the damages might be reduced to $21 billion [= $25bn × 5/6], or 1.6% in share-price terms [= $21bn/$1303bn].

A further question would be: what is the extent to which fossil companies should be held responsible? What is their responsibility compared to users who burn the fuel, such as motorists in cars, or individuals heating their homes? Considering motor vehicle emissions, it would seem disingenuous to argue that it is all the fault of the motorist driving the car—in practice, their choice is whether they require a car. Fossil fuel free cars are relatively expensive in the present day, and not readily available over the historical period analysed. Much responsibility lies with the industrial suppliers to provide efficiency gains and alternative technologies to enable fossil-free transport. That does not excuse users, but the level of responsibility of each party has yet to be established. For example, private motorists generate non-industrial emissions. For users to take some responsibility, the allocation could be based on estimates of the current split between industrial and non-industrial emissions.

In 2015, about 70% of all anthropogenic emissions and 91% of global industrial emissions were fossil related (Griffin 2017). Thus, around 77%

[= 70% × 100%/91%][3] of all anthropogenic emissions were industrial, leaving 23% non-industrial emissions unaccounted for. If the 2015 figures are taken as representative of the split between industrial and non-industrial emissions, even though this proportion could easily vary over time, then the 9.5% of damages attributable to the seven firms in the analysis above ($25 billion) should perhaps be reduced to $19 billion [= $25bn × 0.77], resulting in a reduced—but still substantial—detriment to their share prices of 1.5% [= $19bn/$1303bn].

As previously mentioned, it would be necessary to consider the extent to which non-industrial emissions are a consequence of industrial emissions. After all, it is the companies that provide most of the greenhouse-gas-emitting products that private individuals use. The analysis also omits Scope 2 emissions resulting from energy used by a company, including electricity, steam, heating and cooling, although in global terms, these would be caught by the emissions of utility companies providing these services.

The above arguments highlight two aspects: firstly, the proportion of damages that should be attributed to global warming, estimated at five-sixths based on the Hurricane Harvey data above; and secondly, the split between extractor and user responsibility, here estimated at 77%. On this basis, the initial damage estimate of $25 billion above should potentially be reduced by both factors. Thus, the 9.5% of damages attributable to the seven firms listed should perhaps be reduced to $16 billion [calculated as $25bn × (5/6) × 0.77]. As a percentage of the market capitalisations of the seven firms in question, this figure still amounts to a share-price detriment of 1.2% [$16bn/$1303bn]. In combination, all these figures above still fit within the 1–2% share-price detriment mentioned above and do not alter the overall conclusion. These results are summarised in Table 3.3.

In terms of the scope of extreme weather events explored, this chapter only looks at hurricanes affecting the United States. Clearly, intense storms with strong winds and high precipitation occur in many parts of the world. Therefore, the global damages associated with these events could well be a multiple of those estimated costs above. That said, other factors, such as

[3] If we denote the fossil fuel industry as emitting $F$ tonnes of greenhouse gases in 2015, then $F = 0.91G$, where $G$ was global industrial emissions. Further, $F = 0.7A$, where $A$ was all anthropogenic emissions. Equating $0.91G = 0.7A$, thus $G = (0.7/0.91)A = 0.77A$. So around 77% of anthropogenic emissions were industrial, meaning that 23% were non-industrial.

**Table 3.3** Estimated 2017 Atlantic hurricane season hypothetical damage contributions expressed in billion dollars and as a percentage of the combined firm market capitalisations (see main text), with and without allowance for estimated hurricane baseline levels and producer-versus-user responsibility

| | *No allowance for increase above estimated hurricane baseline levels* | *Allowance for increase above estimated hurricane baseline levels (adjustment factor = 5/6)* |
|---|---|---|
| No allowance for producer-versus-user responsibility | \$25 billion<br>1.9% | \$21 billion<br>1.6% |
| Allowance for producer-versus-user responsibility (adjustment factor = 0.77) | \$19 billion<br>1.5% | \$16 billion<br>1.2% |

changing wind shear conditions, could lead to a less frequent overall TC count. On the other hand, the analysis also neglects sea level rise associated with global warming, which has the capacity to cause huge damage to affected areas. In other regions, droughts and heat waves leading to agricultural losses, water scarcity and stresses on human health are expected to rise (National Academies of Sciences, Engineering, and Medicine 2016).

## Legal Aspects

No legal precedent currently exists for climate damage liability from extreme weather events (Otto et al. 2017) and the Paris Agreement appears to make little mention of loss and damage estimates associated with climate change as a basis for liability; however, it may be established in the future (Thornton and Covington 2016). Thus, the barriers to a successful compensation case for climate damages are substantial, but with the science of attribution developing, the possibility of legal action remains. For major insurance companies or governments footing extreme weather event damage bills, the prospect of multibillion-dollar pay-outs may put focus on whether the legal barriers could be overcome, since this may allow them to pass on costs.

Alternatively, governments may consider raising the funds to cover climate damages by a range of indirect measures, possibly including carbon emissions taxes, carbon permit schemes or fuel duties based on carbon intensity. Proceeds from these measures could be set aside by governments to cover specific climate-related problems. Additionally, the implementation of such measures would have the potential to raise the prices of carbon-intensive energy sources and products, which would have the beneficial consequence of reducing demand for carbon-intensive products and thus accelerate the development of lower-carbon alternatives.

The need for climate science to inform other areas of wider society outside academia (including investors and legal experts) is now more crucial than ever. Despite the legal barriers mentioned above, there has been a spate of court cases regarding global warming (Levin 2018). Therefore, it is extremely important to ensure that legal and corporate parties have a robust scientific understanding of the results and knowledge boundaries of climate research when representing their clients in legal cases.

In early 2018, San Francisco and Oakland attempted legal action against oil corporations, including Chevron, ExxonMobil, Shell and BP, claiming they were responsible for damages related to global warming (Levin 2018). During the trial, the judge took the unusual step of convening a formal "tutorial" on global warming, allowing experts and the oil companies to answer key questions. Chevron's representative accepted that there was no debate about climate change, quoting the Intergovernmental Panel on Climate Change (IPCC) and the conclusion of AR5 SPM (Fifth Assessment Report, Summary for Policy Makers, IPCC 2013) that it is "extremely likely" that humans have been the dominant cause of warming since the mid-twentieth century, and claiming that the problem was international and that individual corporations were not liable. The Chevron representative said that "climate change is a global issue that requires global engagement and global action", and that "production and extraction" activities are not responsible for increases in emissions, but rather they are due to "economic and population growth", adding that it is the way people are living their lives (Levin 2018). Environmentalists noted that the assessment ignored cumulative emissions, that the United States was the biggest carbon polluter in history, and that Chevron was relying on outdated reports from 2012 (Levin 2018). Furthermore, environmentalists insisted that severe weather incidents were becoming more intense, with 17 of the last 18 years being the warmest on record (Levin 2018). However, the case was dismissed in June 2018 on the grounds that the matter fell within the competencies of the legislative authorities rather than that of the judiciary, also noting that the fossil fuel industry has brought many benefits to the world despite its major role in climate change (Slav 2018).

On 9 January 2018, the City of New York also filed a climate change lawsuit against BP, Chevron, ConocoPhillips, ExxonMobil and Royal Dutch Shell (Mooney and Crookes 2018). In June 2018, the oil companies asked a judge to throw out the case (van Voris 2018), arguing that a federal court was not the proper forum to regulate the global energy industry. The judge accepted their case, dismissing it on 19 July 2018 (Pierson 2018), with the judge saying that climate change should be addressed through federal regulation and foreign policy.

In another instance, on 2 July 2018, Rhode Island, the smallest US state, filed a case against 21 oil companies, including Exxon, Chevron and ConocoPhillips, for contributing to climate change and damaging the state's coastline, marine ecosystem and economy, according to the state's Attorney General, Peter Kilmartin (Slav 2018). The Attorney General stated that Rhode Island was especially vulnerable to climate change due to sea level rise and increases in severe weather patterns as seen in the last few years.

Given the outcomes of previous cases, the chances of success are uncertain, but Rhode Island has been ambitious by being the first US state to sue the oil industry for the effects of climate change. Regardless of the outcomes, the cases may weaken the illusion that the oil industry is too big to take on. Even if in the Californian and New York cases, oil companies have maintained that the issue of climate change does not belong in court, but with the legislative authorities of the country (Slav 2018), the repeated litigation may undermine their moral position. Regardless of the legal outcome, the City of New York stated that it would start seeking ways to divest its $189 billion pension schemes out of fossil fuel companies in a responsible way, consistent with fiduciary obligations (Mooney and Crookes 2018). In this respect, while legal cases to date may not have made progress, the change in attitude among large institutional investors does point to ethical and sustainable investing as a means of promoting change. Other instances, such as a recent court case of a Peruvian farmer against the German energy company RWE, highlight that we may only be at the beginning of a series of legal conflicts.

To an ethical and sustainable investor, the successes of oil companies in legal cases may look like something of a Pyrrhic victory[4] when a state pen-

[4] Pyrrhus of Epirus defeated the Romans in the battle of Asculum in 280 BC, but suffered such heavy losses that ultimately his campaign failed. Thus, he "won the battle, but lost the war".

sion scheme simply decides to disinvest from the firms in question. Ethical investors can encourage market forces to affect behavioural change when legal cases do not.

## How Should Investors React?

It is hard to say how rapidly investors should respond to the possibility of companies having or deciding to make contributions for damages associated with global warming caused by their past emissions.

Should investors react at all? Cautious investors might be concerned, particularly if they are uncertain how much these risks are priced into the relevant companies' shares. Market participants seek to anticipate investment opportunities and avoid risks ahead of competitors, making markets forward-looking. Investors must, therefore, make judgements and forecasts about the economy and other developments to gauge investment outcomes in the face of incomplete information. Imperfect or fragmented information results in a wide range of views, which cannot, of course, all be correct. However, as other investors will seek to anticipate trends, market participants do not have the luxury of waiting for certainty to develop, since by then markets will have already responded and share prices will have adjusted (Rayer 2018). Thus, any movement towards an active liability regime could risk shares in such companies becoming stranded assets, with other investors being reluctant to buy them, except at a significant discount—a fact that oil companies are aware of (Supran and Oreskes 2017). Given the mounting evidence, investors may question whether these risks are appropriately priced into high-$CO_2$-emitting companies' shares.

## Conclusion

Potential liabilities for damages from extreme weather events due to emissions may be under-represented in share prices of firms in carbon-intensive sectors. As an example, the authors consider the 2017 Atlantic hurricane season, which had estimated damages of $265 billion. Considering the emissions of the top seven carbon-emitting publicly listed companies, under a hypothetical climate liability regime, these firms might increasingly see costs of around 1–2% of their market capitalisations (or equivalent reductions to share price) from North Atlantic hurricane seasons.

The chapter starts by reviewing US hurricane damages and the relationship with hurricane categories, before looking at the climate science linking extreme weather events to global warming. To conceptualise this link, the atmosphere-ocean system can be considered as a global-scale heat engine, which can be expected to run "faster" or with greater "intensity" as temperature increases. Detailed discussions then follow to link the science behind global warming with the intensity and frequency of tropical cyclones, precipitation, storm surge risk, floods, droughts and heatwaves. The science shows an emerging consensus that the frequency of the most intense storms will increase with global warming.

In some quarters, acceptance that human activities are the cause of climate change as a result of carbon dioxide (and other greenhouse gas) emissions has been strongly resisted, by "climate deniers". This is despite overwhelming evidence from the climate science community that global warming is occurring, with human activity being the primary cause (AGW). Over 97% of peer-reviewed scientific papers on global warming support the AGW consensus. Public perception appears not to reflect this, with "false" balance in the media helping perpetuate a sense of doubt. Several aspects of "climate denier" activities are discussed, including pressure put on scientists and whether fossil companies have deliberately promoted doubt. The question of framing information is also explored, noting how terms such as "climate change" are less emotive, but may less accurately reflect the gravity of the emerging climate catastrophe than "global warming" or other more powerful terms.

The damages from the 2017 Atlantic hurricane season are linked to the recent cumulative emissions of 7 of the top 25 emitting entities that are publicly owned companies and collectively responsible for 9.5% of Scope 1 and 3 emissions between 1988 and 2015. By allocating hypothetical damages based on cumulative emissions, the costs of the 2017 Atlantic hurricane season can be seen to amount to 1.9% of the market capitalisations of the seven firms mentioned. This level of damages refers to only a single year (2017), one type of extreme weather event (hurricanes) and a single geographic locality (the Atlantic). Thus, inclusion of other climate-related extreme weather events could be expected to result in significantly higher costs, amounting to a much higher percentage of the seven firms' market capitalisations. Further, as global warming intensifies, more powerful extreme weather events would be expected.

As hurricanes existed before the onset of human-caused global warming, allowance should be made for a baseline level, with only the additional frequency or intensity of hurricanes to be considered. Precipitation levels from Hurricane Harvey are used to estimate what an appropriate baseline level might be. As a result, the costs of the 2017 Atlantic hurricane season were reduced to 1.6% of the market capitalisations of the seven firms mentioned.

A further question relates to the responsibility of the fossil producer firms (the seven firms considered) against the responsibility of those using their products. Based on 2015 figures for the split between industrial and non-industrial anthropogenic emissions, it is suggested that 77% of the costs should be allocated to the fossil producer firms. Using this factor in isolation suggests that costs of the 2017 Atlantic hurricane season would amount to 1.5% of the seven firms' market capitalisations. If both the hurricane baseline level and the appropriate share of producer responsibility are considered, the costs of the 2017 Atlantic hurricane season are reduced to 1.2% of the market capitalisations of the seven firms mentioned. The figures above all sit within the range of 1–2% of the market capitalisations of the seven producer firms.

At present, no legal precedent exists for climate damage liability from extreme weather events; however, it may be established in future. Currently, costs are borne by governments or insurance companies, who may wish to consider whether the legal barriers could be overcome, since it may allow them to pass on costs. Governments could also consider raising funds to cover climate damages by indirect measures such as taxes, permits or duties. These could also raise the prices of carbon-intensive energy sources and products and thus accelerate the development of lower-carbon alternatives.

Several court cases regarding global warming are reviewed, highlighting the need for climate science to inform areas of society outside of academia. Lawyers and companies need a robust understanding of the results and knowledge boundaries of climate research when representing their clients. Thus far, the legal cases have been deemed to lie outside the competencies of the courts in question.

Although no legal cases to date have established a climate damage liability, some actors have backed up legal action with investment policies. The City of New York is seeking to divest its $189 billion pension schemes out of fossil companies in a way consistent with fiduciary responsibilities. This highlights a crucial role that ethical investors can play by using market forces to affect behavioural change when legal cases do not.

Investors must consider how rapidly they should respond to the possibility of fossil companies having or deciding to make contributions for damages associated with global warming caused by their past emissions. It is uncertain to what extent climate risks are priced into fossil companies' share prices, and cautious investors might be concerned. Any movement towards an active liability regime could risk shares in fossil companies becoming stranded assets, with other investors reluctant to buy them, except at a significant discount. Given the mounting evidence, investors may question whether these risks are adequately priced into high-$CO_2$-emitting companies' shares.

**Acknowledgements** The authors would like to thank Dr Richard Millar of the University of Oxford for his involvement in the development of early versions of the material presented in the chapter as well as Dr Pete Walton of the University of Oxford for helping develop the contacts for this cross-disciplinary collaboration. They would also like to thank the anonymous reviewers for their helpful feedback.

## References

Adams, P., Aquilina, M., Baker, R., Brambley, W., Nava, A., Pathak, S., et al. (2016). *Full disclosure: A round-up of FCA experimental research into giving information*. Financial Conduct Authority. Retrieved from https://www.fca.org.uk, Occasional Paper 23.

Allen, M. R. (2016). Drivers of peak warming in a consumption-maximizing world. *Nature Climate Change, 4*. https://doi.org/10.1038/NCLIMATE2977.

Ballinger, A. P., Merlis, T. M., Held, I. M., & Zhao, M. (2015). The sensitivity of tropical cyclone activity to off-equatorial thermal forcing in aquaplanet simulations. *Journal of the Atmospheric Sciences, 72*, 2286–2302. https://doi.org/10.1175/JAS-D-14-0284.1.

BBC. (2017a, October 25). *BBC wrong to not challenge climate sceptic Lord Lawson*. Retrieved November 13, 2017, from http://www.bbc.co.uk/news/uk-41744344.

BBC. (2017b, December 18). *Ofcom to investigate BBC climate change interview*. Retrieved December 21, 2017, from http://www.bbc.co.uk/news/entertainment-arts-42400653.

Bhatia, K., Vecchi, G., Murakami, H., Underwood, S., & Kossin, J. (2018). Projected response of tropical cyclone intensity and intensification in a global climate model. *Journal of Climate*. https://doi.org/10.1175/JCLI-D-17-0898.1.

Blake, E. S., & Gibney, E. J. (2011). *The deadliest, costliest, and most intense United States tropical cyclones from 1851 to 2010 (and other frequently requested hurricane facts).* Miami: NOAA Technical Memorandum NWS NHC-6, National Weather Service, National Hurricane Center.

Boykoff, M. T., & Boykoff, J. M. (2004). Balance as bias: Global warming and the US prestige press. *Global Environmental Change, 14*, 125–136.

Carrington, D. (2019, May 17). Why the Guardian is changing the language it uses about the environment. *The Guardian*. Retrieved August 14, 2019, from https://www.theguardian.com/environment/2019/may/17/why-the-guardian-is-changing-the-language-it-uses-about-the-environment.

Christensen, J. H., Kanikicharla, K. K., Aldrian, E., An, S., Cavalcanti, I. F., de Castro, M., et al. (2013). Climate phenomena and their relevance for future regional climate change. In T. F. Stocker, D. Qin, G. K. Plattner, M. Tignor, S. K. Allen, J. Boschung, … P. M. Midgley (Eds.), *Climate Change 2013: The physical science basis. Contribution of Working Group I to the fifth assessment report of the intergovernmental panel on climate change* (pp. 1217–1308). Cambridge, UK and New York, NY: Cambridge University Press. https://doi.org/10.1017/CBO9781107415324.028.

Cohen, J., Pfeiffer, K., & Francis, J. A. (2018). Warm Arctic episodes linked with increased frequency of extreme winter weather in the United States. *Nature Communications, 9*, 869. https://doi.org/10.1038/s41467-018-02992-9.

Cook, J., Nuccitelli, D., Green, S. A., Richardson, M., Winkler, B., Painting, R., Way, R., Jacobs, P., & Skuce, A. (2013). Quantifying the consensus on anthropogenic global warming in the scientific literature. *Environmental Research Letters, 8*(024024), 7.

Cook, J., Oreskes, N., Doran, P. T., Anderegg, R. L., Verheggen, B., Maibach, E. W., Carlton, J. S., Lewandowsky, S., Skuce, A. G., Green, S. A., Nuccitelli, D., Jacobs, P., Richardson, M., Winkler, B., Painting, R., & Rice, K. (2016). Consensus on consensus: A synthesis of consensus estimates on human-caused global warming. *Environmental Research Letters, 11*(048002), 7.

Dietz, S., Bowen, A., Dixon, C., & Gradwell, P. (2016). Climate value at risk of global financial assets. *Nature Climate Change, 6*, 676–679. ISSN: 1758-678X, https://doi.org/10.1038/nclimate2972.

Durack, P. J., Wijffels, S. E., & Matear, R. J. (2012). Ocean salinities reveal strong global water cycle intensification during 1950 to 2000. *Science, 336*(6080), 455–458. https://doi.org/10.1126/science.1212222.

Ekwurzel, B., Boneham, J., Dalton, M. W., Heede, R., Mera, R. J., Allen, M. R., & Frumhoff, P. C. (2017). The rise in global atmospheric CO2, surface temperature, and sea level from emissions traced to major carbon producers. *Climatic Change, 144*, 579–590.

Emanuel, K. (2013). Downscaling CMIP5 climate models shows increased tropical cyclone activity over the 21st century. *Proceedings of the National Academy of Sciences, 110*(30), 12219–12224.

Emanuel, K. (2017a). A fast intensity simulator for tropical cyclone risk analysis. *Natural Hazards, 88*(2), 779–796. https://doi.org/10.1007/s11069-017-2890-7.

Emanuel, K. (2017b). Assessing the present and future probability of Hurricane Harvey's rainfall. *Proceedings of the National Academy of Sciences of the USA*. https://doi.org/10.1073/pnas.1716222114.

Emanuel, K., & Sobel, A. (2013). Response of tropical sea surface temperature, precipitation, and tropical cyclone-related variables to changes in global and local forcing. *Journal of Advances in Modeling Earth Systems, 5*, 447–458. https://doi.org/10.1002/jame.20032.

Erta, K., Hunt, S., Iscenko, Z., & Brambley, W. (2013). *Applying behavioural economics at the Financial Conduct Authority*. Financial Conduct Authority. Retrieved from https://www.fca.org.uk, Occasional Paper 1.

Francis, J. A., Vavrus, S. J., & Cohen, J. (2017). Amplified Arctic warming and mid-latitude weather: Emerging connections. *WIREs Clim Change, 8*, e474. https://doi.org/10.1002/wcc.474).

Google. (2018). *Google finance*. Retrieved August 6, 2018, from https://www.google.com/.

Griffin, P. (2017). *The Carbon Majors Database, CDP Carbon Majors Report 2017*. London: CDP (Carbon Disclosure Project).

Hartmann, D. L., Tank, A. M., Rusticucci, M., Alexander, L. V., Brönnimann, S., Charabi, Y. A., Dentener, F. J., Dlugokencky, E. J., Easterling, D. R., Kaplan, A., Soden, B. J., Thorne, P. W., Wild, M., & Zhai, P. (2013). Observations: Atmosphere and surface. In T. F. Stocker, D. Qin, G. K. Plattner, M. Tignor, S. K. Allen, J. Boschung, et al. (Eds.), *Climate change 2013: The physical science basis. Contribution of Working Group I to the fifth assessment report of the intergovernmental panel on climate change* (pp. 159–254). Cambridge, UK and New York, NY: Cambridge University Press.

Haustein, K., Allen, M. R., Forster, P. M., Otto, F. E., Mitchell, D. M., Matthews, H. D., & Frame, D. J. (2017). A real-time Global Warming Index. *Scientific Reports, 7*, 15417. https://doi.org/10.1038/s41598-017-14828-5.

HRH The Prince of Wales, Juniper, T., & Shuckburgh, E. (2017). *Climate change*. London: Ladybird Books, Random House.

IPCC. (2013). *Climate change 2013: The physical science basis. Contribution of Working Group I to the fifth assessment report of the intergovernmental panel on climate change 2013*. Cambridge, UK, and New York, NY: Cambridge University Press. Retrieved from www.ipcc.ch.

Iscenko, Z., Duke, C., Huck, S., & Wallace, B. (2014). *How does selling insurance as an add-on affect consumer decisions?* Financial Conduct Authority. Retrieved from https://www.fca.org.uk, Occasional Paper 3.

Johnson, D. (2017, September 24). *Is this the worst hurricane season ever? Here's how it compares.* (*TIME*). Retrieved November 13, 2017, from http://time.com/4952628/hurricane-season-harvey-irma-jose-maria/.

Keeling, C. D., Piper, S. C., Bacastow, R. B., Wahlen, M., Whorf, T. P., Heimann, M., et al. (2001). *Exchanges of atmospheric $CO_2$ and $^{13}CO_2$ with the terrestrial biosphere and oceans from 1978 to 2000.* I. Global aspects, SIO Reference Series, No. 01-06, Scripps Institution of Oceanography, San Diego, 88 pages.

Khouakhi, A., & Villarini, G. (2017). Attribution of annual maximum sea levels to tropical cyclones at the global scale. *International Journal of Climatology, 37*(1), 540–547.

Knutson, T. R., McBride, J. L., Chan, J., Emanuel, K., Holland, G., Landsea, C., Held, I., Kossin, J. P., Srivastava, A. K., & Sugi, M. (2010). Tropical cyclones and climate change. *Nature Geoscience, 3*, 157–163.

Knutson, T. R., Sirutis, J. J., Zhao, M., Tuleya, R. E., Bender, M., Vecchi, G. A., Villarini, G., & Chavas, D. (2015). Global projections of intense tropical cyclone activity for the late twenty-first century from dynamical downscaling of CMIP5/RCP4.5 scenarios. *Journal Climate, 28*(18), 7203–7224.

Krosinsky, C., Robins, N., & Viederman, S. (2012). *Evolutions in sustainable investing: Strategies, funds and thought leadership.* Hoboken, NJ: John Wiley & Sons.

Lakoff, G. (2010). Why it matters how we frame the environment. *Environmental Communication, 4*(1), 70–81. https://doi.org/10.1080/17524030903529749.

Laliberté, F., Zika, J., Mudryk, L., Kushner, P. J., Kjellsson, J., & Döös, K. (2015). Constrained work output of the moist atmospheric heat engine in a warming climate. *Science, 347*(6221), 540–543.

Leach, N. J., Millar, R. J., Haustein, K., Jenkins, S., Graham, E., & Allen, M. R. (2018). Current level and rate of warming determine emissions budgets under ambitious mitigation. *Nature Geoscience, 11*, 574–579.

Lehmann, J., Mempel, F., & Coumou, D. (2018). Increased occurrence of record-wet and record-dry months reflect changes in mean rainfall. *Geophysical Research Letters.* https://doi.org/10.1029/2018GL079439.

Levin, S. (2018, March 21). Climate science on trial as high-profile US case takes on fossil fuel industry. *The Guardian.* Retrieved March 22, 2018, from https://www.theguardian.com/environment/2018/mar/21/climate-science-lawsuit-san-francisco-sues-chevron.

Lewandowsky, S., Oreskes, N., Risbey, J. S., Newell, B. R., & Smithson, M. (2015). Seepage: Climate change denial and its effect on the scientific community. *Global Environmental Change, 33*, 1–13.

Lin, N., Kopp, R. E., Horton, B. P., & Donnelly, J. P. (2016). Hurricane Sandy's flood frequency increasing from year 1800 to 2100. *Proceedings of the National Academy of Sciences, 113*(43), 12071–12075.

Lukacs, P., Neubecker, L., & Rowan, P. (2016). *Price discrimination and cross-subsidy in financial services.* Financial Conduct Authority. Retrieved from https://www.fca.org.uk, Occasional Paper 22.

Medhaug, I., Stolpe, M. B., Fischer, E. M., & Knutti, R. (2017). Reconciling controversies about the 'global warming hiatus'. *Nature, 545*, 41–56. https://doi.org/10.1038/nature22315.

Mooney, A., & Crookes, E. (2018, January 10). New York sues big oil companies over climate change. *Financial Times.* Retrieved August 1, 2018, from https://www.ft.com/content/4de8e4fc-f62b-11e7-88f7-5465a6ce1a00.

National Academies of Sciences, Engineering, and Medicine. (2016). *Attribution of extreme weather events in the context of climate change.* Washington, DC: The National Academies Press.

National Hurricane Center. (2018). *Costliest U.S. tropical cyclones tables updated.* Miami: National Oceanic and Atmospheric Administration.

Oreskes, N. (2004). The scientific consensus on climate change. *Science, 306*, 1686.

Oreskes, N. (2007). The scientific consensus on climate change: How do we know we're not wrong? In *Climate change, what it means for us, our children, and our grandchildren* (pp. 65–99). Cambridge, MA: MIT Press.

Oreskes, N., & Conway, E. M. (2010). *Merchants of doubt.* New York: Bloomsbury Press.

Otto, F. E., Skele, R. B., Fuglestvedt, J. S., Berntsen, T., & Allen, M. R. (2017). Assigning historic responsibility for extreme weather events. *Nature Climate Change, 7*, 757–759.

Peixoto, J. P., & Oort, A. H. (1992). *Physics of Climate.* New York: American Institute of Physics. ISBN-10: 0883187124.

Pew. (2012). *More say there is solid evidence of global warming.* Washington, DC: Pew Research Center for the People & the Press.

Pierson, B. (2018, July 19). Oil majors win dismissal of New York City climate lawsuit. *Reuters.* Retrieved August 1, 2018, from https://www.reuters.com/article/us-new-york-climatechange-lawsuit/oil-majors-win-dismissal-of-new-york-city-climate-lawsuit-idUSKBN1K931T.

Porritt, J. (2001). *The world in context: Beyond the business case for sustainable development.* Cambridge: HRH The Prince of Wales' Business and the Environment Programme, Cambridge Programme for Industry.

Rahmstorf, S., Box, J. E., Feulner, G., Mann, M. E., Robinson, A., Rutherford, S., & Schaffernicht, E. J. (2015). Exceptional twentieth-century slowdown in Atlantic Ocean overturning circulation. *Nature Climate Change, 5*, 475–480. https://doi.org/10.1038/NCLIMATE2554.

Rayer, Q. G. (2018). Market crises: Should we discuss them more – including with our clients? *Review of Financial Markets, Q1*, 66–69.

Rayer, Q. G., & Millar, R. J. (2018a, February 8). Investing in extreme weather conditions. *Citywire Wealth Manager* (429), 36.

Rayer, Q. G., & Millar, R. J. (2018b, June 11). Hurricanes hit company share prices. *Citywire New Model Adviser* (596), 18.

Rayer, Q. G., & Millar, R. J. (2018c). Investing in the climate. *Physics World, 31*(8), 17.

Risbey, J. S., Lewandowsky, S., Cowtan, K., Oreskes, N., Rahmstorf, S., Jokimäki, A., et al. (2018). A fluctuation in surface temperature in historical context: Reassessment and retrospective on the evidence. *Environmental Research Letters, 13*(123008., doi.org/10.1088/1748-9326/aaf342).

Scripps Institution of Oceanography. (2019). *The keeling curve*. Retrieved February 4, 2019, from https://scripps.ucsd.edu/programs/keelingcurve/.

Simpson, R. H. (1974). The hurricane disaster potential scale. *Weatherwise, 27*(169), 186.

Skeie, R. B., Fuglestvedt, J., Berntsen, T., Peters, G. P., Andrew, R., Allen, M., & Kallbekken, S. (2017). Perspective has a strong effect on the calculation of historical contributions to global warming. *IOP, Environmental Research Letters, 12*(2), 024022.

Slav, I. (2018, July 3). *Rhode Island launches anti-oil lawsuit.* (oilprice.com). Retrieved July 4, 2018, from https://oilprice.com/Latest-Energy-News/World-News/Rhode-Island-Launches-Anti-Oil-Lawsuite.html.

Steffen, W., Rockström, J., Richardson, K., Lenton, T. M., Folke, C., Liverman, D., Summerhayes, C. P., Barnosky, A. D., Cornell, S. E., Crucifix, M., Donges, J. F., Fetzer, I., Lade, S. J., Scheffer, M., Winkelmann, R., & Schellnhuber, H. J. (2018). Trajectories of the earth system in the anthropocene. *PNAS, 115*(33), 8252–8259. https://doi.org/10.1073/pnas.1810141115.

Stern, N. (2006). *Stern review executive summary.* London: New Economics Foundation.

Supran, G., & Oreskes, N. (2017). Assessing ExxonMobil's climate change communications (1977–2014). *Environmental Research Letters, 12*(8), 084019.

Taylor, K. E., Stouffer, R. J., & Meehl, G. A. (2012). An overview of CMIP5 and the experiment design. *Bulletin of the American Meteorological Society, 93*, 485–498. https://doi.org/10.1175/BAMS-D-11-00094.1.

Thornton, J., & Covington, H. (2016). Climate change before the court. *Nature Geoscience, 9*, 3–5.

UN FCCC. (2015). *Adoption of the Paris agreement.* United Nations Framework Convention on Climate Change.

United States Search and Rescue Task Force. (2018). *Hurricanes.* Retrieved October 2, 2018, from http://www.ussartf.org/hurricanes.htm.

van Oldenborgh, G. J., van der Wiel, K., Sebastian, A., Singh, R., Arrighi, J., Otto, F., et al. (2017). Attribution of extreme rainfall from Hurricane Harvey, August 2017. *IOP Environmental Research Letters, 12*, 124009. Retrieved from http://iopscience.iop.org/article/10.1088/1748-9326/aa9ef2.

van Voris, B. (2018, June 13). Oil companies ask to throw out New York's climate change Lawsuit. *Bloomberg*. Retrieved August 1, 2018, from https://www.bloomberg.com/news/articles/2018-06-13/oil-companies-ask-to-throw-out-new-york-s-climate-change-lawsuit.

Vecchi, G. A., & Villarini, G. (2014). Next season's hurricanes. *Science, 343*(6171), 618–619. https://doi.org/10.1126/science.1247759.

Walsh, K. J., McBride, J. L., Klotzbach, P. J., Balachandran, S., Camargo, S., Holland, G., Knutson, T., Kossin, J., Lee, T., Sobel, A., & Sugi, M. (2016). Tropical cyclones and climate change. *Wiley Interdisciplinary Reviews: Climate Change, 7*(1), 65–89.

Woodruff, J. D., Irish, J. L., & Camargo, S. J. (2013). Coastal flooding by tropical cyclones and sea-level rise. *Nature, 504*(7478), 44–52.

Zielinski, S. (2015, January 29). *Climate change is altering the global heat engine.* Retrieved from https://www.smithsonianmag.com/science-nature/climate-change-altering-global-heat-engine-180954079/.

CHAPTER 4

# Mapping Out When and Where Climate Risk Becomes a Credit Risk

*James Leaton*

## Introduction

The growing attention on climate risk by the financial system has resulted in an increasing focus on definitions and reference points for financial institutions. As a result, the Financial Stability Board created a taskforce that published recommendations on climate-related financial disclosure (Financial Stability Board 2017). The taskforce differentiates between the two main types of climate risk: transition risk and physical risk. This chapter discusses each in turn and how they relate to potential credit risk.

Credit risk analysis is concerned with assessing the ability of an entity to continue servicing its debt. It results in a focus on factors which have a material financial impact on the creditworthiness of a debt issuer, for example, related to profitability and leverage ratios. Separate to this type

The views expressed in this chapter are those of the author, and not necessarily those of Moody's.

J. Leaton (✉)
London, UK
e-mail: James.Leaton@moodys.com

 
T. Walker et al. (eds.), *Ecological, Societal, and Technological Risks and the Financial Sector*, Palgrave Studies in Sustainable Business In Association with Future Earth, https://doi.org/10.1007/978-3-030-38858-4_4

of analysis, there is a growing interest in financial products that demonstrate a positive or reduced impact on the environment and society. These products are looking at the impact in a different direction—the external impact of an entity—which may or may not have any financial significance for its creditworthiness. Indeed, the distinction is captured in the concept of 'double materiality', which is applied as an example in the European Union's proposals for non-financial reporting (European Commission 2017). The continuing presence of environmental externalities demonstrates that in many situations, the polluter is not made to pay, and therefore having a large negative impact on the environment does not necessarily result in a material financial cost. Not all environmental impacts will have a consequence for credit risk.

Whilst there is some crossover in terms of the approaches taken to identify climate risks, it should be noted that these risks can manifest themselves in different parts of the capital markets when viewed through an investor lens. Hence, the focus and interests of debtholders may not always align with those of the shareholders in the same company. This situation can be explained by the different exposure to potential upside and risk that results from holding equity versus bonds. For example, an equity-holder may be supportive of increasing borrowing to grow long term; however, a bondholder will consider the increased leverage from taking on extra debt and the increased risk that a borrower will be unable to make interest payments.

From a climate risk perspective, exposure and risk may also be concentrated in different areas. For example, equity investors may prioritise the companies with the largest market cap and the largest emissions as a focus for engagement. These were major factors in determining the companies included in the Climate Action 100 list being used by a coalition of investors to co-ordinate engagement on climate risk (e.g., Climate Action 100 2017). Fixed-income investors may be more concerned with smaller companies with lower credit ratings, which are more susceptible to default and would result in higher losses in the event of a default.

Fixed-income investors should also consider how risk may be transferred between asset classes. If there is an expectation that public entities will bail out the private sector actors, then it should be reflected in the risk analysis. This situation occurred in Alberta, Canada, where Kinder Morgan, the developer of a proposed pipeline, has achieved a reduced risk profile and lower leverage by selling the Trans Mountain project to the federal government for CAD$ 4.5 billion when opposition made progress impossible in 2018 (Morgan 2018). As a result, the risk became elevated for the Canadian government, which took over the costs of project construction, and for the province of Alberta, which has future royalties at risk.

This type of risk transfer also demonstrates why an overarching framework is needed to capture climate risk instead of analysts looking at issuers in isolation. The UNEP (United Nations Environment Programme) Finance Initiative worked with a number of banks to develop a high-level framework that lays out a useful approach for understanding the potential exposure of a lending portfolio to climate risk, which includes transition scenarios, portfolio impact assessment, and borrower-level calibration (UNEP Finance Initiative 2018). These banks are now trialling these approaches to test if they are fit for purpose.

Consideration of climate risk for fixed-income investors has come later than for equity investors. As a result, there is limited evidence regarding how climate risk relates to credit risk. Firstly, many studies are based on 'ESG scores' (environmental, social, and governance), which do not necessarily focus on the most material credit issues, but include metrics relating to historical impact (e.g., $CO_2$ emissions), governance (e.g., corporate policies on climate change), or disclosure (e.g., the information published on these issues). The evidence available largely indicates that there is no strong correlation between these environmental scores and credit indicators, let alone any clear causal relationship (e.g., see Barclays 2018). The picture is further confused by scores that combine the environmental, social, and governance factors, which may in fact cancel each other out.

Secondly, the types of risk analysed present data challenges compared to established financial metrics with decades of historical data, such as debt default rates. Transition risk, by its nature, implies a change occurring. This definition means that using three-year trailing average performance as an indicator is not going to designate when the transition is starting. Historical physical climate change data is available and has been applied to some financial products, such as natural catastrophe insurance. However, the data can present challenges in terms of getting the granularity and predictive capacity desired. The distribution of physical climate events that occur in consecutive years has no respect for the long-term average probability statistics.

Systems for addressing climate risk can provide frameworks for identifying and understanding relative exposure to the different types of risk. Yet, no crystal ball can predict exactly where and when climate risks will impact the market. Financial regulators are also working to understand how to assess the systemic climate risk to markets and the exposure of financial institutions, with many central banks and regulators now members of the Network for Greening the Financial System (Network for Greening the Financial System 2019). As scrutiny is increasingly placed on this area, so are the tools being developed to meet the requirements of the regulated financial sector.

## Identifying Transition Risk

Transition risk relates to the policy, technology, and market changes that accompany the shift to a low-carbon economy. These categories are the three main transmission channels through which analysts think about transition risk. The pace and scale of this transition is uncertain, which influences how credit analysts may think about it.

History tells us that sectors undergoing a transition often underestimate the speed at which it happens, as evidenced by incumbents sticking to the same strategies, perhaps in denial of the changes occurring around them. Whilst most transitions do not manifest as overnight wholesale changes, a fundamental switch in the direction of travel can be enough to pose serious challenges. For example, a market moving from growth to decline requires a different strategy, can affect marginal producers significantly, and may weaken prices across the board. This dynamic also makes capital investments questionable and may lead to difficult decisions about how and when to deal with overcapacity.

### *US Coal Mining Sector Example*

To take the US coal mining sector as an example, the industry failed to recognise a structural decline in demand for its product. This decline occurred because of policy factors (emissions standards), technology changes (cheaper renewables), and market factors (cheaper shale gas). Disclosures to investors at the time continued to talk up their assets and identify export markets as a plan B. The outcome was that most of the large US pure coal mining companies filed for bankruptcy protection in 2016, leading to capital restructuring (Moody's 2019b).

Table 4.1 provides the credit rating migration over time as the structural challenges impacted the US coal mining industries. Most companies saw their credit ratings bottom out in 2016, and only Arch Coal achieved

**Table 4.1** Moody's credit ratings for US coal mining companies 2014–2018

| *Company* | *Moody's credit rating over time* | | |
|---|---|---|---|
| | *2014* | *2016* | *2018* |
| Arch Coal Inc. | B3 | C | Ba3 |
| Bowie Resource Partners LLC | B2 | Caa1 | Caa1 |
| Cloud Peak Energy Resources LLC | Ba3 | Caa2 | Caa1 |
| Foresight Energy LLC | B2 | Caa3 | B3 |
| Murray Energy Corporation | B2 | Ca | B3 |
| Natural Resource Partners LP | B1 | B3 | B3 |
| Peabody Energy Corporation | Ba2 | Ca | Ba3 |
| Westmoreland Coal Company | Caa1 | Caa3 | Caa3 |

Source: Moody's Investor Services (2018e)

the rating it had in 2014 again by 2018. The companies had to file for Chap. 11 bankruptcy protection and/or to implement significant restructuring in order to continue operations.

The degree of financial impact the companies experienced depended on many factors, including:

- the degree of exposure to metallurgical coal for steel production, which diversified risk;
- the relative profitability/margin of the production;
- the location of the production and potential for exports; and
- the degree of existing leverage from merger and acquisition (M&A) activity in recent years.

This example also demonstrates that if the transition is not recognised, then an industry with concentrated risk can very quickly start defaulting on its loans.

### *Transmission Channels*

As demonstrated by the US coal mining sector example, there are three primary ways in which carbon transition risk can manifest itself.

**Policy:** The regulation of emissions or the government support of low-carbon alternatives can create policy risk for carbon-intensive activities. Different mechanisms provide varying levels of certainty in terms of the emissions outcome, with market-based measures less certain. The most definitive policy mechanisms indicate a phase-out of a particular activity over a given timeline. For example, in a number of European countries, governments have indicated the year by which coal will cease generating power. This may in fact result in earlier closures, as there is little incentive to keep investing and cheaper alternatives are already available. Carbon pricing mechanisms provide a market signal; however, whether this signal triggers a switch in generation depends on the relative commodity prices for coal and gas, other policy measures, and the overall emissions cap being applied. It may also be necessary to consider how easy it is for the emitter to pass this cost down the value chain, reducing the impact on its own margins.

Support for the sales of electric vehicles through purchase subsidies or production targets represents a risk for those who delay developing these technologies. Emissions regulations across China, Europe, and California give extra credits for electrified vehicles, which is rewarding those who have invested early. This example demonstrates how environmental regulation is starting to require major capital investment or impose material penalties for non-compliance. Moreover, a significant revenue stream for Tesla is sales of emissions credits to conventional auto manufacturers, which is an extra revenue source derived from being a leader in producing electric vehicles. These policy measures are therefore not negative financially for all participants in the market.

**Technology:** It is difficult to predict the disruptive force that is technology. Most analyses will focus primarily on relative cost to ascertain when a technology might start gaining market share or putting pressure on incumbents. Technology can also surprise markets when it changes something fundamental about consumers' behaviour and consumers' desire. There is some evidence suggesting that the energy sector and energy modellers have been behind the curve in projecting how fast renewable energy costs might fall (Carbon Tracker 2015, 2017b).

For example, the cost of technologies such as lithium batteries, solar panels, and wind turbines has fallen faster than many expected, leading to a faster uptake and earlier deployment. This progress is critical for cost optimisation models of the energy system, which will select the cheapest option to meet energy demand. Figure 4.1 shows how the cost of solar photovoltaic units has fallen by 88% over the last nine years (Lazard 2018).

It is important to recognise that the energy transition is not just about doing the same thing in a different way; it is also about doing things better or through different relationships. This is where traditional sector

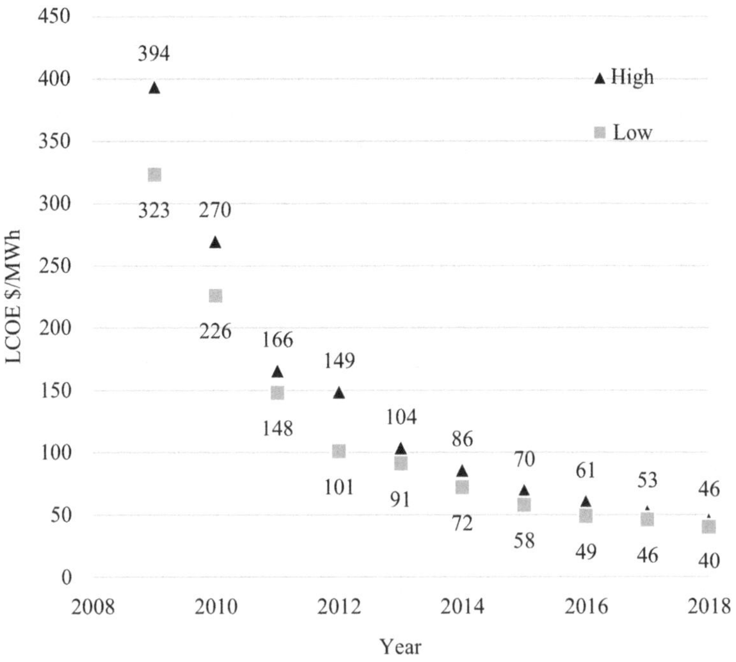


**Fig. 4.1** Unsubsidised solar photovoltaic levelised cost of energy (LCOE). (Source: Lazard (2018), modified representation)

classifications start to blur, as energy solutions may come from broader technology or communications companies seeking to leverage their customer base or datasets, rather than from within the incumbent sector. Alongside these disruptions appear more traditional and incremental improvements in efficiency and existing technology that are less likely to disrupt markets, but can contribute to weakening demand and reduced emissions over a longer period.

**Market:** Ultimately, consumer preferences can drive a number of markets, which are hard to predict. Consumer choice can both accelerate and hinder the low-carbon transition. Indeed, reputational risk is increasingly linked to environmental performance, and customers can increasingly select 'greener' options. The maturity of the market is also important to consider, as established markets with existing infrastructure may take longer to turn over the legacy in place. Growth markets where particular products/services are not established can see more rapid take-up of new solutions. Large institutions, whether public or private, can also act as buyers who want to reduce their own carbon exposure. There are increasing volumes of power purchase agreements being signed by corporations or local governments wishing to secure their own low-carbon power supply. This kind of contract certainty with large credit-worthy counterparties also reduces the risk for low-carbon projects. Project finance lending in the power sector has seen ten-year cumulative default rates lower for green (5.7%) than for non-green (7.5%) projects in recent years as a result of these kinds of structures as the low-carbon transition gains traction (Moody's Investor Services 2018a).

It can be difficult to separate these three transmission channels in practice, as they are mutually reinforcing. The driving factor may depend on the stage a sector is at in terms of the cycle of policy supporting technology, which makes it cheaper and in turn increases consumer uptake. The other form of transition risk on the horizon is climate liability, with growing numbers of lawsuits being brought against government and corporate actors. This event risk has yet to manifest itself in most jurisdictions as legal systems process these new types of claims.

### *Sector Prioritisation*

From a credit perspective, investors and rating agencies think about different types of debt issuers and the characteristics they have. Rating agencies have different methodologies for different asset classes and for different corporate sub-sectors. The approach to thinking about the credit implications of climate risk for a sovereign debt issuer might be very different to that applied to a large corporation and different again for an infrastructure project. In each case, it is possible to prioritise types of issuers or sectors which are exposed to higher levels of risk.

**Sovereign risk:** As would be expected, more macro variables are being considered for assessing sovereign risk than for individual corporations. For example, some sovereigns are reliant on fossil fuel royalties and exports to contribute to GDP. The limited diversification of these economies leads them to be more exposed to transition risk. Using scenarios here can help to understand the potential downside to business if a more rapid transition occurs (Moody's Investor Services 2018d).

Table 4.2 shows the impact on the sovereign credit ratings for oil and gas exporting countries when applying the International Energy Agency's Sustainable Development Scenario. The shaded areas indicate where a

**Table 4.2** Moody's estimated sovereign credit ratings under a low-carbon scenario

| Countries | Current | 2025 | 2030 | 2040 |
|---|---|---|---|---|
| Angola | B3- Caa2 | B3- Caa2 | B3- Caa2 | Caa2 - C |
| Azerbaijan | Ba1 - Ba3 | Ba1- Ba3 | Ba1 - Ba3 | Ba3 - B2 |
| Bahrain | Ba2 - B1 | Ba2 - B1 | Ba2 - B1 | Ba2 - B1 |
| Republic of the Congo | Caa2 - C | Caa2 - C | Caa2 - C | Caa2 - C |
| Gabon | Caa1 - Caa3 | Caa1 - Caa3 | Caa1 - Caa3 | Caa2 - C |
| Kazakhstan | Baa2 - Ba1 | Baa2 - Ba1 | Baa2 - Ba1 | Ba2 - B1 |
| Kuwait | Aa3 - A2 | Aa3 - A2 | Aa3 - A2 | A1 - A3 |
| Nigeria | B1 - B3 | B1 - B3 | B3 - Caa2 | B3 - Caa2 |
| Norway | Aaa - Aa2 | Aaa - Aa2 | Aa1 - Aa3 | Aa1 - Aa3 |
| Oman | Baa2 - Ba1 | Baa3 - Ba2 | Ba3 - B2 | B3 - Caa2 |
| Papua New Guinea | B1 - B3 | B1 - B3 | B3 - Caa2 | B3 - Caa2 |
| Qatar | Aa3 - A2 | A1 - A3 | A1 - A3 | A3 - Baa2 |
| Russia | Baa2 - Ba1 | Baa2 - Ba1 | Baa2 - Ba1 | Baa2 - Ba1 |
| Saudi Arabia | Aa3 - A2 | A1 - A3 | A3 - Baa2 | Ba1 - Ba3 |
| Trinidad & Tobago | Baa3 - Ba2 | Baa2 - Ba1 | Baa2 - Ba1 | Baa3 - Ba2 |
| United Arab Emirates | Aa2 - A1 | Aa2 - A1 | Aa2 - A1 | A3 - Baa2 |

Source: Moody's Investor Services (2018d)

change of two or more notches from the current rating occurs due to the different demand levels and prices in this scenario.

In such a scenario, analysts need to differentiate between the relative cost base of the assets and understand the royalty and tax regime, which may offer more protection to some producers in a low-demand, low-price scenario. On the flip side, countries with significant fossil fuel import bills may reduce their exposure to imports by developing domestic renewable alternatives. In any long-term scenario, there is an opportunity for players to respond to the transition occurring, limit impacts, and potentially maximise opportunities. However, this option may be restricted if everyone is trying to do it at once, or if there are limited capacity/resources available.

**Corporate risk:** Sector exposure to the low-carbon transition is largely dependent on the position of or exposure to the hydrocarbon value chain. Some companies may have fossil fuels as their primary product (oil and gas producers), whilst others may be dependent on them for their business (utilities), or to use their products (transport) or supply their services (engineering contractors). On top of this, financial institutions have a portfolio exposure. This exposure is likely to be representative of the market as a whole unless financial institutions have some particular geographical or sector concentration.

In prioritising focus for assessing credit risk, it therefore makes sense to identify the sectors where transition is already occurring or expected to occur within the next few years, which ensures that efforts are directed towards sectors that require most attention. However, sector classifications cannot be perfect, and there will always be some cases that require special attention or do not fit generalisations. For example, large industrial conglomerates may sit under anonymous holding companies, which do not immediately flag up as having high-risk activities as they are diluted amongst a large portfolio of interests. A heatmap is one of such approaches to use analytical knowledge to create a framework that identifies relative exposure to this issue (Moody's Investor Services 2018b).

Table 4.3 lists the sectors that were identified by Moody's credit analysts as having high or elevated exposure to carbon regulation. The amount of rated debt (as published in September 2018) is indicated for each sector, with utilities, oil and gas companies, and transport-related companies forming the majority of the debt covered.

**Table 4.3** Sectors identified as having high or elevated risk exposure to carbon regulation in the Moody's environmental heatmap in 2018

| *Risk category* | *Sector* | *Rated debt (US$ bn)* |
|---|---|---|
| High risk | Unregulated utilities & power | 504 |
| | Coal mining & terminals | 13 |
| Elevated risk | Oil & gas—integrated | 714 |
| | Regulated power utilities | 673 |
| | Auto manufacturers | 466 |
| | Oil & gas—independent | 470 |
| | Surface transport & logistics | 241 |
| | US Public/Co-operative power utilities | 204 |
| | Chemicals | 119 |
| | Auto suppliers | 94 |
| | Building materials | 91 |
| | Steel | 88 |
| | Oil & gas—refining | 68 |
| | Airlines | 67 |
| | Shipping | 24 |
| | Asset-backed securities—aircraft | 10 |

Source: Moody's Investor Services (2018b)

Each sector is different in how its carbon transition risk manifests itself. It is important to consider the objective of the analysis here. Some investors may be looking for a single metric across hundreds or thousands of corporates as a simple indicator. However, this is unlikely to provide a good measure of carbon transition risk. Carbon foot-printing is one tool that can produce this type of metric; however, it is better suited to measure the impact on the environment than the credit significance of carbon transition. There is an established methodology used to account for carbon emissions, which categorises emissions as Scope 1, 2, or 3, depending on how direct the emissions are to the entity accounting for them (WRI 2004). This methodology serves well to avoid double counting, but does not necessarily capture all relevant exposures or their financial materiality.

For example, most organisations have not historically captured the emissions that result from product use, as there is limited reporting under Scope 3 emissions. This means that for extractive companies under Scopes 1 and 2, they would only report a small fraction of the lifecycle emissions from their products, which would not reflect the significance that curtailing demand for carbon-intensive commodities might have. Recent pressure has led some hydrocarbon producers to report a broader scope of emission impacts, including the use of their products, which raises interesting questions about future liability claims. Sector-specific metrics are therefore important to ensure that main credit impacts are addressed.

The timing of the energy transition is also an important element, with some sectors more advanced or moving faster than others. The European utility sector offers an example of an industry that has undergone significant changes over a decade. It also shows how it is difficult to isolate the impact of the low-carbon transition from other factors. In this case, declining power demand, a shift away from nuclear in Germany post Fukushima, and the financial crisis all provided important context to the decarbonisation that occurred (Moody's Investor Services 2018e).

As a result of the factors identified above, the average Moody's credit rating for European utilities fell three notches over the decade to 2018, from A2 to Baa2. This is a much more gradual erosion of credit quality than seen for the US coal mining example. However, even this gradual decline has still left the sector in a poor position to finance the ongoing transition as a result of declining credit ratings. Given the importance of cost of capital for cleaner technologies, this can place incumbent utilities at a disadvantage to new participants from other sectors.

The low-carbon energy transition requires significant capital investment to deliver changes. Each sector has a typical lag time which impacts how quickly the sector can align with the transition. For example, it can take at least three years to design a new car from scratch, with extra complexity added with the adjustment to increased electrification of vehicles. In transportation, if a shipping or airline company has an existing fleet of vessels or aircraft, then it will have to consider the costs of accelerating replacement. When it comes to oil and gas, the development process for such projects can range from decades for big complex ones to months for US shale expansions. Increasing uncertainty about the status of the carbon transition at the point in the future when a new project is expected to start generating returns should impact how capital deployment risk is assessed.

Within a sector there may be significant variations or limited options for diversification. Some entities may already have decided to focus on a particular end of the green/brown spectrum. In Europe, for example, there has been significant merger and acquisition activity reorganising generation portfolios into different divisions. These business units are then clearly in different modes of operation with a clear strategy, rather than risking confusion or conflict. However, if an industry has very similar portfolios, then it may be harder to differentiate. Technological advances in one company may also be offset by geographical market advantages of another.

As with any kind of risk assessment, once the risk exposure and magnitude are established, it is usual to consider what mitigation measures may be in place. This is typical of credit analysis, which considers factors such as contractual terms, insurance, counterparties, and other measures that can alter risk associated with debt. Here, it would be salient to consider diversification into carbon-neutral or carbon-positive activities or plan to reduce portfolio exposure to carbon-intensive activities. In some sectors, it may be relevant to review investment into research and development, or the ability to pass on costs to customers.

### *Scenario Analysis, Sensitivity Analysis, Stress Testing*

To understand how different transition scenarios may affect companies, it can be useful to apply a range of techniques to demonstrate the extent of any financial impact. Scenario analysis adjusts multiple variables to create alternative futures to help users. Scenarios are not predictions of the future; their purpose is to help users understand the potential range of outcomes. Typically, in credit analysis, this outcome is the impact on a fundamental credit ratio. Sensitivity analysis involves changing a single variable to assess the impact. For example, a range of carbon prices could be used to understand how this variable affects earnings. In addition, stress testing typically starts with a predetermined outcome in terms of a level of stress and works backwards to establish the changes required in performance to produce it. For example, a leading question might be, 'What would be required to cause a credit rating downgrade or a default?'

Moody's recently produced an analysis of the potential fines car manufacturers could receive if they fail to comply with $CO_2$ emissions standards for 2020–2021. This document adjusts the level of fleet emissions reductions achieved by companies, using different methods to demonstrate the penalties that would result. The combined penalties across the rated group of companies range from an estimated €2.4 billion in the rapid transition scenario, to €5.9 billion in the moderate scenario, and up to €11.2 billion if the transition is slow (Moody's Investor Services 2019a).

This kind of sensitivity analysis shows the material incentive companies have to avoid non-compliance, in this case, billions of euros for some companies. The analysis is thus not meant to be a prediction; it informs why companies are likely to take mitigation action to avoid these scenarios. For example, companies may cease production of their most polluting models, subsidise and promote low-emissions models, or pool fleets with other companies to achieve compliance. They may also choose to pay the fine if they consider it a lower cost option.

The value of these tools is that they provide a forward-looking view, rather than summarising what has already happened. Corporations are always reluctant to place too much weight on forward-looking information, which is covered by the usual legal disclaimers in annual reports. Using these insights into the future can fill some gaps in corporate disclosure and enable comparison on a consistent basis. It also gets past the challenge of trying to compare disclosures from different companies and whether they are based on the same assumptions (e.g., discount rates, commodity prices, market growth, etc.).

It is typical to apply a number of scenarios to understand the range of potential outcomes. The risk of an entity selecting their own scenario is that they choose one that is favourable to them. One example of this would be a diversified mining company asking each business unit to test performance in a low-carbon future. The coal division picks a scenario with strong carbon capture and storage deployment, the gas division picks a scenario with significant gas generation growth, the uranium division picks a scenario with high nuclear build, and the lithium division picks a scenario with rapid electric vehicle growth driving battery demand. Whilst all these scenarios may be possible in isolation, it is unlikely that planning based on the best-case scenario for each division will improve risk management or inform strategic choices. It can demonstrate potential strengthening of credit positions or the extent of potential opportunities, but it will not give insight into the potential downside.

Having reference scenarios for companies to use is therefore something financial regulators have considered, as it would also help them and the financial institutions they oversee to assess systemic risk and understand the relative levels of risk. Again, as the above mining company example indicates, there are multiple scenarios that could lead to similar outcomes in terms of overall emissions and thus global warming. Therefore, having a range of scenarios is useful to prevent biases in the analysis. In doing so, it can be possible to include reference scenarios as well as other scenarios of a company's own choosing in order to not restrict the analysis being conducted. The Institutional Investors Group on Climate Change has produced a guide to apply climate scenario analysis which explores some of these issues (Institutional Investors Group on Climate Change 2019).

Alignment with a particular scenario is hard to measure. This difficulty has been discussed in relation to the attempts to define low-carbon benchmarks or products, or to apply science-based targets (Science Based Targets Initiative 2015). These approaches tend to rely on the assumption that all entities are reflective of the overall system, and therefore the overall target that the system must meet is relevant for all entities. This assumption can certainly be used as a starting point to understand the changes needed in a sector; however, credit analysts will want to understand the context of operations for a particular operator, in terms of markets, positioning, and cost structure.

For example, Saudi Aramco recently published a bond prospectus which explains that having some of the lowest lifting costs for oil production in the world meant that they were in a stronger position to be the last producer standing than most independent producers (Saudi Aramco 2019). This view is applying an economic logic on top of the climate science to determine a market-based outcome, rather than a simpler equitable approach where the required emissions cuts are applied equally. The impact of reducing emissions will likely be greater on some parties than others. This approach mirrors the methodology applied by Carbon Tracker

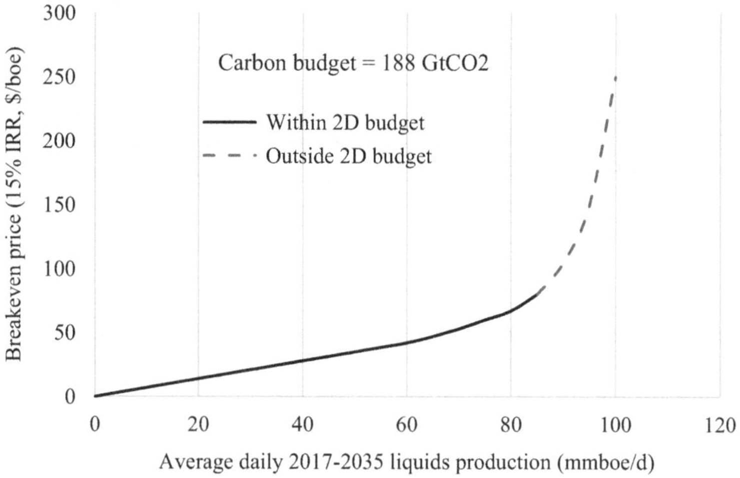


**Fig. 4.2** Carbon supply cost curve for global oil supply indicating the volume consistent with a carbon budget to limit global warming to 2 °C. (Source: Carbon Tracker (2017a), modified representation)

in its carbon supply cost curves, which map out the lowest cost of coal, oil, and gas production and equate to a specific level of cumulative emissions, that is, a carbon budget (Carbon Tracker 2017a).

Figure 4.2 shows a supply cost curve for potential oil projects ranked according to breakeven cost. A cut-off is applied which shows the break-even cost for the marginal project to produce the volume of oil that would result in 188 Gt $CO_2$ over the period 2017–2035. This figure is based on a particular scenario with a mix of coal, oil, and gas which has a 50% change of limiting global warming to 2 °C.

## Mapping Physical Risk

Changes to the earth's climate are already occurring, which means that assessments of current risk exposure need to be updated to reflect both the increasing frequency and severity of acute events, and the acceleration of chronic trends. Beyond current exposure, there is also an interest in longer-term scenarios to indicate where risks are expected to increase in the future. For example, the median risk of US commercial properties being hit by a category 4 or 5 hurricane has already risen by 137% since

1980, with modelling indicating that this will increase by 275% if no further action is taken to mitigate climate change (Blackrock & Rhodium Group 2019). The financial industry has some experience of applying historical climate data in the insurance industry to estimate potential losses from extreme weather events and develop related products. However, many of the physical risks are manifesting in developing countries, where insurance is not widespread and the data and models are not yet available.

### *Climate Data Applicability*

Understanding the exposure to physical risks is easier for certain types of issuers than others from a credit perspective. For sovereign issuers, it is possible to apply country-level data to understand the impact on climate-sensitive sectors, which are important for the GDP, for example. In the United States, there is sufficient granularity of data to map differentials in exposure for municipal entities on some physical risk indicators (Blackrock & Rhodium Group 2019).

At the other extreme, having a complex multinational with multiple assets, businesses, and supply chains makes it harder to understand the specific locations where there is material financial exposure to physical risk, especially if data relating to either the assets or the risk exposure is unavailable.

Understanding physical risks needs to go beyond the headline numbers to the underlying data. For example, global average temperature rises are often referenced, which may not seem like large increases. Within these scenarios, however, the most extreme regional temperature increases will be multiples of the global average, having a much greater impact. Similarly, annual average increases may not tell the whole story about the number of extreme events or the period of time for which a threshold is exceeded.

### *Dealing with Both Events and Trends*

Longer-term trends are in some ways easier to model and factor into credit analysis, as long as the speed of change is well understood. A range of outcomes can also be modelled to cover more rapid changes than the consensus or understand at what point the change has a material effect. For example, changing temperature patterns is one variable that can be modelled in this way to understand potential impacts; however, this may have to include information on changing seasonality, the number of extreme-high-/low-temperature days, and so on. The impact on relevant sectors, such as agriculture or power, can then be analysed.

The increasing frequency and severity of extreme weather events in the future can also be modelled, but it may be harder to factor into credit analysis. While it is possible to identify which region has a higher probability of a certain-strength hurricane, the model cannot tell which region will actually experience one next year. Long-term probabilities, such as 1-in-a-100-years event, do not inform short-term predictions. This unpredictability makes it difficult to integrate this type of event risk into credit analysis. Hence, the impact of hurricanes or floods on credit ratings can only be seen post event.

### *The Case of the California Wildfires*

The increased frequency of conditions which are conducive to wildfires is increasing losses. Recent years have seen extended hot and dry seasons with delayed winter precipitation. Precipitation in the fall dampens vegetation acting as a preventative measure. If this rainfall is delayed, it leaves vegetation exposed to warmer, drier air for longer, making it more susceptible to fires. Higher average temperatures in the summer have also heightened the drying of vegetation. Additionally, heavy rainfalls in the preceding winter contribute to a greater volume of vegetation, providing more fuel for fires. If the fires coincide with strong winds, this mix can increase the scale of the damage and hamper efforts to tackle the fires (Bedsworth et al. 2018).

The hottest and driest summers have been registered in the last 20 years, including 2017 and 2018. Data from the US National Oceanic and Atmospheric Administration since 1895 shows how recent summers have seen average temperatures several degrees higher and with several inches less precipitation than average (Borunda 2018).

Table 4.4 shows the date of the 20 largest fires experienced in California in terms of structures damaged, according to the California Fire Department. This data indicates that three-quarters of the largest 20 events since records began have occurred from 2000 onwards.

However, the contribution of a changing climate is only one factor in determining the financial losses. An increasing number of structures have become exposed to wildfires as the population migrates to the wildland-urban interface (WUI). The US Department of Agriculture Forest Service reported that the number of houses in the WUI increased by 41.1% across the United States between 1990 and 2010, with some states affected more

**Table 4.4** The date of the 20 largest fires recorded in California in terms of structures damaged

| *Fire name* (cause) | *Date* | *Acres* | *Structures* | *Deaths* |
|---|---|---|---|---|
| 1 Camp Fire *(under investigation)* | November 2018 | 153,336 | 18,804 | 85 |
| 2 Tubbs *(under investigation)* | October 2017 | 36,807 | 5636 | 22 |
| 3 Tunnel—Oakland Hills *(Rekindle)* | October 1991 | 1600 | 2900 | 25 |
| 4 Cedar *(human related)* | October 2003 | 273,246 | 2820 | 15 |
| 5 Valley *(electrical)* | September 2015 | 76,067 | 1955 | 4 |
| 6 Witch *(power lines)* | October 2007 | 197,990 | 1650 | 2 |
| 7 Woolsey *(under investigation)* | November 2018 | 96,949 | 1643 | 3 |
| 8 Carr *(human related)* | July 2018 | 229,651 | 1604 | 8 |
| 9 Nuns *(under investigation)* | October 2017 | 54,382 | 1355 | 3 |
| 10 Thomas *(under investigation)* | December 2017 | 281,893 | 1063 | 2 |
| 11 Old *(human related)* | October 2003 | 91,281 | 1003 | 6 |
| 12 Jones *(undetermined)* | October 1999 | 26,200 | 954 | 1 |
| 13 Butte *(power lines)* | September 2015 | 70,868 | 921 | 2 |
| 14 Atlas *(under investigation)* | October 2017 | 51,624 | 783 | 6 |
| 15 Paint *(arson)* | June 1990 | 4900 | 641 | 1 |
| 16 Fountain *(arson)* | August 1992 | 63,960 | 636 | 0 |
| 17 Sayre *(misc.)* | November 2008 | 11,262 | 604 | 0 |
| 18 City of Berkeley *(power lines)* | September 1923 | 130 | 584 | 0 |
| 19 Harris *(under investigation)* | October 2007 | 90,440 | 548 | 8 |
| 20 Redwood Valley *(under investigation)* | October 2017 | 36,523 | 546 | 9 |

Source: California Fire Department

than others (Martinuzzi et al. 2015). This trend increases the value of the assets at risk and any potential insurance or liability claims. The entities which bear the financial liability, are then determined by the legal regime in place in that location and the circumstances of the fire. In California, the application of inverse condemnation to utilities, even where no negligence was found, meant it was the utilities who were the de facto insurer for fires in 2017 and 2018. As a result, the Californian utility PG&E filed for bankruptcy protection in January 2019 due to the scale of wildfire liabilities it had to cover.

### *Physical Risk Mitigation*

In determining the impact on credit strength, analysts consider several mitigating factors, such as investment in adaptation, insurance, expected bailouts, and potential liabilities. After reviewing the impact on US cities a year after major floods or hurricanes, one can see that it is possible for a city to be in a better position than before the event (Moody's Investor Services 2018c). This could be a result of a combination of factors: federal bailouts, investments in new infrastructure, improved resilience and response plans, and insurance pay-outs. It could therefore be argued that US locations that have already experienced an extreme weather event are better placed going forward than those that have not.

The financial impact is therefore transferred elsewhere and is more manageable if it is being diluted amongst much larger federal budgets and insurance portfolios. In countries without funding for federal agencies or widespread insurance cover, cities and regions take much longer to recover, and local economies may suffer for prolonged periods as a result. Analysts need to trace where the financial liability falls. At present, some governments, such as the US federal administration, have a history of bailing out local governments when events occur. There is some debate as to whether this will continue indefinitely if losses keep increasing. Some US cities are already using 'resilience bonds' to use the capital markets to secure funding for improving infrastructure. For example, San Francisco and Washington DC have issued 'green bonds' to fund stormwater management infrastructure, and Harris County, Texas issued a 'flood bond' to finance flood prevention works after experiencing Hurricane Harvey in 2017.

Some locations are also investing in adaptation measures, which will reduce exposure to losses in the future. For example, cities such as Cape Town are already suffering water shortages due to the increased frequency of drought events. This situation resulted in economic losses due to reduced agricultural outputs, lower water revenues, and lost tourism income, as well as further knock-on effects on financial institutions and the wider economy (UBS 2018). At the same time, the city had to increase expenditure to improve the water infrastructure. This combination was credit-negative for the city for a period of time.

Following the shortages, local administrations have initiated programmes to improve water management, reduce consumption, and augment supply, which are reflected in the vulnerability assessment of Cape Town. This case shows that when a water shortage occurs, there is a visible incentive to invest in solutions. However, these solutions may come too late to minimise losses. There is still a major shortfall in investment in climate resilient infrastructure elsewhere; however, analysts are starting to recognise the benefits of reduced vulnerability in their credit assessments, which helps justify expenditure.

## Conclusion

Integrating climate risk into credit analysis is an evolving field, with the tools and data required still being developed and refined. Physical and transition climate risks are increasingly material for creditworthiness, with scenario and sensitivity analyses useful approaches to understand potential future exposure. The ability of entities to transfer risk or pass on costs makes it essential to have a system view that can understand where impacts may ultimately land across the capital markets.

Event risk will continue to present a challenge, even with better analytical tools, as no one can predict in advance exactly where and when extreme weather events will occur. Trends in terms of changing energy technologies and climatic conditions are easier to identify. For these trends, the challenge lies in assessing whether the individuals running companies or governments are making the necessary adjustments, or just betting on the status quo. The experimental nature of the approaches being applied to examine the credit impacts of climate risk confirms that this field is still at an early stage.

## References

Barclays. (2018). *ESG: Investing in credit*. Retrieved from https://www.investmentbank.barclays.com/content/dam/barclaysmicrosites/ibpublic/documents/our-insights/ESG2/BarclaysIB-ImpactSeries4-ESG-in-credit-5MB.pdf.

Bedsworth, L., Cayan, D., Franco, G., Fisher, L., & Ziaja, S. (2018). *Statewide Summary Report*. California's Fourth Climate Change Assessment. Publication number: SUM-CCCA4-2018-013.

Blackrock & Rhodium Group. (2019). *Getting physical: Assessing climate risks*. Retrieved from https://www.blackrock.com/us/individual/literature/whitepaper/bii-physical-climate-risks-april-2019.pdf.

Borunda, A. (2018, November). *See how a warmer world primed California for large fires*. National Geographic. Retrieved from https://www.nationalgeographic.com/environment/2018/11/climate-change-california-wildfire/.

Carbon Tracker Initiative. (2015). *Lost in transition*. London. Retrieved from https://www.carbontracker.org/.

Carbon Tracker Initiative. (2017a). *2 Degrees of separation*. London. Retrieved from https://www.carbontracker.org/.

Carbon Tracker Initiative. (2017b). *Expect the unexpected*. London. Retrieved from https://www.carbontracker.org/.

Climate Action 100. (2017). Retrieved from http://www.climateaction100.org/.

European Commission. (2017). *Guidelines on non-financial reporting*. Brussels.
Financial Stability Board. (2017). *Final report: Recommendations of the task force on climate-related financial disclosures*. Retrieved from https://www.fsb-tcfd.org/publications/final-recommendations-report/.
Institutional Investors Group on Climate Change. (2019). *Navigating climate scenario analysis*. Retrieved from https://www.iigcc.org/download/navigating-climate-scenario-analysis-a-guide-for-institutional-investors/?wpdmdl=1837&refresh=5d3c726774fa01564242535.
Lazard. (2018). *Lazard's levelized cost of energy analysis – version 12.0*. Retrieved from https://www.lazard.com/media/450784/lazards-levelized-cost-of-energy-version-120-vfinal.pdf.
Martinuzzi, S., Stewart, S. I., Helmers, D. P., Mockrin, M. H., Hammer, R. B., & Radeloff, V. C. (2015). *The 2010 wildland-urban interface of the conterminous United States*. Research Map NRS-8. Newtown Square, PA: U.S. Department of Agriculture, Forest Service, Northern Research Station. Retrieved from https://www.nrs.fs.fed.us/data/wui/state_summary/#wui-houses.
Moody's Investor Services. (2018a). *Default and recovery rates for project finance bank loans, 1983–2016: Green projects demonstrate lower default risk*. London.
Moody's Investor Services. (2018b). *Environmental risks – Global: Heat map: 11 sectors with $2.2 trillion debt have elevated environmental risk exposure*. London.
Moody's Investor Services. (2018c). *Local government – Texas: Hurricane Harvey damage fails to stop revenue growth in most affected areas*. New York.
Moody's Investor Services. (2018d). *Sovereigns – hydrocarbon exporters: Carbon transition manageable for most; significant credit pressure in event of more ambitious transition*. Frankfurt.
Moody's Investor Services. (2018e). *Unregulated utilities and power companies – global: Carbon transition brings risks and opportunities*. New York.
Moody's Investor Services. (2019a). *Automakers look to electrification to avoid billions in emission-related fines*. London.
Moody's Investor Services. (2019b). *Cross-sector – global: Frequently asked investor questions about environmental, social and governance issues*. London.
Morgan, G. (2018, May 29). Canada buys Kinder Morgan's Trans Mountain pipeline for $4.5 billion –but can we sell it? *Financial Post*. Retrieved from https://business.financialpost.com/commodities/energy/ottawa-buys-trans-mountain-pipeline-for-4-5-billion-but-can-it-sell-it.
Network for Greening the Financial System. (2019). *First comprehensive report*. Retrieved from https://www.banque-france.fr/sites/default/files/media/2019/04/17/ngfs_first_comprehensive_report_-_17042019_0.pdf.
Saudi Aramco. (2019). *Bond prospectus*. Global Medium Term Note Programme, Dhahran, Saudi Arabia.
Science Based Targets Initiative. (2015). *Sectoral decarbonization approach: A method for setting corporate emission reduction targets in line with climate science*. London.

UBS. (2018). *Water scarcity – special focus on Cape Town*. Retrieved from https://www.ubs.com/content/dam/WealthManagementAmericas/cio-impact/cio-longer-term-investments.pdf.

UNEP Finance Initiative. (2018). *Extending our horizons: Assessing credit risk and opportunity in a changing climate*. Retrieved from https://www.unepfi.org/wordpress/wp-content/uploads/2018/04/EXTENDING-OUR-HORIZONS.pdf.

WRI—World Resources Institute. (2004). *Greenhouse gas protocol*. Washington, DC.

CHAPTER 5

# Designing Insurance Against Extreme Weather Risk: The Case of HuRLOs

*Martin Boyer, Michèle Breton, and Pascal François*

## Introduction

Hurricanes are among the most catastrophic natural events. Even though the number of hurricane landfalls appears stable in the United States, with an average of 18 per decade since 1900 (NHC 2018), they tend to be more and more costly. According to the National Hurricane Center (NHC), 13 out of the 18 hurricanes that caused more than US$10 billion (inflation-adjusted) of damage since 1900 occurred during the last 15 years despite a 10-year lull between 2006 and 2015. Table 5.1 reports the hurricanes that caused the biggest financial damage in the United States since 1900.

We thank Sahar Guesmi and Matthieu Robillard for excellent research assistance. Financial support from HEC Montréal is gratefully acknowledged.

M. Boyer • P. François (✉)
Department of Finance, HEC Montréal, Montreal, QC, Canada
e-mail: martin.boyer@hec.ca; pascal.francois@hec.ca

M. Breton
Department of Decision Sciences, HEC Montréal, Montreal, QC, Canada



T. Walker et al. (eds.), *Ecological, Societal, and Technological Risks and the Financial Sector*, Palgrave Studies in Sustainable Business In Association with Future Earth, https://doi.org/10.1007/978-3-030-38858-4_5

**Table 5.1** Costliest mainland United States tropical cyclones, 1900–2017

| *Rank* | *Hurricane* | *Regions hit* | *Year* | *Category* | *Damage* |
|---|---|---|---|---|---|
| 1 | Katrina | SE FL, LA, MS | 2005 | 3 | 160 |
| 2 | Harvey | TX, LA | 2017 | 4 | 125 |
| 3 | Maria | PR, USVI | 2017 | 4 | 90 |
| 4 | Sandy | Mid-Atlantic & NE U.S. | 2012 | 1 | 70.2 |
| 5 | Irma | FL | 2017 | 4 | 50 |
| 6 | Andrew | SE FL, LA | 1992 | 5 | 47.79 |
| 7 | Ike | TX, LA | 2008 | 2 | 34.8 |
| 8 | Ivan | AL, NW FL | 2004 | 3 | 27.06 |
| 9 | Wilma | S FL | 2005 | 3 | 24.32 |
| 10 | Rita | SW LA, N TX | 2005 | 3 | 23.68 |
| 11 | Charley | SW FL | 2004 | 4 | 21.12 |
| 12 | Hugo | SC, USVI, PR | 1989 | 4 | 18.09 |
| 13 | Irene | Mid-Atlantic & NE U.S. | 2011 | 1 | 14.985 |
| 14 | Frances | FL | 2004 | 2 | 12.936 |
| 15 | Agnes | FL, NE U.S. | 1972 | 1 | 12.516 |
| 16 | Allison | N TX | 2001 | TS | 11.815 |
| 17 | Betsy | SE FL, SE LA | 1965 | 3 | 11.152 |
| 18 | Matthew | SE US | 2016 | 1 | 10.3 |
| 19 | Jeanne | FL | 2004 | 3 | 9.9 |
| 20 | Camille | MS, SE LA, VA | 1969 | 5 | 9.776 |
| 21 | Floyd | Mid-Atlantic & NE U.S. | 1999 | 2 | 9.62 |
| 22 | Georges | USVI, PR, FL, MS, AL | 1998 | 2 | 9.06 |
| 23 | Fran | NC | 1996 | 3 | 7.9 |
| 24 | Diane | NC | 1955 | 1 | 7.63 |
| 25 | Opal | NW FL | 1995 | 3 | 7.614 |
| 26 | Alicia | N TX | 1983 | 3 | 7.47 |
| 27 | Isabel | Mid-Atlantic | 2003 | 2 | 7.37 |
| 28 | Gustav | LA | 2008 | 2 | 6.96 |
| 29 | Celia | TX | 1970 | 3 | 6.026 |
| 30 | Frederic | AL, MS | 1979 | 3 | 5.712 |
| 31 | Iniki | Kauai, HI | 1992 | 4 | 5.487 |
| 32 | Long Island Express | NE US | 1938 | 3 | 5.279 |
| 33 | NC/VA 1944 | Mid-Atlantic | 1944 | 3 | 4.927 |
| 34 | Carol | NE US | 1954 | 3 | 4.198 |
| 35 | Marilyn | USVI, PR | 1995 | 2 | 3.402 |

Damage is expressed in US$ billions after accounting for inflation to 2017 dollars

Source: National Hurricane Center. Category "TS" stands for tropical storm

Due to the growth of hurricane occurrence and the costly damages associated with them, important literature has been devoted to the assessment of hurricane risk and to their trajectories (see inter alia, Jewson and Hall 2007, Nakamura et al. 2015, Kriesche et al. 2014, and the references therein). Approaches to predict hurricane outcomes can be divided into two main streams: meteorological and probabilistic methods. Meteorological methods (see for instance Gray et al. 1992) are based on complex models of natural phenomena, while probabilistic methods (static or dynamic) rather rely on historical frequencies (see Bove et al. 1998; Epstein 1985; Vickery et al. 2000; Jewson and Hall 2007; Bonazzi et al. 2014). Both approaches aim at assessing the probability of catastrophic events in a given area.

The reason why so much energy has been devoted to predicting this natural phenomenon is that insurance against catastrophic risk, such as hurricanes, wind storms, and tsunamis, is an important concern for homeowners. The concern is especially latent for homeowners in the south-east United States, around the Gulf of Mexico, and in the western North-Pacific.[1]

The increase in concern is due in part to the increased concentration of insured risk in coastal regions vulnerable to climatic catastrophes,[2] leading to an increase in the cost of rebuilding communities, and to a reduction in the ability of the insurance industry to financially support such losses in these regions. The potential insurer insolvency risk associated with major climatic catastrophes creates an important entry barrier since newcomers in the hurricane and catastrophic insurance market must have large amounts of capital available. This entry barrier led Froot (2001) to conclude that the market for catastrophic risk suffers from supply restrictions that can be partly explained by the market power exerted by traditional reinsurers.

To supplement the traditional insurance market, financial instruments called Insurance Linked Securities have emerged in the 1990s and early 2000s (see Cummins and Barrieu 2013). Such instruments are also known as catastrophe options and catastrophe bonds, industry loss warranties, and sidecars, all of which are financially competitive when compared to traditional reinsurance (see Ramella and Madeiros 2007).

[1] See the hurricane generation models of Hall and Jewson (2007) and Rumpf et al. (2009) for the case of the North Atlantic, and of Rumpf et al. (2007) and of Yonekura and Hall (2011) for the case of the western North-Pacific.

[2] According to Pielke et al. (2008) the hurricanes that landed in Miami in 1926 resulted in losses of 760 million dollars. If such a hurricane were to hit the Miami agglomeration today, the financial losses would amount to approximately 150 billion dollars (or 102 billion 2004-dollars according to Kunreuther and Michel-Kerjan 2009). Hurricane Katrina, which hit New Orleans in 2005, caused damages estimated at 108 billion dollars according to the National Oceanic and Atmospheric Administration.

Moreover, and in contrast to traditional insurance contracts, they can be designed in a way to have very low moral hazard and credit risk (Ramella and Madeiros 2007). Such interesting design features come, however, at the cost of increasing the instruments' basis risk (Doherty 1997). One new instrument is the HuRLO (Hurricane Risk Landfall Option), launched in 2008 by Weather Risk Solutions (WRS), that allows investors to take positions on hurricane landfall in a similar way as in pari-mutuel first-by-the-post horse race betting. While the interest in catastrophe bonds and other insurance-linked securities has been growing steadily (Cummins 2008, 2012), the literature on the hurricane-risk market itself is not extensive. Using data from the Hurricane Futures Market, Kelly et al. (2012) study the traders' perception and the trading dynamics according to available information on hurricane risk. They conclude that relative-demand pricing is consistent with a Bayesian update of beliefs according to information released by various official meteorological centers.

The objective of this paper is to analyze the operation of the HuRLO market by modeling the decisions of rational risk-averse decision-makers who want to hedge against catastrophic losses. Using the HuRLO as a motivating example, Ou-Yang (2010) and Ou-Yang and Doherty (2011) compare pari-mutuel[3] and traditional insurance for risk-averse expected utility maximizing hedgers. They compute the optimal dynamic hedge of a single agent in an economy where the decisions of the other players are assumed to be exogenous. Moreover, they examine the properties of the equilibrium on that market when agents and risks are symmetrical. They find that a pari-mutuel mechanism leads to under-insurance. They also find that a pari-mutuel setting can be advantageous when transaction costs of traditional insurance are high and when information asymmetry problems are rampant.

[3] The pari-mutuel mechanism was invented by Pierre Oller in 1865 in order to limit the profit of bookmarkers who were then controlling the betting industry in France. Since 2002, many investment banks have used a pari-mutuel mechanism for wagering on various economic statistics; odds on these statistics have been shown to be efficient forecasts of their future values (Gürkaynak and Wolfers 2006). The pari-mutuel market microstructure is analyzed by Lange and Economides (2005) who show the existence of a unique price equilibrium and find many advantages of pari-mutuel over the traditional exchange mechanism. A pari-mutuel auction system for capital markets is proposed by Baron and Lange (2007).

With respect to HuRLOs in particular, Wilks (2010) describes their market structure, and the mechanism and adaptive algorithm used to price the options. He shows that the proposed price adjustment mechanism converges rapidly to the market participants' beliefs about the outcome probabilities. Meyer et al. (2008, 2014) study the behavior of participants in an experiment of a simulated hypothetical hurricane season, during which they are allowed to trade in both primary and secondary HuRLO markets. Meyer et al. (2008, 2014) look into the potential bias traditionally observed in pari-mutuel betting. They find that market prices converge to efficient levels and that biases are not significant at the aggregate level. A priori, it therefore seems that HuRLOs should be a perfect additional tool for hedging catastrophic loss in the Southeast United States, and in the state of Florida in particular.

Our contribution to the literature is twofold. We first examine the effectiveness of pari-mutuel insurance, as Ou-Yang and Doherty (2011), but in a more realistic setting, with dynamic trading, price updating, and strategic interactions between market participants. In addition, unlike Meyer et al. (2008, 2014), our model involves agents characterized by concave utility functions acting optimally, albeit possibly with limited foresight.

The HuRLO market provides investors with the opportunity to hedge against, or speculate on, the risk that a specific region in the Gulf of Mexico and on the East Coast of the United States will be the first to be hit by a hurricane (or that no hurricane will make landfall in the continental United States) during a year. Many characteristics of HuRLOs distinguish them from traditional insurance, including the fact that the payment received doesn't depend on an individual's financial loss (or lack thereof), nor on the price paid for such protection. And, because of the pari-mutuel setting, HuRLOs have characteristics that distinguish them from standard derivatives such as: (1) the absence of counterparty and liquidity risk; (2) the absence of an underlying traded asset; and (3) a market-demand-based payoff function.

HuRLOs are interesting for both hedging and speculating purposes. On the hedging side, HuRLOs could be useful to agents (individuals, firms, or otherwise) that own assets in hurricane-prone and thus vulnerable areas. Speculators could also participate in that market by taking advantage of differences in market-based and objective landfall probabilities. As a competitor for traditional reinsurance products, HuRLOs have important merits: since the risk is limited to the invested capital, no counterparty is needed to assume the position opposite to what the insurer/reinsurer desires, and there is essentially no need for a probability or a loss appraisal since the payoff depends on market-wide factors that all but eliminate adverse selection and moral hazard issues.

Despite such advantages and the HuRLOs' complementarity with other forms of natural catastrophe hedging instruments, the market for HuRLOs has not taken off. According to the Weather Risk Solution website,[4] HuRLOs are not presently (2016–2019) available for trading.

Given the particular price formation mechanism in the HuRLOs market, one interesting question is the possible presence of strategic issues: when buying HuRLO for insurance purposes, should one place a single order, or buy options sequentially? Should one be the first to trade, or wait to observe the trades of other players? To address this question, we study the behavior of many agents facing potential losses from hurricanes. Our model of the HuRLO market is dynamic, and we explicitly account both for the impact of individual players' decisions on the option price and for risk aversion in the face of catastrophic losses. As in Ou-Yang and Doherty (2011), agents are nonstrategic investors who maximize their utility by assuming exogenous prices and stakes of other players. We model their behavior during simulated hurricane seasons to evaluate various investment strategies in terms of sequence and size of purchases. Our simulations reveal that the order type, sequence, and order packaging have a significant impact on the price paid, and on the number of traded options. Therefore, HuRLO contracts appear to be difficult to evaluate and to purchase optimally. This seriously questions the ability of the HuRLO market to act as an effective insurance mechanism.

The rest of the paper is organized as follows. Section "Hurricane Risk Landfall Options" gives details on the HuRLO product and market organization and on the price adjustment mechanism. Section "A Simulation Experiment" reports on the implementation and results of the simulation model. Section "Recommendations and Public Policy Implications" elaborates on recommendations and public policy implications. Section "Conclusion" concludes.

[4] www.weatherrisksolutions.com (last visited in January 2019).

## Hurricane Risk Landfall Options

HuRLOs are binary options on the occurrence of hurricane landfall in various regions during a given hurricane season; 75 of these options are available: 74 correspond to a given county or area (thereafter identified as counties), and the "null" option corresponds to the case where none of the 74 options received a payoff before the end of the hurricane season. When the National Hurricane Center (NHC) issues a hurricane warning because the hurricane is closing in on a specific county, trading is suspended until the hurricane makes landfall or the immediate threat vanishes. Options are automatically "exercised" when a hurricane hits one county.[5]

When this landfall occurs, holders of the winning option (corresponding to the hit county) receive a payoff (i.e., the option matures in-the-money) while holders of all the other options receive nothing (options mature out-of-the-money). At the end of the season, the holders of the null option of all the series[6] that have not yet materialized receive a payoff, while all the other options are worthless (since risk pools are separated for different series, payoffs of the null option differ across series). When a hurricane hits two counties, it is considered as a second hurricane if the contact points are more than 150 nautical miles apart.

HuRLOs are priced to reflect market demand. This contrasts with classical pari-mutuel settings where the price of a claim is constant and independent of the demand for a given position. When the outcome is realized, the total mutual reserve is shared equally among the owners of the winning claim, irrespective of the price they paid for their option. Thus, if at a given date and for a given series we observe the market price of option $k$ ($\pi_k$), the total mutual reserve ($M$), and that $m_k$ options of type $k$ were purchased in the primary market, then the payoff of a stake if outcome $k$ is realized ($R_k$), the (decimal) odds of outcome $k$ ($O_k$), and the implied market probability ($q_k$) are given by[7]:

[5] To qualify, a hurricane must be identified as such by the NHC and must cause more than 1 million dollars damage according to EQECAT (now part of Corelogic).

[6] A new series of options is launched every time a new hurricane is identified by the National Hurricane Center.

[7] A list of notations for all parameters and variables used in this paper is provided in Appendix 1.

$$R_k = \frac{M}{m_k} = \frac{\sum_k \pi_k m_k}{m_k}$$

$$O_k = \frac{R_k}{\pi_k} = \frac{M}{\pi_k m_k}$$

$$q_k = \frac{\pi_k m_k}{\sum_k \pi_k m_k} = \frac{1}{O_k}.$$

In a classic pari-mutuel setting, the corresponding $R_k$, $O_k$, and $q_k$ values are obtained by fixing $\pi_k = c$ for all $k$ so that $M = c\sum_k m_k$ and $q_k = m_k / \sum_k m_k$.

Each HuRLO series is "seeded" by a financial institution that buys an equal number of each option (say 1), at a price that reflects the historical probabilities of the possible outcomes (see the Table 5.6 in Appendix 2 for a summary of the historical probabilities in the United States). As options are bought on the primary market, prices adjust dynamically to the collective trading of market participants, reflecting the relative demand for the various options. As a result, when an order for a block of identical options is executed, the price of each option in the block is increasing, while the prices of all the other options are decreasing, reflecting the increasing total relative demand for this option.

This dynamic adjustment mechanism is not considered by Ou-Yang and Doherty (2011), who are solving a static optimization problem for a single agent, under perfect information on odds across all areas. Accordingly, they model the decision problem faced by an individual who "places his stake at the end of the wagering period after all other participants have placed their stakes." Assuming a stake of $x$ dollars in option $k$ when the mutual reserve is $M$ and the total stakes on outcome $k$ placed by other participants is $M_k$, the payoff to the agent becomes

$$R_k(x) = x\frac{M + x}{M_k + x}$$

if outcome $k$ is realized. In other words, in a static world, all the mutual reserve is shared according to the amount wagered rather than to the number of options held, since the price of each option is constant so that $\pi_k = c$. This yields an analytical characterization of the optimal stake using first-order optimality conditions.

Even under the assumption of perfect information, if the last player in a small market decided to invest $x$ to buy a block of HuRLOs for a given county, all of these options would need a different price to reflect the increasing demand, and these successive prices are needed to express the payoff as a function of $x$. If that is not the case, then one has to assume that an agent's demand is too small to influence prices.

The adaptive algorithm to set HuRLO prices in "practice" is described by Horowitz et al. (2012). The market price of each HuRLO is adjusted dynamically, each time a security is bought on the primary market. Thus, when a HuRLO of type $k$ is bought, a smoothing parameter is used to increase its price and decrease the price of all the other HuRLOs. This adjustment ensures that the total of all HuRLO prices is equal to their (time-adjusted) nominal value, while maintaining the payoff $R_k$ as close as possible to this amount. Because the market for HuRLOs is operating during a significant time horizon, a capitalization factor is used to compensate participants for opportunity costs, rewarding early entries and penalizing late ones. More precisely, denote by $r$ the annual rate reflecting the time-value of money, by $c$ the nominal value of the option, and by $t$ the date, measured in years since the initialization of the market. An investor purchasing an option for $\pi_k$ dollars at date $t$ expects a payout in the neighborhood $ce^{rt}$ if outcome $k$ occurs at date $t$, so that the total of all option prices $\sum k\ \pi_k$ is equal to $ce^{rt}$. Consequently, if the market is in equilibrium, the number of options of all types should be approximately equal. This adjustment process is described in detail in Appendix 3.

Wilks (2010) examines the behavior of market probabilities implied by option prices in the setting of the HuRLO market. Using simulations where the most favorably priced HuRLO is purchased, he shows that the pricing algorithm responds promptly to participants beliefs. He does not, however, provide any rationale for choosing dynamic market probabilities rather than the classical pari-mutuel setting where the price of claims is held constant.

The following two figures illustrate the relative behavior of the two systems over time, measured in transactions, when participants in the market are buying the option with the highest expected payoff, according to their beliefs. In Fig. 5.1, we assume that prices are constant, whereas we assume adaptive prices in Fig. 5.2. We assume in these two figures three possible outcomes whose initial probabilities of occurrence are given or believed to be (10%, 30%, 60%) for outcomes 1, 2, and 3, respectively. The initial mutual reserve is set to 900,000\$. During the first 150 transactions,

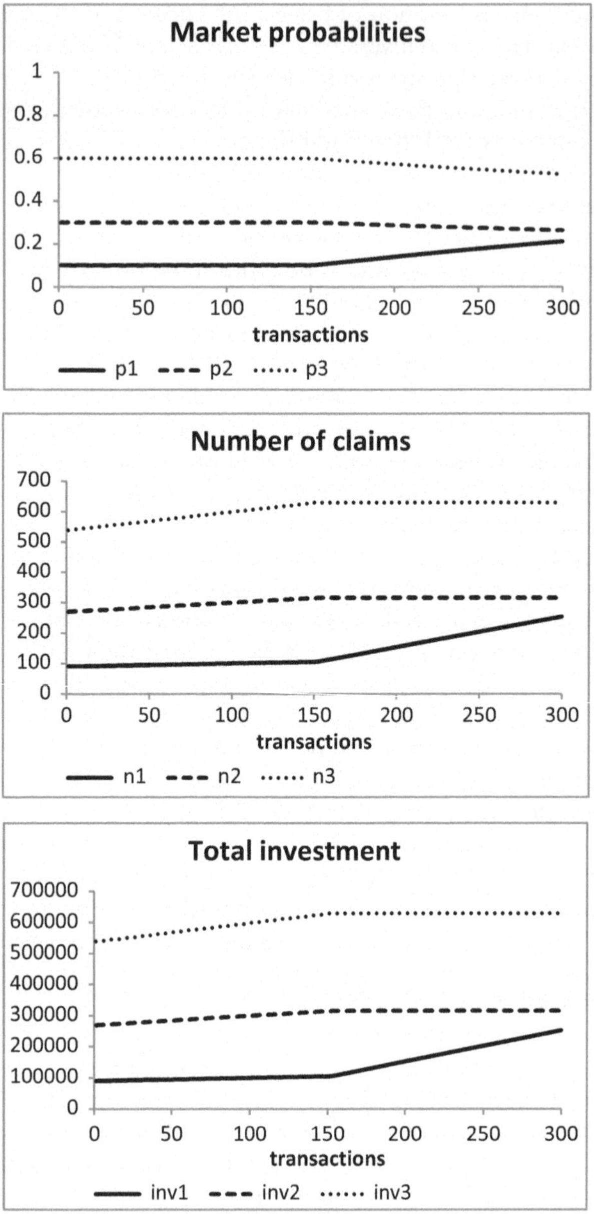


**Fig. 5.1** Market evolution as a function of transactions with *constant* prices. (Parameters are $M_0$ = \$900,000, $p_0 = (0.1, 0.3, 0.6)$, $p_{150} = (0.85, 0.1, 0.05)$)

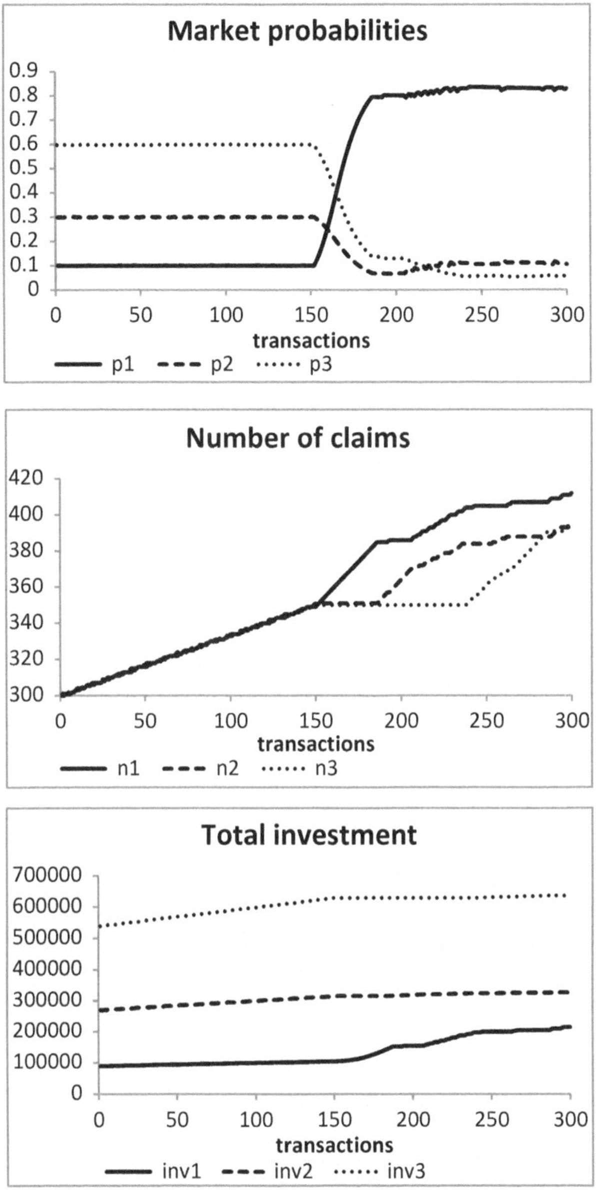


**Fig. 5.2** Market evolution as a function of transactions with adaptive prices. (Parameters are $M_0$ = \$900,000, $p_0 = (0.1, 0.3, 0.6)$, $p_{150} = (0.85, 0.1, 0.05)$)

outcome probabilities remain at (10%, 30%, 60%). Between transactions 150 and 151, public information is released, changing the participants' beliefs to (85%, 10%, 5%) for outcomes 1, 2 and 3 respectively.

This experiment makes it apparent that the adaptive price market (Fig. 5.2) is reacting much more promptly to changes in beliefs than the fixed-priced market (Fig. 5.1). After 300 transactions, the odds in the fixed-price market are still very far from the objective probabilities, while the market-based odds implied by the adaptive prices reflect closely even dramatic changes in objective probabilities. This is particularly interesting for the smooth functioning of a climatic catastrophe market, where forecasts can change dramatically over a very short time period. Another advantage of the adaptive-pricing algorithm is the fact that, when prices adjust smoothly, option holders have a good idea of the payoff they will receive if they hold a winning option, and therefore of the amount of insurance they hold. That is not the case with classical fixed-priced pari-mutuel bets.

Let us now compare Fig. 5.2 with Fig. 5.3 where we examine the case of adaptive prices when orders are executed for blocks of 10 options. Since blocks of options are executed sequentially, prices update after each single purchase. This means that market participants do not know precisely the total cost of their order at the time it is placed. One can observe that, because market probabilities adjust quickly, block orders can have a significant impact on prices.

## A Simulation Experiment

We now simulate and observe the behavior of players and the evolution of the HuRLO market during typical hurricane seasons. As in Ou-Yang and Doherty (2011), we assume that players do not anticipate the impact of their decisions on the decisions of other players and on the evolution of the final payoff. Accordingly, at a given decision date, players deciding about purchasing an option or a block of options only consider the current state of the system and evaluate the options' final payoff by assuming that they are making the last purchase on the primary market.

In our setting, players can buy options in three series of HuRLOs and can purchase options on the primary market at distinct moments during the hurricane year, depending on the number of hurricanes. The players involved in the market are risk-averse investors who may have vulnerable assets in various counties.

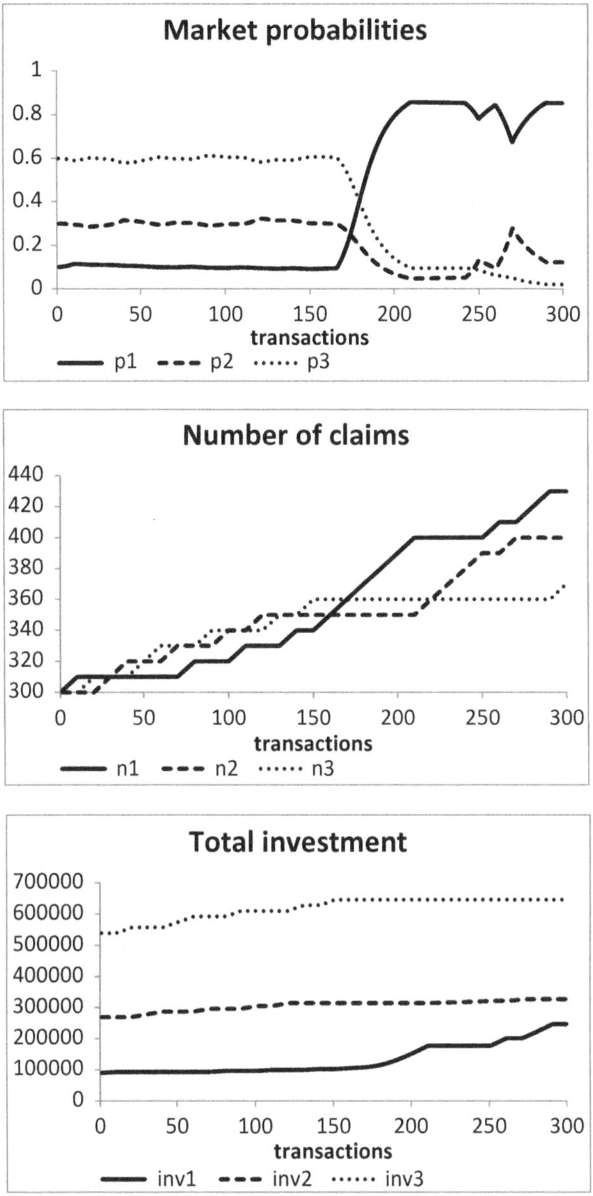


**Fig. 5.3** Market evolution as a function of transactions with adaptive prices, when orders are placed in blocks of 10 options. (Parameters are $M_0$ = \$900,000, $p_0 = (0.1, 0.3, 0.6)$, $p_{150} = (0.85, 0.1, 0.05)$)

This simulation model allows us to experiment with different investment strategies. These strategies are myopic, in the sense that players solve a static decision problem each time they have the possibility to buy an option. However, we give them repeated access to the market during the season, allowing them to increase their stake as the prices of options evolve. We conduct a large number of experiments using a representative data set.

### *Assumptions*

A1: Probabilities of hurricane formation and landfall do not change during the season (recall that trading is suspended when a hurricane warning is issued).

A2: For each potential hurricane forming in the season, we distinguish two stages: (1) Before the hurricane has formed, and (2) When a hurricane is present in the Atlantic Basin but has not yet landed or vanished. We further assume that only one hurricane can be present in the Atlantic Basin at any given moment.

A3: All players have CRRA utility with the same Arrow-Pratt coefficient of relative risk aversion.

A4: In each successive phase of the hurricane season, transactions take place sequentially and market data is updated after each single purchase.

Hurricane formation is assumed to be governed by a Poisson process with intensity $\lambda = 3$ to match with the number of series that we are using.[8] The probability $p_k$ that a hurricane makes landfall in county $k$, given that one is present in the Atlantic Basin, is supposed to be known by market participants. Given the probability of hurricane formation and landfall (see Appendix 2), players can compute at any decision stage the probability $P_{jk}$ that an option $k$ of series $j$ will be the winning option (i.e., mature in-the-money). This probability depends on the remaining duration $d$ of the hurricane season, on the number $h$ of series that have already been executed, and on the actual presence ($l = 1$) or absence ($l = 0$) of a hurricane in the Atlantic Basin (details are given in Appendix 4). Using the initial state of the hurricane season, as given by historical landfall probabilities, and the seeder portfolio of options, one can then calculate the current market

[8] In reality, it seems that $\lambda$ is between 5 and 6. See http://climateaudit.org/2007/01/14/more-evidence-that-hurricanes-are-the-result-of-a-poisson-process/ (last visited on February 22th, 2019).

prices, the total mutual reserve, and the number of options in the three HuRLO series, as a function of *d*, *h*, and *l*.

Players' utility is given by the concave CRRA function $U(W) = W^{1-\gamma}/(1-\gamma)$. We shall assume that players have a total utility that is equal to the expected utility of their final wealth in each of the *k* counties. In other words, for a given player *i* with current wealth $W_i$, the expected utility will be given by

$$Y_i = \sum_{k=1}^{K} p_k \frac{\left(W_i - L_{ik}\right)^{1-\gamma}}{1-\gamma} + p_0 \frac{\left(W_i\right)^{1-\gamma}}{1-\gamma}$$

where $L_{ik}$ is Player *i*'s expected loss if a hurricane makes landfall in county *k*.

Therefore, when considering the possibility to buy an option *k* in series *j* given the values of *d*, *h*, and *l*, a player observes the state of the market, that is, the total mutual reserve $M_j$, and vectors containing the number of each type of options $m_j$ and market prices $\pi_j$ in series *j*, along with the probability $P_{jk}$. Players also consider their wealth $W_i$ and the number of each option *k* in series *j* they own. Because the market price vector $\pi_j$ applies only to the next option purchased, it is not possible to find an analytical expression for the optimal wager of Player *i*. However, it is easy to determine whether or not purchasing a single option *k* in series *j* would increase a player's expected utility, assuming this would be the last transaction in the market, by considering the marginal impact $\mu_{ijk}(\cdot)$, computed as the difference in expected utility for Player *i* due to the purchase of a single option *k* in series *j* (see Appendix 5).

A market simulation typically involves many players, each of whom has positive marginal impact $\mu_{ijk}$ for many options *k* in many series *j*. Even if one agent assumes to be the only investor in the market, it may still be interesting to buy many options, and the order in which these purchases are made will influence the total cost. The order in which purchases are made can also alter the composition of an investor's portfolio of options (because the $\mu_{ijk}$'s will change after each purchase).

In our experiments, we allow the players to use various specific investment strategies, in order to assess the importance of strategic issues in the HuRLO market. These strategies are displayed in Table 5.2. Strategies S1 and S2 pertain to the size of the order, while strategies S3, S4, and S5 pertain to the choice among options. Accordingly, the purchase order of a

**Table 5.2** Set of possible strategies used by player $i$

| *Strategy* | *Definition* |
|---|---|
| $S_1$ | Player $i$ places an order for a single option. |
| $S_2$ | Player $i$ places an order for a block of options, updating $\mu_i$ after each purchase. |
| $S_3$ | Player $i$ chooses randomly among all the options with positive $\mu_{jk}$. |
| $S_4$ | Player $i$ chooses the option with the highest (positive) $\mu_{jk}$. |
| $S_5$ | Player $i$ chooses the option with the lowest (positive) $\mu_{jk}$. |

single player $i$ having computed the vector $\mu_i$ given the current state of the market is described by a strategy pair. On each transaction day, the order in which players are given access to the market is determined randomly, and players are offered the possibility to trade as long as they are interested.

The simulation consists of generating a large number of hurricane seasons, discretized in days. Players are given the opportunity to trade each day. The option prices, the mutual reserves, and the number of live options are updated, following each trade, using the algorithm presented in Appendix 3. The simulation algorithm is detailed in Appendix 6.

### *General Results from the Simulations*

We present our observation of the evolution of the market under various scenarios about the strategies used by the players. We thus report representative results obtained with a model involving four players, four counties at risk for a hurricane landfall, and three option series. The HuRLO market is initialized with an initial mutual reserve of $1,000,000 used to purchase an equal number of each option at prices set to what can be viewed as historical landfall probabilities. For the sake of the simulation, these landfall probabilities are set to $p_1 = 0.2, p_2 = 0.15, p_3 = 0.25, p_4 = 0.22$. The complement, which corresponds to the probability that a given hurricane does not make landfall is given by $p_0 = 0.18$. Parameter values are $c = 1000$, $r = 0$ and $\gamma = 0.5$ and a seeding fee of 3% is taken from the mutual reserve at a settlement date. Results are based on 200 repetitions of the simulation algorithm and are robust to changes in parameter values.

We conducted five experiments using the same simulation data (200 trials) to assess whether the HuRLO-purchasing strategies have any significant impact on the market as a whole. In experiments E1 and E2 all players use the same strategy, while in experiments E3, E4, and E5, one of

**Table 5.3** Set of experiments in trading

| *Experiment* | *Definition* |
|---|---|
| $E_1$ | All players use strategies $S_1$ and $S_4$. |
| $E_2$ | All players use strategies $S_2$ and $S_4$. |
| $E_3$ | Player 1 uses strategy $S_1$ and $S_4$, the others use $S_1$ and $S_3$. |
| $E_4$ | Player 1 uses strategy $S_1$ and $S_4$, the others use $S_1$ and $S_5$. |
| $E_5$ | Player 1 uses strategy $S_2$ and $S_4$, the others use $S_2$ and $S_5$. |

**Table 5.4** Number of options and total mutual reserve in the three series

| | *Number of options* | | | *Total mutual reserve ($)* | | |
|---|---|---|---|---|---|---|
| *Experiment* | *Series 1* | *Series 2* | *Series 3* | *Series 1* | *Series 2* | *Series 3* |
| $E_1$ | 120.2 | 104.2 | 143.9 | 25,810 | 21,467 | 27,381 |
| $E_2$ | 676.1 | 655.6 | 508.4 | 122,337 | 128,852 | 84,491 |
| $E_3$ | 120.6 | 104.2 | 145.6 | 25,919 | 21,456 | 27,630 |
| $E_4$ | 122.4 | 103.1 | 143.1 | 26,315 | 21,249 | 27,266 |
| $E_5$ | 682.1 | 646.6 | 512.5 | 114,766 | 126,723 | 84,786 |

the four players is using a strategy that differs from that of the others. Table 5.3 presents the set of experiments and the strategies used by the players.

Table 5.4 reports the average number of options and the average total mutual reserve, excluding the initial seeding capital, for each series according to the five experiments, characterized by different joint strategies.

A first obvious conclusion is that considerably more interest is generated when players are allowed to order their options by blocks (strategy $S_2$) instead of separately (strategy $S_1$). Both the mutual reserve and the number of options are much larger in experiments $E_2$ and $E_5$ than in experiments $E_1$, $E_3$, and $E_4$. This is surprising since players have the opportunity to buy options every day, and as many times as they want in a single day. We infer from these experiments that the way in which orders are placed is very important, not only for the decision-making player, but also for the activity of the market. In terms of investment and number of options, the global results do not differ much when players are using the same or different ordering strategies.

Table 5.5 reports on the players' average utilities at the end of the hurricane season in the five experiments. These payoffs are computed by

**Table 5.5** Players' utilities

| *Experiment* | *Player 1* | *Player 2* | *Player 3* | *Player 4* |
|---|---|---|---|---|
| $E_1$ | 109 | 106 | 105 | 109 |
| $E_2$ | 404 | 359 | 334 | 327 |
| $E_3$ | 128 | 94 | 103 | 107 |
| $E_4$ | 143 | 92 | 105 | 90 |
| $E_5$ | 402 | 246 | 337 | 399 |

assuming that all players have identical initial wealth and vulnerable properties in all counties. We see that the difference in utility enjoyed by players who are using a "better" strategy than the others can be significant. We also observe that utility is generally higher when players are trading blocks of options ($E_2$ and $E_5$).

From these experiments, we can conclude that, if one decides to participate in the HuRLO market, the timing and ordering of option purchases are important, even when all players are myopic.

### *An Illustrative Example*

Figures 5.4, 5.5, and 5.6 present the evolution of each of the five option prices, of the mutual reserve, and of the number of options purchased over time for one of the trials in the simulation experiment. In the trial illustrated in Figs. 5.4, 5.5, and 5.6, three hurricanes are formed and land on days 113, 187 and 200. Three of the players are using strategy $S_1$–$S_3$, while one of them is using strategy $S_1$–$S_4$. In other words, we are showing the dynamics of one trial of experiment $E_3$. Each day, players are offered, in turn, the possibility to buy a single option. When players are interested in more than one option, they choose randomly (Players 1, 2, 3) or they choose the one with the highest marginal impact (Player 4). The round of offers continues until no player is interested in buying options, which closes the trading day.

Four options (dashed lines) are associated with four different districts. The fifth one (straight line) is the null option. In this trial, three hurricanes are formed and land on days 113, 187 and 200, respectively. The top, middle, and bottom graphs correspond to option prices of the first, second, and third series. The landfall probabilities are kept constant over the year at $p_0 = 0.18$, $p_1 = 0.2$, $p_2 = 0.15$, $p_3 = 0.25$, and $p_4 = 0.22$.

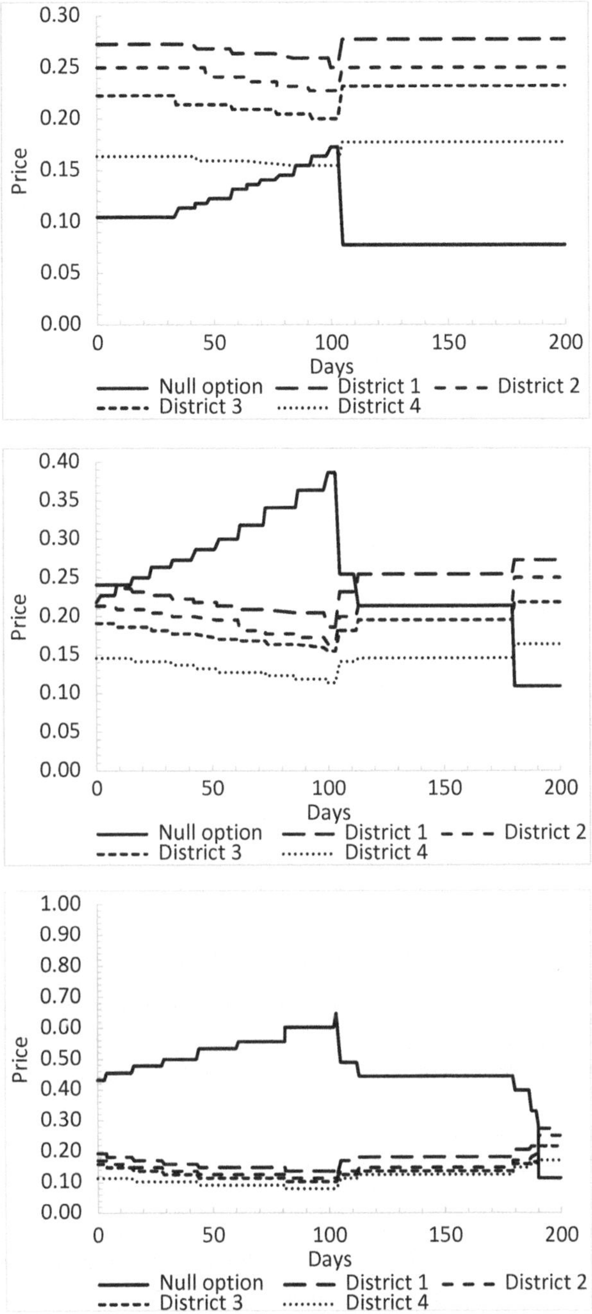


**Fig. 5.4** Evolution of option prices over the season

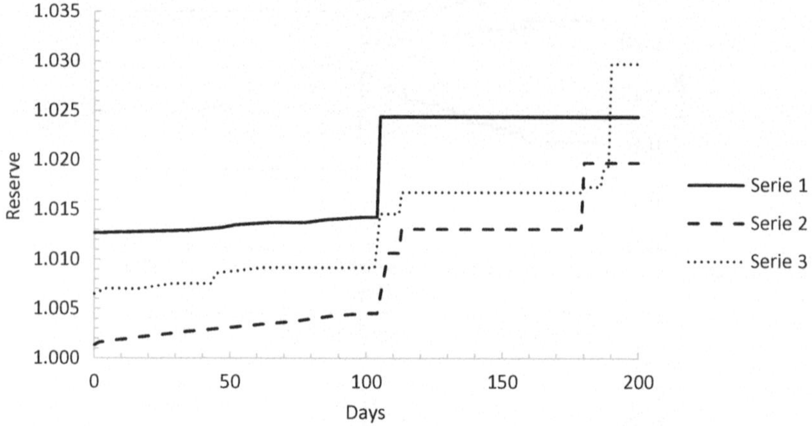


**Fig. 5.5** Size of the mutual reserve in the three series over the season

This example is representative of market evolution over time; we see that prices evolve according to the market demand, and that this demand depends on the time elapsed and on the realization of uncertain events (recall that the $p_k$'s remain constant over time). In particular, while activity in the null option market is regular, most “insurance” options are bought in phases where hurricanes are present in the Atlantic Basin. Obviously, the demand for such options in series 1 is higher than in series 2 and 3. Obviously, the demand for options of series 2 and 3 pick up after options of past series have been settled.

### *Computational Considerations*

The results of our simulation experiments clearly show that the way purchase orders are processed makes a significant difference on the players' utilities and on the market activity. This indicates that strategic considerations should be important for a player wishing to participate in the HuRLO market.

However, one inescapable conclusion from our experiment is the difficulty of identifying an optimal way to purchase HuRLOs. Our simulation experiment involves myopic players, who do not anticipate the impact of their decisions on the decisions of other market participants and on the evolution of the final payoff, and who evaluate their payoff by assuming

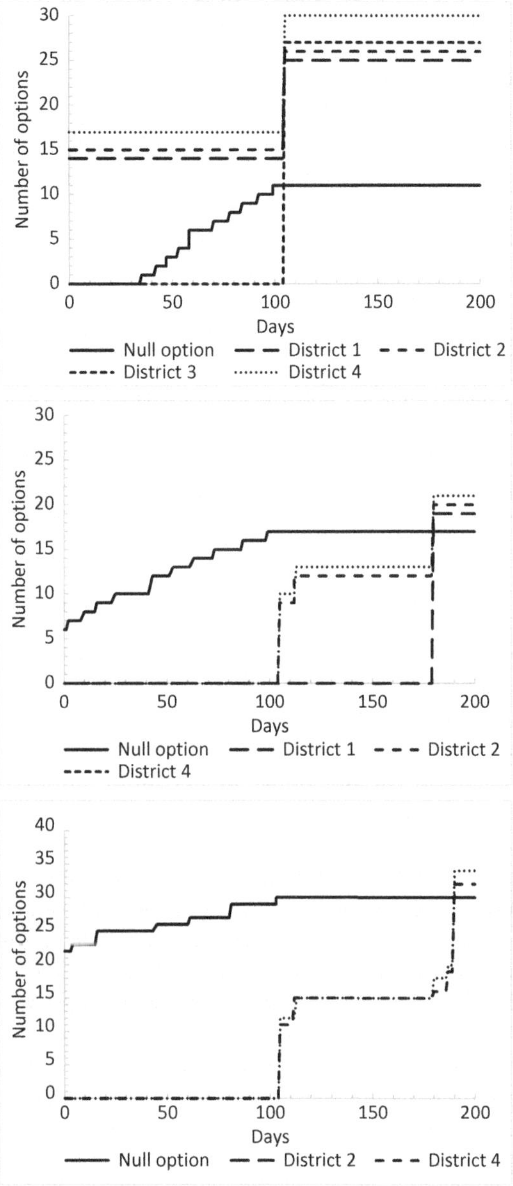


**Fig. 5.6** Number of options in each of the three series over the season

that they are making the last purchase on the primary market. Even in that case, the information required to evaluate any purchasing strategy of Player *i* (that is, how many options of each kind to buy and the sequence in which the orders should be executed) is an observable state vector containing Player *i*'s current wealth, the conditional probability that a hurricane will make landfall in each county, the number of each options of each series owned by Player *i*, the number of each option of each series in the market, the total mutual reserve of each series, and the market price of each option in each series.

In a normal HuRLO market offering 3 series of 75 options (one per county plus the null option), purchase orders are vectors of dimension 225, with combinatorial possible sequences, while the state vector is of dimension 754. Finding the best response of a player to fixed strategies of other players, or finding the equilibrium strategy in a market populated by rational farsighted players, may be a very difficult problem. The use of a simulation approach is probably the only way to gain some insight about the strategic issues present in the HuRLO market.

## Recommendations, and Public Policy Implications

One interesting feature of the pari-mutuel approach to managing hurricane risk is that there seems to be very little demand for such market design. In particular, as pointed out by Ou-Yang and Doherty (2011), pari-mutuel insurance has several merits with respect to insurance markets, including the possibility of becoming an interesting alternative to traditional insurance. Pari-mutuel insurance can be sought as an alternative when traditional insurance has high transaction costs, is too expensive, and is plagued with informational problems, or when it is simply not available. With respect to the Florida catastrophic and weather risk market, the development of such an alternative to traditional insurance products would appear to have a high potential. One could even imagine that the Florida market would be ready for the introduction of such a risk management tool that is neither plagued by moral hazard nor adverse selection problems. Moreover, in an active HuRLO market, insurers would bear no counterparty or default risk, and they do not need to invest in further loss and cost appraisals. That is why it was natural to think, in 2008 when such a market was introduced, that HuRLOs would perform well in Florida, with 75 HuRLOs being possibly traded (74 coastal counties, plus the null). No transactions seem to have occurred on this market after 2009. The question is why would such a market find no traction in the financial and risk management world?

One possible reason for the absence of a market is that there were not enough "speculators" who were willing to take a position on there being no hurricane that would make a landfall so that natural hedgers could not be able to get enough return of their market positions in HuRLOs. This is similar to saying that the initial seed to lift the market (which was 5 million dollars in 2009) was not large enough to attract speculators and players with no stake in the Florida hurricane market to "buy" the null contract. Without enough speculators (or risk neutral investors) populating the HuRLO market, it is possible that this market fell into a "no-trade theorem" gap (see Milgrom and Stokey 1982) where prices were adjusting to new information in such a way that there was essentially no money to be made by entering a transaction. The "no-trade theorem" states that if all players are rational and all players receive the same information at the same time (in our case, hurricane trajectory), then a market that is designed to give an efficient equilibrium will find to have very little (or no) volume of transactions. It seems that the market for HuRLOs embedded all these conditions.

Another reason why the market for HuRLOs did not find much traction with entities exposed to hurricane risk in Florida is that positions on where a hurricane would make landfall could be done continuously up until the point where the option paid. In other pari-mutuel settings, such as horse races, betting stops at some time well before the state of the world is realized. If one was able to take positions on a horse while the race is going on, no one would have an incentive to "invest" in a horse before more information is learned throughout the race. This creates tension between risk management based on prior probability and risk management based on posterior probability. In the case of HuRLOs, the tension is made worse by betting against other players than the house (a similar discussion could be constructed around the game of roulette).

For the market to run appropriately, there needs to be important changes to the current structure to reduce both the "no-trade" problem and the tension between prior and posterior probabilities and beliefs. From a broader perspective, it seems to us that a central planner could play a key role in this market by providing the necessary seed money for the market to be active. The central planner could then use the HuRLO market as a soft commitment device to pay only the seed amount, and no more, when a storm hits some coastal area. At the same time, the central planner could put together similar markets for similar events such as an earthquake in California, typhoons in the Pacific and winter storms in Europe. With enough seed capital from some public source, new players, who have only indirect natural catastrophe exposures, could become interested in this pari-mutuel market. Another potential nudge on this market would be to force insurers who are involved in writing Hurricane risk insurance in Florida to hold a certain basket of such options in a way that would be similar the managing of carbon-emission trading schemes. Without a more capital intensive presence of the insurance industry or of local governments, there is little that pure speculators can do to see this market take off.

## Conclusion

In this research, we examined one particular market design: Hurricane Risk Landfall Option (or HuRLOs), which seeks to become an alternative to traditional insurance and reinsurance contracts. These pari-mutuel markets for hurricane risk were launched in 2008 by Weather Risk Solutions, but never found enough players to make the market liquid or dynamic enough to effectively help with managing hurricane risk. One reason may be that HuRLOs are not pure pari-mutuel products since their payoffs do not depend directly on the amount wagered.

To assess why the market never took off, we investigated whether negative strategic issues were too detrimental to the market when a player decided to invest in HuRLOs. We showed that the order, sequence, and packaging of an order make a difference in the price paid, and in the number of options held by players. This highlights a major drawback of HuRLOs as an insurance product, that is, HuRLOs are very difficult to evaluate and to purchase optimally. In addition, it is important to note that speculators are really needed for the HuRLO market to work. Indeed, if the only options bought correspond to counties where the hurricane risk is high, then there is a real possibility that properties in these counties will be underinsured. In the limit, if there is only one county where hurricanes can strike, then without speculators buying the null option, there is no insurance at all since, in that scenario, what the investors will recover will be exactly what they put in the pool.

As a last remark, we would like to point out that we did not consider the choice between buying insurance or buying options in the sense that we assumed that the only available hedge against losses are the HuRLOs. Also, we did not examine in our simulations whether market participants would prefer to acquire other types of securities. We assumed that investors could only buy HuRLOs, and they would do so whenever it would increase their expected utility. The choice between traditional and pari-mutuel insurance may be simplified somewhat if one assumes that the payoff of a winning option should be near its par value in a well-functioning market. However, the question of how and when to buy pari-mutuel insurance remains open.

## Appendix 1: List of Parameters and Variables

| *Notation* | *Definition* |
|---|---|
| $K$ | Number of counties, indexed by $k \in \{1,\ldots, K\}$. |
| $I$ | Number of players, indexed by $i \in \{1,\ldots, I\}$. |
| $J$ | Index of the option series, $j \in \{1, 2, 3\}$. |
| $W_i$ | Current wealth of player, $i \in \{1,\ldots, I\}$. |
| $p_k$ | Conditional probability that a hurricane present in the Atlantic Basin will make landfall in county $k$. For $k = 0$, $p_0 = 1-\sum_k p_k$ is the probability that it will not make landfall. |
| $L_{ik}$ | Potential (expected) losses of player $i$ in county $k$, where $L_{i0} \equiv 0$. |
| $c$ | Nominal value of a HuRLO. |
| $R_{jk}$ | Payoff of an option $k$ in series $j$ if outcome $k$ is realized. |
| $O_{jk}$ | Decimal odds of outcome $k$ in series $j$. |
| $q_{jk}$ | Implied market probabilities for outcome $k$ in series $j$. |
| $P_{jk}$ | Probability that option $k$ of series $j$ will mature in-the-money. |
| $n_{ijk}$ | Number of each option $k$ of series $j$ owned by player $i$. |
| $m_{jk}$ | Number of each option $k$ of series $j$ in the market. |
| $M_j$ | Total mutual reserve of series $j$. |
| $\pi_{jk}$ | Market price of option $k$ of series $j$. |
| $\Upsilon_i$ | Expected utility of agent $i$. |
| $\gamma$ | Risk aversion parameter. |
| $r$ | Annual discount rate. |
| $d$ | Time remaining until the end of the hurricane season. |
| $H$ | Number of series that have already been executed. |
| $l$ | Indicator of the presence of a hurricane. |
| $\lambda$ | Annual expected number of hurricanes. |

## Appendix 2: Hurricane Landfall Probabilities in the United States

For each of the 11 Atlantic regions of the United States, Table 5.6 presents the probability that a named storm, a hurricane, or an intense hurricane will make landfall in a given year.

Under a Poisson distribution, the probability that at least one storm makes landfall is given by the complement probability that no storm makes landfall: $1 - P(0) = 1 - \exp(-x/d)$, where $x$ is the number of named storms or hurricanes or intense hurricane to make landfall in that particular region over a span of $d$ years according to historical records.

## Appendix 3: Price Updating Algorithm

The market is seeded by the purchase of an equal number of each option (say 1) at a price that reflects historical probabilities of the possible outcomes (see Appendix 2). Each time an option of type $b$ is bought, the market price vector of HuRLOs is updated using an adjustment factor $\alpha$ that ensures that "pricing probabilities" sum to 1 and that the payoff of the last option bought is close to the time-adjusted nominal value. Denote by $\beta = \exp(rt)$ the capitalization factor applied to account for the time elapsed since the initialization of the market, and by $\xi_k$ the pricing probabilities, $k = 1,\ldots, K + 1$. The updating algorithm is the following:

$$\xi_k \leftarrow \begin{cases} \xi_b + \alpha\xi_b(1-\xi_b) \text{ if } k = b, \\ \xi_k(1-\alpha\xi_k) \text{ otherwise,} \end{cases}$$

$$\pi_k \leftarrow \xi_k \beta c,$$

$$\alpha \leftarrow \begin{cases} 0 \text{ if } \dfrac{M}{m_b} > \beta c, \\ \dfrac{1}{m_b + \pi_b} \text{ if } \dfrac{M}{m_b} = \beta c, \\ A \text{ otherwise,} \end{cases}$$

where $m_k$ and $M$ represent the number of type-$k$ options and the total mutual reserve immediately before the transaction, and where

**Table 5.6** Historical probabilities of hurricane landfall

| *Region* | *Year start* | *Number of years* | *Coastline (km)* | *Number of storms to make landfall* | | | *Probability of at least 1 storm making landfall in the region in a given year* | | | *Probability of no storm making landfall in the region over a 10 year horizon* | | |
|---|---|---|---|---|---|---|---|---|---|---|---|---|
| | | | | *Named* | *Hurricanes* | *Intense hurricanes* | *Named (%)* | *Hurricanes (%)* | *Intense hurricanes (%)* | *Named (%)* | *Hurricanes (%)* | *Intense hurricanes (%)* |
| 1 | 1880 | 136 | 503 | 72 | 43 | 17 | 43 | 27 | 12 | 0 | 4 | 29 |
| 2 | 1880 | 136 | 257 | 27 | 13 | 4 | 19 | 9 | 3 | 12 | 38 | 75 |
| 3 | 1880 | 136 | 666 | 104 | 51 | 23 | 56 | 31 | 16 | 0 | 2 | 18 |
| 4 | 1880 | 136 | 382 | 44 | 19 | 2 | 29 | 13 | 1 | 3 | 25 | 86 |
| 5 | 1900 | 116 | 373 | 26 | 9 | 5 | 22 | 7 | 4 | 9 | 46 | 65 |
| 6 | 1900 | 116 | 483 | 49 | 35 | 16 | 37 | 26 | 13 | 1 | 5 | 25 |
| 7 | 1880 | 136 | 574 | 25 | 11 | 3 | 18 | 8 | 2 | 14 | 45 | 80 |
| 8 | 1851 | 165 | 673 | 83 | 54 | 15 | 41 | 28 | 9 | 0 | 4 | 40 |
| 9 | 1851 | 165 | 527 | 14 | 5 | 0 | 9 | 3 | 0 | 41 | 74 | 100 |
| 10 | 1851 | 165 | 426 | 26 | 15 | 7 | 15 | 9 | 4 | 19 | 40 | 65 |
| 11 | 1851 | 165 | 447 | 9 | 5 | 0 | 6 | 3 | 0 | 56 | 74 | 100 |

$A > 1/(m_b + \pi_b)$. The effect of the smoothing constant $\alpha$ is to increase the pricing probability of option $b$ and to reduce the pricing probabilities of the other options. When $M/m_b > \beta c$, option $b$ is overpriced, and no update is made. When $M/m_b = \beta c$, the smoothing constant corrects for the dilution effect due to the additional claimer for outcome $b$. Otherwise, the option is underpriced, and the smoothing factor should be higher. In our implementation, we used $A = \max\{(M - c\beta m_b)(1 - \pi_b)/M, 1/(m_b + \pi_b)\}$, which has the desirable properties of increasing with the imbalance, decreasing with the total mutual reserve, and decreasing with the pricing probability of option $b$.

## Appendix 4: Computation of the Outcome Probabilities

The probability distribution of the number of new hurricanes that will form until the end of the season is denoted by $\phi_d$, where $d$ is the remaining time in the season. Assuming that hurricane formation is a Poisson process of intensity $\lambda$, the probability that $y$ hurricanes will form until the end of the season is then given by:

$$\phi_d(y) = \frac{(\lambda d)^y \exp(-\lambda d)}{y!}.$$

The probability $P_{jk}(d, h, l)$ that option $k$ in series $j$ will be the winning option depends on the remaining time in the season, on the number of series that have already been settled, and on the presence or absence of a hurricane. For $j = 1$ and $h = 0$, it is given by:

$$P_{1k}(d,0,0) = \sum_{y=1}^{\infty} \phi_d(y)\, p_k \sum_{s=0}^{y-1} p_0^s, \text{for } k = 1,\ldots,K,$$

$$P_{1k}(d,0,1) = p_k + p_0 \mathrm{E}\left[P_{1k}(d + D,0,0)\right], \text{for } k = 1,\ldots,K,$$

where $D$ is a random variable representing the presence time of a hurricane. Here, an option $k$ in the first series will be executed if one hurricane or more is formed, and the first one to land does so in county $k$. Clearly, $P_{1k}(d, h, l) = 0$ for $h \geq 1$. Similarly, for $j = 2$ and $h = 0$ we get:

$$P_{2k}(d,0,0)=\sum_{y=2}^{\infty}\phi_d(y)\,p_k\sum_{s=0}^{y-2}C_{s+1}^{1}p_0^{s}(1-p_0),\text{for } k=1,\ldots,K,$$

$$P_{2k}(d,0,1)=p_0\mathrm{E}\left[P_{2k}(d+D,0,0)\right]+(1-p_0)\mathrm{E}\left[P_{2k}(d+D,1,0)\right],\text{for } k=1,\ldots,K,$$

$$P_{3k}(d,h,l)=P_{2k}(d,h-1,l),\text{for } h\geq 1.$$

Notice that there is exactly one winning option in each series, so that

$$P_{j0}(d,h,l)=1-\sum_{k=1}^{K}P_{jk}(d,h,l).$$

## Appendix 5: Computation of Marginal Impact

The computation of the marginal impact of buying an option is presented for the case of a single series ($J$ = 1). When more than one series are offered, the computation is done in a similar way, accounting for the fact that an option $k \neq 0$ in series $j$ can only be a winning option if the null option is not the winning option in series $j-1$.

If Player $i$ does not buy option $b$, expected utility is given by:

$$A=\sum_{k=0}^{K}P_k(d,h,l)\,U_i\left(W_i-L_{ik}+\frac{n_{ik}}{m_k}M\right),$$

where $L_{i0}=0$.

On the other hand, if Player $i$ buys option $b$, expected utility is given by:

$$B=\sum_{k=0,k\neq b}^{K}P_k(d,h,l)\,U_i\left(W_i-\pi_b-L_{ik}+\frac{n_{ik}}{m_k}M\right)$$
$$+P_b(d,h,l)\,U_i\left(W_i-\pi_b-L_{ib}+(n_{ib}+1)\frac{M+\pi_b}{m_b+1}\right).$$

The marginal value of investing in option $b$ is therefore:

$$\mu_{ib}(d,h,l,M,\pi,m,n_i,W_i)=B-A.$$

## Appendix 6: Simulation Algorithm

1. Read parameters and initialize the market using $p$, yielding $M^0$ and $m^0$. Initialize the options held by all players to $n_{ik}{}^0 = 0$ for $I = 1,\ldots,$ $I$ and $k = 0,\ldots, K$. Set $d = 1$, $h = 0$ and $l = 0$.
2. Using the hurricane model, generate hurricane dates, durations, and outcomes during the hurricane season.
3. Compute probabilities $P_{jk}$ at $(d, h, l)$ and select randomly an ordering $O$ of the players.
4. For $I = 1,\ldots, I$

    a. Determine the purchase order for Player $O(i)$ according to her strategy,
    b. For each transaction by player $O(i)$, update market variables,
    c. When purchase order of Player $O(i)$ is completed, set $i = i + 1$.

5. If $d = 0$, stop. Otherwise, update $h$ and $l$ according to the hurricane scenario realization. Set $d = d - 1/365$ and go to 3].

## References

Baron, K., & Lange, J. (2007). *Pari-mutuel applications in finance: New markets for new risks.* Basingstoke: Palgrave Macmillan.

Bonazzi, A., Dobbin, A. L., Turner, J. K., Wilson, P. S., Mitas, C., & Bellone, E. (2014). A simulation approach for estimating hurricane risk over a 5-yr horizon. *Weather, Climate and Society, 6*, 77–90.

Bove, M. C., Elsner, J. B., Landsea, C. W., Niu, X., & O'Brien, J. J. (1998). Effect of El Nino on U.S. landfalling hurricanes, revisited. *Bulletin of American Meteorological Society, 79*, 2477–2482.

Cummins, J. D. (2008). CAT bonds and other risk-linked securities: State of the market and recent developments. *Risk Management and Insurance Review, 11*, 23–47.

Cummins, J. D. (2012). CAT bonds and other risk-linked securities: Product design and evolution of the market. *The Geneva Reports: Risk and Insurance Research, 5*, 39–61.

Cummins, J. D., & Barrieu, P. (2013). Innovations in insurance markets: Hybrid and securitized risk transfer solutions. In G. Dionne (Ed.), *Handbook of insurance.* Boston: Kluwer Academic Publishers.

Epstein, E. S. (1985). *Statistical inference and prediction in climatology: A Bayesian approach.* Springer. Meteorological Monographs.

Doherty, N. A. (1997). Financial innovation in the management of catastrophe risk. *Journal of Applied Corporate Finance, 10*(3), 84–95.

Froot, K. A. (2001). The market for catastrophe risk: A clinical examination. *Journal of Financial Economics, 60*(2), 529–571.

Gray, W. M., Landsea, C. W., Mielke, P. W., & Berry, K. J. (1992). Predicting Atlantic seasonal hurricane activity 6–11 months in advance. *Weather and Forecasting, 7*, 440–455.

Gürkaynak, R., & Wolfers, J. (2006). *Macroeconomic derivatives: An initial analysis of market-based macro forecasts, uncertainty, and risk.* National Bureau of Economic Research Working Paper, no. 11929. Cambridge, MA: National Bureau of Economic Research.

Hall, T. M., & Jewson, S. (2007). Statistical modelling of North Atlantic tropical cyclone tracks. *Tellus, 59A*(4), 486–498.

Horowitz, K. A., Bequillard, A. L., Nyren, A. P., Protter, P. E., & Wilks, D. S. (2012). *U.S. patent No. 8,266,042.* Washington, DC: U.S. Patent and Trademark Office.

Jewson, S., & Hall, T. M. (2007). Comparison of local and basin-wide methods for risk assessment of tropical cyclone landfall. *Journal of Applied Meteorology and Climatology, 47*(2), 361–367.

Kelly, D. L., Letson, D., Nelson, F., Nolan, D. S., & Solís, D. (2012). Evolution of subjective hurricane risk perceptions: A Bayesian approach. *Journal of Economic Behavior & Organization, 81*(2), 644–663.

Kriesche, B., Weindl, H., Smolka, A., & Schmidt, V. (2014). Stochastic simulation model for tropical cyclone tracks with special emphasis on landfall behavior. *Natural Hazards, 73*, 335–353.

Kunreuther, H., & Michel-Kerjan, E. (2009). The development of new catastrophe risk markets. *Annual Review of Resource Economics, 1*, 119–137.

Lange, J., & Economides, N. (2005). A pari-mutuel market microstructure for contingent claims. *Journal of European Financial Management, 11*(1), 25–49.

Meyer, R. J., Horowitz, M., Wilks, D. S., & Horowitz, K. A. (2008). *A mutualized risk market with endogenous prices with application to U.S. landfalling hurricanes.* Working Paper 2008-12-08, Risk Management and Decision Processes Center, The Wharton School of the University of Pennsylvania.

Meyer, R. J., Horowitz, M., Wilks, D. S., & Horowitz, K. A. (2014). A novel financial market for mitigating hurricane risk. II. Empirical validation. *Weather, Climate, and Society, 6*, 318–330.

Milgrom, P., & Stokey, N. (1982). Information, trade and common knowledge. *Journal of Economic Theory, 26*(1), 17–27.

Nakamura, J., Lall, U., Kushnir, Y., & Rajagopalan, B. (2015). HITS: Hurricane intensity and track simulator with North Atlantic ocean applications for risk assessment. *Journal of Applied Meteorology and Climatology, 54*, 1620–1636.

National Hurricane Center (2018). Retrieved from https://www.nhc.noaa.gov/.

Ou-Yang, C. (2010). *Managing catastrophic risk by alternative risk transfer instruments.* University of Pennsylvania Publicly accessible Dissertations 220. Retrieved from http://repository.upenn.edu/edissertations/220.

Ou-Yang, C., & Doherty, N. (2011). *Pari-mutuel insurance for hedging against catastrophic risk.* Wharton School Working Paper # 2011-08.

Pielke, R. A., Jr., Gratz, J., Landsea, C. W., Collins, D., Saunders, M. A., & Musulin, R. (2008). Normalized hurricane damage in the United States: 1900–2005. *Natural Hazards Review, 9*(1), 29–42.

Ramella, M., & Madeiros, L. (2007). Bermuda sidecars: Supervising reinsurance companies in innovative global markets. *Geneva Papers on Risk & Insurance, 32*(3), 345–363.

Rumpf, J., Weindl, H., Höppe, P., Rauch, E., & Schmidt, V. (2007). Stochastic modelling of tropical cyclone tracks. *Mathematical Methods of Operations Research, 66*(3), 475–490.

Rumpf, J., Weindl, H., Höppe, P., Rauch, E., & Schmidt, V. (2009). Tropical cyclone hazard assessment using model-based track simulation. *Natural Hazards, 48*(3), 383–398.

Vickery, P. J., Skerlj, P., & Twisdale, L. (2000). Simulation of hurricane risk in the U.S. using an empirical track model. *Journal of Structuring Engineering, 126*(10), 1222–1237.

Wilks, D. S. (2010). *A novel financial market structure for mitigating hurricane risk.* Proceedings of the 20th Conference on Probability and Statistics in the Atmospheric Sciences.

Yonekura, E., & Hall, T. M. (2011). A statistical model of tropical cyclone tracks in the western North Pacific with ENSO-dependent cyclogenesis. *Journal of Applied Meteorology and Climatology, 50*(8), 1725–1739.

CHAPTER 6

# The Evolving Risk Management Opportunity and Thinking Sustainability First

*Stephen Kibsey, Stéfanie D. Kibsey, Amr Addas, and Cary Krosinsky*

## Introduction

The objective of this chapter is to demonstrate how ESG-sustainability (Environment, Social, Governance) is evolving through the influence of numerous initiatives, task forces, new concepts, taxonomies, disclosure, education, and training by listing many of these driving forces. This chapter first addresses evolving concepts related to ESG-sustainability, followed by a description of some of the realities attached to sustainability, and finishes with a look inside what is supporting the evolution of ESG-sustainability.

The field of ESG-sustainability is evolving at a rapid pace in the corporate and investment sectors. The clarification of the corporation's and investor's fiduciary duty pertaining to ESG-sustainability factors needs to

S. Kibsey (✉) • S. D. Kibsey • A. Addas • C. Krosinsky
Concordia University, Montreal, QC, Canada
e-mail: stefanie.kibsey@concordia.ca; amr.addas@concordia.ca; cary.krosinsky@yale.edu



T. Walker et al. (eds.), *Ecological, Societal, and Technological Risks and the Financial Sector*, Palgrave Studies in Sustainable Business In Association with Future Earth, https://doi.org/10.1007/978-3-030-38858-4_6

be achieved to reduce ambiguity and confusion in the planning of a business or an investment strategy. Progressing into the future, professional managers will experience a transition in their traditional roles to include more socio-environmental related tasks. Though the categories of socio-environmental risks and opportunities are limitless, a few are currently being highlighted in the business and investment sector such as climate change, diversity, and cybersecurity. To deal with these and many other ESG-sustainability issues, government task forces and nongovernment organizations are being created to set guidelines and frameworks for decision-makers; taxonomies are enabling decision-makers to clarify and certify green investments; accounting and disclosure guidance on sustainability activities are being developed to enhance reporting on sustainability goals and targets set by corporations and investment firms; and education and training needs for professionals in decision-making roles are evolving as the transition toward sustainable finance continues to accelerate. Consequently, the field of risk management will need to adapt to the new realities of integrating ESG-sustainability issues, and new opportunities will develop. A need for ESG-sustainability to be a first consideration in the investment process and risk management monitoring will thus create a transformation for professionals, academics, and educators.

Institutional investors, bankers, insurers, as well as corporations in all types of industry segments are key actors who are eager to understand how guidelines, policies, and regulations will frame sustainable finance in years to come. Several regions such as the European Union, the United Kingdom, Canada, and China, to name a few countries, are making strides to embrace sustainability and deal with climate change. As the framing becomes clearer, the actors will need tools to identify, evaluate, mitigate, and report on material ESG-sustainability issues and opportunities. The development of these tools will require basic, acceptable, standardized taxonomies (classifications of criteria for green and social needs), which will be the underlying foundations for further advancement in sustainable finance. The concept of "Think Sustainability First" (High-Level Expert Group 2018) in finance and investing is analogous to "Think Safety First" in industrial settings. Just as safety is a fundamental element in the culture of many industrial sectors, policymakers are looking to make sustainability the fundamental element in the financial sector's culture. The premise of ensuring that capital is allocated with sustainability in mind will be a cultural agent of change needed for the adoption of the SDGs (Sustainable

Development Goals) (https://www.un.org/sustainabledevelopment/sustainable-development-goals/) and for the transition to a low carbon economy.

## Evolving Concepts

### *Evolving Need to Clarify Fiduciary Duty*

How does a businessperson or an investment manager truly decide on what his or her responsibility is beyond maximizing profits and returns? The concept of being a good corporate citizen is well understood in the corporate and investment sectors, but there can be times when business and investment decision-makers need to make trade-offs between profit and socio-environmental issues. This is where a clear understanding of fiduciary duty can help decision-makers act responsibly without the fear of improperly carrying out their obligations and desires to be good corporate citizens.

As a starting point, a definition is in order. According to Business Dictionary, fiduciary duty is: "A legal obligation of one party to act in the best interest of another. The obligated party is typically a fiduciary, that is, someone entrusted with the care of money or property." This, as with all definitions, is open to interpretation. However, acting in the interests of another requires the one party taking on this responsibility to clearly understand these interests. For a corporation, the management and board are working for the shareholders to maximize the value of the enterprise, but it is difficult to understand the shareholders' socio-environmental interests. Similarly, for investment managers, despite a clear investment policy accepted by their clients, socio-environmental issues and return maximization may conflict with each other.

Decision-makers are obliged to achieve financial success, but the decision is not always clear in the case that some return or profit are sacrificed for socio-environmental success. Likewise, it is not clear if the pursuit of maximizing financial return and profit at the expense of good corporate citizenship is counter to fulfilling one's fiduciary duty. However, taking on the responsibility to identify, evaluate, and mitigate risks that could affect the value of the assets with which the manager is entrusted means that the manager should consider financial as well as extra-financial risks on the financial impact because socio-environmental factors do matter. The concept of fiduciary duty needs to be re-calibrated as policy, regulation, and science become dominant drivers of influence in finance and investing.

Developing investment strategies in the new era of thinking of sustainability first requires the evolution of some critical components, such as formal education, construction of beliefs, and acceptance of a progressive culture within an organization. Within this framework, investors will be more prone to allocate capital with the intention of getting an optimal return within a reasonable risk budget and a positive embedded social or environmental impact.

The Commonwealth Climate Law Initiative has efforts in Canada to clarify fiduciary duty as it pertains to socio-environmental information and with a focus on climate change. According to this initiative, decision-makers in business and investment firms are expected to assess socio-environmental risks under their fiduciary duty (Sarra and Williams 2019). As the board of directors must oversee the management of all business risks, they must also include those affecting the long-term sustainability of the business. Risk management for business entities and investment firms relies on various inputs, such as academic research, professional training and certification, consultancy reports, seminar and conference learning, and experience on the job, just to name a few. The practitioner who needs to make decisions hopes to employ strategies to mitigate the material risks. In some cases, the planning of an ESG strategy can be achieved by searching for a business or investment opportunity to counteract those risks. Fiduciary duty is a responsibility that requires expertise on many subjects, but how does the practitioner learn about new emerging risks before they materialize or negatively affect the investment or business?

The challenge is further compounded by the culture in academia whereby scientific research is often aimed at fulfilling the need for a greater understanding and acceptance from the researchers' academic peers rather than those who make strategic decisions in business and investments. If decision-makers and practitioners delay strategies until the research is accessible through the general media, chances are that there is little time to prepare a risk management strategy to mitigate the risk in question.

Even with a clear understanding of fiduciary duty, where do business and investment decision-makers source the information, get their education, or find inputs to analyze extrafinancial issues? A typical starting point is the World Economic Forum (World Economic Forum 2019). Though this is a good source as a starting point, the practitioner still needs a credible, scientific source to effectively design a strategy. This is where the challenges begin to amplify. A science-to-practice gap exists, in particular with risks associated with an issue like climate change (Kasperson and

Berberian 2011). Decision-makers can be quite unaware of relevant research, especially if an intermediate has not read the academic research and put it into the practitioners' arena of information sourcing.

The need for intermediaries (middlepersons) between the "headlines and the footnotes" is a reality. For ESG-sustainability related risks, middlepersons can be nongovernmental organizations (NGO). NGOs are constantly being developed and take on investment managers as members or signatories, as is the case for UNPRI and Ceres. These organizations and several more nongovernmental organizations promote the integration of ESG-sustainability in business and investments. Governments are also lending a hand by setting up and supporting task forces. Since it seems logical that decision-makers want to maximize all material inputs into an analysis, they must apply best practices on every possible occasion, including ESG-sustainability material information. Decision-makers who prefer not to include ESG-sustainability issues in their decision-making analysis are simply taking on a greater risk than those who do. Furthermore, to fulfill the fiduciary duty, a decision-maker needs the relevant information on several material ESG-sustainability topics and themes.

### *Evolution of Material Issues and Scenario Analysis*

Decision-makers need to focus on material issues and not waste their time researching topics, which will not affect their decision-making process. The Sustainability Accounting Standards Board (SASB) has constructed frameworks for decision-makers to focus on material issues depending on a business' sector or industry. It sets the stage for sustainability disclosure and reporting. Moreover, scenario analysis as an important component of reporting is being recommended by The Task Force on Climate-Related Financial Disclosure (TCFD) (Task Force on Climate-Related Financial Disclosures 2017). Many organizations are not yet equipped with the tools and knowledge to either apply known scenarios or create customized ones. Furthermore, the importance of the TCFD cannot be underestimated; it is the recommended climate change disclosure framework for corporations and financial institutions. So, using principles and guidelines set out by SASB and TCFD, decision-makers at businesses and investment firms can be more transparent on sustainability issues and show they are fulfilling their fiduciary obligations to stakeholders.

The TCFD is key to helping corporate sustainability report and disclose ESG issues and opportunities in a more standardized fashion to investors and other stakeholders. It focuses on disclosure around governance, strategy, risk management, and metrics related to climate change. The readers of the reporting by businesses are also actively demanding this type of disclosure. Shareholders are increasingly demanding public companies to disclose operational risks related to climate change, according to a recent publication by The Chartered Professional Accountants of Canada (CPA 2017). Based on the filings in 2015 of 75 listed Canadian companies, the report finds that: (1) less than one third of companies made specific disclosures of board or senior management oversight of climate-related issues; (2) only one quarter of companies disclosed proactive strategies to deal with the transition to a low-carbon economy; (3) climate-related disclosures focused most commonly on risks related to greenhouse gas emissions regulations, and physical-risk disclosures were limited; and (4) the majority of climate-related disclosures did not include financial metrics or targets (CPA 2017, pp. 21–27).

### *Evolving Responsibilities for Executives and Decision-Makers: Change Management*

Integrating ESG-sustainability at an investment firm will change the nature of the portfolio manager's and analyst's traditional roles. Whereas it was common for the portfolio manager and analyst to concentrate solely on financial information, they now need to collect, understand, and integrate nonfinancial factors into their investment thesis going forward. The challenge is that the disclosure from businesses may be not at a sufficiently detailed level to give the portfolio manager and analyst the necessary transparency on material issues they wish to assess in order to make a final decision.

According to Colgren (2017), the value of an organization far exceeds what financial statements show as 80 percent of the valuation of a company actually depends on the worth of its intangible assets. Accordingly, by simply restricting themselves to the balance sheet, decision-makers are looking at a very small portion of the full value of a business or investment. These intangibles can constitute various nontraditional sources of value. A firm's social license, good governance, and environmental stewardship can be possible material value drivers that escape the balance sheet. It is obvious that traditional approaches to valuation are no longer sufficient going forward, and changes in approaches mean changes in traditional roles for those who disclose valuation information and those who analyze it.

The risk management opportunity will either fashion itself through executives specializing in ESG as their main function and collaborating with a traditional function or integrating ESG within a traditional role (Gibassier et al. 2018). The ability to account for ESG-sustainability factors and the measurement of progress and impacts will be new and evolving tasks for CFOs and other executives and operators. In the past, accountants made efforts to integrate nonfinancial values in their reporting and disclosure. Now the challenge is to incorporate the nonfinancial information in an integrated report. The proliferation of targeting SDGs will set the need to innovate accounting frameworks and provide a context for accounting development opportunities (Bebbington and Unerman 2018).

Let us not be naïve and think that the only changing role will be that of the CFO or in the accounting field. For ESG-sustainability to be truly institutionalized in a business or investment firm, it needs to become part of the culture and spread throughout the whole organization, including its stakeholders. Champions of the cause will need to make sure that all employees are on board. To do so, the evolution of educational and training programs including the concepts of sustainability is essential. Education will help employees build conviction and strong beliefs, which should help nurture a sustainability culture within the organization. Of course, buy-in from the top is an absolute condition for success. Change in management will be a necessary driving force within organizations. Senior managers and operators can adopt approaches and conduct an analysis aligned with ESG-sustainability in their decision-making. Moreover, the need for some ESG-sustainability specialist within the firm will be conducive to achieving success as they can supply information and guidance. As measurement and disclosure may become challenging duties, new competencies will be called upon.

## Evolving Realities

### *Examples of Evolving Issues Transforming Risk Management*

There is possibly an endless aggregated number of evolving risk issues in the world, but among those, some will be more in the limelight. Furthermore, the three issues highlighted here are material for almost every business regardless of the sector. This is where the concepts of fiduciary duty, materiality, and change management come to play in real issues.

*Climate Change*

The risks related to climate change and the challenges to sustain our way of life on this planet have added new elements to the field of risk management at corporations and investment firms. As the evolution of risk management related to climate change progresses, decision-makers in both businesses and investment firms need to learn the basic science underlying the issue. However, middlepersons and organizations have played an important role in packaging the information in a common language. For example, though the science of heat absorption by carbon dioxide was explained over 150 years ago by scientists, it is only more recently that the finance community has started to acknowledge the issue of climate change in a more comprehensive fashion. The middleperson, Nicolas Stern, who brought an understanding of the science of climate change which was developed over two centuries and helped the finance community understand the issues and challenges, sets a good example of how investment risk management needed to adapt to new opportunities in which sustainability is central (Stern 2014).

The evolution of ESG-sustainability and the transformation of risk management issues into opportunities with thinking sustainability as a priority have been influenced by some renown economists such as Mark Carney, Governor of the Bank of England since 2013 and Chairman of the Financial Stability Board from 2011 to 2018. Carney was instrumental in passing a profound and influential message in his now famous comments: "A classic problem in environmental economics is the tragedy of the commons," and "Climate change is the tragedy of the *horizon*" (Carney 2015). His influence has set the tone for an accelerated development in risk management related to climate change which has recently become the focus point of emerging risk analysis. Carney's influence layered on what Al Gore, the Nobel Peace Prize winner in 2007, communicated has set the stage and continues to promote the need to act for climate change. Gore's documentary *An Inconvenient Truth* was part of a campaign to educate people about global warming and undoubtedly brought the findings of science from the footnotes to the headlines. One of the underlying drivers of the evolution of ESG-sustainability risk management is thus these influential personalities who have undertaken the task to understand the academic research and translated it into an easy comprehensible form for decision-makers in the financial sector. Following these influences, the popularity of disclosing carbon emissions by businesses and carbon footprinting by investment firms grew substantially (CDP 2016; UNPRI

2016). Some investors have started setting investment strategies with targets to participate in the low carbon economy transition. Within the realm of ESG risks, the risks associated with climate change are now taking priority.

As risks become opportunities, the 2007 report by the Canadian Business for Social Responsibility (CBSR) first indicated that putting the world into a low-carbon economic transition could potentially have economic benefits. Ten years later, the CBSR 2017 report describes the new business opportunities for the regulatory development and cost reductions for businesses transitioning to a low carbon economy (Klar and Rotchild 2017). Recent initiatives on climate change disclosure are amplifying the need for more community engagement and economic incentives to support a transition to a low-carbon economy. The financial risk of increasing carbon taxation, the physical risk of more frequent and intense flooding, and the transitional risk of stranded hard and human assets are examples of risks requiring full assessment and continuous monitoring. Current offsets for investors include allocating capital to green real estate, renewable energy, and electrified modes of transportation. Investment analysis requires an understanding of protocols which define various scopes of carbon emissions, certification of green investments, and descriptions of the life cycle of products.

*Diversity and Inclusion*

A great example of an ESG-sustainability issue that is being transformed from a risk to an opportunity is diversity and inclusion. In relation to the studies dealing with talent and human resources, diversity and inclusion is of interest to the risk manager. Indeed, the lack of diversity and inclusion in the workforce can be a concern for the investment analyst who is evaluating the management of a corporation. For example, the Canadian Centre for Diversity and Inclusion's (CCDI) mission is to help the workplaces to be inclusive, free of prejudice and discrimination (https://ccdi.ca/). Diversity, as any asset, needs to be valued. It is also important to understand that diversity without inclusion is not worth very much.

When considering diversity and inclusion, just concentrating on gender representation on corporate boards—though a good starting point—is not sufficient. The whole workforce at an organization should be examined, including stakeholders. Diversity includes different races, cultures, personalities, ages, and cognitive approaches to problem solving, to name a few. The ability of a risk manager to be able to assess the risk or opportunity of diversity and inclusion requires training and understanding which may not be found in traditional organizations. There lies a challenge for risk management to evolve.

*Cybersecurity*
Cybersecurity is a fairly new ESG-sustainability risk that straddles the border between governance and social issues. The vulnerability of being invaded by an unauthorized third party into one's cyberspace is of great concern to businesses as well as governments and individuals. Organizations take various means to be resilient to cyber-attacks, yet hackers continue to develop new methods of possible entry (Centre for Risk Studies, University of Cambridge 2018). Transparency through disclosure on this issue is extremely thin and for good reason. Businesses are reluctant to disclose too much information about their cybersecurity as hackers could use this very information to devise an attack. As a result, investors who are trying to assess the vulnerability and resilience of a business they wish to invest in are left in the dark (https://www.unpri.org/). However, businesses need to be resilient in the face of ruthless hackers and must ensure that best practices, a strong cyber culture, and insurance play a role in their defense. For any growing concern to remain sustainable without cyber interruptions, the risk management of the organization must be applying best practices known in the industry and have the appropriate resources in place. The risk manager must develop the necessary skills to assess the cyber risks.

### *Presence of the Sustainable Development Goals*

The Sustainability Development Goals have been very influential as tangible goals for investors and businesses. These goals can play on the conscience of decision-makers and can help define opportunities. Since the Brundtland Report published in 1987, the need for a more detailed framework or blueprint was satisfied by the SDGs in 2012, which replaced the Millennium Goals (MDG) of 2000. The SDG framework addresses global challenges related to poverty, inequality, climate, peace and justice, and other issues and sets goals to be achieved by 2030 (https://www.un.org/sustainabledevelopment/sustainable-development-goals/). The SDGs are playing a significant role in the evolution of risk management and how decision-makers are being influenced. The participation of the business and investment sectors is greatly needed to achieve progress toward these goals.

Given the extensive number of goals set out, institutions that would consider adopting SDGs tend to pace themselves and choose perhaps one or two of the goals rather than try to accomplish all seventeen. Some asset managers try to focus mostly on climate change given that it is the most measurable and urgent issue. Businesses try to align their strategy with the issues that they may be able to resolve with their services and products or the way they produce them. The challenge is to measure the outcome or impact for a targeted goal.

Some industries are making great efforts to tackle the SDGs, and associations from the industry are supporting these initiatives. For example, within the mining industry, the Minerals Council of Australia has published a report as "… the first step in a long-term program of work to better understand and share how Australia's minerals industry is contributing—and can keep contributing—to sustainable environmental outcomes and safe, healthy, prosperous and resilient communities" (MCA 2018). This support helps individual mining companies to participate in the achievement of the SDGs. Furthermore, investors are being supported by initiatives such as The Global Impact Investing Network which has formed a network of asset owners and managers who wish to target these goals and help build a sustainable future (Global Impact Investing Network 2019). There is no doubt that businesses and investment firms now face a "wicked" problem (Rittel and Webber 1973). Traditional strategic planning approaches are probably not up to the task when it comes to SDGs. Therein lies the opportunity for academics, decision-makers, and middle-persons to collaborate on finding new approaches for strategic planning.

## The Evolution of Support for ESG-Sustainability

### *Examples of Task Forces Influencing the Evolution*

The creation of task forces is a good example of how policymakers and governments have contributed to the evolution of ESG-sustainability. In 2018, reports from the High-Level Expert Group (HLEG) in the European Union and the UK Green Finance Taskforce gave a huge boost to moving forward key policies that are needed to meet the challenges of environmental and social issues. The HLEG's reports present recommendations for changes in the European financial system to be more sustainable, and a strategy is being developed to encourage sustainable investing (High-Level Expert Group 2018). The UK Green Finance Taskforce also encourages changes in the financial sector to integrate sustainable investing (Green Finance Taskforce 2018). In Canada, an expert panel on sustainable finance was put together in 2018. An interim report was produced in the Fall of 2018, followed by consultation sessions in five Canadian cities. The final report was released in June 2019 with fifteen recommendations built around three pillars for policymakers (Environment and Climate Change Canada 2018, 2019). These task forces generally act as intermediaries with the objective of ensuring that businesses and investors prioritize the transition to ESG-sustainability. This is typically done via consultation with decision-makers and recommendations on aligned policies to regulators and governments. These task forces set the tone and help create the context for success in ESG-sustainability for all sectors and industries.

### *Development of a Green Taxonomy of Opportunities*

As the management of risks related to climate change is becoming better understood, the opportunity to put capital investments into assets which are categorized as green and contribute to a transition to a low-carbon economy allows decision-makers to place ESG-sustainability as a priority. A taxonomy or list of criteria to categorize investments as green requires research and a credible third party to classify types of assets. The green bond market has become an extremely interesting investment segment providing an opportunity to earn a return on products which deliver a positive environmental impact. For example, the Climate Bond Initiative helps define and categorize such opportunities through its taxonomy of green investments. These services have helped investors focus on this specific ESG-sustainability theme (Climate Bond Initiative n.d.).

The opportunity to capitalize on the disruption in the energy market as the issue of climate change gains momentum continues to grow. The need for alternative sources of low-carbon emitting energy sources and energy efficiency gives investors an opportunity to put capital to work. To ensure credibility, the green bond market has precise principles called The Green Bond Principles whose guidelines include transparent disclosure and places the bond market in a key role in funding projects that contribute to environmental sustainability (Green, Social and Sustainability Bonds n.d.).

### *Educational Needs to Ensure a Transition and Evolution*

ESG-sustainability in business and investments requires multidisciplinary expertise in fields, such as environmental studies, sociology, law, geopolitics, psychology, management, accounting, finance, and investment. The challenge is not only to have a basic understanding of these fields but also to be able to understand how they all work in a system. This systems concept is well known in ecological sciences, but perhaps less so in finance. Systems thinking, which focuses on a system's interrelated parts, could therefore help decision-makers better understand the complexity of sustainability. As systems thinking is an approach that considers how components of a system act and contribute to a whole, it is particularly useful in addressing complex or wicked problems which often arise and deal with sustainability issues (Systems Thinking n.d.). Thinking of sustainability first in an investment strategy requires understanding the many components related to different fields and depending on the type of investment, different components may be more important than others.

Furthermore, there is a definite need for a sustainability center in universities, a place where the different disciplines feeding into ESG-sustainability can be centralized and then dispatched to the traditional fields of management, accounting, finance, economics, marketing, and investment analysis. A good analogy is mathematics which typically is a department of its own in educational institutions. Mathematics is used in many subjects such as chemistry, psychology, engineering, accounting, economics, and biology. It can also come under different names: arithmetic, algebra, calculus, etc. Likewise, ESG-sustainability can be used in various subjects, including engineering, architecture, finance, and accounting among others and can appear under many names: responsible or impact investing, corporate social responsibility, ESG, and sustainability to name a few. Therefore, sustainability centers should be introduced in universities to increase collaboration between departments. Furthermore, the academically produced tools and publications need to be transformed into products which the decision-makers can easily understand and learn how to use. Centers dedicated to this purpose would help advance the evolution of the integration of ESG-sustainability in financial decisions and risk management.

As businesses and investment firms continue to take on ESG-sustainability strategies, the need for aligned education will undoubtedly grow. Teaching ESG-sustainability to a board member, a portfolio manager, an external management director, or ESG-Sustainability specialist will require different approaches. For example, investment professionals tend to specialize in asset classes, so teaching them ESG-sustainability will require to take this into account. Also, in businesses, education will need to be customized depending on the industrial segment in which the company operates.

## Conclusion

Despite the challenges presented, optimism in converting emerging risks into opportunities truly lies in developing an understanding of the ESG-sustainability (environmental, social, governance) approaches and issues. Many initiatives put forward by middlepersons and government and non-government organizations have helped pave the way for decision-makers to change behavior and modify traditional approaches to make them more adaptable to the realities of the future. Going forward, the evolution of ESG-sustainability rests on the back of quality education to ensure thinking sustainability first is incorporated in all business and investment plans.

The transition and inclusion of ESG-sustainability issues in of the field of risk measurement and management of emerging risks continue to be promising. The integration of ESG-sustainability strategies in businesses and investment firms has demanded new methodologies in the field of risk assessment. ESG-sustainability issues related to climate change, diversity, and cybersecurity, to name a few, have also created opportunities for both businesses and investment firms as decision-makers attempt to manage these issues. Furthermore, due to the importance of many of these emerging risks and opportunities, the demand for enhancing risk disclosure standards for corporations and financial institutions and the need for new regulations, laws, and clarifications are growing. The creation of task forces and the development of taxonomies are being put in place at such a great pace that some businesses and financial firms are embroiled in an "alphabet soup" (an overabundance of acronyms representing the large number of initiatives). Many are still struggling with the concepts of scenario analysis and outcome measurement from the SDGs.

Furthermore, the need for formal education in the field of ESG-sustainability is slowly replacing the self-schooling of professionals to ensure the standardization of language and comparable methodologies and competencies. In the meantime, so-called intermediaries (middlepersons) have been interpreting scientific findings on emerging risk issues for the benefit of decision-makers. Intermediaries tend to be nongovernmental organizations, foundations, or individuals concerned about specific ESG-sustainability issues and have taken it upon themselves to transfer the knowledge from academia to the practicing decision-makers. Their means of communication is less likely to be academic journals, nor do they often use the general media. The conduit of choice for professionals to learn about ESG-sustainability tends to be through memberships as active partners or signatories and to a cause directed at a specified segment of society or industry. Many questions remain open-ended: will this evolution enhance capitalism to the point it becomes more harmonized with environmental and social issues, and will business models become balanced between profit and purpose so return on investment is a combination of money and intention? Will we achieve thinking about ESG-sustainability as a priority in concert with economic viability? For now, within this grand evolution of putting sustainability first, developed concepts supported by taskforces, initiatives and individuals are being used by decision-makers to not only manage risks but also recognize great opportunities.

## References

Bebbington, J., & Unerman, J. (2018). Achieving the United Nations Sustainable Development Goals: An enabling role for accounting research. *Accounting, Auditing & Accountability Journal, 31*(1), 2–24. https://doi.org/10.1108/AAAJ-05-2017-2929.

Carney, M. (2015). *Breaking the tragedy of the horizon – climate change and financial stability:* Speech by Mr. Carney, Governor of the Bank of England and Chairman of the Financial Stability Board, at Lloyd's of London, London, 29 September 2015. Retrieved from https://www.bis.org/review/r151009a.htm.

CDP. (2016). CDP's full GHG emissions dataset. Providing modelled and reported emissions covering over 5,500 companies. Retrieved from https://www.cdp.net/en/investor/ghg-emissions-dataset.

Centre for Risk Studies, University of Cambridge. (2018). *Cyber risk outlook 2018.* Retrieved from https://www.jbs.cam.ac.uk/faculty-research/centres/risk/publications/space-and-technology/cyber-risk-outlook-2018/.

Climate Bond Initiative (CBI). (n.d.). Retrieved from https://www.climatebonds.net/policy.

Colgren, T. D. (2017, February 1). Expanding the accounting ecosystem. *Strategic Finance.* Retrieved from http://sfmagazine.com/post-entry/february-2017-expanding-the-accounting-ecosystem/.

CPA—Chartered Professional Accountants Canada. (2017). *State of play: Study of climate-related disclosures by Canadian public companies*. Retrieved from the CPA https://www.cpacanada.ca/en/business-and-accounting-resources/financial-and-non-financial-reporting/sustainability-environmental-and-social-reporting/publications/climate-related-disclosure-study.

Environment and Climate Change Canada. (2018). *Interim report of the Expert Panel on Sustainable Finance*. Retrieved from the Government of Canada http://publications.gc.ca/site/eng/9.863536/publication.html.

Environment and Climate Change Canada. (2019). *Final report of the Expert Panel on Sustainable Finance: Mobilizing finance for sustainable growth*. Retrieved from the Government of Canada http://publications.gc.ca/collections/collection_2019/eccc/En4-350-2-2019-eng.pdf.

Fiduciary duty. In *BusinessDictionary*. Retrieved from http://www.businessdictionary.com/definition/fiduciary-duty.html.

Gibassier, D., Arjaliès, D.-L., & Garnier, C. (2018). Sustainability CFO: The CFO of the future? *The Association of Accountants and Financial Professionals in Business*. Retrieved from https://www.imanet.org/insights-and-trends/external-reporting-and-disclosure-management/sustainability-cfo-the-cfo-of-the-future?ssopc=1 and https://www.ivey.uwo.ca/sustainability/news/2018/12/sustainability-cfo/.

Global Impact Investing Network. (2019). Achieving the sustainable development goals: The role of impact investing. *GIIN*. Retrieved from https://thegiin.org/research/publication/sdgs-impinv.

Green Finance Taskforce. (2018). *Accelerating green finance* (report). Retrieved from https://www.gov.uk/government/publications/accelerating-green-finance-green-finance-taskforce-report.

Green, Social and Sustainability Bonds. (n.d.). Retrieved from https://www.icmagroup.org/green-social-and-sustainability-bonds/.

High-Level Expert Group. (2018). *Financing a sustainable European economy* (final report). Retrieved from the European Commission https://ec.europa.eu/info/publications/180131-sustainable-finance-report_en.

Kasperson, R. E., & Berberian, M. (2011). *Integrating science and policy, vulnerability and resilience in global environmental change*. London: Earthscan.

Klar, D., & Rotchild, L. (2017). Climate change guide for business 2.0. *CBSR*. Retrieved from https://irp-cdn.multiscreensite.com/6a4e36b0/files/uploaded/climate-change-guide-2.0.pdf.

MCA—Minerals Council of Australia. (2018). *Sustainability in action: Australian Mining and the United Nations Sustainable Development Goals* (report). Retrieved from https://minerals.org.au/news/australia%E2%80%99s-world-class-minerals-industry-shows-global-leadership-sustainability.

Rittel, H. W. J., & Webber, M. (1973). Dilemmas in a general theory of planning. *Policy Sciences, 4*(2), 155–169. Retrieved from http://www.jstor.org/stable/4531523.

Sarra, J. P., & Williams, C. A. (2019). Time to act: Response to questions posed by the expert panel on sustainable finance on fiduciary obligation and effective climate-related financial disclosures. *SSRN*. Retrieved from https://papers.ssrn.com/sol3/papers.cfm?abstract_id=3335530.

Stern, N. (2014). *Why are we waiting? The logic, urgency, and promise of tackling climate change*. Cambridge and London: The MIT Press.

Systems Thinking. (n.d.). Retrieved from http://learningforsustainability.net/systems-thinking/.

Task Force on Climate-related Financial Disclosures (TCFD). (2017). Recommendations of the task force on climate-related financial disclosures (final report). Retrieved from https://www.fsb-tcfd.org/publications/final-recommendations-report/.

UNPRI—United Nations Principles for Responsible Development. (2016, September 5). Montréal Carbon Pledge: Accelerating investor climate disclosure. Retrieved from https://www.unpri.org/climate-change/montreal-carbon-pledge-accelerating-investor-climate-disclosure/602.article.

World Economic Forum (WEF). (2019). The global risks report 2019 (14th edition). Retrieved from World Economic Forum https://www.weforum.org/reports/the-global-risks-report-2019.

PART II

# Societal Risks

CHAPTER 7

# Terrorism and Trading: Differential Equity and Bond Market Responses During Violent Elections

*Allan Dwyer and Tashfeen Hussain*

## Introduction

The efficient-market hypothesis holds that securities markets are efficient, unbiased, and instantaneous in their treatment of material information flows. In other words, in liquid and well-regulated stock markets there do not exist any arbitrage opportunities that would allow an investor to make above average returns without a commensurate rise in risk. Most of the headline research in this field, however, has looked at the mature, liquid, developed-country stock markets, principally those of the United States. The wider reality may be somewhat messier, especially in the emerging traded asset markets of the Global South. Emerging markets present particularly esoteric market information systems. The assessment of political risk, for example, is more complex for developing nations such as Nigeria and Pakistan.

A. Dwyer (✉) • T. Hussain
Department of Accounting and Finance, The Bissett School of Business, Mount Royal University, Calgary, AB, Canada
e-mail: adwyer@mtroyal.ca; thussain@mtroyal.ca





T. Walker et al. (eds.), *Ecological, Societal, and Technological Risks and the Financial Sector*, Palgrave Studies in Sustainable Business In Association with Future Earth, https://doi.org/10.1007/978-3-030-38858-4_7

It can be proposed that stock and bond markets amount to a massive crowd-sourcing mechanism for assessing and acting upon changes in political risk. Both academics and practitioners have yet to fully appreciate the country risk-assessment function played by markets. This chapter assesses financial market responses to reports of electoral violence during the 2013 general election in Pakistan. The election is used herein as an event study to assess how stock and bond traders responded to confirmed acts of political violence during and after the campaign. An additional line of enquiry involves an observation of differential responses to electoral violence by domestic investors in comparison with international players. Insights into both the theoretical efficacy of the efficient-market construct as well as the particularities of Pakistan at this point in its democratic journey are assessed. The chapter proposes ways in which academics and policy makers might use financial market responses and information flows to improve their understanding of political violence. It also explores the ways in which political risk is expressed by different types of investors in various financial markets.

## Efficient Markets, Information Flow, and Risk

Efficient markets theory is relevant to this chapter insofar as it provides a platform for assessing how the Pakistan bond and stock markets responded to information flows of an unpredictable but material nature. The entire "market efficiency" conversation begins and ends with the arrival of information in the market and the ways in which market participants process and act upon it. Fama (1970) insists that it is important to know whether or not markets are efficient because "the ideal is…a market in which…investors can choose among the securities that represent ownership of firms' activities under the assumption that security prices at any time 'fully reflect' all available information" (Fama 1970, p. 383). Investors need to know that market prices are fair and completely reflective of the many factors that could adversely affect investments. They can thus allocate investment capital with confidence that the prices they are paying for securities are close to the fair value of the underlying assets, and that those prices reflect all known risks. There have been numerous critiques of Fama's efficient markets contention since it was proposed. It is generally accepted at present that there are different forms or intensities of efficiency: weak, semi-strong, and strong. These gradations of market efficiency differ according to the types of information that are (or are not) incorporated into securities prices. For example, do market prices reflect all historical information about the asset? Do they reflect other forms of currently available public and private information? At present, it is generally accepted by both financial practitioners and academics that markets rapidly incorporate new *public* information into prices, at the very least. It is important to note that "efficiency" in this context does not equate to "rational" (Malkiel 2003, p. 60). Markets absorb information rapidly, but not always *accurately*. Markets are highly efficient but quite unpredictable, and "fake news" can lead to the repricing of a traded asset as quickly as genuine news.

The term "markets" is, of course, an oversimplification meant to signify the global complex of trading systems, investors, issuers, and instruments that characterize the current era of financialized capitalism (Lapavitsas 2009; Fine 2014). There are numerous types of securities exchanges, some of which exist only in computer networks. The proliferation of financial instruments and contracts in recent years is a subject of much discussion in the political economy literature, especially in reference to the financial crisis of 2007 and after. Though it is not the purpose of this chapter to reflect on the ethics of globalization, it is worth noting that the analysis in the present chapter would not be possible without the subject country, Pakistan, having issued high-yielding US dollar sovereign debentures. The ubiquity and utility of "fictitious capital" in the form of traded equities and foreign-currency bonds are the context within which the present analysis is undertaken. Indeed, it provides a new avenue by which one type of information flow, namely news of electoral violence, can be assessed.

Sovereign bonds present eloquent expressions of country risk. When interest rates in the overall economy are rising (or falling), bond prices drop (or rise) because newly issued bonds are offering higher (or lower) rates of interest to new buyers. The rate of interest offered can also be seen as a reflection of the riskiness of the country in question. Higher risk countries are required to offer high interest rates on their bonds in order to entice investors to buy them. The riskier the asset, the higher the required market return, as investors demand a higher investment return to compensate them for the perceived risk of the investment. The principal fear for bond investors is that a negative event will occur and lead to a cessation of interest payments to investors. Credit rating agencies (CRAs) stand amid financial markets as epistemic communities providing standardized, model-driven assessment of country risk. The credit ratings process, especially in the case of emerging market issuers, has faced much critical discourse in recent years (Block and Vaaler 2004). Celebrity political risk specialist Ian Bremmer has expressed it this way: economic and political risks describe whether the country *can* pay its debt versus whether the country *will* pay its debt (Bremmer 2005).

Finally, volatility as a measure of risk is another way of thinking about how information enters securities market and is acted upon by traders and other market participants. A simple mathematical calculation such as a standard deviation, when measured on a rolling basis on the same data series over time, indicates periods of sudden market agitation. During these episodes, buyers and sellers are less discriminating with the prices where they are willing to execute orders. The result is a wider band of executed prices, or "prints," and helps measuring the market impact of information arrival without reference to whether securities prices moved upward or downward. Volatility is a standard way of measuring the impact of information flows on markets.

## The Credit Ratings Process and Country Risk

The principal way that country risk is assessed and discounted is the formal credit ratings process, although a significant literature in the fields of financial economics and finance has emerged to question the efficacy of existing systems of credit risk analysis. Credit rating agencies have come under academic scrutiny recently for the role they may have played in recent financial crises and to question whether conventional ratings processes correctly gauge the country risk of emerging market issuers in particular (Tichy 2011; Jaramillo and Tejada 2011; Scholtens 1999; Block and Vaaler 2004). As an alternative to credit ratings, some researchers of developing-nation debt have sought to isolate the components of country risk out of the price structure of the derivative securities contracts that are associated with many sovereign bonds, the insurance contracts known as credit default swaps (CDSs). The structure of these exotic securities renders them an important proxy for the risks that are otherwise hard to identify. For example, Longstaff et al. (2011) find that 64% of the variation in the prices of emerging market CDSs (and by extension, the underlying sovereign bonds) can be explained by global factors, particularly those related to the US stock and bond markets. In other words, emerging markets are viewed as being riskier when US markets are struggling. Remolona et al. (2008a, b) have also concentrated on CDS prices for emerging market bonds and similarly discovered that sovereign risk is driven by a number of factors, such as country-specific fundamentals and global risk aversion on the part of investors. Emerging market debt (EMD) appears to be viewed by investors as exotic and highly risky, but the source of that risk is often close to the investors' own home market, especially in the case of the United States. Remolona et al. zero in on the credit ratings and default histories of a set of emerging market issuers to derive an alternative measure of sovereign default risk. Their conclusions confirm that the sovereign and country risk of EMD issuers is a complex structure of different types and levels of risk that are not measured by traditional credit rating methods. Block and Vaaler (2004) find that CRAs tend to downgrade developing country ratings more often in election years than at other times and that perceptions of risk tend to be higher before elections than after. This view implies that an ostensibly positive event, a democratic election, may be perceived negatively by CRAs and forces emerging democracies to pay higher interest rates on issued bonds. The picture that emerges from this literature is that the global financial markets, far from being efficient and unemotional venues for the identification and subsequent pricing of the risks of sovereign debt instruments are, in fact, characterized by a distinct inability to uniformly gauge the risk of investing in emerging markets. Elections, in particular, offer a data-rich opportunity to seek out new ways in which investors respond to changes in country risk (Santiso 2013).

The largest holders of sovereign bonds are major international institutional investors. The greatest risk for those who invest in EMD instruments is that the government-issuer in question will, in the face of uncertainty or instability, stop making its interest payments or refuse to pay back the loan principal at expiry. A government's decision to suspend interest payments on internationally traded bonds is entirely political and always made with reference to a complex of internal economic and social challenges. CRAs claim to predict the likelihood of these events, but the system employed by CRAs is uniform across issuers. The sovereign debt of Pakistan, for example, is assessed on the same set of metrics as is the debt of Canada. Pakistan, however, has a distinctly different political, economic, social, and especially human security landscape than Canada. This risk landscape may not be wholly captured by formal credit rating models. A country like Pakistan has less fiscal room to maneuver, in particular, when faced with extreme challenges such as natural disasters, dissent requiring increased policing, or epidemics. Therefore, the credit rating processes and the resulting measures may not be the optimal way to measure default risk in emerging economies.

There is a robust literature in political science on the concept of political risk in the form of state failure and its prediction. Much of this scholarly work has a direct relevance to the financial-economic literature around the issue of sovereign default risk in emerging markets, yet economists interested in sovereign default have not yet adopted a multidisciplinary perspective. Political instability as predicted by the Goldstone et al. (2010) model presents as one of its unfortunate outcomes the suspension of debt payments. Paul Collier's seminal work on the role of economics and resource scarcity as contributors to civil war and state failure, especially in Africa, would seem to have direct relevance to the question of sovereign credit quality in emerging markets (Collier and Hoeffler 2002, 2004). Collier's *The Bottom Billion* (2007) famously proposes that there are four "traps" that keep countries from developing good governance and push them toward economic failure and conflict. In essence, the upstream causes of each of Collier's development traps are human insecurities of various types and in various sensitivities, such as political violence. Bremmer (2006) posits that country risk can be understood through an amorphous and notional spectrum (the "J-curve") where differing degrees of socio-political openness dictate which countries will succeed in the long term, and which will struggle. The model has been popular in the mass media, though it acts more as an ex post facto method for explaining why the North Koreas and Iraqs of the world have taken the courses they did than as an instrument for the prediction of political violence and thus country risk.

While economists have not embraced the political science literature on political risk, violence, and state failure, they *have* addressed the issue of bond default and its connection to political processes in isolation from that literature. Hatchondo and Martines (2010) highlight that sovereign debt repayment decisions are "determined by public officials" and thus might be affected by such things as elections and civil wars. They find that only in the case of Argentina's sovereign default in 2001 did a popular political risk measure show an increase in risk after a creditor-friendly government was replaced by a debtor friendly government. Dixit and Londregan (2000) propose in a two-stage model whereby governments calculate the domestic electoral impact of debt defaults and subsequent increases in taxes. Much of the recent literature looks at the issue of domestic versus international investor perceptions, a key point of distinction since the two constituencies have the power to impact national political outcomes differently. External creditors are feared due to the dangers that arise from reputational decline, and domestic investors may bring in-country forces to bear that can cause civil strife or even regime change. In the particular case of emerging markets, Cuadra and Sapriza (2008) find that political instability leads to demands by the marketplace for higher investment returns as a form of compensation for the increased risk of default, an important conclusion that supports efficient markets theory in general, and the idea that financial markets perform an important role in parsing large amounts of information and then signaling to observers an assessment of changing country risk conditions.

The theoretical literature cited here points to an opening in the research frontier: the flow of price data from the bond and stock markets should offer empirical confirmation of the increase and decrease of country risk. Since it is an iron law of financial economics that securities markets quickly incorporate new information into asset prices by selling risky instruments and buying safer instruments with relatively less risk, in theory, the bond and stock markets should be data-rich sources of information about country risk (Fabozzi 2005). There are far more bond investors, traders, and analysts watching and acting on developments in emerging markets everyday than there are political scientists with an interest in country risk. It should be noted that the political risk conclusions that these traders express via financial markets are as democratic and well-considered as those of any CRA or academic analyst.

## Pakistan and the 2013 Election

As stated earlier, elections in emerging or frontier markets present important opportunities to observe how investors update their country risk assessments as vital information enters the markets. Pakistan's general election on May 13, 2013 was heralded by observers as a benchmark in that nation's long transition to democracy. It was the first time that an elected government in Pakistan replaced another elected government without the interim intervention of Pakistan's military. The nation saw a record turnout in elections for the National Assembly as well as for the four provincial assemblies in Punjab, Sindh, Balochistan, and Khyber Pakhtunkhwa. The election was deemed fair by a number of international observation missions, though not without some irregularities (European Union 2013; National Democratic Institute 2013). The Pakistan Institute for Peace Studies (PIPS), an NGO, reported after the election that there were 298 deaths and 885 injuries during and immediately after the

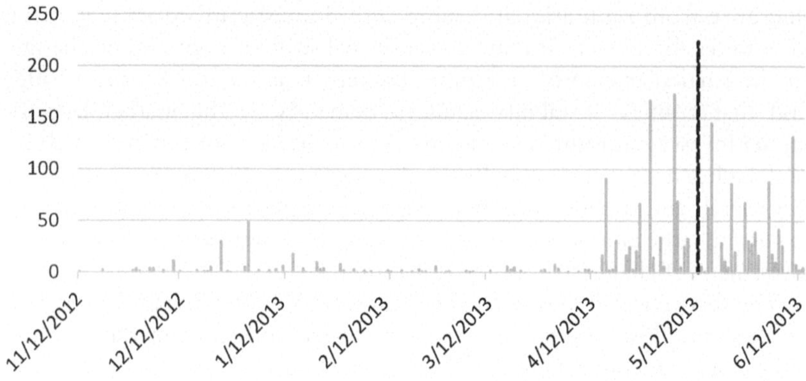


**Fig. 7.1** Political casualties (deaths and injuries), 2013 Pakistan election

election campaign (PIPS 2013, p. 1). These figures relate to victims classified as party leaders and candidates as well as party workers (see Fig. 7.1). These casualties emerged from a total of 148 terrorist attacks and 97 acts of political violence as categorized by PIPS researchers. The majority of this election-related violent activity occurred in Karachi, though there were also significant incidents in Balochistan, Khyber Pakhtunkhwa, and the Federally Administered Tribal Areas. Most incidents reported as terrorist attacks by PIPS were perpetrated by Tehreek-e-Taliban Pakistan (TTP), generally known as the Pakistan Taliban, and occurred in the month of April and two weeks before the May 13th vote. Given nuclear-armed Pakistan's important strategic and historic place in South Asia, international organizations and other governments closely watched the election process in Pakistan. US President Obama congratulated Pakistan on its "historic peaceful and transparent transfer of civilian power" (US Department of State 2013).

Another key constituency watching the election with interest was the international financial markets. In recent years, Pakistan has increasingly become drawn into international financial arrangements, like so many other emerging or developing economies. The Karachi Stock Exchange (KSE) was one of the top global performers during the pre-election period, and Pakistan's outstanding US dollar Eurobond issues saw some price appreciation during the months prior to the vote. Both stock and bond markets experienced some volatility during the election period, and it is that volatility, or rather the possible source of that volatility, that is the focus of this chapter.

Pakistan holds an important place in Asian strategic structures and dialogues. The ongoing conflict with India, the recent appearance of China as friend and benefactor, the proximity to perennial newsmaker Afghanistan, and the capricious American interest in and localized strategic dependence upon Pakistan all make for great scholarly fodder. Independent of the technical financial questions being pursued in the present chapter, Pakistan is in and of itself deserving of serious enquiry. Stephen Cohen has proposed that in order to understand Pakistan's place in the world, the country should be viewed along two planes (Cohen 2004). First, there is the "idea" of historic Pakistan as an indispensable refuge for India's Muslims. Politicians and aspiring leaders communicated a narrative of threat and exclusion that supported a program of independence for South Asian Muslims in the waning, chaotic final years of the Raj. A second, distinctly different theme in modern Pakistan's history is the manufactured international image of the country as an unstable nuclear-armed entity with a worrying history of shaky democratic periods interspersed with relatively benign authoritarian military administrations. Christine Fair suggests that Pakistan continues to wrestle with foundational issues such as the appropriate role of Islam in national governance, the place of ethnic minorities, an appropriate democratic role for the armed forces, and the balance of power between Islamabad and the country's assorted provinces and regions (Fair 2011a). Fair suggests that Pakistan is viewed as both a victim of terrorism as well as, admittedly, an on-again off-again friend of certain Islamist nonstate actors (Fair 2011b). Cohen similarly points out that Pakistan has avoided Muslim authoritarianism and suggests that one way to understand the country is to consider it as a form of South Asian, Muslim version of Israel (Cohen 2004). T.V. Paul proposes that Pakistan struggles with what can be termed a "geostrategic curse" (2014). Due to the scary neighborhood in which Pakistan resides, political leaders have pushed economic and social developments to the back burner as they have accepted aid from various external courtiers, most notably, the United States. Under Paul's model, "rentier" elites in Pakistan have overinflated the threat of war with India in order to entrench themselves in positions of influence (p. 18).

Of particular interest for the present study is the place of elections in Pakistan. In his study of the divergent political histories of India, a robust democracy, and military-autocratic Pakistan, Philip Oldenburg points out the serious questions of legitimacy surrounding every election in Pakistan's history (Oldenburg 2010). In Pakistan, elections are viewed by urban power brokers and regional elites as an extension of age-old systems of kinship and intertribal rivalry, as well as a chance to gain access to government largesse (Lieven 2011). Elections in Pakistan are characterized in a general sense by unelected institutions going to great lengths, often to the point of violence, to retain power rather than see it change hands according to the democratic will of the polity. It follows then that nonstate actors, such as terrorist groups, would use elections as an opportunity to broadcast their agenda as well as intimidate or eliminate political groups who oppose their view of what Pakistan is or should be.

Pakistan, then, is a special case: a developing economy with unique geometries of origin and a long history of persistent, though frustrated democratic aspiration. The 2013 election was heralded by many as a successful democratic exercise. Pakistan presents a rare opportunity for analysis in that it has an assemblage of liquid, active financial markets of various asset classes in conjunction with an electoral tradition that is particularly contested, and on occasion, violent. The 2013 election in particular was an excellent chance to observe how unscheduled, election-related information (namely the numerous acts of violence perpetrated against party workers and candidates) was processed and acted upon by financial markets.

## Data on Electoral Violence

Financial markets respond in various ways to material information flows, not only through buying and selling bonds and shares, but also through changes in the patterns of market volatility as well as notable increases or decreases in volumes of securities traded. Starting, then, from the base assumption that informed observers may be communicating valuable information via the performance of securities markets, the Pakistan 2013 general election was selected as an event study.

The underlying issuers of the principal traded asset types, stocks and bonds, can expect a disruption of future cash flows in the event of political instability and the related damage to economic activity. The prospect of depressed corporate earnings due to civil strife sends stock prices down. For their part, bond investors demand higher yields to compensate for burgeoning risks, which is achieved through the sale of bonds and thus lowers bond prices. In the case of Pakistan, the two markets, stock and

Eurobond, are characterized by very different investor bases. The domestic Karachi stock market caters primarily (about 90%) to domestic investors. Due to Pakistan's relative dearth of large investible corporations, foreign investors in the Karachi exchange are not major participants and the vast majority of investors are local traders and speculators.

Daily closing data for the KSE 100 Index was collected for the six months before the election and the one month after the election in order to calculate daily percentage moves in the index for eventual comparison to unanticipated news in the form of election violence data. The 2013 election was highly anticipated in Pakistan, and election-related announcements and activity started some months before the actual voting date of May 13.

The one month of additional data collection post-election was deemed necessary since acts of violence related to voting can continue for some time after polling day in Pakistan. Indeed, violent actors seek to disrupt the process of government formation or try to settle scores from the election.

As for the other asset type covered in this chapter, Pakistan's Eurobonds are held by foreign investors through investment funds in the large financial capitals (see Table 7.1). Eurobonds issued in denominated currencies, such as Euros or US dollars, are viewed by emerging economies as highly

**Table 7.1** Top 10 holders of Pakistan's 2016, 2017, and 2036 USD Eurobonds (Maturities)

| *7.125% of 2016* | *6.875% of 2017* | *7.875% of 2036* |
|---|---|---|
| First Private Investment | UBS | Grantham Mayo Van Otterloo |
| Ashmore Investment Mgmt | JP Morgan | Pictet Funds |
| ING International | Pictet Funds | Universal Investment Lux |
| UBS | Goldman Sachs Group | ING International Advisory |
| Mediolanum International | Nordea Bank AB | Vontobel Asset Management |
| Eaton Vance Management | ARCA SGR SPA | GAM Holdings Ltd |
| SEI Investments Fund | Wallberg Investment SA | Generali Fund Management |
| FMR LLC | Ashmore Investment Mgmt | Russell Investments Ireland |
| Ashmore Group PLC | Dekabank Deutsche Girozen | Bank Julius Baer & Co. |
| Pacific Life Insurance | Eastspring Investments | T Rowe Price Associates |

Source: Bloomberg Financial Markets. Data current as of May 2015

prestigious. During the period of the 2013 election, the government of Pakistan had three US dollar Eurobonds outstanding. Their maturities were 2016, 2017, and 2036. These three bond issues pay interest to holders in the amounts of 7.125%, 6.875%, and 7.875%, respectively. The bonds are very liquid in the sense that they are easily obtained from or sold back to an elite set of banker-dealers located in the major Western financial centers. The bonds trade throughout each market day and the data appear on the Bloomberg Financial Markets service. The daily closing price of each bond was collected for the same period as the KSE (above): the six months prior to and one month after the election date. The Pakistan stock and Eurobond markets, then, are eager consumers of information and should be responding to negative forms of information flow.

Data on electoral violence was procured by PIPS. PIPS collects data on violence in Pakistan via a network of volunteers, mostly journalists, based around the country. The data is assembled and expertly parsed in a central location. PIPS publishes information on violence according to perpetrator, target, location, number of injuries and deaths, and locations down to the township level. They also include a media source for every incident. Perpetrators, for example, can be criminal gangs, various Islamist extremist groups, separatist parties from the tribal areas and Balochistan, or sometimes elements of the government. Targets can range from military installations to government workers, party and political workers, businesses owners, and others. We observe the data for financial market responses on concurrent days to the first reports of violence as well as with one- and two-day lags between violent act and market price performance. We are looking for evidence of a relationship between the acts of electoral violence and the two large financial markets, and whether the stock and bond markets responded in a differential way. We also analyze changes in market volatility as well as volume of shares traded in Karachi for any evidence of responses related to acts of electoral violence.

## Discussion

Figure 7.2 shows the volume of shares traded on the KSE around the time of the election. There is a distinct increase in volume *after* the election as opposed to before. This is an indication of heightened trading activity after the election—both buying and selling activity. This volume information has no directional value in the sense that there is no accompanying signal from the market that the election was viewed either positively or

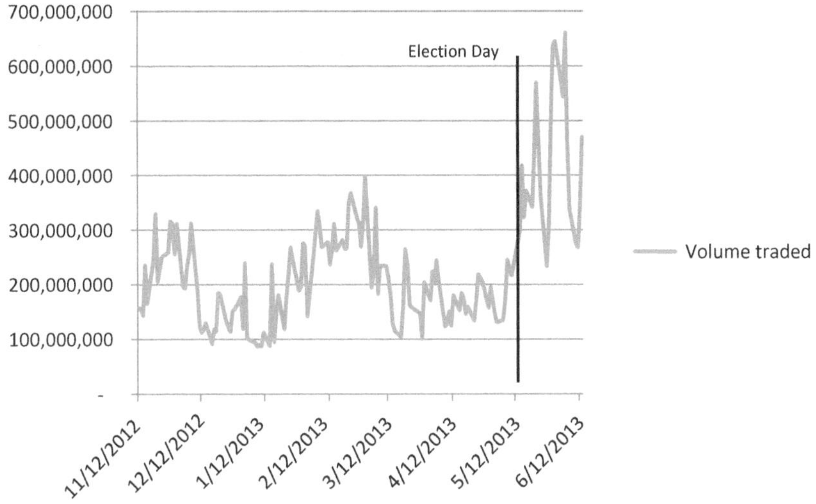


**Fig. 7.2** Volume traded, KSE

negatively by the market; it simply shows that trading activity increased. Figure 7.3 shows the overall level of stock prices in the period under study, as measured by the KSE Index. The KSE traded steadily higher throughout the time of the election, seemingly unconcerned that violent acts could have a dampening effect on economic activity and hence on corporate earnings and ultimately stock prices. Volume traded is a "neutral" factor; it merely points to the increased interest in stock investment, but it is taken in conjunction with the chart of consistently rising stock prices around the time of the election. The conclusion appears to be that KSE investors as overwhelmingly domestic actors shrugged off violence during the campaign, maybe because they have become desensitized to it. Perhaps levels of violence were much lower than expected, which accounts for the lack of a negative reaction in the form of a stock sell-off.

Another way of thinking about how stock investors responded to unexpected information flows in the form of acts of violence in 2013 is to look at the effects on the volatility of stocks on the KSE during and shortly after the campaign. Figure 7.4 shows the graph of the volatility of prices on the KSE at that time. Like volume changes, volatility (measured in this chapter by standard deviation of the previous three days' closing price of the KSE) is independent of market direction. The volatility measure also shows a

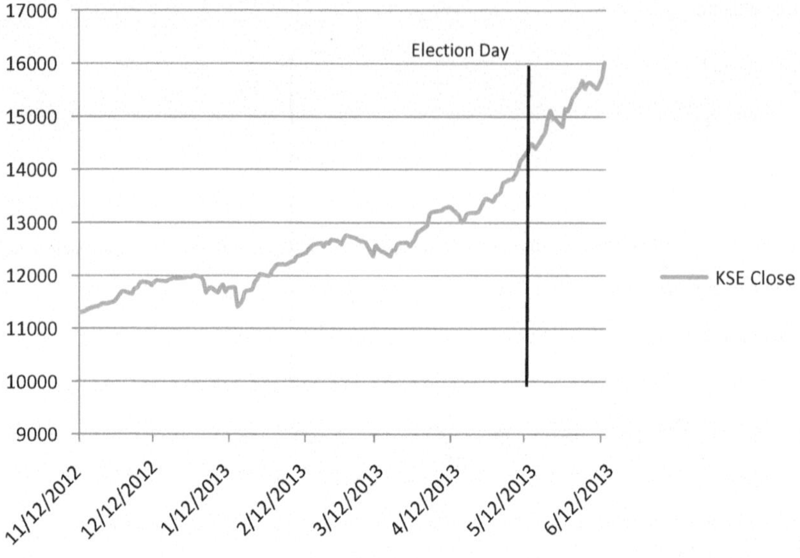


**Fig. 7.3** KSE closing prices

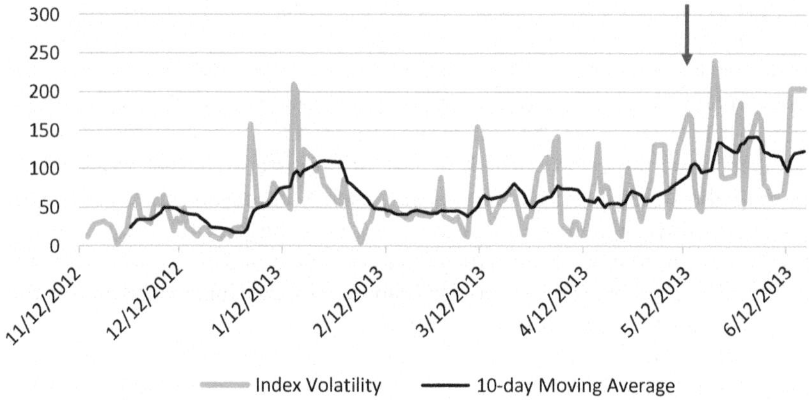


**Fig. 7.4** KSE Index volatility, average

distinct increase in the volatility or degree of variation of stock prices around election day. Volatility can be affected by many things, including sudden large difference in the prices at any time on the market. For example, during a regular quiet trading day the bid and offer levels of stocks are closely aligned. Traders are carefully placing buy and sell orders very close to where the most recent trades have gone through or "printed." But in a volatile market, perhaps at a time of crisis, buying and selling levels tend to be more scattered and imprecise. This phenomenon might have been happening with the KSE around election day. It appears that both KSE volume and volatility were significantly affected by violent events leading to casualties during the election. There was a significant increase in volume traded in the days following the election.

In financial economics, volatility in financial markets is traditionally associated with risk. Increased volatility means increased uncertainty for investors, because a higher volatility signifies that the range of potential returns is spread more widely. Increased volatility means that market predictability, such as it is, is impeded. Equity market investors looking for predictable gains are thus thwarted. So, within the context of a rising market, violent acts are expressed in the equity market in terms of a greater level of investment risk, even within the context of a steadily rising market. It is important to note, however, that equity investors in Pakistan did not see acts of violence as threatening to future corporate earnings in the country, otherwise the KSE would have been sold off. There is a distinct pattern in both equity volatility as well as KSE volume (both "price neutral" indicators) of a burst of activity around the actual election day and then lasting for the month afterward. This pattern may be because, though the election results were a source of both positive and negative concern for equity markets (depending on the investor), investors as a whole increased their share dealing in the context of a rising market. That rising market is an overriding expression of investor directional sentiment, overwhelmingly positive, in the months before and just after the election.

Bond market responses, on the other hand, were quite curious. As shown in Fig. 7.5, the two longer-dated bonds (2017 and 2036 expiry) responded significantly and immediately to acts of violence. The mathematics of bonds makes it likely that the longest dated of the two would have the most drastic responses to material news flow. The longer the period to maturity means more payments being discounted at the risk rate for that bond. Bond prices and yields move in opposite directions. Figure 7.5 shows how bonds began to sell off around the time the election

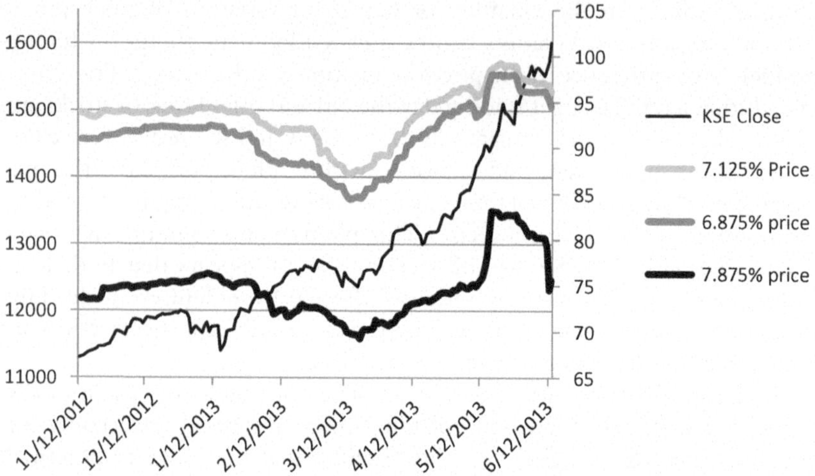


**Fig. 7.5** KSE Index (left axis) and bond prices for 2016, 2017, and 2036 maturities (right axis)

was called, on February 3, 2013. This selling reflects the perception of increased risk during the election campaign on the part of investors. The activity was reversed about a month before the election, ironically at a time when political violence increased. The Pakistan bonds rose into election day, the corresponding drop in yields perhaps an expression of relief by investors that perhaps, despite scattered acts of violence, the democratic exercise was proceeding apace. Interestingly, immediately after the election, bond prices spiked up, likely on reflection of relief in the bond market that the election had "worked" and that a workable result had been achieved. Yet, violence continued, as indicated in Fig. 7.1, in typical score-settling Pakistani fashion, and the bond market took note, eventually selling off sharply one month after election day.

## Conclusion

The diversion of bond prices from stock prices in the weeks after the election is noteworthy. International investors (bond investors) likely deemed some news that surrounded the election as being unsuitably risky in a way that domestics (equity investors) did not, especially as political violence continued. This perception may be due to the higher sensitivity to blood in the streets that foreign players would have, as opposed to locals for whom the tragedy of violence is all too familiar.

The proposition that securities markets are efficient in how they treat and act upon random inflows of information is tentatively affirmed in this chapter. In the case of Pakistan and that nation's important 2013 election, it appears that equity markets acted on information with a time lag, while bond markets, the preserve of sophisticated and networked international investors, responded very quickly, and perhaps even capriciously, to acts of violence. These reactions may be because the types of investors who are willing to buy the sovereign debt instruments of Pakistan and other emerging markets are going to be particularly attentive to news-flow during election periods. And they are apparently more sensitive to the ways in which violent acts during elections reflect on overall country risk. For their part, domestic stock investors seemingly shrugged off the bad news. They did respond by increasing the volumes traded in the market and the wider ranges of pricing levels to deal within during the course of the trading day, as measured by volatility. Both the stock and bond investors expressed a sense of heightened risk, though in distinctly different ways.

The research approach and tentative findings of this chapter may be of use to both policy-oriented observers of elections, both academics and people in the public sector in and beyond Pakistan. If bond and stock markets are efficient, then they might be classified as a type of ready-made and easily accessed crowd sourcing mechanism for seeing the differential effects of electoral violence at different times and in different places. Stock and bond markets are political risk metrics that are accessible to the "rest of us" who are nonspecialist observers of places like Pakistan. Stock markets are concerned about corporate earnings and overall economic conditions. In the case of Pakistan in 2013, these observers showed only agitation during acts of violence but kept their positive view of future corporate earnings. They expressed this by continuously bidding up the KSE. Perhaps there is a threshold of violence prior to which equity traders refuse to be deterred. Or maybe Pakistan is a place where equity traders are inured to the unfortunate ubiquity of violence. It bears noting that the KSE is located in Karachi, a notoriously unstable metropolitan area marked by high levels of both criminal and Islamist violence. The traders live there like everyone else, in a climate of near-constant violence (Inskeep 2012). The mere fact that a democratic election was proceeding on schedule may have been viewed by local actors as being more important than the spate of otherwise predictable violence.

This chapter may open the door to new ways of thinking about country risk for financial market operators as well. Traditionally, experts in the operations of financial markets have not been interested in much other than verifiable and efficacious measures of investment risk. If market responses to violence can be deemed to have certain patterns, then it is likely that market operators will quickly capitalize on these as profit-making opportunities. Though the purpose of this chapter is not to identify new trading strategies or inputs for hedge funds, there is a sense in which a newly liberalized market, such as Pakistan, offers a new frontier for both bond and stock investors. Investment banks and investment funds spend a lot of resources trying to "figure out" places like Pakistan.

In an era of globalized, efficient finance capital, new opportunities for gain are quickly grasped and acted upon. This chapter offers new information about how domestic observers of violence in Pakistan react to reports of unrest during elections. In a country where political violence is endemic and where elections especially are a time of concentrated, politically motivated assaults, domestic observers seem strangely inured. Still, it is important not to read too much into this, as equity market players are not "typical" Pakistanis. Like many developing nations, the domestic stock market of Pakistan is peopled in large part by speculators and fast-money stock operators. The market is not as well-regulated as those in the major financial capitals. However, it may be said that the stock market responses represent the sentiments of more "hardened" observers of Pakistan's affairs. For their part, sophisticated international investors appear to be more sensitive to headline-making violence and act quickly and directionally to what they perceive as dangerous times. Pakistan's use of the international bond markets is one component of wider global processes of financialization. It should be remembered that the bond market transmits the message of risk to wider international audiences than does the domestics-heavy KSE. This reach is one unfortunate downside of the wholesale financialization of emerging nation governments and their budgeting processes. Developing nations can access global markets for necessary funds from global investors who are eager for new opportunities to diversify their portfolios. However, global markets monitor these investments and become highly sensitive to anything that endangers credit quality. They can act quickly to sell bonds when their perception of risk changes, as we have seen for Pakistan before and after the important 2013 election. This act of selling drives up the risk rating of the bonds and thus the required investment return. The result of Pakistan's electoral violence is that foreign investors will demand higher interest rates the next time Pakistan taps international markets for funds and Pakistan will have no choice but to pay.

## References


Block, S., & Vaaler, P. (2004). The price of democracy: Sovereign risk ratings, bond spreads and political business cycles in developing countries. *Journal of International Money and Finance, 23*, 917–946.

Bremmer, I. (2005). Managing risk in an unstable world. *Harvard Business Review, 83*(6), 51–60.

Bremmer, I. (2006). *The J-curve: A new way to understand why nations rise and fall.* New York: Simon & Schuster.

Cohen, S. (2004). *The idea of Pakistan.* Washington, DC: The Brookings Institution.

Collier, P. (2007). *The bottom billion: Why the poorest countries are failing and what can be done about it.* New York: Oxford University Press.

Collier, P., & Hoeffler, A. (2002). On the incidence of civil war in Africa. *Journal of Conflict Resolution, 46*(1), 13–29.

Collier, P., & Hoeffler, A. (2004). Greed and grievance in civil war. *Oxford Economic Papers, 56*(4), 563–583.

Cuadra, G., & Sapriza, H. (2008). Sovereign default, interest rates and political uncertainty in emerging markets. *Journal of International Economics, 76*, 78–88.

Dixit, A., & Londregan, J. (2000). Political power and the credibility of government debt. *Journal of Economic Theory, 94*, 80–105.

European Union. (2013). *Final report: Pakistan 2013.* Brussels: European Union Election Observation Mission.

Fabozzi, F. (2005). Bond pricing, yield measures and total return. In F. J. Fabozzi (Ed.), *The handbook of fixed income securities* (pp. 73–105). New York: McGraw Hill.

Fair, C. (2011a). Addressing fundamental challenges. In S. P. Cohen (Ed.), *The future of Pakistan.* Washington, DC: The Brookings Institution.

Fair, C. (2011b). Why the Pakistan army is here to stay: Prospects for civilian governance? *International Affairs, 87*(3), 571–588.

Fama, E. (1970). Efficient capital markets: A review of theory and empirical work. *Journal of Finance, 25*, 383–417.

Fine, B. (2014). Financialization from a marxist perspective. *International Journal of Political Economy, 42*(4), 47–66.

Goldstone, J. A., Bates, R. H., Epstein, D. L., Gurr, T. R., et al. (2010). A global model for forecasting political instability. *American Journal of Political Science, 54*(1), 190–208.

Hatchondo, J. C., & Martines, L. (2010). The politics of sovereign defaults. *Economic Quarterly, 96*(3), 291–317.

Inskeep, S. (2012). *Instant city: Life and death in Karachi*. New York: Penguin Books.

Jaramillo, L., & Tejada, C. M. (2011). *Sovereign credit ratings and spreads in emerging markets: Does investment grade matter?* IMF Working Paper WP/11/44. Washington, DC: International Monetary Fund.

Lapavitsas, C. (2009). Financialized capitalism: Crisis and financial expropriation. *Historical Materialism, 17*, 114–148.

Lieven, A. (2011). *Pakistan: A hard country*. New York: Public Affairs.

Longstaff, F. A., Pan, J., Pedersen, L. J., & Singleton, K. J. (2011). How sovereign is sovereign credit risk? *American Economic Journal: Macroeconomics, 3*(2), 75–103.

Malkiel, B. (2003). The efficient market hypothesis and its critics. *Journal of Economic Perspectives, 17*(1), 59–82.

National Democratic Institute. (2013). *The 2013 national and provincial assembly elections in Pakistan*. Washington, DC; Bangkok: National Democratic Institute; Asian Network for Free Elections (joint).

Oldenburg, P. (2010). *India, Pakistan, and democracy: Solving the puzzle of divergent paths*. London: Routledge.

Paul, T. V. (2014). *The warrior state: Pakistan in the contemporary world*. New York: Oxford University Press.

PIPS. (2013). *Elections 2013: Violence against political parties, candidates and voters*. Islamabad: Pak Institute for Peace Studies.

Remolona, E. M., Scatigna, M., & Wu, E. (2008a). A ratings-based approach to measuring sovereign risk. *International Journal of Finance & Economics, 13*(1), 26–39.

Remolona, E. M., Scatigna, M., & Wu, E. (2008b). The dynamic pricing of sovereign risk in emerging markets: Fundamentals and risk aversion. *Journal of Fixed Income, 17*(4), 57–71.

Santiso, J. (2013). *Banking on democracy: Financial markets and elections in emerging countries*. Cambridge, MA: The MIT Press.

Scholtens, B. (1999). On the comovement of bond yield spreads and country risk ratings. *Journal of Fixed Income, 8*(4), 99–103.

Tichy, G. (2011). Credit rating agencies: Part of the solution or part of the problem? *Intereconomics, 46*(5), 232–262.

US Department of State. (2013). *Statement of U.S. President Barack Obama on the Pakistan elections*. Islamabad: US Embassy Islamabad.

CHAPTER 8

# The Effect of Corporate Tax Avoidance on Society

*Gio Wiederhold*

## Introduction

This chapter addresses the interaction of tax avoidance and global well-being. Both fields have been subject to much research, but their intersection has not been covered as thoroughly.

Paying as little tax as legally possible appears to be a rational game. Most individuals participate and are not shocked when corporations do it as well. While the effects of tax avoidance are broad, views of the participants are parochial. Organizations concerned with the social welfare of individuals complain about having insufficient funds; while corporations do well. Politicians gather votes by proclaiming corporations should pay more. Business economists complain about taxes throttling business and limiting employment.

All views may be right, even though they conflict with each other.

G. Wiederhold (✉)
Stanford University, San Francisco, CA, USA
e-mail: gio@cs.stanford.edu



T. Walker et al. (eds.), *Ecological, Societal, and Technological Risks and the Financial Sector*, Palgrave Studies in Sustainable Business In Association with Future Earth, https://doi.org/10.1007/978-3-030-38858-4_8

## Tax Avoidance Schemes: Elements and Participants

### *Overview*

This chapter only deals with tax avoidance and legal schemes to avoid paying taxes, and not with direct, illegal tax avoidance, as misrepresenting or misclassifying income. The adoption of tax avoidance schemes is complex and relies on professional advice. To meet their customers' expectations, advisors to individuals and corporations are expected to play an effective game (Wiederhold 2013). To gain insight into those games we will describe the participants.

Taxes are paid by individuals and businesses. All want to pay as little as possible, with an occasional exception (Politi 2011). Businesses, especially large corporations, have means that are not accessible to individuals. Those corporations will be multinational, through their ownership of corporations resident in other countries. Since a decision made in the nineteenth century in the state of New Jersey, corporations have been able to own other corporations (Tarbell 1904). That right has crossed state and national borders (Dill 1898). Such controlled foreign corporations (CFCs) provide a powerful mechanism to minimize taxes on corporate income by exploiting differences in taxation and its oversight in different jurisdictions.

Being owned, a CFC has no freedom in deterring the owner's actions, even if they are inimical to its own well-being. A CFC can even be terminated at will (Eslinger 2018). With the 2011 citizen's united decision (USSC 2010), corporations have even been endowed with personhood, although with one notable exception—in the City of London—they have not been given the right to vote directly (Clarke 1999). Furthermore, on direction of their owners, corporations have the resources to influence local elections more than individuals.

There appears to be a conflict with the notion of corporate personhood, one that is conveniently ignored. The formal abolition of slavery in the US in 1885 prohibits ownership of other persons (Allain 2012) and the biblical 1st commandment and laws in all countries prohibit killing. However, such actions are accepted when owners deal with owned corporate persons.

Given that corporations can own and control other corporations, anywhere in the world, and that those owned corporations can own further corporations, we find that many multinational corporations control more than a hundred dependent corporations, each established to fulfill some corporate purpose. The definition of ownership differs as well. A subsidiary corporation may be owned by multiple parents, perhaps by a 1% share giving control, but letting 99% of its profits flow to the other parent. Rules that determine ownership relevant to taxation differ as well, even within the US Federal tax code, but even more among US states and other countries. The rules are often revised attempting to address prior tax leaks (Brady 2017), but corporations will react quickly. The 2019 tax act (TCJA) tries to repatriate accumulated offshore funds to the US, but schemes to avoid visibility are already in the works. Some schemes move funds to novel taxhavens, but developing countries are unlikely to benefit. Inconsistencies with prior international arrangements raise issues as well (Athanasiou 2018).

Wealthy individuals participate in similar schemes. They are also, often advised to set up legal entities in remote places. Their bankers will help them and identify places where small corporations are easy and cheap to set up, and then perform the actions that otherwise require a corporate financial department (Fitzgibbon 2018). Having one's wealth kept in a business avoids many inheritance taxes, since corporations do not die and can be taken over by one's progeny, a comforting situation for worried parents. We will now focus on corporations.

### *Intermediaries*

Effective exploitation of laws and regulations for tax avoidance typically requires multiple intermediaries. A transfer of money out of one's home country must be explainable. An intermediary should be set up in a credible place of business.

For example, suppose that Mr. Albert Miller is advised to set up a subsidiary company in Zug, a Swiss canton. This company, A.MCo, will perform consulting for his mechanical engineering business (Zuckman 2015). The fact that it has no employees and no real estate makes its operations cheap and almost invisible to sympathetic Swiss cantonal administrators. The Swiss federal government depends mainly on a cut from cantonal taxes. The A.MCo will be paid for its services, actually rendered by Albert himself via the internet, reducing Albert's US income. Keeping money in a Swiss bank is not very profitable, so A.MCo uses a Luxembourg investment firm, which mainly invests in US stocks, since these have a high rate of return.

This approach is also used by individuals in many developing countries. When scaled up, there may be an actual advisor, say on growing and marketing cocoa beans. Such valuable advice warrants high payments but avoids questions about unwarranted transfers of funds. Zuckman estimates that 30% of Africa's wealth is held off-shore. The accumulated funds are invested where they garner reliable profits, rarely in Africa, where the owners already experience high risks.

That simple scheme would become more noticeable if employed at a larger scale by corporations. Instead of transferring overvalued service payments offshore, they transfer assets that can yield income, say the rights to intellectual property (IP) as patents and know-how. The foreign entity must pay for that right, at a cost that is referred to as a transfer price. Keeping transfer prices fair has been an issue for over 90 years (Churchill 1972), but has become crucial in the last 30 years, commensurate with the growth of the internet and the emphasis on intangible products.

## *Transfer of Tangibles*

Physical, tangible products have prices and values that can be estimated by comparison. If a manufacturer ships machinery to its offshore CFC for subsequent sale or lease to an overseas customer, a price charged to independent US customers for such machinery, called the arms-length price, will be known.

Though booking much less US income to save taxes might be noticed, any costs for adaptions needed for foreign operations that should yield higher prices may be ignored. The transfer price will then be a bit less than its foreign CFC should pay, so that less US taxes are due, and the low-taxed offshore profits will be a bit higher.

In the 1970s, an important factor in global trade, the shipping costs, started to become negligible. Today, a loaded 40-foot shipping container can be transported from any harbor to any other harbor in the world for about $1000. Parts used in assemblies of complex goods may make multiple voyages. As a result, local industries have lost an important cost advantage over foreign competition.

### *Tariffs*

Levying tariffs on imports can generate income in lieu of taxes and protect internal industries. They can be important for nations that do not have effective alternate tax systems. Developing countries often use tariffs on incoming goods to protect their growing industries. Developing nations in the British Commonwealth, for instance, have long been favored by its larger members for this reason. Such tariffs have been accepted, but when a nation transitions to a more developed state, as signified by joining the World Trade Organization (WTO), protective tariffs become less acceptable.

Tariffs are not effective for intangibles, where only one transfer is required. For modern manufactured goods that use parts and IP from many countries, a fair imposition of tariffs is complex and its effect, hard to assess.

Tariffs are also easy to misuse. Some developing countries may be held hostage by tariff threats, while smaller countries without substantial export of tangibles cannot be threatened by tariffs. For instance, Switzerland's unwillingness to share financial information has been threatened with tariffs, but some policy adjustments sufficed to make them disappear.

It is also tempting to use a tariff to offset advantages due to preferential taxes and credits provided by competing manufacturing countries. For instance, substantial tariffs were imposed by the US on imported washing machines, lobbied for by Kenmore corporation. Those increased the prices of all machines for US consumers by about 25%. The tariffs hurt some southeast Asian companies, assembling low-cost machines (Tankersley 2019). Tariffs levied by developed nations may be particularized to supplying the goods. Manufacturers will respond by reshipping and relabeling the goods. The WTO is supposed to be an arbiter, but it acts slowly and is easily ignored.

While tariff wars are mainly fought by major countries, they nevertheless affect all global trades. Since fairness and politics now interact, we will ignore tariffs for now.

### *Transfer of Intangibles*

Modern industry depends on intangibles: formulas, designs, recipes, software, data, and know-how for producing valuable goods. One box of intangibles can be used to create millions of tangible items, such as medicines or cell phones. Consider a pharmaceutical company developing a new drug. The research to develop a new drug will be supported by the local government. But when it becomes likely that the drug will be successful, the rights to profit from the drug, which is due to the inherent IP, can be transferred offshore to the company's CFC (Drucker 2010).

What is a fair transfer price for such IP? As there are no similar sales, there is no comparable arms-length price used as a basis to estimate a fair transfer price for the IP. Corporate analysts may have a good hunch, such as $1 billion in each of the next ten years. However, the corporate accountants only deal with facts: the company has spent $40 million annually for five years on relatable drug research. A 25% profit margin sounds great. They, and the government's tax agents, hence consider an estimated transfer price of a reasonable $250 million. If, however, the analysts were correct, the CFC will, in ten years, be able to book the excess offshore, $9.75 billion gross revenue from the drug, before some manufacturing and distribution costs. But nobody can be certain about that amount.

For online-only companies that only create intangible products, such schemes are even easier. Their products are primarily entertainment or information, supplied freely in return for personal information made available to advertisers. The cost of initial creation of their products only requires smart people with computers, no costly research labs, and little access to prior patents. The value of IP rights to be transferred offshore is even less certain (Wiederhold et al. 2010). Actual manufacturing costs, namely shipping copies over the internet, are negligible. However, the software and related data must be maintained to keep its value as underlying systems, security threats, and user expectations change. I estimated such costs, incurred annually, to be as much as 20% of prior spending (Wiederhold 2016).

The smart people and contractors needed for software and data maintenance can work anywhere, while being paid out of income collected in the corporate home country. Workers at remote sites, such as India and the Philippines, provide much of the needed services for the US and European clients. The pool of young people in emerging countries with an adequate education and English language competency enables them to participate and earn well. The local governments do not profit from the local CFCs, since any IP created offshore is assigned to the payors, namely the CFCs' parent companies. Corporate guidance can minimize profits of offshore CFCs in high-tax jurisdictions by charging high royalties for the base IP that had already been transferred to other low-tax locations. Countries like India do not protest, in part because increasing local employment is a good thing, and in part because their bureaucrats do not understand how IP transfers affect them (Wiederhold 2017).

When dealing with future profits of internet companies, estimates of future income are again crucial. Substantial tax avoidance is enabled by misestimation. The actual computations are quite complex and require assignment of IP-generating resources, capitalization of past costs, and discounting of future income, but the concept remains the same. Those complexities hide any intentional misestimation of transfer prices, so that the boundary where tax avoidance becomes tax evasion is hard to discern.

### *Dependence on Valuations of Intellectual Property*

As shown, the major problem in valuing any property is that its value depends on the future net income, namely the future revenues minus the costs incurred. For intellectual property, future income will depend on the number of paying users, which in turn will vary with its perceived uniqueness, protection from imitators, ongoing reliability, and adaption to emerging trends (Wiederhold 2006). Those amounts can be huge. Twitter was valued at $12 billion at its initial public offering (IPO) in 2013 (Damodaran 2013). Shortly before, the company had transferred the right to all of its overseas incomes to its offshore CFC at a small fraction of that expectation. Since all of Twitter had less than $0.5 billion in annual revenues at that time and was still losing money, its overseas CFC could not afford to pay rational transfer price, nor could its home base business afford the taxes due on it. A challenge was dropped.

In the section below "Taxation of IP Transfers by Royalty", we suggest an approach that replaces one-time transfer price taxation with royalty-based taxation to avoid this problem.

## Places Involved in Tax Avoidance

### *Classification of Places Involved in Tax Avoidance*

We showed that successful tax avoidance requires using a variety of locales; some will be in established developed countries, others in developing countries that have specific resources, and some in countries that cannot be classified as either, but that can profit from playing a role in the game of tax avoidance (Weyzig and Dijk 2009). As a result, classifying countries by their state of development does little to inform us how they contribute to tax avoidance. An alternative is to classify them according to the role they play in international trade using the following categories: rich countries (29), globalizers (24), and nonglobalizers (48) (Dollar and Kraay 2004).

Ireland, certainly a rich and well-developed country, is often seen as a tax haven due to its low 12.5% corporate tax. But since the average tax paid by major US corporations on their world-wide net income is a mere fraction of that, there must be more to it, and there is. Ireland has true territorial taxation. This means that an Irish company with a subsidiary outside of Ireland pays no Irish income taxes on income booked at that CFC located outside of its territory. What are good places to have such secondary CFCs?

There are a number of miniature countries, which I will refer to as Palm Islands, that profit significantly from hosting secondary CFCs. Many are part of the British Commonwealth and have trustworthy institutions and adequate communications. Asian equivalents are Vanuatu and Mauritius. It makes sense for them to host businesses that require few resources and are willing to pay some residence and registration fees.

These countries also gain some employment from businesses servicing the firms that establish a formal presence there. They devise laws and regulations that will benefit such external transactions but affect few locals. Hosting many such businesses even allows some Palm Islands to levy no income taxes at all. Such arrangements promote development, including cheaper labor for tourist facilities. The tourists, some nominally there for business meetings, support local development as well.

The Double Irish strategy is then a three-country strategy where the parent corporation establishes a primary CFC in Ireland, and have that Irish subsidiary establish a secondary CFC in a Palm Island. For that Palm Island, CFC will hold the rights to income-generating IP. Since the primary CFC has little income to report to its parent, few taxes are paid in Ireland and no income is reported to the parent corporation.

While the price of corporate IP rights being transferred to Palm Islands is minimized, income and spending from accounts there for external investments will be large. Not being subject to income tax means that nothing is officially reported. Analyses of capital flows have shown that the annual per capita income and spending in countries that are willing to be secondary tax havens can be millions of dollars, distorting global summaries for developing countries (Clausing 2019).

The discrepancies certainly seem suspicious to authorities in customer countries who note incredible high revenues from Palm Islands; as a result, such companies are stigmatized, and politicians are pressured to act.

That concern leads to the Dutch Sandwich strategy. To provide trust, the locations used for customer billing and collecting payments should be familiar to consumers. Within the European Union (EU), the Netherlands and Luxembourg are now the prime initial destinations for payments. Service companies there distribute the revenues. After paying for local manufacturing, marketing, and distribution costs, and any sales taxes due in the purchasers' countries, the profits are directly transferred to the secondary CFCs on the Palm Islands. This transaction avoids informing the primary CFC about profit transfers and prevents independent Irish observers from wondering why Ireland is seen as being complicit in tax avoidance schemes. Knowledgeable politicians there can plausibly ignore the flow of funds that are transferred directly to offshore Irish companies.

For smaller Asian countries, Singapore and Hong Kong perform similar roles. Panama serves this purpose in South America too for the UK and London in particular (Steverman 2019). The island nation of Mauritius serves foreign and Indian tax avoiders investing in India, covering nearly 40% of investment in India (Bahree and Ball 2016). Because of their roles they are viewed as being complicit in tax haven arrangements as well.

China has managed to keep payments within its country. In India, local businesses will collect payments, but little control is exerted by its government on the revenue flow (Wiederhold 2017).

### *Sales Taxes as a Special Case*

Sales taxes are mainly used to pay for local services, as roads and security. Some sales taxes are hard to collect in developing countries where much trade goes on in markets and street stalls that are hard to regulate. Still, the businesses that supply tangible goods to points-of-sale can be identified.

Sales taxes present different issues from income taxes. While corporate profits are transferred to locations where taxes are harder to collect, sales are local and visible to tax authorities. Even internet companies competing with local businesses cannot hide them effectively. Avoiding sales taxes was possible in the US for out-of-state sales, but such intra-US sales tax avoidance is going away. Internationally, the situation is more fluid. Sales of goods from countries that do not levy sales taxes can make that benefit available to purchasers, upsetting local businesses.

Companies that supply intangibles present a different challenge. Much of their information products are free to consumers, and their income comes from advertisers, who may be local or remote. Many ads presented in developing countries are for branded goods sold to customers worldwide, and such income is not locally visible.

Frustration about the inability to tax internet information providers has led countries, primarily in the European Union, to consider a new taxation concept, referred to as digital taxes. Their collection metric is close to the consumers' sales base, but their collection would be from the information providers, those that can now hide their profits from taxation.

## Actions to Mitigate the Tax Avoidance Issues Raised

### *Overview*

The issues of imbalance of wealth are widely discussed, and the fact that imbalanced taxation contributes to the problem is broadly recognized. However, many treatises on developing countries do not treat the role of taxation and tax avoidance in a broad context. Individual senior politicians there may be identified and ostracized. The fact that many individuals and corporations participate in aggressive tax avoidance and evasion is seen as a given. Though the practice is not unique to developing countries, it certainly affects countries with low governmental revenues more.

Observing tax evasion causes groups that try to aid developing countries, as NGOs, to be suspicious of government officials in developing nations. External efforts to improve internal governance have had limited success and breed resentment. Consequently, formal channels are often ignored by NGOs, and work-arounds are devised to help the people in needs.

We look briefly at some current actions and proposals to make taxation fairer and consider how those proposals interact with developing nations. A universal requirement is open access to information.

### *Taxation of IP Transfers by Royalty*

As shown, transfer pricing, as practiced, distorts income flows. But businesses transferring assets, for any reason, have a legitimate complaint of the current method of transfer price taxation. The tax is levied at the time of transfer, not when the benefits of the transfer are realized, leading to future benefits being aggregated. We observed in the earlier example that there is a wide range of possible future income associated with an IP item, as a patent or drug formulation. Since the future is intrinsically uncertain, there is no trustworthy information, so that it makes no business sense to assign a fixed current value to it. But since taxation practice requires a single current value to be taxed, businesses will fight for a minimal estimate. In our earlier example, based on the negotiated value of $250 million and a 20% rate, the tax to be paid becomes $50 million.

In commercial transactions, valuable long-term transfers involving uncertainties are handled by royalty agreements. The rate is set based on the relative contribution of the transferred assets, often IP, into the indefinite future.

We propose that a tax based on future income can be set using the current tax rate over the same future using a proportional royalty. Annual actual information is used in each of the future years. In the example, a royalty-based tax based on the optimistic projection of $10.0 billion future revenues by the analysts, would, over time, yield $2.0 billion to the government. If the drug in the example turns out to be unsuccessful, much less tax would be collected, and that is fair as well.

Using such a business-like approach causes the pressure on the company, created by a huge instant tax bill due to an IP transfer, to disappear. In terms of transfer-pricing concepts, both the amount and the method become realistic in terms of arms-length principles. But as long as businesses are successful in convincing tax authorities to accept minimal instant transfer prices for taxation, there is little incentive to move to a more rational long-term tax collection approach.

## *OECD Efforts*

The Organization for Economic Co-operation and Development (OECD), based in Paris, has been concerned that tax avoidance has reduced the base of taxable corporate profits and increased the burdens on individual taxpayers (OECD 2015). Since the OECD is primarily composed of developed nations of the G20, its objectives can be questioned by observers in developing countries. While countries within the EU have been supportive, other nations, and NGOs trying to assist those nations, have viewed some of its actions with suspicion, although increasing fairness should benefit all nations.

### *Identifying Tax Havens*

In 2000, an OECD effort was to identify tax havens. A criterion was that countries should share information about suspected tax avoiders. Once the countries signed an agreement with at least 12 other countries to share information on request, they would be taken off the list of being tax havens. As a result, we find now amazing bilateral agreements among countries that would never be interested in each other's tax records (Oyedele 2016). By 2009, the list had dwindled from 31 to 3. Now none are left. Even then, the results often wind up being favorable to businesses, since the tax havens could now claim to have been blessed by the OECD (Shaxson 2016).

The concept is also simplistic: tax evasion strategies do not rely on single jurisdictions. Multilateral agreements among groups of Palm Islands countries and G20 countries would be more effective, but the broader approach has not been politically acceptable, including to US legislators. It is an issue that few of their voters understand.

Another problem with most bilateral agreements is that information has to be provided only if the requesting country has a "reasonable suspicion." But without initial access to the data, it is hard to make a case. The release of the Panama Papers did create such suspicions. The US developed a broader approach (FATCA), using the importance of access to US banks to force the sharing of information. While significant loopholes exist, it is widely derided (Pomerleau 2014).

*Base Erosion and Profit Shifting (BEPS)*
The OECD has been more effective with providing guidance to governments so that their approach to taxation would be consistent, including proposals regarding base erosion and profit sharing (BEPS). Some BEPS proposals realize that developing countries have different problems and goals and encourage the United Nations (UN) to participate (Johnston 2019).

In 2017, comments were welcomed on BEPS proposals to deal with transfer pricing. Subsequently a summary of the practices of 50 countries was published (OECD 2018). Some of these documents are affecting planning in the EU. To take effect, individual countries would have to change laws and regulations, but their politicians have little motivation, and their voters are more excited by novel tax proposals.

## *European Efforts*

Public pressures for fair taxation in Europe have been increasing as examples of extreme corporate avoidance became public. Since fairness implies a particular point of view, the OECD documents have provided some common guidance.

*Pressure on British Overseas Territories (BOT)*
Since many of the Palm Islands are part of the British commonwealth, the EU had convinced the UK government to put pressure on its overseas territories to publish the list of the registered holdings and their beneficial owners. Some governments are formally complying, while others are

protesting. The outcome is unclear, but it is likely that some corporate tax avoiders may move to more hospitable locales, or if they are content with local services, at least shift formal ownership to an intermediary corporation or LLC in yet another country, so that they will be harder to identify.

However, with the British exit from the EU, that pressure will vanish and financial managers in the City of London will feel relief. Overall the UK will be motivated to be competitive in attracting financially savvy businesses, while much of its own industry is controlled by offshore multinationals. It is likely that its offshore territories will feel less pressure as well.

*Pressure on European Countries*

Pressures have also been exerted on EU members that are seen to abet systemic tax avoidance, such as Ireland, the Netherlands, and Luxembourg (Weyzig and Dijk 2009). Such accusations of being a tax haven have been taken seriously by the public, but in many regards, changes have been cosmetic (Groot and Eikelenboom 2013). Politicians must consider the well-being of local businesses and the broad public; the EU, not having tax authority itself, can only lobby for fairness.

A similar situation exists in Switzerland, where taxation is a cantonal issue and the Swiss federal government has only limited influence. Earlier attempts to alter the situation have been defeated by the voters, but more recent laws give the federal government more control.

Countries outside the EU have little influence, and developing countries even less, even if much of their wealth is in accounts held within Europe and invested there.

## *Apportionment of Revenues*

As we have seen, multinationals will shift income to low-tax jurisdictions to avoid paying these fees, therefore depriving others of tax revenues. Since internal financial transfers are hard to track, an alternate approach to determine taxable revenues is to use apportionment.

Apportionment is a method when many jurisdictions claim a right to tax income by allocating the total among each other using a set formula (Zelinsky 2018). A common example is road taxes for trucks and buses. An interstate trucker will submit records of miles driven in each of the states; the states can then decide how to tax their share of the income. They could also decide to levy the total at the same tax rate and split the taxes collected, making it easier for the trucking businesses. Here the basis for the apportionment formula is simple to agree on: miles driven.

When other metrics are to be included—for instance, truck weight, type, axles, number of passengers carried, and so on—the formula used becomes more complex. Lengthy negotiations have been needed for states to agree. Still, any metrics agreed on are visible and avoid letting the taxpayer decide what business expenses matter and should determine taxes.

The European Commission has proposed the use of apportionment to deal with income from multinational corporations (Bettendorf et al. 2009). Instead of having all revenue collected in say Luxembourg, a favored venue, and taxed according to its laws and regulations, the total revenue (Common Consolidated Corporate Tax Base) would be split up according to the location of the resources that are seen to contribute to revenue in each European country. The proposed metrics for the allocation are: sales, salaries, and capital, in equal proportion. Countries can still tax the attributed revenues as they desire and compete, however, they wish, but they will not lose their tax base to competing countries.

The metrics used here ignore IP, except to the extent that the salaries of IP-generating personnel is factored in (Wiederhold 2011). Existing intellectual capital (IP and experts who use it) is unlikely to become a metric, since even when booked, it is valued inconsistently. Where IP rights have been transferred to tax havens, they should be valued only at the declared transfer price to avoid perpetuating the imbalance where IP rights allow now 55% of US foreign profits to be booked in small compliant countries with widely differing stages of development.

### *Digital Taxes*

As mentioned above, the frustration of not being able to effectively tax internet businesses is creating an increasing urgency to adopt a new, digital tax scheme, also referred to as a digitalization tax, an internet tax, and even narrower, a GAFA (Google, Apple, Facebook, and Amazon) tax. It could help developing countries obtain some revenues.

The digital tax is to be levied at a low but fixed rate on the gross income, that is, the total local sales revenue of major businesses at their top-level. What is being sold, where the products are created and maintained, what is transferred internally, and the costs of delivery are ignored in the digital tax, since those factors are too easy to manipulate, as we have seen in our analysis of transfer pricing. Getting all EU members to agree will be hard, even while they all are suffering from questionable transfer pricing for their intellectual properties.

While apportioning would identify the share of the taxable income owed to the EU, digital taxes also require identification of the points of sales. This data is available whenever sales taxes are distributed. Even at the 3% rate proposed, a digital tax could add billions of dollars to major companies' tax bills (Minkoff 2018). The proposed criteria for being considered a major company are very specific; major companies must have more than €7 million in annual revenues, more than 100,000 users, and more than 3000 contracts (e.g., advertisers) in the EU. These limits reduce the quantity of objections, but they have little to do with tax principles.

The concept of the digital tax will be challenged as it violates traditional taxing of concepts: namely, that only profits should be taxed and that profits should be allocated to the companies that create the goods. Issues of intra-company pricing disappear, reducing work for advisors.

Countries outside of the EU that are even more frustrated may find a digital tax attractive as well, but they would adjust the limits appropriately. The recently established African Trade Union is certainly a candidate, since it might resolve a revenue issue that is hard to deal with by their individual members.

### *Brexit*

The effects of the Brexit, the UK leaving the European Union, are hard to foresee. The UK, and within it, the City of London, a 3-square km enclave in central London, the town, will no longer be subject to EU regulations. The city has maintained strong connections with smaller countries, such as the British Overseas Territories (including various Palm Islands) but also Gibraltar, the Channel Islands: Jersey and Guernsey (not part of the EU), and the Isle of Man. While Queen Elisabeth II is the Lord of Mann, the Isle of Man is neither part of the EU nor the UK, although it has a defense treaty and a customs union with the UK. The variety of related jurisdictions support aggressive tax avoidance.

Brexit will strengthen the position of the city, and hence of the UK, to support questionable capital transfers. The contentious issue of the border between the republic of Ireland and Northern Ireland is mainly about the movement of people and tangible goods, whereas intangibles do not face this issue.

Other emerging countries hoping to gain opportunities if British Overseas Territories were to be reined in by EU pressures will now have to look to larger, less effective bodies, such as the UN, to impose global pressure.

### *Openness*

Hiding information is an important part of avoiding scrutiny. Registering companies, but not publishing who the actual participants are, is the first step. Corporations can have arbitrary names as they do not have to show a birth certificate, passport, or ID card as natural persons do when establishing residency or engaging in significant financial transactions.

The most aggressive effort toward openness has been by the US government. The FATCA regulation requires identification of US resident owners and their holdings in US and foreign banks. FATCA penalizes noncooperative banks with a 30% tax in their US revenues. Some banks have given up serving US residents, but major banks find it hard to avoid having activities in the US.

## Conclusion

Aggressive tax avoidance and outright tax avoidance deprive governments of resources to improve infrastructure and education everywhere. These practices also engender distrust in the fairness of government, further reducing the motivation to be straightforward. Developed countries have and are strengthening mechanisms to fight the losses of income and investment capital. However, smaller developing countries have little leverage over their business partners and are suffering more. Some have used the opportunity to be complicit in tax haven schemes, however they remain in a perilous situation; trusting advice from expert firms that participate in setting up wealth transfer schemes is certainly risky. Large developing countries all occupy specific positions, depending on the strength of their internal governance. Making an honest effort to understand tax avoidance can help countries at large.

While this chapter cannot take the risk of predicting the future, it aims to present the factors that can be manipulated by the various participants who will determine the future.

## References

Allain, J. (2012). *The legal understanding of slavery: From the historical to the contemporary*. Oxford: Oxford University Press.

Athanasiou, A. (2018). *Study shows: Canada has much to lose from TCJA*. Tax News.

Bahree, M., & Ball, D. (2016). Island tax haven roils India's ways. *The Wall Street Journal*.

Bettendorf, L., Devereux, M.P., Horst, A., Loretz, S., & Mooij, R. A. (2009). Corporate tax harmonization in the EU. *CPB Discussion Paper #113*.

Brady, K. (2017). *H.R.1 0 – An Act to provide for reconciliation pursuant to Titles II and IV of the concurrent resolution on the budget for fiscal year 2018*. 155th Congress of the USA. Kevin Brady (sponsor). 22 December 2017.

Churchill, W. (1972). Tax avoidance. *Hansard of the House of Commons, 205*, 85–87.

Clarke, W. (1999). *How the city of London works*. Sweet and Maxwell.

Clausing, K. (2019). *Open, the progressive case for free trade: Immigration and global capital*. Cambridge, MA: Harvard University Press.

Damodaran, A. (2013). *Musings on markets – Twitter announces IPO: The valuation*. Retrieved from http://aswathdamodaran.blogspot.com/2013/10/twitter-announces-ipo-valuation.html.

Dill, J. B. (1898). *The statutory and case law applicable to private companies*. New York: Baker, Voorhis, & Co.

Dollar, D., & Kraay, A. (2004). Trade, Growth, and Poverty. *Economic Journal, 114*, 22–49.

Drucker, J. (2010). Globe-trotting profits, U.S. companies dodge $60 billion in taxes with global odyssey. *Bloomberg Businessweek*.

Eslinger, B. (2018). HP treated startup like slaves, Jury Told as trial wraps. *Law 360*.

Fitzgibbon, W. (2018). Zimbabwe's list of alleged offshore offenders includes panama papers shell companies. *International Consortium of Investigative Journalists*.

Groot, G., & Eikelenboom, S. (2013). Fiscale BV's Onder de Loep Genomen. *Het Financieele Dagblad*.

Johnston, S. S. (2019). UN to mull value creation in digital economy tax work plan. *Tax Notes*.

Minkoff, Y. (2018). Tech giants may face billions in new taxes. *The Wall Street Journal*.

OCED. (2015). Aligning transfer pricing outcome with value creation, Actions 8-10. OECS/G20 Base Erosion and Profit Shifting Project.

OCED. (2018). Transfer pricing country profiles. Retrieved from https://www.oecd.org/ctp/transfer-pricing/transfer-pricing-country-profiles.htm.

Oyedele, T. (2016). Nigeria joins 30 other countries to sign tax cooperation agreement for automatic sharing of country-by-country information. *PWC Nigeria Tax Blog*.
Politi, J. (2011). White house chief defends "Buffet Rule". *Financial Times*.
Pomerleau, K. (2014). Foreign Account Tax Compliance Act (FATCA) goes into force today. *The Tax Foundation*.
Shaxson, N. (2016). Report: The treaties that cut taxes in the poorest countries. *Tax Justice Network Blog*.
Steverman, B. (2019). The wealth detective. *Bloomberg Businessweek*, pp. 46–51.
Tankersley, J. (2019). Trump's washing machine tariffs stung consumers while lifting corporate profits. *The New York Times*.
Tarbell, I. M. (1904). The history of the standard oil company. *McClure Phillips*.
*US Supreme Court: Citizens United V. Federal Election Commission*. (2010). 558 U.S. 310. Retrieved from https://supreme.justia.com/cases/federal/us/558/310/.
Weyzig, F., & Dijk, V. (2009). Incoherence between tax and development policies. *Third World Quarterly, 30*(7), 1259–1277. Netherlands.
Wiederhold, G. (2006). What is your software worth? *Communications of the ACM, 49*, 65–75.
Wiederhold, G. (2011). Follow the money, how does industry pay programmers' salaries when the required intellectual property is offshored? *Communication of ACM, 54*(1), 65–74.
Wiederhold, G. (2013). *Valuing intellectual capital, multinationals, and tax havens*. Management for Professionals. New York: Springer Verlag.
Wiederhold, G. (2016). Unbalanced data leads to obsolete economic advice. *Communications of the ACM: Viewpoint, 59*(1).
Wiederhold, G. (2017). *Very few people understand the value of IP*. Edited Interview Transcript of STRAIGHT TALK, India Business Journal, April 2017. Recorded and transcribed by Prakash Attili, Infosys.
Wiederhold, G., Gupta, A., & Neuhold, E. (2010). Offshoring and transfer of intellectual property. *Information Resources Management Journal (IRMJ), 23*(1), 74–93.
Zelinsky, E. A. (2018). *How wayfair opens the door to taxing internet sales*. Oxford University Press.
Zuckman, G. (2015). *The hidden wealth of nations*. Chicago: University of Chicago Press.

CHAPTER 9

# Planning for the Carbon Crisis: Reimagining the Power of the US Central Bank and Financial Institutions to Avert a Twenty-First-Century Climate and Financial Disaster

*Carla Santos Skandier*

## Introduction

The year 2018 was crucial for the climate movement: the anticipated 1.5°C special report (SR 1.5) was released. The report by the Intergovernmental Panel on Climate Change (IPCC)—the United Nations (UN) body for assessing climate science—looked at the impacts of a 1.5°C increase in temperature compared to pre-industrial levels and the pathways for decarbonization (Roy et al. 2018).

Although the report put forward a really daunting timeframe—12 years to significantly transform our energy, land, and economic systems—it also highlights that limiting global heating to 1.5 °C, instead of the common target of below 2 °C, is society's best change to address social and economic inequalities

C. S. Skandier (✉)
The Democracy Collaborative, Washington, DC, USA
e-mail: csantos@democracycollaborative.org

 
T. Walker et al. (eds.), *Ecological, Societal, and Technological Risks and the Financial Sector*, Palgrave Studies in Sustainable Business In Association with Future Earth, https://doi.org/10.1007/978-3-030-38858-4_9

(Roy et al. 2018, p. 447). Most of these conclusions are built on the acknowledgment that climate change impacts have the potential to act as threat multipliers to regions and communities already vulnerable to high poverty levels. These regions are especially vulnerable as they often rely on activities such as agriculture to make a living and have less capacity to recover from extreme weather events (Roy et al. 2018, p. 55).

Despite the analysis provided by the SR 1.5 report on the connection between climate change and economic impacts, it omitted the climate-related risks to the financial sector and its social, environmental, and economic feedback loop. It thus missed a great opportunity to raise the issue of stranded assets, which can negatively impact society and stymie climate action progress if not properly addressed.

Stranded assets in the financial world are assets that are no longer able to provide the returns expected when initial investments were made (Caldecott et al. 2016). Assets can become stranded for a number of reasons such as changes in regulation and market conditions. The carbon bubble, a term coined by the London-based think tank Carbon Tracker Initiative, describes it as capital markets holding the listed companies' fossil fuel reserves that cannot be burned in order to stay within society's remaining carbon budget, that is, the limited amount of greenhouse gases (GHG) we still can emit for a 50-50 chance to limit temperature increases to 1.5 °C this century (Campanale et al. 2011). With as much as 85 percent of the fossil fuel reserves needing to remain in the ground and related infrastructure unused to keep society within climate safety goals (see Fig. 9.1), consequently a portion of the reserves already accounted for in the capital markets will not be able to provide any financial return (Muttitt 2016, p. 6).

In order to create an economy that can move away from a fossil fuel-based production as well as react to the effects of climate change already baked into our earth's system, we will need a financially stable society. While the proposed Green New Deal (GND) resolution has the ability to provide a framework for climate action over the next decade, we must also look at the steps needed to deflate and prepare for a potential burst of the carbon bubble that could limit fossil fuel reserve exploitation and a sharp shift to renewable energy generation sources (US Congress 2019). The deep entrenchment of fossil fuel companies in the financial market could have implications that reverberate across the economy, much like the housing crisis, and therefore damage our social and economic institutions. This reliability could make the challenge of transitioning to a carbon-free, equitable society all more daunting.

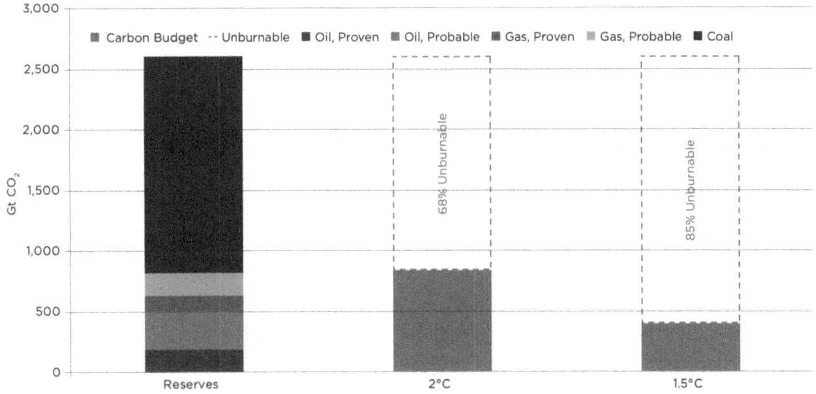


**Fig. 9.1** Global fossil fuel reserves compared to carbon budgets for a likely chance of 2 °C and a medium chance of 1.5 °C. (Source: Muttitt (2016, p. 15). Reproduced with permission)

## Buckling Up for the 2020s (and the Potential Next Financial Crisis)

A decade after the Great Recession we are facing a new potential financial crisis with the climate-induced bubbles looming. To make sure that we are well prepared for the climate and financial challenges of our fossil fuel dependency, we need to understand where we are in terms of crisis-preparedness and what we still haven't learned from the precedent financial crisis.

### *The Missing Signs of Fossil Fuel Stranded Assets*

September 2018 marked the tenth year since Lehman Brothers collapsed, a date that also marks the beginning of the Great Recession. In spite of the passage of the 2010 Dodd-Frank Wall Street Reform and Consumer Protection Act (Dodd-Frank Act),[1] aimed at making the system less prone to crises and more resilient, a key piece of what ultimately led to a twenty-first century financial crisis remains largely unaddressed. Why were the many signs of a growing bubble mounting in the system ignored?

[1] 111th Congress Public Law 203 (2010).

There is a vast list of potential bubbles that face the financial markets today—from those related to climate change and exogenous forces to others focused on the financialization of the economy—which makes it hard to prepare for each one of them. The carbon bubble stands out as particularly concerning because the assumptions that the bubble is built upon also condemn us to more climate change. Concerns about fossil fuel stranded assets have been brushed off under the false assumption that those assets will not be stranded in the near, medium, or even long term because society will need to continue extracting oil, gas, and coal indefinitely to meet growing demand. This mentality is exemplified in the forecast that the top five global publicly traded oil and gas companies—ExxonMobil, Royal Dutch Shell, Chevron, BP, and Total—will make over US$110.4 billion in oil and gas investments in 2019 (InfluenceMap 2019, p. 3). The argument is even stronger in a country such as the United States, where the regulatory environment not only allows extraction, but also enables further fossil fuel expansion. As a result, instead of working to mitigate the worst impact of climate change and use it as the best opportunity to promote equity, the United States has now become the world's top oil and gas producer. It is expected to account for 60 percent of the global growth in oil and gas production between now and 2030 (Trout and Stockman 2019, pp. 5–6).

What companies and the US government are missing is that the threat of stranding fossil fuel assets is not limited to policy change. The bursting of the housing bubble in 2008, for instance, was triggered by a series of compounding and related actions, very much including enabling policy. This included a combination of financial industry deregulation, permission granted to banks to engage in hedge funds, and increasing incentives for homeownership—paired with aggressive industry tools, like creating interest-only loans accessible to subprime borrowers (Amadeo 2019). It is well known that a number of reasons beyond policy and regulation can also leave assets stranded, such as a fluctuation in commodity prices or extreme weather events, that change conditions from when investments were first made. In all cases, it is easy to see how fossil fuel assets could be stranded.

Although the United States has plenty of oil and gas to continue extraction for many years to come, they are coming largely from unconventional sources, particularly from shale reserves that require hydraulic fracturing (fracking) technology (Trout and Stockman 2019). But fracking has been a controversial endeavor, with many pointing out that several fracking sites have not yet proven to be financially sustainable. In fact, 60 of the biggest fracking companies have accumulated between 2012 and 2017 a negative cash flow of $9 billion per quarter (McLean 2018, p. 89). And without fossil fuel subsidies, the situation becomes even more challenging. In 2017, when prices per barrel of oil were at US$50 (prices in 2018 are slightly higher, at US$58), 40 percent of the Permian Basin, 59 percent of the Williston Basin, and 73 percent of offshore, federally administered fields in the Gulf of Mexico would not have been economically viable without subsidies (Erickson et al. 2017, p. 18). Combined with the dropping costs of renewable technology and potential electrification in other sectors, such as transportation and heating, it becomes clear that economic pressure is mounting on fossil fuel assets (IRENA 2019, p. 9).

The same is true from an infrastructure perspective. As average global temperatures increase, extreme weather events are expected to become more intense and frequent, putting a growing pressure in centralized fossil fuel reserves and infrastructure. A clear example is Hurricane Harvey's landfall in Texas in 2017, which led to the closure of oil refineries throughout the state (Rapoza 2017). Yet, physical constraints go well beyond extreme weather events. Other effects, such as water availability, are also a concern as fracking can at times demand as much as 9 million gallons of water to trigger the flow of oil and gas into a well, putting a further constraint in parts of the country that are already facing prolonged droughts (Gallegos et al. 2015, p. 5840). Of 40,000 oil and gas wells drilled since 2011, three quarters were in water-scarce areas and 55% were experiencing drought (Freyman 2014).

There is also one less spoken potential factor for stranding assets: social change. Pressure for climate action continues to mount across the globe, including the promising rise of a movement of youths not willing to compromise their future. In the United States, a growing movement aims at reducing the fossil fuel industry's economic and political power, increasing the investors' perception of the dangers surrounding fossil fuel extraction and use, and revoking the fossil fuel projects' social license. This includes the 350.org's seven-year-long divestment campaign, the shareholder activism that led to fossil fuel investors passing a resolution in 2017 for ExxonMobil to disclose climate-related risks to its business, and the other more straightforward efforts such as protests against specific fossil fuel projects like the Dakota Access Pipeline (McKibben 2019).

It is no coincidence that despite the US administration's successful efforts to dismantle environmental legislation and advance an agenda that enables companies to continue their business, a growing momentum around climate action is building. After a sit-in orchestrated by the youth-led organization Sunrise Movement in the office of the House of Representatives' Speaker Nancy Pelosi calling on Democratic leadership to react to the urgency of the climate disaster; Senator Ed Markey and Congresswoman Alexandria Ocasio-Cortez introduced a joint resolution on the GND. The plan's goals, a direct response to IPCC's SR 1.5 findings, are supported by 92 percent of Democratic Party registered voters, and 64 percent of Republican registered voters (Leiserowitz et al. 2019, p. 4).

Although such poll results do not necessarily translate into policy adoption in American politics, the social pressure to revoke the social license of the fossil fuel industry has been building in the 2020 election cycle—a presidential election year. This increases the likelihood of successful litigation against the fossil fuel industry, signs of which are increasingly apparent as more court cases are brought against fossil fuel companies, including examples like New York, Rhode Island, and Massachusetts suing Exxon Mobil for the cost of climate change damages (Hasemyer 2019).

Furthermore, the sole focus on regulation as a means of stranding assets ignores the fact that oil, in particular, is controlled by an international market in which almost all nations across the globe have signed and committed to the Paris Agreement (of course, as of 2017 the United States had initiated the process to withdraw from the agreement). With the increasing role, the United States expects to play in fossil fuel exportation, how other countries implement their Paris Agreement commitments (even if insufficiently), and their reactions to changes in demand, technology, and market prices will also affect the decisions on which US fossil fuel assets will turn out to be stranded.

The threat of stranding assets is therefore not only tied to a shift in regulation in the United States but also to the fossil fuel industry confronting threats on many fronts including pending litigation, uneconomic extraction tactics, and lowering costs of renewables, as well as a changing international market based on regulatory commitments made by multiple countries to transitioning to green energy resources. Hoping for fossil fuel investments to provide 100 percent of their expected return at this point is not only wishful thinking, but also a collective delusion considering the vast number of pressure points that will, sooner rather than later, change perceptions and ultimately force a correction in the financial market.

### *The Systemic Nature of the Carbon Bubble*

If fossil fuel companies reflected their real value, that is, considering the actual burnable carbon associated with their reserves as well as the potential pressure of court cases, it would have a ripple effect throughout the financial system. As quantified by CitiGroup in 2015, the carbon bubble could put at risk as much as $100 trillion in current wealth, many times more the housing bubble that triggered the Great Recession which is estimated somewhere between $6 and 25 trillion (Curmi et al. 2015, p. 8; Porter 2014). In the same year, the Bank of England's (BoE) Governor Mark Carney estimated that the carbon threat could potentially constrain close to a third of the equities and assets of the Financial Times-Stock Exchange 100 companies (Carney 2015, p. 8).

The astronomic numbers raised many concerns, and since then a group of over 30 central bankers and supervisors, including from the BoE and European Central Bank, launched the Network for Greening the Financial System (NGFS) to further look into the issue of climate-related risks in the financial sector. In October 2018, the network released its first progress report, recognizing the financial risks imposed by climate change and the key role central banks have in securing a resilient financial system. As the report further states, the timeline for the materialization of those risks is still uncertain, but due to the major threat to the financial system, extensive action must be taken today to lessen future impacts (Central Banks and Regulators Network for Greening the Financial System 2018, p. 3).

Although the US Federal Reserve (Fed) has remained largely silent on the issue, including its nonparticipation in the NGFS, experts are starting to look at the carbon bubble's implications for the country. There are plenty of signs of concerns as the US figures as a top fossil fuel exporter and a late climate policy adopter. Due to these attributes, the United States can be considered a "loser" country, the classification includes those countries that will be disproportionately impacted by a significant wealth loss due to fossil fuel stranded assets (Mercure et al. 2018, p. 588).

The commitment to fossil fuel expansion by the US government is also reflected in its banks, who dominate the world's fossil fuel financing. The 2019 "Banking on Climate" report concludes that JP Morgan is the world's worst banker for climate change, followed by Wells Fargo, Citi, and Bank of America (Kirsch et al. 2019). Together, these four US banks have poured well over US$500 billion between 2016 and 2018 into fossil fuel companies and projects—JP Morgan alone was responsible for roughly

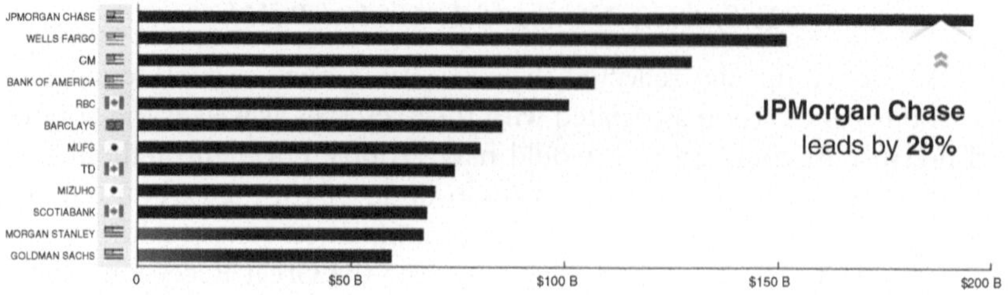


**Fig. 9.2** Stakes of global banks in financing the fuel industry. (Source: Kirsch et al. (2019, p. 8). Reproduced with permission from Rainforest Action Network)

US$196 billion—and remain the top banks committed to further expand fossil fuel production (see Fig. 9.2) (Kirsch et al. 2019, p. 7). In a scenario of an unplanned shut down of the industry, these US banks may face default on the many loans made to fossil fuel companies.

According to the Carbon Tracker Initiative, the NY Stock Exchange had the highest concentration of fossil fuels in their exchanges in 2013, with 215 gigatons of equivalent carbon dioxide ($GtCO_2$) listed: 36 $GtCO_2$ from coal, 33 $GtCO_2$ from gas, and 146 $GtCO_2$ from oil (Leaton et al. 2013, p. 15). The NY Stock Exchange stands as one of the stock exchanges with the largest potential for carbon-intensive growth in the world. According to the study at the time, it could possibly reach 366 $GtCO_2$, which was at the time almost 70 percent of the *global* carbon budget for a 50 percent likelihood of not exceeding 1.5 °C (see Fig. 9.3) (Leaton et al. 2013, pp. 18–19). Considering the leading role US companies take in oil and gas production, and the US banks' poor record in green investments by continuously financing fossil fuel projects, it is hard to imagine that the US stock market's exposure to fossil fuel stranded assets has become any less troublesome in 2019.

Taking into account the systemic threat of the burst of the carbon bubble to the financial system, it is easy to conclude that just as it happened during the mortgage crisis, the worst impacts will not be borne by those that initiated it, but instead will significantly cripple the common people. The carbon bubble burst will affect average people's investments—including those held in the pension and retirement funds—and potentially decimate millions of jobs, threatening the stability of communities across the country.

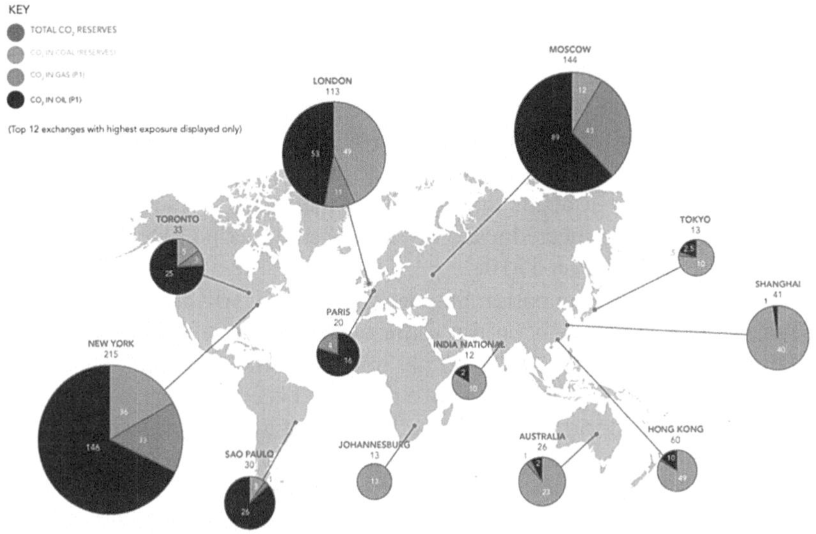


**Fig. 9.3** $GTCO_2$ of current coal, oil, and gas reserves listed on the world's stock exchanges. (Source: Leaton et al. (2013, p. 18). Reproduced with permission)

## Harnessing the Federal Reserve's Power

### *The Federal Reserve's Role in US Financial Markets*

With the ever-growing issue of the carbon bubble, there is no federal agency better equipped to deal with the problem than the agency in charge to ensure a healthy and stable US financial system (Federal Reserve 2019, p. 1). Established over 100 years ago, the Federal Reserve Bank's (Fed) inception was to provide stability to monetary and financial systems and to protect against the continuous financial stresses—such as the Panic of 1907 or banks withdrawals—that plagued the early twentieth century banking system. In addition to providing the country with a central bank system, the Fed was assigned with a dual mandate of maintaining price stability and low unemployment. In the aftermath of the 2008 crisis, the Dodd-Frank Act added a third explicit mandate: to regulate systemic risk and preserve systemic financial stability (Watchel 2010).

The third mandate calls for strengthening the regulatory regime of firms that could potentially destabilize the US financial system and negatively impact the wider economy. To achieve that goal, the Dodd-Frank Act established the Financial Stability Oversight Council (FSOC), with the function of identifying systemically important financial institutions (SIFIs) to be under the Fed's supervision. To identify SIFIs, the FSOC looks at one of two sets of standards, either at the material financial distress (First Determination Standard) or at the potential threat to financial stability due to nonbank financial firms' nature, scope, size, scale, concentration, interconnectedness, or activities (Second Determination Standard) (12 CFR Part 1310).

For the First Determination Standard, the FSOC will assess if the nonbank financial company is on the verge of insolvency or financial default. Additionally, it looks at the potential impact of the company's financial difficulties on the economy when in a distressed economic period. For the Second Determination Standard, the FSOC will look at a number of criteria, such as the firm's exposure, when taking into consideration the total consolidated assets, credit-default swaps outstanding, further derivatives, liabilities, total debt outstanding, leverage ratio, and substitutability. For outstanding debt, FSOC applies the threshold of US$20 billion, leverage ratio of total consolidated assets of 15 to 1, and for substitutability FSOC will consider matters such as the firm's market share and if competitors are likely to suffer the same stress (12 CFR Part 1310).

Although the financial stability mandate is an important step to avoid a 2008 crisis re-run, the amendments have failed to recognize one of the key reasons behind the Great Recession: there was a cascade of failures by actors outside the direct financial system that imposed a threat on the financial stability of the entire system. As adopted, the Dodd-Frank Act and subsequent regulations allow the Fed, following the recommendations of the FSOC, to oversee activities beyond the banking sector. Yet, the Fed's mandate for regulations is limited in its power over nonbank financial institutions and large bank holding companies. While a full analysis of systemic threat from fossil fuel firms is outside of the scope of this chapter, a quick look at the definitions and criteria adopted for the First and Second Determination Standards shows that fossil fuel companies could indeed fit into the broader definition of firms that can pose a threat to the financial stability of the country. By restricting the kinds of institutions over which the Fed has power, the amendments ignore the possibility of the Fed to prevent or mitigate a bubble burst of toxic assets such as the ones on fossil fuel companies' balance sheets.

As previously pointed out, the carbon bubble's reach is far, meaning that the majority of people are at some level connected to the impending carbon bubble in the financial markets. Two key examples are the collection of pension and retirements funds that take advantage of the stock market to ensure a sound fund for future pensioners, and the people who have a health or home insurance sold by companies that diversify their risks by investing in the stock market. It thus becomes hard to make the case that the Fed should not, under a macro-prudential analysis, at least be aware that companies other than banking and nonbanking financial institutions have the potential of threatening the financial stability of the whole system. This is especially true considering its threefold mandate to maximize employment, stabilize prices, and ensure financial health to the system.

Worst yet, the Fed's limited reach in terms of actors inherent in systemic risks also ignores the recent memory of the Great Recession, when many sectors beyond the financial were also in line for vast amounts of bailout money due to the system-wide risk they posed. Take, for example, the automotive industry: the government created the Automotive Industry Financing Program to provide bailouts and save the troubled industry. If the sector would have been allowed to bankrupt, it would have put further stress into an already weak financial system, negatively impacting the American economy. Together, the program injected over US$80 billion in the industry, mostly directed to General Motors and Chrysler (US Department of Treasury n.d.), which were facing potential bankruptcies that could have led to the losses of more than 1 million jobs nationwide (Ingrassia 2011, p. 224).

If the carbon bubble is heading toward another collapse like that of the mortgage crisis with potentially even more stranded assets, we will need something better than last-minute bailout programs. With the carbon bubble's potential to create a crisis several times larger than the 2008 crisis, it is time to harness the Fed's responsibility *and* policy weapons to break through the vicious pathway of destruction that fossil fuel companies have built. As the carbon bubble continues to mount, US central bankers and regulators must take measures to confront the growing threat of fossil fuel dependency, not only to the ecological and social systems but also to the financial system. These measures include ensuring that financial institutions under its supervision are diminishing and mitigating their exposures to noxious assets and recognizing that proactively acting on behalf of the society can be the best way to deflate the bubble at this point in time.

What follows are a set of suggestions on how to best understand and mitigate the carbon bubble in the time we have left.

### *The Need for Climate-related Risks in Individual and Macro-prudential Supervision*

There are many steps that the Fed can take to better understand potential climate-related risks in the US financial system. A first step would be to engage in the ongoing international conversations around the topic by voluntarily joining the NGFS. A second step is to start assessing the extent to which its supervised institutions are exposed to fossil fuel stranded assets in order to create plans to limit the crisis. In this direction, the Fed can emulate the BoE's plan to include in its stress tests the resilience of US banks and insurers against the impact of climate change (Bank of England 2019).

Yet, those are just preliminary steps to understand how intrinsic and problematic the issue of the carbon bubble in the American financial system is. The Oxford Sustainable Finance Programme's Director Ben Caldecott lists a number of other available tools that can be adopted today to manage the risks of overexposure to high-carbon investments, including increasing the capital requirements for carbon assets to manage their increased risks (Caldecott 2011). A similar suggestion, "a brown penalizing factor," is proposed by London-based organization New Economy Foundation, by which central banks could introduce additional capital requirements for fossil fuel-intensive loans. This penalizing factor would make loans for risky carbon-intensive projects more expensive and less attractive, therefore reducing the number and types of these loans (Van Lerven 2018).

The Carbon Tracker Initiative has also provided numerous proposals to improve transparency and to facilitate the monitoring of the stranded assets risks from the extractive sector. The Initiative suggested in its 2013 report the following proposals: to demand that extractives companies report their fossil fuel reserves' $CO_2$ potential; to include among FSOC's activities a stress test of the reserves current levels and production plans against climate safety scenarios and a report on their current market status; and, for regulators, to develop long-term equity markets that can deal with systemic risks using climate change risk as a test case to demonstrate they have succeeded (Leaton et al. 2013, pp. 23–25).

## Plan to Resolve Failing Energy Companies

Another amendment to the Dodd-Frank Act extends the Federal Deposit Insurance Corporation (FDIC)'s power to take over failing banks to SIFIs (Title II Section 204). Without wading into the merits of an orderly liquidation authority related to financial institutions, the same principle could be applied in a positive manner to the needed resolution of fossil fuel companies with the explicit goal of orderly deflating the carbon bubble.

This resolution could be done in the following way.[2] Considering the previous recommendations, the Fed would identify systemically important fossil fuel firms that are imposing a systemic threat to the stability of the financial system. After these companies are identified, the Fed would proactively resolve them by supporting the federal government in acquiring the majority of these companies' assets. Once in control of these companies, the federal government would be able to immediately:

1. Stop all new exploration, preventing new fossil fuel infrastructure lock-in and consequently the further expansion of the carbon bubble;
2. Plan for the managed decline of existing fossil fuel extraction in accordance with climate safety goals, thus starting the process of deflating the carbon bubble;
3. Write noxious assets off the financial system, accelerating the deflation of the carbon bubble; and
4. Offer a reasonable exit option, especially to institutional investors, such as pension and retirement funds, thus allowing them to orderly move away from fossil fuel bad assets without adverse ripple effects on the future of workers.

The Fed would guide the pathway to wind down the fossil fuel related companies. The Fed's commitment to this goal would also provide the policy tool to finance the resolution of fossil fuel companies, that is, "quantitative easing" (QE).[3] The combined enterprise value of the top 10 US publicly traded fossil fuel companies in 2019, including ExxonMobil, Chevron, and ConocoPhillips, was just below the US$1 trillion benchmark (see Fig. 9.4). Considering that in the aftermath of the 2008 crisis

[2] The steps outline is an oversimplification of how fossil fuel companies' resolution would take place, but it aims to provide a framework on how it could be implemented.

[3] "Quantitative easing" refers to the process by which the Fed increases the money supply in the economy, usually by purchasing financial assets in the market.

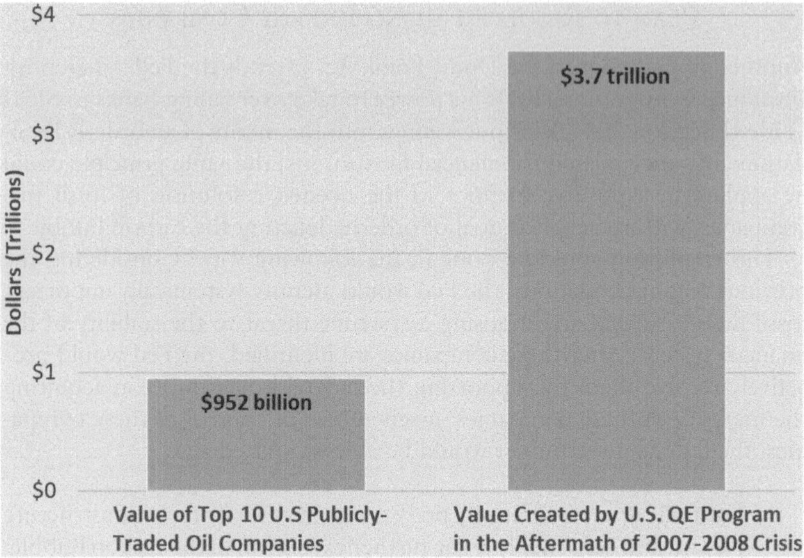


**Fig. 9.4** Quantitative easing for the planet versus quantitative easing for Wall Street

the Fed created over US$3.5 trillion to write off bad assets from banks and other financial institutions and ease the economy (Schulze 2017), it seems that proactively deflating a bubble that could be significantly greater than the Great Recession—and for potentially a quarter of the price—is a great decision for both our financial system and the climate.

Although we raise many of the similarities to the Great Recession and of the tool used by the Fed, Quantitative Easing, it is important to note that the proposal presented here is fundamentally different from the series of bailouts implemented a decade ago. Most importantly, the write-off is not a "rescue plan" for a troublesome sector, implemented only for them to regain power (much like the financial sector that ten years later is bigger and more consolidated than ever). Instead, the proposed *buyouts* would significantly shift the ownership structure of the targeted companies into public hands to explicitly eliminate all business related to the fossil fuel industry. In taking a controlling financial stake and actively taking business decisions (unlike the 2008 takeovers), we can manage the decline of the industry, planning a just transition for workers and communities that stand most affected by the elimination of the fossil fuel industry.

The concept of buying out fossil fuel companies and putting the federal government in charge of winding down their respective assets may seem an aggressive plan to some. However, the longer we wait to take on this major systemic risk, the more difficult it will be to mitigate and address economic and environmental impacts caused by a heavily dependency on carbon-intensive services and products. If we want to meaningfully deflate the carbon bubble before we run the risk of it bursting, a federal takeover is not only reasonable, but also our best financial option to secure a proactive rescue plan that puts Main Street and the world at its center instead of allowing high-income CEOs to come out unscathed as the rest of the economy treads water (as seen in 2008).

## A Re-envisioned Financial System

Mitigating climate change and deflating the looming carbon bubble, while transitioning to a sustainable society, requires more than the Fed alone can accomplish. New and re-envisioned financial institutions will need to absorb the old system and to provide the mechanisms that ensure that the transition is democratically and equitably financed, in alignment with the proposed GND resolution. In particular, we need to consider the potential role that public financial institutions and the federal government—federal government takeovers is by no means an unusual feature of American history—can play to counterpoint the vast private market that helped create and continues to expand a risky bubble in the system. What follows is a vision of two set of financial institutions that could start shifting the path away from climate and financial destruction together.

### *Green Investment Bank*

A Green Investment Bank (GIB) is a publicly owned and controlled financial institution with the purpose of providing financing to climate-friendly sectors and projects, in particular to those aimed at reducing greenhouse gas emissions and energy use. Targeted projects are often prescribed in the banks' mandate and financed through direct funding and lending mechanisms such as grants, loans, and investments. In more recent years, GIBs have also engaged in the work of enabling and formalizing secondary green markets by issuing additional mechanisms, such as green bonds. Because GIBs are often nationally owned—and backed by the federal government—they tend to have a great credit rating, which enables them to provide long-term, low-interest loans as well as enhance the credit quality of bonds to meet regulatory capital requirements of institutional investors. In addition, GIBs have the advantage of being able to capitalize the profits from their activities into the public benefit, which could then be re-invested into new projects that further advance green transition projects (Brown 2019b).

A US GIB could play a key role in deflating the carbon bubble in two meaningful ways. First, a US GIB could be in charge of holding fossil fuel companies' equities and cleaning the open market from their stranded assets. Second, a US GIB would provide a market for institutional investors, such as pension and retirement funds, to roll over their stocks toward fossil fuel-free investments in an orderly fashion without negatively impacting the future of American teachers, nurses, and governmental employees (something like an asset-swap program). In this scenario, the pension funds, with the help of the federal government, could easily eliminate its carbon bubble risk by shedding its fossil fuel investments and redirecting that investment into the Green Investment Bank.

The creation of a nationally owned investment bank to finance the needed projects is by no means a new idea. For the implementation of the 1930s New Deal, President Franklin Roosevelt used the recently created Reconstruction Finance Corporation (RFC), which had a function similar to an investment bank. With the initial capital stock of $500 million, the RFC was able to extend its credit to over US$40 billion, and support a number of key infrastructure projects, including roads, bridges, dams, and electricity during its 25 years of existence (Brown 2019a, pp. 288–289).

While the United States has never re-created a similar institution, Germany has relied greatly on its fully state-owned development bank—Kreditanstalt für Wiederaufbau (KfW)—to play a catalytic role in financing its green energy revolution. By leveraging financial mechanisms such as grants, 30-year low-interest loans, and green bonds, KfW was responsible for providing all of the funding for Germany's solar photovoltaic sector between 2007 and 2009. Together with Germany's network of public banks, they accounted for over 72 percent of the financing that resulted in an increase in renewables in the country's electricity mix, jumping from 6 percent in 2000 to 41 percent by 2017 (Brown 2019b).

### *Public Banks*

Public banks are financial institutions that provide services similar to those offered by private, commercial banking institutions, such as investing, lending, and deposit services. Because they are publicly owned, they have some key differences (here we focus particularly on state and municipal ownership). First, their activities are guided for and by public purposes, creating opportunities for the democratization of money creation and allocation. As a result, public banks often have different incentive structures, pay scales, interest rates, and investment mandates. They can, for example, finance infrastructure and generate projects critical for the green transition at much lower interest rates than commercial banks or the bond market, ensuring lower energy rates throughout the country (Bozuwa and Hanna 2019). Secondly, public banks can also support community energy projects and low-income-household retrofits usually deemed unattractive to private investors, significantly alleviating energy poverty of residents, and regain control over energy decisions. With the decision-making process closer to the people, public banks can also convene participatory processes to identify local and regional just-transition priorities in alignment with a green economy.

Public banks also play a complementary role to GIBs as they are depository institutions, which means that public banks have the capacity to leverage their capital up to 10 times in a similar fashion to traditional banks. The creation of state and municipal-owned public banks would then provide state and local governments as well as people the possibility to shift their accounts and savings away from private banks that have been lending to stranded projects. Consequently, public banks would deliver a safer option for their business, reduce the capacity of private banks to finance catastrophic projects, and increase the financing available for state and local transition initiatives.

The concept of public banks is not alien to the United States, home to two state-owned public banks: The Bank of North Dakota (BND) and Territorial Bank of American Samoa. While the Territorial Bank of American Samoa is only a couple years old, the BND has been around for 100 years, providing loans and banking services as well as serving as a reliable and affordable source of capital to community banks and credit unions across the state. In addition, the BND played a crucial role in managing the impacts of the 2008 financial crisis in the state by increasing its local lending—all while having an annual return on investments between

17 and 23 percent in the ten years following the financial crisis (Brown 2019a, p. 146). However, the lack of a just transition mandate for the state and the bank has translated into a not-so-good—to say the least—record on sustainable projects. Without that intentional conciseness and precise arrangements, a public bank—or any public institution for that matter—can fall into the paradigm of supporting destructive projects, such as the Dakota Access Pipeline, under the fallacy of job creation, a narrative pushed by the pipeline company.

The Bank of North Dakota's support to fossil fuel projects shows that the creation of public institutions must be strongly attached to policy and regulatory framework to point their activities in the right direction. This is a role that could be started by the Fed, but also more largely expanded through the adoption of federal, state, and local policies such as the GND. Costa Rica's national-owned public bank, simply known as Banco Popular, has been used as an instrument for the green transition. Structured as a public worker-owned cooperative, Banco Popular has been able to intentionally advance the country's established social and environmental goals by developing special lending products, such as eco-savings and eco-products, to fund at low-interest rates environmental-friendly projects like residential solar panels, sustainable water supply systems, energy-efficiency retrofitting, and conservation projects (Marois 2017, pp. 5 and 7).

## Conclusion

There are numerous signs indicating that fossil fuel companies have created—and continue to expand—a dangerous bubble inside the financial system by investing in fossil fuel related products and therefore feeding the possibility of stranded assets. To address the issue in the United States, the Fed is positioned as the federal institution tasked with dealing with systemic risk and should anticipate and react prior the burst of the carbon bubble. By joining the NGFS and evaluating the resilience of American banks and other financial institutions through a climate stress test, the Fed would be taking some of the key steps to better understand the threat of climate-related financial risks. Yet, due to the limited time left to prevent a potential burst of the carbon bubble, the Fed could—and should—go beyond and proactively provide the federal government with a resolving plan to deal with these failing fossil fuel firm's inherent systemic risk in a way that would, at once, deflate the carbon bubble, provide a reasonable exit option to institutional investors, especially those in charge of the future of US workers, and avert climate catastrophe.

Together with the creation and the repurpose of financial institutions to serve the public interest, such as GIB and a network of public banks, these measures would start to move society past fossil fuels and toward a sustainable, democratic, and equitable society, from the financial sector up.

## References


Amadeo, K. (2019). Causes of the 2008 global financial crisis. *The Balance*. Retrieved September 14, 2019, from https://www.thebalance.com/what-caused-2008-global-financial-crisis-3306176.

Bank of England. (2019). *Bank of England to disclose assessment of how it manages climate-related financial risk in the 2019/20 annual report*. London, UK.

Bozuwa, J., & Hanna, T. (2019). Democratize finance, euthanize the fossil fuel industry. *Jacobin*. Retrieved March 29, 2019, from https://jacobinmag.com/2019/03/green-new-deal-financing-fossil-fuels.

Brown, E. (2019a). *Banking on the people: Democratizing money in the digital age*. Washington, DC: Democracy Collaborative.

Brown, E. (2019b). The financial secret behind Germany's Green Energy Revolution. *Truthdig*. Retrieved March 29, 2019, from https://www.truthdig.com/articles/the-financial-secret-behind-germanys-green-energy-revolution/.

Caldecott, B. (2011, July 12). Why high-carbon investment could be the next sub-prime crisis. *The Guardian*. Retrieved March 29, 2019, from https://www.theguardian.com/environment/2011/jul/12/high-carbon-investment.

Caldecott, B., Harnett, E., Cojoianu, T., Kok, I., & Pfeiffer, A. (2016). *Stranded assets: A climate risk challenge*. Inter-American Development Bank Monograph 481. Washington, DC: Inter-American Development Bank.

Campanale, M., Leggett, J., & Leaton, J. (2011). Unburnable Carbon: Are the world's financial markets carrying a carbon bubble? *Carbon Tracker Initiative*.

Carney, M. (2015). *Breaking the Tragedy of the Horizon (Speech)*. London, UK: Lloyd's of London.

Central Banks and Regulators Network for Greening the Financial System (NGFS). (2018). First progress report.

Curmi, E., Rahbari, E., Prior, E., Kleinman, S., Channell, J., Jansen, H. ... Kruger, T. (2015). Energy Darwinism II: Why a low carbon future doesn't have to cost the earth. *Citigroup*. Retrieved from https://cusdi.org/wp-content/uploads/2016/02/ENERGY-DARWINISM-II-Why-a-Low-Carbon-Future-Doesn%E2%80%99t-Have-to-Cost-the-Earth.-Citi-GPSI.pdf.

Erickson, P., Down, A., Lazarus, M., & Koplow, D. (2017). Effect of government subsidies for upstream oil infrastructure on U.S. oil production and global $CO_2$ emissions. Stockholm Environment Institute Working Paper No. 2017-02. Retrieved from https://mediamanager.sei.org/documents/Publications/Climate/SEI-WP-2017-02-US-oil-and-gas-production-subsidies.pdf.

Federal Reserve. (2019). Overview of the Federal Reserve system. Retrieved March 29, 2019, from https://www.federalreserve.gov/aboutthefed/files/pf_1.pdf.

Freyman, M. (2014). Hydraulic fracturing and water stress: Water demand by the numbers. Retrieved March 29, 2019, from https://www.ceres.org/sites/default/files/reports/2017-03/Ceres_FrackWaterByNumbers_021014_R.pdf.

Gallegos, T., Varela, B., Haines, S., & Engle, M. (2015). Hydraulic fracturing water use variability in the United States and potential environmental implications. *Water Resources Research, 51*, 5839–5845.

Hasemyer, D. (2019, July 22). Fossil fuels on trial: Where the major climate change lawsuits stand today. *Inside Climate News.* Retrieved from https://insideclimatenews.org/news/04042018/climate-change-fossil-fuel-company-lawsuits-timeline-exxon-children-california-cities-attorney-general.

InfluenceMap. (2019). Big oil's real agenda on climate change: How the oil majors have spent $1bn since Paris on narrative capture and lobbying on climate. London, UK. Retrieved from https://influencemap.org/report/How-Big-Oil-Continues-to-Oppose-the-Paris-Agreement-38212275958aa21196dae3b76220bddc.

Ingrassia, P. (2011). *Crash course: The American automobile industry's road to bankruptcy and bailout – and beyond.* New York, NY: Random House.

IRENA (International Renewable Energy Agency). (2019). Renewable power generations costs in 2018. Retrieved from https://www.irena.org/-/media/Files/IRENA/Agency/Publication/2019/May/IRENA_Renewable-Power-Generations-Costs-in-2018.pdf.

Kirsch, A., Opeña, J., Marr, D., Marr, G., Aitken, G., Hamlett, C., Louvel, Y., Masson, L., Saldamando, A., Stockman, L., Cushing, B., & Houska, T. (2019). Banking on climate change: Fossil fuel finance report card 2019. *Rainforest Action Network, BankTrack, Indigenous Environmental Network, Sierra Club, Oil Change International, and Honor the Earth.* Retrieved from https://www.banktrack.org/download/banking_on_climate_change_2019_fossil_fuel_finance_report_card/banking_on_climate_change_2019.pdf.

Leaton, J., Ranger, N., Ward, B., Sussams, L., & Brown, M. (2013). Unburnable carbon 2013: Wasted capital and stranded assets. *Carbon Tracker Initiative & The Grantham Research Institute, LSE.* Retrieved March 29, 2019, from https://www.carbontracker.org/reports/unburnable-carbon-wasted-capital-and-stranded-assets/.

Leiserowitz, A., Maibach, E., Rosenthal, S., Kotcher, J., Goldberg, M., Ballew, M., et al. (2019). *Politics & global warming, December 2018*. New Haven, CT: Yale University and George Mason University.

Marois, T. (2017). How public banks can help finance a green and just energy transformation. *Transnational Institute*. Retrieved from https://www.tni.org/files/publication-downloads/how_public_banks_can_help_finance_a_green_and_just_energy_transformation.pdf.

McKibben, B. (2019). Money is the oxygen on which the fire of global warming burns. *The New Yorker*. Retrieved September 14, 2019, from https://www.newyorker.com/news/daily-comment/money-is-the-oxygen-on-which-the-fire-of-global-warming-burns.

McLean, B. (2018). *Saudi America: The truth about fracking and how it's changing the world*. New York, NY: Columbia Global Reports.

Mercure, J. F., Pollitt, H., Viñuales, J., Edwards, N., Holden, P., Chewpreecha, U., et al. (2018). Macroeconomic impact of stranded fossil fuel assets. *Nature Climate Change, 8*, 588–593.

Muttitt, G. (2016). The Sky's Limit: Why the Paris Climate goals require a managed decline of fossil fuel production. *Oil Change International*. Retrieved from http://priceofoil.org/content/uploads/2016/09/OCI_the_skys_limit_2016_FINAL_2.pdf.

Porter, E. (2014, 21 January). Recession's true cost is still being tallied. *New York Times*. Retrieved from https://www.nytimes.com/2014/01/22/business/economy/the-cost-of-the-financial-crisis-is-still-being-tallied.html.

Rapoza, K. (2017, August 30). Hurricane Harvey forces even more Texas oil refineries to close. *Forbes*. Retrieved from https://www.forbes.com/sites/kenrapoza/2017/08/30/hurricane-harvey-forces-even-more-texas-oil-refineries-to-close.

Roy, J., Tschakert, P., Waisman, H., Abdul Halim, S., Antwi-Agyei, P., Dasgupta, P. … Suarez Rodriguez, A. G. (2018). Sustainable development, poverty eradication and reducing inequalities. In V. Masson-Delmotte, P. Zhai, H.-O. Pörtner, D. Roberts, J. Skea, P. R. Shukla … T. Waterfield (Eds.), *Global Warming of 1.5°C. An IPCC Special Report on the impacts of global warming of 1.5°C above pre-industrial levels and related global greenhouse gas emission pathways, in the context of strengthening the global response to the threat of climate change, sustainable development, and efforts to eradicate poverty*. In press.

Schulze, E. (2017, November 24). The fed launched QE nine years ago – these four charts show the impacts. *CNBC*. Retrieved from https://www.cnbc.com/2017/11/24/the-fed-launched-qe-nine-years-ago%2D%2Dthese-four-charts-show-its-impact.html.

Trout, K., & Stockman, L. (2019). Drilling towards disaster: Why U.S. oil and gas expansion is incompatible with climate limits. *Oil Change International*. Retrieved from http://priceofoil.org/content/uploads/2019/01/Drilling-Towards-Disaster-Web-v3.pdf.

US Congress, House, *Recognizing the duty of the federal government to create a Green New Deal*, 116gh Congress, 1st Session, introduced in House 7 February 2019. Retrieved September 14, 2019, from https://apps.npr.org/document.html?id=5731829-Ocasio-Cortez-Green-New-Deal-Resolution.

US Department of Treasury. (n.d.). Automotive industry financing program. Retrieved March 29, 2019, from https://www.treasury.gov/initiatives/financial-stability/programs/Other%20Programs/aifp/Pages/autoprogram.aspx.

Van Lerven, F. (2018). Greening the banks: The Bank of England is taking climate change seriously. *New Economics Foundation*. Retrieved from https://neweconomics.org/2018/12/greening-the-banks.

Watchel, P. (2010). Dodd Frank and the Fed. NYU Stern. Retrieved August 20, 2018, from https://w4.stern.nyu.edu/blogs/regulatingwallstreet/2010/07/doddfrank-and-the-fed-kermit-s.html.

CHAPTER 10

# Economic Risks from Policy Pressures in Montreal's Real Estate Market

*Carmela Cucuzzella and Jordan Owen*

## Introduction

Real estate development projects can be seen miles away by spotting the cranes in the skyline. Montreal has seen a rise in the appearance of these cranes. Citizens may see the towers being built but they may not understand how complex it is for the developer to get to that stage. The real estate development process is not a linear trajectory of independent and well-defined tasks; it's a complex process where the output of one report changes the decisions made at subsequent phases of development; it is an ongoing and recursive process. The political process that provides the permits to a real estate development project is not different. City officials and developers are constantly engaged in intense conversations about how to

C. Cucuzzella (✉)
Concordia University, Design and Computation Arts, Montreal, QC, Canada
e-mail: carmela.cucuzzella@concordia.ca

J. Owen
Massachusetts Institute of Technology, Cambridge, MA, USA
e-mail: jvowen@mit.edu



T. Walker et al. (eds.), *Ecological, Societal, and Technological Risks and the Financial Sector*, Palgrave Studies in Sustainable Business In Association with Future Earth, https://doi.org/10.1007/978-3-030-38858-4_10

better build the city; together they aim to arrive at a consensus. In many cases, city officials have the power to inhibit or stop projects entirely if they do not satisfy the needs and/or desires of the community. In Montreal, city officials have just recently implemented by-laws and regulations that significantly hinder real estate development profits and opportunities. This chapter explores the impact of these emerging policy changes on the economic viability of the real estate development market in Montreal.

The United Nations published a report in 2019 stating that by 2050, 68% of the world's population is projected to be urban (United Nations 2019). A major implication of this increased urbanization is that in order to provide an equitable quality of life, cities will have to better accommodate for people of different demographics, income levels, and family sizes. It is no surprise that social, affordable and family housing policies are being revised in most major cities throughout Canada, including in the City of Montreal. New municipal housing regulations have gained importance as most cities become increasingly unaffordable. This influx of new urban dwellers will also have implications in the way that people move around the city, with increased population will come increased pollution, carbon emissions, noise, and automobile congestion. Therefore, mobility will have to become more sustainable. Without rethinking collective transport, cities could become inhabitable. The North American tradition of relying on a car must be removed from our collective thinking. New methods of sustainable mobility are being introduced in many major cities across Canada, in Montreal the new Réseau Express Métropolitain (REM) will be introduced in 2021.

Both of these initiatives for the City of Montreal, increased collective transport through the city's REM program and social housing, are key characteristics of a vibrant and sustainable urban condition. The REM transportation program will require approximately $6 billion in investment from the city. The city will be building one main line that spans from the Rive-Sud, crosses downtown at the McGill station toward Canora. The line will then split into three locations, 1) YUL Airport, 2) Sainte-Anne-De-Bellevue and 3) Deux-Montagnes. (Montreal 2019) This new high-speed transport system will service a predominant north-south trajectory along with services in the west of Montreal, all of which are currently missing in the public transport system of Montreal. The proposed REM layout in relation to the current metro system in Montreal will improve connectivity in public transport and may help reduce the use of cars for daily urban commutes (United States Department of Transportation 2002). Improved social housing by-laws are necessary to provide stable and healthy living conditions to growing families (Habitat for Humanity 2019). It is, therefore, important to include both in the infrastructure development plans of any city. The City of Montreal is planning the inclusion of these new services by taxing the real estate developers through the REM tax and the Inclusion of Affordable Housing by-law (the 20-20-20 by-law). Developers must plan for the changing regulations, since they will have a significant impact on the financial viability of new real estate development projects.

This chapter aims to respond to the question, how can developers navigate the regulations to maximize the financial viability of a real estate project? There are many new regulations being implemented in Montreal, such as the 20-20-20 by-law and the REM tax, explained in subsequent paragraphs in this chapter; however, this chapter will focus solely on the impacts of the social housing component of the 20-20-20 by-law. This component has become increasingly important for cities since the aim of such by-laws is to make cities more inclusive and accessible. Though the by-laws are developing in different ways in cities around the world, this chapter focuses only on the introduction of the social housing by-law in Montreal. We address this in three steps. First, we briefly describe the growth experienced in the real estate market to date in Montreal. Second, we outline the new policy changes for affordable housing and transit. And finally, we explore the financial impact of the three ways in which the social housing by-laws can be enforced. We conclude with a summary of our findings.

## Drivers of Real Estate Economic Growth in Montreal

The Montreal real estate development market has seen tremendous growth over the past five years. Numerous towers are under construction, bringing thousands of new units on the market (Marotte 2018). In fact, a research report from PricewaterhouseCoopers (PwC) shows that condominium and rental units under construction have grown from 101,314 units in 2007 to 163,357 units in 2017 ("Rental" and "Condo" for Canada 2007 and 2017 in Table 10.1). This represents approximately a 60% growth over the last 10 years, compared to the new home market which has stagnated over the same period ("Homeowners" for Canada 2007 and 2017 in Table 10.1). Rental rates in the downtown area have surpassed $3.00 per square foot[1] and condominiums are selling out at

[1] Based on an analysis of rental prices for the downtown area in Montreal for 2018–2019.

**Table 10.1** Inventory under construction across Canada, by intended market

| | *2007 Homeowner* | *2007 Rental* | *2007 Condo* | *2012 Homeowner* | *2012 Rental* | *2012 Condo* | *2017 Homeowner* | *2017 Rental* | *2017 Condo* |
|---|---|---|---|---|---|---|---|---|---|
| Toronto | 15,164 | 2353 | 27,953 | 14,785 | 2987 | 51,039 | 18,534 | 6663 | 45,152 |
| Vancouver | 3680 | 582 | 20,842 | 5289 | 1695 | 15,924 | 5053 | 7944 | 29,124 |
| Montreal | 3650 | 5199 | 5383 | 3062 | 2205 | 13,326 | 2150 | 9562 | 11,267 |
| Edmonton | 7026 | 600 | 8576 | 5225 | 2100 | 4598 | 4803 | 1831 | 3738 |
| Calgary | 6072 | 121 | 8527 | 4092 | 975 | 5849 | 4066 | 1058 | 5174 |
| Ottawa | 3210 | 170 | 1571 | 2270 | 445 | 2696 | 3311 | 1856 | 2184 |
| Quebec City | 720 | 1216 | 465 | 661 | 1365 | 1533 | 483 | 3439 | 1356 |
| Winnipeg | 837 | 937 | 686 | 1257 | 844 | 982 | 1644 | 1676 | 1801 |
| Halifax | 766 | 1180 | 523 | 931 | 2234 | 462 | 671 | 3026 | 453 |
| Saskatoon | 1059 | 99 | 860 | 1401 | 246 | 1292 | 847 | 143 | 563 |
| **Canada** | **54,754** | **16,462** | **84,852** | **50,080** | **21,290** | **105,622** | **55,402** | **49,132** | **114,225** |

Note: Adapted from Kelly et al. (2019, p. 12)
The bold values are the totals for Canada, as a country

averages of over $800 per square foot.[2] This is unheard of in the Montreal market and has caused land values to surge upward of $125 per square foot on the Floor Area Ratio (FAR).[3] Developers in Montreal, namely Brivia, Canderel, Devimco, DevMcGill, and Mondev, have benefited from this trend, generating equity on large scale deals.[4]

There are at least three drivers fueling this growth. The first is net migration which has increased the potential pool of buyers and is projected to keep growing, with an estimated 225,000 new migrants moving to Montreal between 2018 and 2022 (Kelly et al. 2019), most of them are predicted to be international.

The second driver increasing new housing demand is sustained low interest rates across Canada (Canada 2019). As illustrated in Figs. 10.1 and 10.2, Canadian interest rates have been dropping consistently since the early 1990s and have stabilized at around 2% in 2019 (Trading Economics 2019). These low rates are very favorable for investors, since they allow developers to borrow large sums of money without being penalized on high interest. Furthermore, real estate buyers are more inclined to purchase homes or condos because the carrying costs are less. The increased demand in home and condo purchases will cause the prices of real estate to rise. Therefore, lower interest rates cause real estate prices to rise.

**Fig. 10.1** Canadian interest rates 1990–present. (Adapted from "Canadian Interest Rate 2019," Trading Economics)

[2] Based on an analysis of condo prices for the downtown area in Montreal for 2018–2019.
[3] These prices are based on interviews with developers in Montreal.
[4] Based on conversations with each of these developers in Montreal.

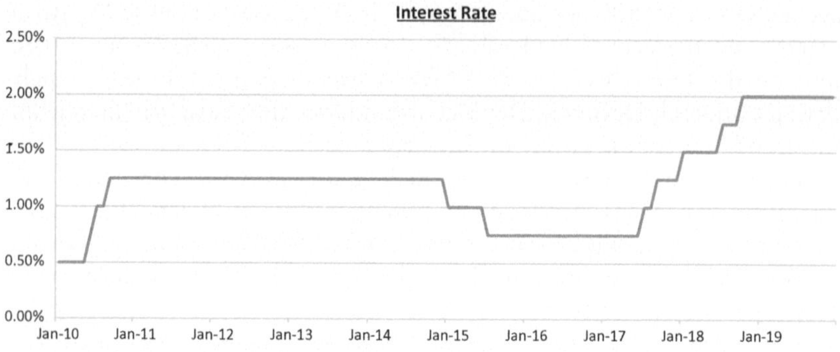


**Fig. 10.2** Canadian interest rates 2008–present. (Adapted from "Canadian Interest Rate 2019," Trading Economics)

**Table 10.2** Different housing option prices from 2015 to 2020

| | *2015* | *2016* | *2017* | *2018 (F)* | *2019 (F)* | *2020 (F)* |
|---|---|---|---|---|---|---|
| *Starts* | | | | | | |
| Single-detached | 2402 | 2499 | 2771 | 2650 | 2650 | 2600 |
| Multiples | 16,342 | 15,335 | 21,985 | 20,600 | 20,350 | 20,150 |
| Total starts | 18,744 | 17,834 | 24,756 | 23,250 | 23,000 | 22,750 |
| *Housing market* | | | | | | |
| Centris # sales | 39,209 | 41,307 | 44,396 | 46,300 | 47,350 | 47,700 |
| Centris avg. price ($) | $332,497 | $344,508 | $364,438 | $383,500 | $402,500 | $410,000 |
| Mortgage rates (5-Year %) | 4.67% | 4.66% | 4.78% | 5.27% | 5.80% | 6.00% |
| Monthly mort. payment | $1283.85 | $1328.70 | $1425.08 | $1584.88 | $1762.74 | $1834.45 |
| *Rental market* | | | | | | |
| Two-Bed avg. rent ($) | $760 | $791 | $782 | $790 | $800 | $810 |

Note: Adapted from "Housing Market Outlook: Quebec Region," in Housing Market Information, by CMHC 2018, Canada: Canada Mortgage and Housing Corporation

A third driver is the increase in single-family housing prices. Table 10.2, adapted from the CMHC, predicts a 4% increase in housing prices from 2015–2020, directly impacting the purchasing power of clients. Given the predicted mortgage rates, assuming a 25% down payment and a 25-year amortization, monthly mortgage payments are estimated to increase from

$1283 in 2015 to $1834 in 2020 (see Table 10.2), representing a 7.4% in annual growth for single-family homes (CMHC 2018). Conversely, the estimated increase in rent for the same period is only 1.3% annually. Furthermore, the average condo price in Montreal for 2018 was $328,000, while the average single-family home was $383,500 (Lau 2019). This trend has caused many home buyers to either purchase condos or remain in rental properties, further driving condo and rental prices upward.

In summary, the three factors pushing the real estate market growth are: increased net migration, low interest rates, and increasing single-family housing prices.

## Emerging Policies Impacting Real Estate Growth

This growth is promising for developers; however, it does not come without risks. City officials have, in some ways, hindered the real estate development market by enforcing by-laws that have an impact on the economic viability of a project. Namely the *Réseau Express Métropolitain* (REM) tax, the Strategy for Inclusion of Affordable Housing (also known as the 20-20-20 regulation) (Arquin and Pignoly 2019), and borough demands on architecture design, all introduce increased economic risks in the development of urban housing projects.

In the case of the REM, if a new development project is located within a one-kilometer radius of a REM high-speed transport station, the development project is taxed at a rate of $11 per buildable square foot above grade.[5] In 2019, only 65% of the total REM tax will be charged, which equates to $11 per buildable square foot. By 2021, the REM tax will have increased to $17 per buildable square foot, which will be indexed by the consumer price index thereafter. In other words, after 2021 this $17 tax will increase by the rate of inflation. This tax is enforced for any development project within a one-kilometre radius.

The Strategy for Inclusion of Affordable Housing, known as the 20-20-20 regulation, is projected to be enforced by the Fall of 2019. As it is becoming too expensive for the average income family to live in the City of Montreal, the municipality had to regulate development to make housing widely accessible. This new regulation affects only multiple residential (multi-res) developments and varies depending on the total units planned

[5] Buildable square feet are calculated by adding up the total square feet per floor. Above grade refers to all floors excluding the basement.

(see Table 10.3) The 20-20-20 by-law refers to the three different types of housing: social, affordable, and family housing. (Arquin and Pignoly 2019).[6]

Social housing is the construction of subsidized housing for Montreal residents on welfare. Depending on the size of the project, the City of Montreal chooses between a financial contribution, an on-site donation or an off-site donation. A financial contribution is calculated by taking the total number of units in the project multiplied by 20% and the resulting number of units is taxed at $20,000 per unit. An on-site donation is a parcel of land that is dedicated to the social housing requirement given to the city and must fit 20% of the total number of units in the project. Finally, an off-site donation is a parcel of land not directly connected to the project, also given to the city, and fits 22% of total proposed units for the social requirement.

Affordable housing refers to a rental or purchase price below the ceiling price established by the City of Montreal, which can only increase by a maximum of 2% per year for the first 5 years, afterward it's regulated by the Housing Authority (Quebec 2019). Appendix 1 outlines the ceiling prices for condo and rental units. Affordable housing is not required for projects of less than 50 units. For projects with more than 50 units, the proportion of units attributed to affordable housing changes according to the location (downtown or other territories). For example, if a proposed project has 100 units, 15 units will have a ceiling price and 5 of these units will be 3-bedroom family units.

Finally, family housing refers to a unit that provides sufficient space to host a family; this size is set at a minimum of 925 square feet in Downtown Montreal (Arquin and Pignoly 2019), and 1033 square feet in the outskirts of Montreal (Arquin and Pignoly 2019). The regulation requires that 5–10% of a project's total units to be 3-bedroom family units depending on location (see Table 10.3).

The implication of the Strategy for Inclusion of Affordable Housing alone represents a commitment by the developer to <u>dedicate 50%</u> of any new development project with more than 50 units to affordable and social

[6] The main difference between social housing and affordable units are that social housing needs to be on a separate lot from the rest of the project. The social housing units are built by the developer and sold to the city at cost to manage. On the other hand, affordable units are spread throughout the proposed project and the units to be considered affordable are chosen solely by the developer. There are a set of rules that developers must follow with the price of the affordable units and price increases if it's a rental property. A more detailed outline of affordable units is shown in Appendix 1.

**Table 10.3** Summary of the 20-20-20 by-law

| *Number of units in the project* | *Social housing* | | *Affordable housing* | | *Family housing* | | |
|---|---|---|---|---|---|---|---|
| | *Downtown* | *Other territories* | *Downtown* | *Other territories* | *Downtown* | *Central neighborhoods* | *Outskirts* |
| 5–49 units | Financial contribution | Financial contribution | n/a | n/a | n/a | n/a | n/a |
| 50+ | 20% or financial contribution | 20% on site or 22% off site or financial contribution | 10–15% including 5% family units or financial contribution | 15–20% including 5% family units or financial contribution | 5% | 10% | n/a |

Note: From City of Montreal, in "La Ville de Montréal publie le règlement 20-20-20 sur les logements sociaux, abordables et familiaux," by Anthony Arquin and Agnès Pignoly. Davies

housing. In the following case study, we will outline the financial impact of only the 20% social housing contribution. We do not consider the affordable or family tax implications in this case study. We examine four scenarios: (a) profit before regulations; (b) financial contribution; (c) off-site donation and (d) on-site donation.

## Case Study: New Development Project in Montreal Southwest

Once a developer acquires a property for the purpose to develop a new project, the developer must obtain a demolition permit before starting construction. This requires the preparation of preliminary architecture plans with exterior renderings that must be approved by the city. The city typically has their own architectural and design demands in terms of how they envision the districts.

The incoming by-law, the Strategy for Inclusion of Affordable Housing, empowers the municipalities to issue demolition permits only once an agreement has been signed with the developer regarding social housing. Therefore, the issuance is contingent on the city being satisfied with both the architectural plans and the conformity to social regulation requirement. As previously mentioned, the requirement to include on-site social housing can be replaced with either of two other options: (1) a fee; or (2) a transfer of property to the city. The decision on whether the developers include social housing on site, pay the fee, or transfer a property to the city, is solely up to the municipality. This decision may vary from one project to the next.

To illustrate the impact that social housing regulation has on the economics of real estate development, we outline a case study which includes two sites for a development in the City of Montreal. We chose this case because of two conditions: the social housing agreement with the City of Montreal was recently approved and these two sites were recently acquired by the developer.

For confidentiality, we will name the two sites for this project as Site X and Site Y. Initially, 24 condos were to be developed on Site X and 116 apartments on Site Y. It is important to note that Site X had in-place zoning, meaning developers were permitted to build residential properties, while Site Y is located in a post-industrial area, meaning it had industrial zoning in place. Zoning is a process where the city divides land areas in a municipality into zones (e.g., residential, industrial) in which certain land uses are permitted or prohibited. Industrial zoning refers to an area of the city that is dedicated for industrial development and is ideally intended to isolate disturbances of industrial activity from other areas, such as residential or commercial. Therefore, if a developer proposes a project with a different use than what the area it is zoned for, the city must be open to changing the zoning in place to accommodate the developer's project. The change of zoning is typically a difficult process. In this specific case, since the neighborhood was going through a residential transformation, the city was open to changing its zoning from industrial to residential.

These property purchases (Site X and Site Y) were done in 2018, before the social housing regulations were modified in the city. Even though these regulations are in the final stages of the approval process at the city, they are already being enforced across the boroughs in Montreal. This single shift in regulation is having a major impact on the business models of these projects. For the first time, developers in Montreal are introduced to regulated constraints and taxes for social and affordable housing rather than being able to control 100% of the project. The 20-20-20 regulation constrains approximately 50% (see Table 10.3) of the project to social, affordable and family housing combined. In other words, 50% of the property is controlled by the city and 50% is controlled by the developer. Furthermore, the REM tax, at $11 per square foot, represents an additional tax of approximately 5% of total hard costs, or 15% of the developer's profit.[7]

The following tables outline the evolution of the business plans for this new development project during the negotiation process with the city. The business plans were originally laid out as illustrated in Table 10.4. Some key terms necessary to understand the business plan are the following:

1. <u>Buildable square feet</u>: The volume of square feet necessary to build the property
2. <u>Gross livable square feet</u>: Above ground buildable square feet
3. <u>Above grade</u>: Includes the buildable square feet excluding the parking garage
4. <u>Below grade</u>: The buildable square feet only in the parking garage

[7] Assuming that total hard costs per square foot are $200, the $11 per square foot represents 5% of total hard costs. Hard costs represent only physical materials and labor that is required for construction.

**Table 10.4** Proposed project business plan (before regulations)

| *Site X* | | | *Site Y* | | |
|---|---|---|---|---|---|
| Gross livable square feet (SF) | 83% | 83,991 | Net livable square feet (SF) | 87% | 17,127 |
| Common spaces (parking) | $375 | 18,224 | Common spaces | $350 | 2559 |
| Total buildable SF | $40,000 | 102,215 | Total buildable SF | $30,000 | 19,686 |
| **Revenues (assuming condo)** | | | **Revenues (assuming condo)** | | |
| Net sellable SF | | 69,713 | Net sellable SF | | 17,127 |
| Condo sales | 83,991 | $26,142,199 | Condo sales | 19,686 | $5,994,450 |
| Parking sales (60 spots) | 18,224 | $2,400,000 | Parking sales (9 Spots) | | $270,000 |
| **Total revenue** | | **$28,542,199** | **Total revenue** | | **$6,264,450** |
| **Hard costs** | | | **Hard costs** | | |
| Above grade ($170 per SF) | | $14,278,470 | Above grade ($140 per SF) | | $2,756,040 |
| Below grade ($90 per SF) | | $1,640,160 | Land | | $1,500,000 |
| Land | | $4,200,000 | | | |
| **Soft costs (35% Hard)** | | **$5,571,521** | **Soft costs (30% Hard)** | | **$826,812** |
| **Total costs** | | **$25,690,151** | **Total costs** | | **$5,082,852** |
| **Profit** | | **$2,852,048** | **Profit** | | **$1,181,598** |
| **Total profit of both sites** | | **$4,033,646** | | | |

Note: Synthesis of business plan by authors

5. Net sellable square feet: The total square feet that can be sold to the client, measured from the center of the common walls between units
6. Hard cost: Costs of physical materials that goes into construction
7. Soft costs: Cost of non-physical assets, including financing, permitting, engineers and commission

In order to calculate the profit in a development business plan, as outlined in Table 10.4, expected costs must be subtracted from the total potential revenue. Potential revenue is calculated by multiplying the property's gross buildable square footage by an efficiency ratio. The result is the total square footage that can be sold to the end client. In the case of Site X, the gross buildable square footage is 83,991 square feet, the efficiency ratio is 83%, and the net sellable square footage is 69,713 square feet. The net sellable square footage is then multiplied by a price per foot to sell the condos. In the case of Site X, it is $375 per square foot and the total sales are $26 million. Finally, parking sales must be added: 60 parking spots multiplied by $40,000 per spot equates to $2.4 million, for total sales of $28.5 million.

The next step is to subtract total costs from total sales. As previously described, the gross buildable square footage is the total amount of volume the developer must build. The space above the parking levels is referred to as above grade square feet, while below grade square feet incorporates only the parking levels. Hard costs represent the total physical costs that go into the construction of a new project. Developers estimate total costs by multiplying the above grade square footage by a blended rate per square foot. In the case of Site X, the above grade square feet is 83,991 and the blended hard cost per foot above grade is $170, for a total hard cost above grade of approximately $14 million.

Soft costs are all the non-physical costs that go into the construction of a project, including the architecture fees, engineering fees, and financing fees. A developer will typically analyze the soft costs line item by item, but a quicker solution is to apply a percentage of hard costs to get to the total for soft costs. In the case of Site X, the soft cost as a percentage of hard cost is estimated at 35%, for a total of approximately $5.5 million.

Finally, the land price must be added to the cost section, for a total of $25.7 million dollars in the case of Site X. This represents a profit of $2.8 million for Site X and a cumulative profit of $4 million for both sites. It is important to note that this profit does not include overhead or the new policies such as the REM tax or *Strategy for Inclusion of Affordable Housing*.

Table 10.5 shows the approximate impact of paying the financial contribution and keeping the project as is. The impact is only monetary since it is a one-time fee and doesn't impact the design or layout of the project. The financial contribution is calculated by taking 20% of the total number of projected units—in this case, 140 units. The resulting number of units, 28, is multiplied by a fixed fee of $20,000 per unit, for a total contribution of $560,000. The resulting profit, given a financial contribution, is $3.4 million.

After months of negotiating with city officials, the city requested that social housing units would have to be included on-site or off-site. City boroughs have increasingly been pushing for actual social housing units rather

**Table 10.5** Proposed project business plan (payment of financial contribution)

| | |
|---|---|
| Total profit of both sites (before financial contribution) | $4,033,646 |
| Total # units | 140 |
| 20% of units | 28 |
| Financial contribution per unit | $20,000 |
| Total financial contribution | $560,000 |
| **Total profit after financial contribution** | **$3,473,646** |

Note: Synthesis of business plan by authors

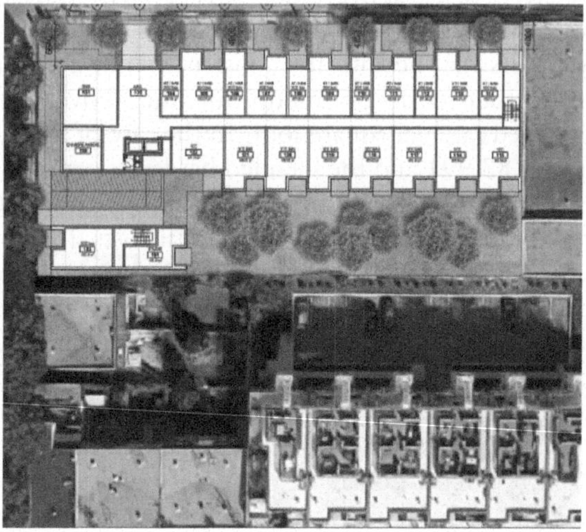

**Fig. 10.3** Site X implantation proposal. (Adapted from architect plans for Site X, 2019. Reproduced with permission)

than the financial contribution, since there is a current shortage of social housing in the City of Montreal (Arquin and Pignoly 2019). It is more difficult to develop a project with on-site social housing rather than to pay the social contribution fee or trade a separate piece of land with the city. This is because devoting a portion of the land on-site to social housing requires mandatory separation and spacing between the social housing units and the remaining building; this leads to a major loss in buildable square footage.

The developer analyzed two potential outcomes for this new project:

1. Selling Site Y to the city for the social housing needs for Site X, and building Site X according to the original design, as illustrated in Fig. 10.3
2. Building social housing on site, as illustrated in Fig. 10.4

**Fig. 10.4** Site X implantation social housing on site. (Adapted from architect plans for Site X, 2019. Reproduced with permission)

As previously mentioned, Fig. 10.3 shows the initial floor plan of Site X presented to the city. It is important to note that before the new social housing regulations, this initial layout would have likely been accepted. Now that social needs are being imposed on developers, and because the site contained more than 50 units, Fig. 10.3's layout was not accepted and a social housing component needed to be designed and planned. Figure 10.4 is a representation of the layout of Site X with social housing drawn on-site. The red rectangle is an actual representation of the floor plate that the social housing building would take if it was built on-site.

In Montreal, social housing that is built on-site must be built with a different entrance and as a separate building (the red floor plate in Fig. 10.4). There are a few drawbacks to this. First, there is a loss in efficiency in terms of land use coverage due to the spacing between the two buildings. Second, there is a loss in net to gross efficiency ratio, as outlined in Table 10.4. The loss is due to the fixed areas that still must be built and are spread over a smaller area of gross buildable square footage, such as the staircases, lobby, and gym that need to be duplicated in the separate social housing building. Third, and possibly the most important drawback, is the social segregation of the inhabitants of the two buildings, since the social housing dwellers are clearly delineated from the non-social housing. What this implies is that there may likely be two quality levels of maintenance, building materials, and common spaces for the two distinct buildings, further highlighting the social discrepancy of the two types of inhabitants. These social drawbacks are a paradoxical outcome. Separating out the social housing in this manner is detrimental from a conceptual and human level.

From a financial perspective, intuitively, a developer knows that building social housing on-site is not the best option. There is an efficiency loss as well as the value of neighboring condominiums decreases due to their proximity to a clearly visible social housing building. The financial implication of developing social housing on-site is illustrated in Table 10.6. The changes that were incorporated in Table 10.6 are as follows: (a) a 5% reduction in gross buildable square footage for the loss in land use efficiency, (b) a 2% reduction in the net to gross efficiency ratio, bringing it down to 81%, and (c) a $5 reduction in the condominium sales price per foot. The result is a total profit of $1.3 million for Site X, representing a 52.72% reduction in total profit.

Alternatively, the city may also accept a land trade with another site in the same borough to compensate for the social housing needs. In this

**Table 10.6** Hypothetical business plan (Project X with social housing on-site)

| | | |
|---|---|---|
| Gross livable square feet (SF) | | 83,991 |
| Common spaces | | 18,224 |
| TOTAL BUILDABLE SF | | 102,215 |
| Social housing needs *(% of total buildable)* | 25% | 25,554 |
| Remaining gross buildable SF *(buildable SF before—social housing needs—5% loss in efficiency)* | | 72,828 |
| Common spaces | | 13,837 |
| Net sellable SF | 81% | 58,991 |
| **Revenues (assuming condo)** | | |
| Net sellable SF | | 58,991 |
| Condo sales | $370 | $21,826,608 |
| Parking sales (40 spots) | $40,000 | $1,600,000 |
| **Total revenue** | | **$23,426,608** |
| **Hard costs** | | |
| Above grade ($160 per SF) | 72,828 | $11,652,510 |
| Below grade ($90 per SF) | 17,674 | $1,590,660 |
| Land | | $4,200,000 |
| **Soft costs (35% hard)** | | **$4,635,110** |
| **Total costs** | | **$22,078,280** |
| **Profit** | | **$1,348,328** |

**Table 10.7** Hypothetical business plan (trading Project Y for social housing needs at Project X)

| | | |
|---|---|---|
| Total buildable SF Site X | | 102,215 |
| **Social housing needs** *(% of total buildable)* | **25%** | **25,554** |
| Land value sold to city *(value / unit at 968.76 SF / unit)* | $12,000 | $316,534 |
| **Land value rounded down according to agreement** | | **$300,000** |
| **Total buildable SF Site Y** | | **23,896** |
| – Social housing needs | | 25,554 |
| = Remaining SF for social housing | | 1658 |
| **Financial contribution per unit (807.3 SF)** | **$11,500** | **$23,614** |
| *Profit after trade* | | |
| **Profit of both projects** | | **$4,033,646** |
| – Profit Site Y | | $1,181,598 |
| + City contribution land | | $300,000 |
| – Financial contribution remaining social needs | | $23,000 |
| – Decontamination + Demolition) | | $200,000 |
| **Total** | | **$2,929,048** |

case, Site Y may be traded for the social housing needs for Site X. Table 10.7 shows the financial implications of this deal.

The social housing needs, defined by the city, represent 25% of the total buildable square footage of a proposed project. Site X has 102,215 buildable square feet, where 25% represents approximately 25,554 square feet. The deal of the trade of Site Y for the social housing needs of Site X is as follows:

1. The developer sells Site Y, decontaminated and demolished at an agreed price;
2. The developer pays a financial contribution for social housing needs not met by the trade; and
3. The developer may build Site X as per the initial layout illustrated in Fig. 10.3.

The city establishes the compensation they will provide to the developer by taking the square footage of the social housing needs and multiplying it by a set value per potential unit. In this case, the social housing needs are 25,554 square feet, the value per unit is $12,000 and the average size per unit is 968.76 square feet. The result is a financial compensation of $316,534, which was rounded down to $300,000. It is important to remember that this case is not hypothetical, meaning the city did round down the compensation to $300,000 rather than pay the full $316,534.[8] Even though the developer purchased Site X for $1.5 million, see Table 10.4, the site was sold to the city for $300,000, representing a loss of $1.2 million.

Next, the developer must pay the financial contribution to the city because of the shortfall in square feet available in Site Y. Again, the social housing needs are 25,554 square feet and Site Y could only fit 23,896 square feet, representing a shortfall of 1658 square feet. A cost per foot is applied to the shortfall to get to $23,000 in financial contribution payable to the city. Finally, a decontamination and demolition budget is estimated at $200,000,[9] which will need to be conducted by the developer prior to the trade. The result is that the profit from both projects went from approximately $4.0 million down to $2.9 million, or a reduction of over 27%.

To summarize, the profit evolution of each option, in order of magnitude of the effect on the total projected profit, is outlined in Table 10.8. The first line represents the base, meaning the projected profit before the social housing component was imposed. The second line represents the projected profit for the financial contribution only, representing a total

**Table 10.8** Profit analysis of three scenarios

| *Analysis* | *Project X* | *Project Y* | *Total* | *Profit reduction ($)* | *Profit reduction (%)* |
|---|---|---|---|---|---|
| Profit before all regulations | $2,852,048 | $1,181,598 | $4,033,646 | $0 | 0.00% |
| Profit with financial contribution only | $2,388,048 | $1,085,598 | $3,473,646 | −$560,000 | −13.88% |
| Profit with land trade | $2,929,048 | $0 | $2,929,048 | −$1,104,598 | −27.38% |
| Profit with social housing on site | $1,348,328 | $558,610 | $1,906,938 | −$2,126,708 | −52.72% |

Note: Scenario synthesis by authors

[8] This is based on conversations with the president of the real estate development company, and verified through their file.

[9] This budget was estimated by the developer and provided to me for completing our hypothetical business plans.

reduction in profit of $560,000, or a 13.88% reduction from the base. The third line item is the profit with the land trade, representing a reduction in profit of $1.1 million, or a 27.38% reduction from the base. Finally, the least attractive option is to build the social housing on site, representing a reduction in profit of $2.1 million, or a 52.72% reduction from the base. Since the option for only a financial contribution was not made available to the developer by the municipality, it is clear what the next best option is: to trade Site Y in exchange for Site X's social housing needs. This reduced the initial projected profit by $1.1 million.

As the City of Montreal has not yet specified the guidelines in terms of which option they will enforce—financial contribution, off-site donation, or on-site donation—developers are put in a position of financial risk, even *before* they can purchase a portion of land. This may result in significant impacts on the development of the city.

## Discussion

In the case presented above, we only examined the economic and financial risks for a developer from the social housing component of the 20-20-20 regulation. This component alone had the potential to reduce net profits by 52.72%, not including the economic impacts of requiring 20% of units be dedicated to affordable housing, 20% to be three-bedroom units, as well as the $11 REM Tax per buildable square foot. For the case studied, a project of 102,215 square feet would represent an additional tax burden of over $1 million dollars. This chapter has sought to highlight the financial risks for development projects associated to a changing political environment. Developers who have not budgeted and planned properly for the new regulations will see a major drop in profitability. However, it is rarely the case that a law increasing taxes and costs affect one side of the equation entirely. As costs related to social housing integration are increasing, so are the prices that developers are selling or renting their condos for, ultimately pushing the increased cost burden onto the end user. A regulation designed to provide affordable housing may end up having the exact opposite outcome.

The question remains: is there a policy which increases affordable housing while stimulating the real estate development industry? Can we satisfy the needs of both the developer and the government, or do we have to choose one or the other? Currently, the political framework is favoring the government, while hindering real estate developers' profits and growth opportunities. This leads to a situation where real estate development stagnates. As a result, the total number of social housing units developed may fall, leading to an unfavorable situation for the government. City officials and economists may debate over the best solution; however, the policy must balance the needs of both the developer and the government to be successful in the long run.

One solution that has been implemented by many cities in the United States, including New York City in 2016 (Tuller 2018), is inclusionary upzoning. Inclusionary upzoning is where the city requires 15% of the units in a new development to be affordable, while allowing the developer greater overall density in their project as compensation (Hickey 2014). The developer is therefore restricted in terms of pricing 15% of the units in their project; however, the overall scale of the project has increased so the economic effect is negligible. In other words, inclusionary upzoning offers cities or boroughs the opportunity to enforce social housing requirements while ensuring the economic feasibility of the project.

In the long run, a social housing policy that places the entire burden on the developers, such as Quebec's 20-20-20 policy today, may result in a worsened economic and even a conflicted political environment. The developers may suffer from lost profits and reduced opportunities, leading to a stagnant development industry. The government may also suffer from a reduction in projected social housing units developed as the economy slows and less units are built. City officials and developers should be collaborating on a solution that provides benefits and growth opportunities for both parties—a win-win situation. Inclusionary upzoning is one solution that some cities have implemented and have proven to be successful (Tuller 2018). However, it is only one solution among others that can be potentially beneficial for both developers and municipalities.

Future research is needed to analyze a variety of social housing policy strategies that will both help increase the development of social housing in Montreal as well as growth opportunities for developers. The upzoning approach adopted by New York City is but one example of a social housing strategy that has attempted to consider both parties. In order to find a long-term solution for Montreal and the province of Quebec that is sustainable for both the developer and the government, collaboration between both parties is necessary.

## Appendix 1: Affordable Units*

Condominium Units

1. Studio units with a maximum sale price including taxes of $200,000
2. One-bedroom units with a maximum sale price including taxes of $250,000
3. Two-bedroom units with a maximum sale price including taxes of $280,000
4. Three-bedroom units with a maximum sale price including taxes of $360,000

Rental Units

1. Studio units with a maximum of $788 per month before taxes
2. One-bedroom units with a maximum of $946 per month before taxes
3. Two-bedroom units with a maximum of $1064 per month before taxes
4. Three-bedroom units with a maximum of $1262 per month before taxes

It is understood that the rents illustrated above will be increased annually by 2% on January 1 of each year. This indexation will be applicable for the first 5 years following the date on which the property is finished and ready for the use for which it is intended.

*This is an extract of the social housing agreement signed between Mondev and the City of Montreal.

## References

Arquin, A., & Pignoly, A. (2019). *La Ville de Montréal publie le règlement 20-20-20 sur les logements sociaux, abordables et familiaux*. Retrieved from https://www.dwpv.com/fr/Insights/Publications/2019/Montreal-publie-reglement-20-20-20.

Canada, B. o. (2019). Canadian interest rates and monetary policy variables: 10-year lookup. *Interest Rates*.

CMHC. (2018). *Housing market outlook: Quebec region*. Retrieved from Canada: Habitat for humanity (Producer). (2019, September 1, 2019). Why is affordable housing important?

Hickey, R. (2014). "Inclusionary Upzoing" Is gaining ground. Here's why. *ShelterForce The Voice of Community Deveopment*.

Kelly, H. F., Warren, A., & Kramer, A. (2019). Emerging trends in real estate 2019: The United States and Canada. *PricewaterhouseCoopers and United Land Institute.*

Lau, R. (2019, January 11). 2018: A record year for Montreal real estate: Survey. *Quebec Global News.*

Marotte, B. (2018, September 27). Four Seasons plans return to Montreal with $250-million hotel project. *The Globe and Mail.* Retrieved from https://www.theglobeandmail.com/real-estate/the-market/four-seasons-targets-return-to-montreal-with-250-million-hotel-project/article32071590/.

Montreal, C. o. (Producer). (2019, September 1, 2019). Building a network for greater Montreal. *Réseau express métropolitain (REM).*

Quebec (Producer). (2019, September 1, 2019). Regie du logement.

Trading Economics. (2019). Canada interest rate 2019. Retrieved from https://tradingeconomics.com/canada/interest-rate.

Tuller, D. (2018). Housing and health: The role of inclusionary zoning. *Health Affairs, Health Policy Brief: Culture of Health.*

United Nations. (2019). *World urbanization prospects the 2018 revision.* Retrieved from https://www.un.org/development/desa/en/news/population/2018-revision-of-world-urbanization-prospects.html.

United States Department of Transportation. (2002). *The importance of public transport, in 2002 status of the nation's highways, bridges, and transit: Conditions & performance.* Retrieved from https://www.fhwa.dot.gov/policy/2002cpr/pdf/ch14.pdf.

CHAPTER 11

# Climate Change and Reputation in the Financial Services Sector

*Robert E. Bopp*

## Rising Relevance of Reputation

### *Relevance*

Buffett and Connors (2010, p. 5) state: "It takes twenty years to build a reputation and five minutes to ruin it. If you think about that, you'll do things differently."

Currently, the term reputation is extensively used, be it in politics or business. Reputation is what everyone worries about in financial institutions, particularly when it comes to climate change. Either one is worried that an institution's reputation is jeopardized, or one is eager to build up

The views expressed in this chapter are those of the author and not necessarily those of Ernst & Young.

R. E. Bopp (✉)
Financial Services, Ernst & Young, Stuttgart, Germany
e-mail: robert.bopp@de.ey.com



T. Walker et al. (eds.), *Ecological, Societal, and Technological Risks and the Financial Sector*, Palgrave Studies in Sustainable Business In Association with Future Earth, https://doi.org/10.1007/978-3-030-38858-4_11

an institution's reputation. In any case, it is crucial to understand that reputation is what we call "reflective" in its nature. Abraham Lincoln circumscribes it as follows: "Character is like a tree and reputation like a shadow. The shadow is what we think of it; the tree is the real thing" (Brooks 1879, pp. 584–587). This simile suggests that reputation is what is *seen* through the observer's eye. Each observers' point of view is different and characterized by many individual experiences, beliefs, thoughts, and perceptions. People cannot grasp reputation. Consequently, people cannot directly invest in it, nor is it possible to protect it.

It becomes complex when someone tries to identify a reputation's reference point (Kadous et al. 2008). Is it a person, for example, an ordinary citizen, or a celebrity? Is it an organization, such as a small, private-owned venture, or a large multinational corporation? Is it an institution, for instance, a public institution, a charitable foundation, or a government entity? Depending on the answer, very different volatility schemata for reputation exist.[1] The more minutely detailed the reference point for a financial institution is, for example, person, board member, and bank, the more volatility can be observed (Imhof 2000).

In spite of it, all reputation stands at the focal point of discussions in many fields of the financial services industry. The rise of modern communication diversifies the group of stakeholders that potentially affect an institution's reputation by using new means and formats. It therefore becomes even more important to understand which stakeholder is relevant in mitigating the positive/negative impact on an institution's reputation. What is the stakeholder interested in by observing the institution and who does the stakeholder reach—by which media channel? How can the institution react to a massive attack that puts the institution's very own existence, its license-to-operate, at stake?

### *Definition of Reputation*

There is no generally accepted definition of reputation (Suchanek 2007). However, there are diverse conceptions throughout different scientific

[1] Depending on the definition, financial risks comprise numerous risks, for example, concentration risk, market risk, interest rate risk, currency risk, equity risk, commodity risk, liquidity risk, refinancing risk, operational risk, country risk, legal risk, model risk, political risk, valuation risk, reputational risk, volatility risk, settlement risk, profit risk, and systemic risk.

disciplines. In economics, it is argued that reputation refers to an incentive structure that requires information about the contract party on the one hand and that is intertemporal and self-enforcing on the other hand (Bauhofer 2004).

Information is the basis for reiterative, relational contracts between economic parties. Thereby all parties suffer incomplete information since perfect information is not achieved at reasonable cost and reasonable effort. Making decisions requires the inclusion of elements of the past and the future. For example, if customers have positively experienced a product in the past, the product benefits from that positive perception. Based on it, the buyers assume that they will benefit from the product with a high reputation in the future. It is through the agreement of the expectation with the experience that the parties will consider to reiteratively invest into this relation (Eisenegger 2004). This means that incomplete, objectifiable information is compensated by subjective experiences.

Reputation derives from various aspects (European Systemic Risk Board 2016). Generally, reputation is synonymous with authenticity, reliability, credibility, trustworthiness, responsibility, liability, and similar expressions. The least common denominator for a definition of reputation is that reputation has value. This value is determined by the sociocultural background of the person that relies, for the decision, on past and future aspects of the counterparts (Pohl and Zaby 2008). For example, products labeled "Made in China" are seen as products of lower quality in the western hemisphere, since this label indicated products of lower quality in the past—compared, for instance, to labels such as "Made in Great Britain" or "Made in Germany." Nowadays, China has developed into an industrial leading nation in Asia. This label is thus seen in the Asian region as a label of quality, as opposed to labels such as "Made in India" or "Made in Vietnam."

For the purpose of this chapter, reputation is understood as a combination of trust, credibility, and integrity. The different aspects are illustrated in Fig. 11.1.

### *Differentiation*

The term reputation is not to be confused with image or brand. For example, there is quite obviously a difference between Apple's image, brand, and reputation. In a nutshell, Apple has a general image of an IT company that anticipates and sets new trends and developments. As a brand, Apple stands for innovative products such as the iPhone, iPad, and iMac.

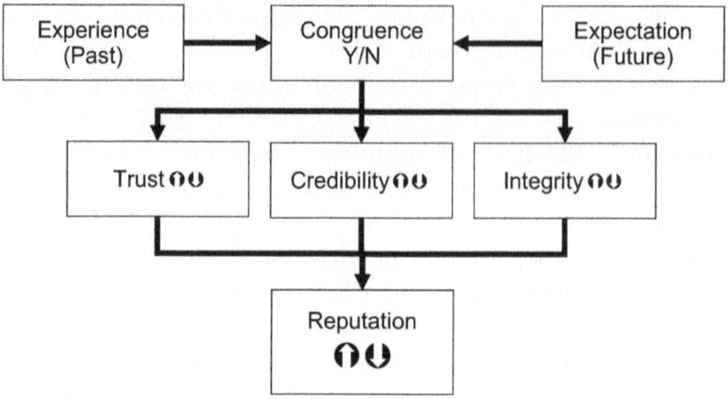


**Fig. 11.1** Aspects of reputation

However, the company's reputation is increasingly determined by how it treats its suppliers and the people who work for them. While image and brand can to a certain degree be controlled objectively by the company, reputation can essentially be experienced subjectively by the corporate environment. The Apple logo transports these different messages to the stakeholder.

It can be stated that image is the overall impression someone receives of the object of observation (Kinter and Ott 2014). People or businesses can influence this impression by positioning themselves in a certain manner. Images can be placed to transport certain messages in order to provoke a specific reaction from the targeted audience group (stakeholder group), for example, the business appears as a responsible employer or as a producer of traditional food. In any case, an image is more like a snapshot of a current phenomenon and therefore focuses on immediate short-term effects. An image can be managed actively, and it is possible to play with various images at once.

The brand contains aspects of reputation and image. It is the most impactful of the three concepts, as it can be determined and controlled directly by the company in terms of product, price promotion, and placement. It integrates individual experiences to distinguish one brand from another. A brand is often recognized through logo, sign, or symbol, for example, Coca-Cola or Pepsi (soft drinks), Mercedes or BMW (cars), and Apple or Windows (computers). It indicates that a product belongs to that brand. Branding is the most immediate and most direct communication of a business.

It is important to note that a person cannot become a brand. In some cases, for example, for fashion designers, pop stars, and artists, people use the term "brand" to describe these celebrities.[2] Here it is important to separate the brand name from the person. The person behind the name, who defines the brand by its image, carries a reputation that reflects his/her character traits.

## New Reputation Dimension for Financial Services

The role of financial services is that of an intermediary for supply and demand of capital. In practical terms, an intermediary receives capital from one market side to invest it on the other side. The capital owner expects that the intermediary acts in his or her interest and manages to get a positive return out of the investment. The market participants will only let an intermediary play that role if he or she is considered trustworthy, credible, and honest—if they believe in his or her reputation. Otherwise, they will try to secure their property by legal contracts. The worse the reputation, the more contracts are needed. Economically, this means that more contracts lead to higher costs, for example, for lawyers and notaries. These transaction costs have a negative impact on the company's cost structure and can lead to economic collapse.

Hence, the intermediary role pretty much depends on the intermediary's reputation. It is crucial to understand and assess the risk exposure of the involved parties in terms of reputation. Financial services need comprehensive and systematic information regarding their business's dependency on the concerns of stakeholders.

Financial services need to understand what is expected of them and how the businesses are perceived by relevant stakeholders regarding environmental, social, and governance (ESG) related topics. The following section outlines a few, brief examples of how ESG, as a new dimension, contributes to the reputation of financial services institutions. The different aspects of reputation are illustrated in Fig. 11.2.

### *Environmental Change*

Climate change with all its consequences for humankind is a major concern for the twenty-first-century population. To mitigate the effects of

[2] See Karl Lagerfeld or Gianni Versace.

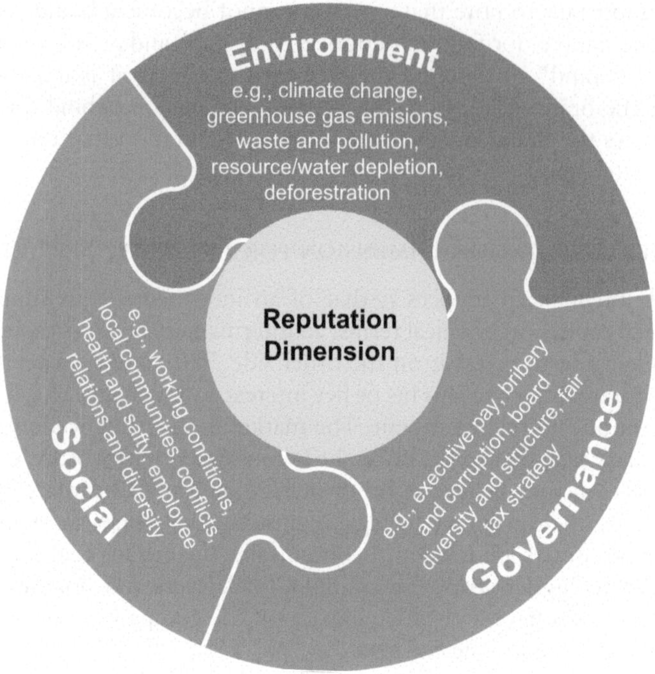


**Fig. 11.2** Environmental, social, and governance criteria

climate change, various institutions and parties are trying to reduce their levels of carbon in the atmosphere to abate global warming. Financial institutions must play a significant role in this development since they must provide the capital to finance the transformation of the economy toward a low carbon industry. This transformation is required to support the goals defined under the Paris Agreement.

At the Paris climate conference (COP21) in December 2015, 195 countries adopted the universal, legally binding global climate deal. The agreement sets out a global action plan to avoid dangerous climate change by limiting global warming to well below 2 °C and pursuing efforts to limit it to 1.5 °C (EU 2017).

To do so, institutions must, according to the Paris Agreement, reduce emissions, increase the use of renewables, and enhance energy efficiency, which require heavy investments, not only from the public but also from the private sector (EU 2019).

Financial services must be transparent. It must be clear for stakeholders to which extent the financial industry depends on the environment and to what extent their business impacts the environment. It damages an institution's reputation and jeopardizes its business model if the institution's perceived business behavior regarding the support of the Paris goals differs from stakeholder expectations.

The difficulty for financial institutions is that they are affected not only by market mechanisms but also by the vast breadth of ecological concerns. Ecological concerns include the depletion of resources and its impact on the environment, the clients' reliance on fossil fuel and related emissions, as well as the engagement with nuclear power plant operators and the financing of renewable energy facilities, such as solar- or hydro-electric power plants.

The question of the obsolescence of a company's product or service is also becoming central to the value ascribed to that company. The long-term view in terms of positive or negative impact on climate change is becoming prevalent amongst counterparties for playing a role as a new dimension of reputation for financial services.

### *Social Pressure*

Human activities are accelerating social concerns, notably in the form of human rights, diversity, inclusion, and loss of species. In terms of reputation, stakeholders are interested to know about an institution's positioning in these areas. They ask if an institution positively impacts society or if it harms individuals or groups by the way it does business.

Human rights as an area of concern is a major dimension to a financial institution's reputation since it includes such considerations as the impact on local communities and the health and welfare of employees. The stakeholders' interest is twofold. On the one hand, they are interested in the way the financial institution acts internally, for example, by implementing and living a corporate responsibility strategy, and on the other hand, how it acts externally, for example, by doing business along a corporate sustainability strategy. These interests bring the area of a company's social responsibilities straight into the financial arena (UN 2019).

Another important aspect driving social concerns is the level of diversity and inclusiveness. These characteristics are becoming key concerns to all stakeholders and refer to an examination of company policies and the way these policies are put into practice by structured monitoring and governance processes. Innovation and agility are seen as the great benefits of diversity and inclusiveness. The reputation of a company is therefore driven by the way a company hires/employs a diverse set of people to stay competitive in a challenging environment and to generate a positive impact through the way they operate.

The external way of looking at a company's reputation is through the way it treats its customers. If a company does not grant or respect the customers' rights, it will face damages through litigation. Consumer protection is a central consideration for stakeholders seeking to understand a company's value, and therefore it is a dimension of reputation for financial services. Social concerns can also result from a firm's attitude toward animal welfare, for example, financing research facilities or cosmetics that rely on animal experimentation in their research and development. These concerns about the welfare of animals are major considerations for stakeholder groups seeking a thorough understanding of a company's principles. Stakeholders are also increasingly interested in less obvious examples of animal welfare, such as species extinction, including bees or butterflies, due to pesticides.

These social concerns are a major dimension of reputation for financial services, even though the impact of a firm is likely to be more a consequential one than an immediate one.

### *Governance Transformation*

The third dimension that impacts the financial services' reputation refers to governance aspects. Reputation will undergo fundamental changes as climate change issues gain importance in terms of binding/non-binding regulations. Governance, especially corporate governance, covers the area of investigation into the rights and responsibilities of a company's management (Wieland et al. 2014). This includes board, shareholders, and the various stakeholders in an institution. Each of them have their personal concerns and topics of interest, and the stakeholders monitor the extent to which these topics are covered as it influences the organization's reputation.

Inward looking, a system of internal procedures and controls makes up the management structure of a company. The balance of power between the chief executive officer (CEO) and the board of directors plays an important role in decision making. While the British tradition combines both roles in one person, the European tradition splits the roles of CEO and chairman (Ooghe and De Langhe 2002). Thus, reputation does have different reference points in different business traditions.

External observers often focus on issues around executive compensation. Financial services institutions are now being asked to list the percentage levels of bonus payments and the levels of remuneration of the highest-paid executives. They are coming under the scrutiny of stakeholders if the information is not properly disclosed or when it causes irritations—reputational damage—due to the contractual agreements, for example, absolute amount, relative amount compared with average salary of average employee, or granted/guaranteed benefits and privileges. Stakeholders might also focus on employee compensation, especially equal pay for employees of all genders. Stakeholders have started to ask for pay gap audits and for the results of those audits to be made available to the public for review. As such, these results may be the starting point for discussion about the reputation of a firm.

As a conclusion, it can be said that ESG aspects have become new elements of reputational dimensions for financial institutions. They are considered "new" dimensions because they receive much more attention in the eyes of relevant stakeholders today than they did in the past. Therefore, a company is better off providing a congruence between postulated behavior and realized business attitude (see Fig. 11.3). Any gap affects the reputation in one way or another.

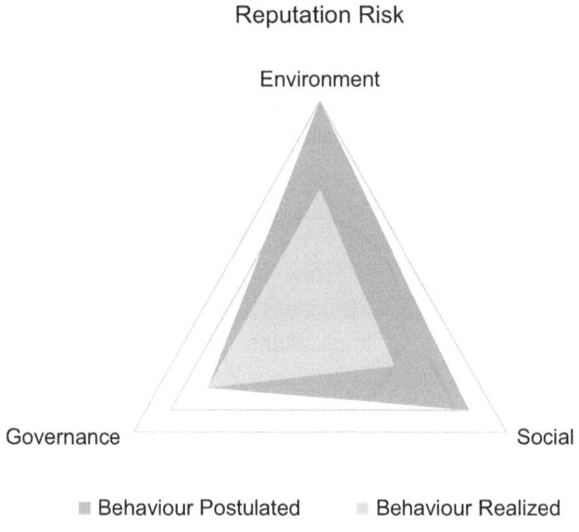


**Fig. 11.3** Reputation risk

## Necessity to Integrate Climate Change to Stay Relevant

### *New Business Implications*

Climate change is an issue with economic implications that are transforming financial services. Among many issues that are important to the financial industry, climate change has been driven to the top of the business agenda. It has introduced many new business implications–illustrated in Fig. 11.4. These implications need to be managed by financial institutions in order to stay relevant (Bouma et al. 2017).

Financial institutions need to respond to new business challenges by addressing carbon costs, calculating the value at stake, and assessing strategic risks from climate change (Schmidheiny and Zorraquin 1998). These actions will lead to new market opportunities in which business processes are transformed, environmental procurement criteria are implemented, or buying patterns for procurement and consumers are changed. Through them, new markets are created and innovation is pushed (Stapelfeldt et al. 2018).

The regulatory environment will adjust to these implications, too. Recent and anticipated regulations and policies need to be addressed and directors' responsibilities are likely to be reassessed (Busch et al. 2016). For example, climate change and its effects urge institutions to cope with

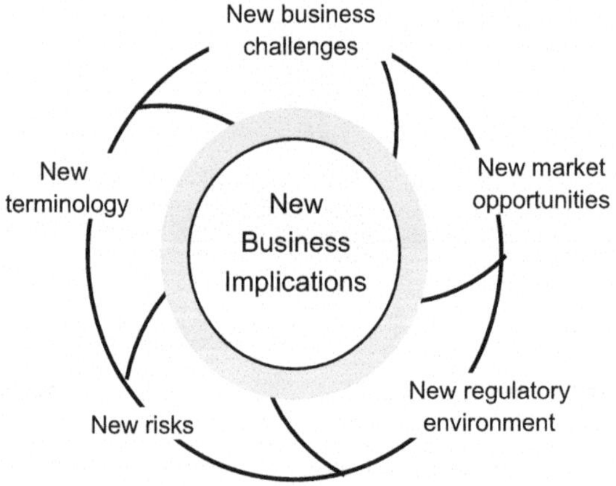


**Fig. 11.4** New business implications

the new risks that arise. This might be done by adjusting or expanding existing risk management systems to the new risk environment by, for example, transitional or physical risk classifications.

### *Strategic Considerations*

As climate change impacts financial services, new strategic considerations need to be managed. Thereby, new risks and opportunities are two sides of the same token. Technically speaking, an event is considered a risk when it comes with a negative value and vice versa—an opportunity comes with a positive value. This definition applies to business risks in general, for example, operational, legal and regulatory, financial, and societal risks, as much as to specific financial services risks in particular, such as credit, market, liquidity, operational, and compliance risks (BaFin 2017).

The nature of climate risks means that the biggest challenge in climate risk management is in assessing the resilience of financial institutions' strategies. Climate risks also have a number of distinctive elements, which require a strategic approach. Mark Carney (2019) spoke of them in terms of:

- Breadth, as climate risks affect multiple lines of business, sectors, and geographies;
- Magnitude, as climate risks impacts are large, potentially non-linear, and irreversible;
- Foreseeable nature;
- Dependency on short-term actions given that the size of future impacts will, at least in part, be determined by the actions taken today; and
- Uncertain time horizon which may stretch beyond traditional business planning cycles.

Financial institutions' reputation can be disrupted by climate risks if they fail to develop a strategic approach to manage these risks. The disruptions need to be managed strategically in a structured manner in order to stay viable as a financial institution. Figure 11.5 presents the relevant strategic dimensions.

In a top-down view, reputation and climate change must be part of the risk culture and communicated from the top to improve the financial institutions' performance. A strong risk governance with an integrated

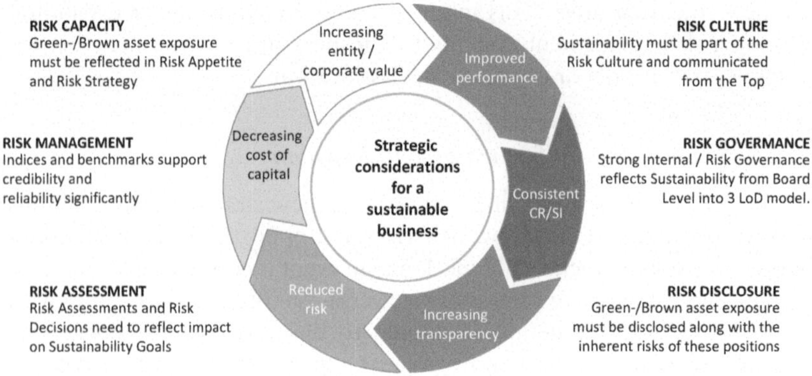


**Fig. 11.5** Strategic considerations in the context of climate change and sustainability

Three-Lines-of-Defense-Model (Eulerich 2012) reflects the board's commitment and ensures consistency regarding corporate responsibility and corporate sustainability. Clear and transparent risk disclosure is crucial for the communication with the stakeholders as they are interested to understand the inherent risks of positions related to climate change.

A bottom-up approach of risk assessments is also required. In doing so, the risk position can be compared to the defined risk goals, and adjustments can be made. The immediate impact of reducing risk positions is the decrease of costs for financial institutions, for example, by using higher ratings for refinancing purposes. The risk management provides the indices and benchmarks to support internal and external rating and scoring models. The derived risk-bearing capacity of an institution determines its capacity to withstand disruptions.

These strategic components support a sustainable business by minimizing, mitigating, or compensating the risk and by maximizing the opportunity for a financial institution exposed to environmental risks and potential reputational damage.

### *Tactical Affirmation*

There are various business implications as financial services understand and act on climate change. Not being aware of new risks—and opportunities—may lead to severe disruptions. Considering the disruptions from a

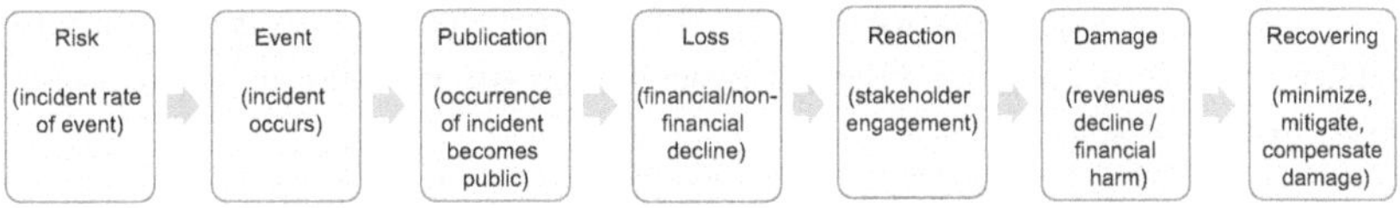


**Fig. 11.6** Risk management–tactical

strategic risk view is as important as managing these risks in a tactical manner. To disregard these interdependencies means that a financial institution will be pushed out of business by competition. An increased focus by stakeholders on the role financial institutions play in relation to climate change further provokes the need for organizations to understand actions. The financial institution's benefit for the economy and for the society is questioned if its ecological role is not clear. Its business model, including its products and services, might become obsolete, and the institution will lose its relevance.

However, such a development does not happen on its own. It is usually the result of a process that must be closely managed on a tactical level (see Fig. 11.6).

Climate change-related risks are, according to the categorization of the Financial Stability Board–Task Force on Climate-related Financial Disclosures (FSB-TCFD), either transitional risks or physical risks (FSB-TCFD 2017). Therefore, risks in general are defined as events with a specific incident rate, as opposed to events without an applicable incident rate. The latter is commonly described as coincidence.

The risk itself becomes a matter of interest if an incident occurs. This might happen, in the sense of a policy or legal risk under the transitional risk categorization when, for instance, a local regulator releases a new regulation on how to structure financial products. The relevance of the risk for the financial institution is given when the regulator's activity becomes available to relevant stakeholders either because it was officially published or because it became publicly known. Only on that basis can a loss in financial or non-financial terms happen. The risk of a new regulation not yet implemented can cause a decline in share price or negatively impact reputation. In any case this loss will provoke an immediate reaction from stakeholders, for example, by selling shares, adjusting proxy voting rules, or administrating active shareholder action (Horster and Papadopoulos 2019). Such reactions will lead to damages for the institution, such as declining revenues, increasing cost, and liability suit.

These tactical implications show the importance to integrate climate change and reputation as relevant aspects into the management processes and procedures.

## Perceived Reputation by Stakeholders

### *Availability of Information*

The availability of information is critical. Stakeholders need information to assess which financial institution can seize the opportunities in a low carbon economy and which are strategically resilient to the physical and transitional risks associated with climate change (Carney 2019).

In the past, it was the role of regulatory authorities to monitor and control market players. They performed their tasks based on rules and regulations laid down in legal frameworks and as hard law. Nowadays, soft law has begun to play an important role in terms of governance, risk, and compliance issues, and it is rooted in standards, principles, and codices to which a person or company agrees to comply with as an act of self-regulation.

As mentioned, stakeholders intend to bring information and experience in accordance with deduce reputation as a basis for future decisions. Against that background, stakeholders broaden their understanding of the financial institution's exposure to climate-related risks by analyzing publicly available information. To evaluate an institution's reputation, more complete, consistent, and comparable information for stakeholders is needed. Increased transparency enables the analysis of climate-related risk. As a response, financial institutions are beginning to disclose how climate-related risks and opportunities financially impact the institution in financial and non-financial publications (FSB-TCFD 2019).

Since it is not the institution's intention to disclose its impact on the environment, it is the task of the observer to come up with an individual assessment. In such an assessment, the given information may serve as a benchmark against the individual values measured. Any deviation between the published information and the individual understanding causes a risk for the institution's reputation. It is therefore of the utmost importance to have clear communication between the relevant parties about certain subject areas.

### *Classification of Information*

The FSB-TCFD provides climate-related classification of information which is widely used (TCFD 2018). It is expected that financial institutions include information with respect to governance, strategy, and risk management as well as metrics and targets.

In terms of governance, an institution is requested to report about the organization's governance around climate risks. It must describe how an organization's board oversees risks, and reputation risk must be mentioned here as a risk category on its own. The management´s role to assess and manage reputation risk must be clearly addressed.

From a strategic point of view, it is necessary to elaborate on the actual and potential impacts of reputation risk. Specifically, its impact on the organization's businesses, its strategy, and its financial planning should be reported in detail. Reputation risk may impact the institution differently in the short, medium, or long term. The stakeholders need to ask whether the organization is prepared to withstand internal or external shocks and disruptions caused by climate-related scenarios.

Disclosed information on risk management sheds a light on the methods used to identify, assess, and manage reputation risk. Reputation risk is thereby integrated into an overall risk management approach. The linkages to other transitional or physical risks are also important to note. Differences in risk management systems vary from defining reputation as individual risk class to including reputation risk under operational risks. The evaluation of reputation depends on the sophistication of the approach. It is either strongly qualitative, for example, describing the circumstances as well as the causes and effects, or quantitatively designed, for example, relying on correlations among different risk categories.

The disclosure on metrics and targets addresses mainly technical details that are relevant to understand the materiality of the provided information, such as the regular use of scenario analysis to test strategic resilience.

An organization informs about the metrics used to assess reputation risk in accordance with its strategy and risk management processes. For example, greenhouse gas emissions are reported for Scope 1, Scope 2, and Scope 3 if appropriate. The stakeholder may use these descriptions to assess a financial institution's risk management and its performance against the targets described and determined under the governance and strategy section.

### *Usability of Information*

Financial institutions must have a clear picture of what they want to disclose and in what form. Before disclosing information, they must foresee how the information can be interpreted or understood by the user to ensure that the user's perception aligns with the intended message behind the information.

Financial institutions must communicate clearly what they intend to do and where they see limitations. It is important not to make false or misleading promises in the disclosures as they will damage credibility, integrity, and trust. A clear statement to what can be done by the institution and what might not be in its scope of responsibility will be perceived by the stakeholder as a sign of transparency and authenticity.

Reputation risk is a discrete risk category and must be managed as such by integrating it into the overall risk management concept, including risk-bearing capacity, risk measurement, and risk mitigation.

Based on the outcome of materiality assessments, it is important to disclose the institution's exposure to ESG themes. One method to prevent the institution from damages caused by reputation risk is a regular and open dialogue with stakeholders. Only then can the information facilitate the stakeholders' perception of an institution's reputation.

However, financial institutions must consider how their businesses would be affected in different physical and transitional risks scenarios. For instance, if there is a tight and strict regulation in place, the transitional risks become more relevant relative to the physical risks. In contrast, if the regulation remains lax, then the physical risks may have a relatively higher relevance. Even though climate scenarios are not forecasted, they can be considered as data-driven narratives that help financial institutions to think through different possible futures. Therefore, the scenario analysis is part of their assessments of the impact of climate risks on their balance sheet and broader business strategies.

## Conclusion

This chapter examined the importance of climate change and reputation for financial services and demonstrated the different ways in which climate change-related risks are of high interest for various stakeholder groups. The investigation demonstrates that climate change impacts an institution's reputation, and thus stakeholders should be attuned to the climate change-related actions of a company.

This study has both practical and theoretical implications. It examined how financial institutions respond to different stakeholders' experiences and expectations. Although there is no common definition of reputation, the study showed how important it is to integrate reputation into risk management methodology.

Firms must either develop their own transitional scenarios or build on commonly available models. Scenarios should be implemented consistently across the business, linking identification of risks and opportunities to climate change and reputation.

It further provides an explanation for the new dimension that reputation has added to the discussion of climate change-related risks: if the financial services provider does not manage climate-related risks appropriately, the institution's reputation is likely to be tarnished to an extent that the company will not stay relevant and, consequently, it will lose its license to operate.

## References


BaFin. (2017). *Rundschreiben 09/2017 (BA) – Mindestanforderungen an das Risikomanagement – MaRisk.* Retrieved April 1, 2019, from https://www.bafin.de/SharedDocs/Veroeffentlichungen/DE/Rundschreiben/2017/rs_1709_marisk_ba.html?nn=9866146.

Bauhofer, B. (2004). *Reputation management. Glaubwürdigkeit im Wettbewerb des 21. Jahrhunderts.* Zürich: Orell Füssli.

Bouma, J., Jeucken, M., & Klinkers, L. (2017). *Sustainable banking: The greening of finance.* Abington: Routledge.

Brooks, N. (1879). Lincoln's imagination. *Scribner's Magazine*, pp. 584–587.

Buffett, W., & Connors, R. J. (2010). *Warren Buffett on Business: Principles from the Sage of Omaha.* Chichester: John Wiley & Sons.

Busch, T., Bauer, R., & Orlitzky, M. (2016). Sustainable development and financial markets: Old paths and new avenues. *Business & Society, 55*(3), 303–329.

Carney, M. (2019). *European Commission Conference: A global approach to sustainable finance* (Bank of England Speech, no. 603). London.

Eisenegger, M. (2004). *Reputationskonstitution in der Mediengesellschaft.* Luzern: VS Verlag für Sozialwissenschaften.

EU. (2017). *Paris agreement.* Retrieved April 1, 2019, from https://ec.europa.eu/clima/policies/international/negotiations/paris_en.

EU. (2019). *Sustainable finance.* Retrieved April 1, 2019, from https://ec.europa.eu/info/business-economy-euro/banking-and-finance/sustainable-finance_en.

Eulerich, M. (2012). Die regulatorischen Grundlagen des Three-Lines-of-Defense-Modells. *Zeitschrift Interne Revision (ZIR), 47*(4), 192–196.

European Systemic Risk Board. (2016). *Too late, too sudden: Transition to a low carbon economy and systemic risk*, Reports of the Scientific Committee No 6, Frankfurt.

FSB-TCFD. (2017). *Final report: Recommendations of the task force on climate-related financial disclosures.* Retrieved April 1, 2019, from https://www.fsb-tcfd.org/publications/final-recommendations-report/.

FSB-TCFD. (2019). *Task force on climate-related financial disclosures: 2019 status report.* Retrieved April 1, 2019, from https://www.fsb.org/2019/06/task-force-on-climate-related-financial-disclosures-2019-status-report/.

Horster, M., & Papadopoulos, K. (2019). *Climate change and proxy voting in the U.S. and Europe.* Retrieved April 1, 2019, from https://corpgov.law.harvard.edu/2019/01/07/climate-change-and-proxy-voting-in-the-u-s-and-europe/.

Imhof, K. (2000). *Öffentlichkeit und Skandal.* München: Juventa.

Kadous, K. et al. (2008). *Is there safety in numbers? The effects of forecast accuracy and forecast boldness on financial analysts' credibility with investors.* Retrieved April 1, 2019, from https://ssrn.com/abstract=1301136 or https://doi.org/10.2139/ssrn.1301136.

Kinter, A., & Ott, U. (2014). *Risikofaktor Social Web – Reputationsrisiken und -chancen managen.* München: Bank-Verlag Medien.

Ooghe, H., & De Langhe, T. (2002). The Anglo-American versus the Continental European corporate governance model: Empirical evidence of board composition in Belgium. *European Business Review, 14*(6), 437–449.

Pohl, M., & Zaby, S. (2008). *Das bankbetriebliche Reputationsrisikomanagement und dessen Umsetzung.* Basel: WWZ-Forum.

Schmidheiny, S., & Zorraquin, F. (1998). *Financing change.* Cambridge, MA: MIT Press.

Stapelfeldt, M., Granzow, M., & Kopp, M. (2018). *Greening finance.* Berlin: LOGOS.

Suchanek, A. (2007). *Ökonomische Ethik.* Tübingen: Mohr Siebeck.

TCFD. (2018). *TCFD 2018 status report.* Retrieved April 1, 2019, from https://www.fsbtcfd.org/publications/tcfd-2018-status-report/.

UN. (2019). *Declaration of Human Rights.* Retrieved from https://www.un.org/en/universal-declaration-human-rights/index.html.

Wieland, J., Steinmeyer, R., & Grüninger, S. (2014). *Handbuch compliance-management.* Berlin: Erich Schmidt.

CHAPTER 12

# Financial Risk Management in the Anthropocene Age

*Bradly J. Condon and Tapen Sinha*

## Introduction

According to the 2018 Intergovernmental Panel on Climate Change (IPCC) report, if global warming continues to increase at the current rate (the so-called business-as-usual scenario) global temperatures are likely to reach 1.5 °C between 2030 and 2052. Limiting global warming to 1.5 °C is affordable and feasible but requires immediate action. Climate-related risks for natural and human systems depend on the magnitude and rate of warming, geographic location, levels of development and vulnerability, and on the choices and implementation of adaptation and mitigation options. Climate-related risks to health, livelihoods, food security, water supply, human security, and economic growth are projected to increase

We gratefully acknowledge ITAM and the Asociación Mexicana de Cultura for their generous support of this research. The opinions expressed in this chapter are the sole responsibility of the authors.

B. J. Condon (✉) • T. Sinha
Instituto Tecnologico Autonomo de Mexico (ITAM), Mexico City, Mexico
e-mail: tapen@itam.mx



T. Walker et al. (eds.), *Ecological, Societal, and Technological Risks and the Financial Sector*, Palgrave Studies in Sustainable Business In Association with Future Earth, https://doi.org/10.1007/978-3-030-38858-4_12

with global warming of 1.5 °C and increase further with 2 °C. Estimates of the global emissions outcome of current nationally stated mitigation ambitions as submitted under the Paris Agreement will result in global warming of about 3 °C by 2100, with warming continuing afterward.

The climate risks that we set out below are very serious. The worst-case scenario is catastrophic. Additionally, climate risks create challenges and opportunities for the financial industry, particularly insurance. In this chapter we first set out the risks posed by climate change, and then we seek some possible solutions to reduce emissions (often referred to as climate change mitigation) and to adapt to climate change. We show that financial markets can be harnessed to reduce emissions through market mechanisms. In particular, markets can put a price on risk. That allows insurance/reinsurance companies to step in with appropriate solutions and create incentives for emissions reductions and climate change adaption. Emissions reductions will reduce the risk of catastrophic climate change. However, some climate change is already inevitable. Therefore, adaptation is essential.

## The Risks from Climate Change

The destabilizing effects of the climate crisis will have both ecological and financial consequences. We examine some worst-case scenarios for the twenty-first century, in order to highlight the importance of managing the risk of catastrophic economic, ecological, and security consequences arising from the worsening climate crisis.

Scientists cannot predict the future climate with precision. The conservative estimates of the IPCC mentioned above are not the only estimates available. For example, one estimate of the range of probabilities points to a global increase of the average temperature of between 2.6 °C (4.7 °F) and 4.8 °C (8.6 °F) between 2000 and 2100 (i.e., in addition to the warming that already occurred up to 2000) (Collins et al. 2013). This does not mean that the extra 1.1, compared to earlier IPCC estimates, will be in the last 50 years until 2100. Rather, it means that the pace and magnitude of climate change are not capable of precise calculations. The range of probabilities depends on the model used, the amount of emissions, and whether a particular amount of climate change leads to events that accelerate climate change further. Land will warm faster than oceans, and the Arctic will warm faster than the tropics (Collins et al. 2013). Climate change could cause abrupt changes, including to the Atlantic meridional overturning circulation (AMOC), the Arctic sea ice, the Greenland ice sheet, the Amazon forest, and the monsoonal circulations, as it has in the past in periods of much slower climate change (Collins et al. 2013). According to a United Nations report released on September 22, 2019, climate impacts are hitting harder and sooner than climate assessments indicated even a decade ago, and interacting tipping points could lead to a cascading effect where the Earth's temperature heats up by a catastrophic 4 °C–5 °C (Kabat et al. 2019).

The melting of the Greenland and Antarctic ice sheets may accelerate into a sudden loss of large amounts of ice, leading to dramatic changes in sea levels and ocean circulation (Bamber et al. 2019; Holland et al. 2019). Indeed, a catastrophic sea level increase is already unstoppable (Englander 2019). In the past, 400 parts per million (ppm) concentration of carbon dioxide ($CO_2$) in the atmosphere coincided with a sea level rise of 16 meters (Dumitru et al. 2019). We have already passed the 410 ppm mark. By 2050, low-lying megacities and small island nations will face extreme sea level events annually; by 2100 extreme sea level events will occur at least annually at most locations under all scenarios (IPCC 2019).

The melting of the Arctic permafrost could rapidly release methane, which would create a feedback loop of increased warming that releases further methane emissions (IPCC 2019). When seawater will have absorbed so much $CO_2$, becoming saturated and unable to absorb any more, the rate of greenhouse warming will increase dramatically. To meet the goal of the Paris Climate Agreement, to limit global warming "to well below 2 °C above pre-industrial levels and to pursue efforts to limit the temperature increase to 1.5 °C above pre-industrial levels," global emissions must peak by 2020 (Revill et al. 2017).

Climate change may also have political and social unrest issues. Drought may have contributed to the war in Syria, which produced a flood of migrants that set the stage for Brexit and other destabilizing political movements in the European Union (EU) (Kelley et al. 2015; Selby et al. 2017; De Châtel 2014). Similarly, climate change may have played a role in the flows of migrants from Central America, through Mexico, to the United States, by making subsistence farming less viable. This event led to other political and economic repercussions as the Trump administration threatened Mexico with trade sanctions for failure to stem the flow of migrants (Grant 2019; CRP, 2019; Kuil et al. 2016).

Science can attribute extreme weather events to climate change, such as the record-breaking heat waves in Europe in June, July, and August of

2019 (Vautard et al. 2019). Vulnerability to climate change varies between countries and between populations within countries, due to factors such as geography, income inequality, capacity to adapt to climate risks, and political systems. For example, the major emerging markets of Brazil, Russia, India, and China (BRIC) face different levels of climate risk locally and create different magnitudes of climate risk globally, as does the United States. Climate change is likely to increase economic inequality between and within these and other countries (Diffenbaugh and Burke 2019).

A recent study has estimated the economic cost of climate change by country, measured as the social cost of carbon per ton of $CO_2$ ($tCO_2$). India's is the highest (US$86 per $tCO_2$), followed by the United States (US$48 per $tCO_2$), Saudi Arabia (US$47 per $tCO_2$), Brazil (US$24 per $tCO_2$), China (US$24 per $tCO_2$), and the United Arab Emirates (US$24 per $tCO_2$). Northern Europe, Canada, and the Former Soviet Union are expected to have a net benefit because their current temperatures are below the economic optimum (Ricke et al. 2018). Another study predicts that the negative impact of climate change on economic growth, measured as the percent loss in gross domestic product (GDP) per capita by 2100 with no climate change mitigation, will be worse for the countries with the greatest temperature increases, which includes Russia (12.46%), India (13.39%), and the United States (14.32%) (Kahn et al. 2019).

China is the largest emitter of greenhouse gases (GHGs) but is making significant progress addressing mitigation. China's total emissions from fossil fuel and industrial processes are projected to peak 5–10 years ahead of its 2030 target in the Paris Agreement, with carbon emissions peaking for most cities at a per capita GDP (in 2011 purchasing power parity) of US$19,000–22,000 (Wang et al. 2019). Locally, air pollution has serious implications for public health in China. Globally, its emissions add to climate risk for all countries.

India's large population of subsistence farmers is vulnerable to floods, droughts, and famines, while India's cities are vulnerable to heat waves and floods. Indeed, climate change has shifted agriculture and subsistence strategies in the Indian subcontinent before, to adopt more drought-tolerant crops, and served as a catalyst for the de-urbanization of the Harappan civilization (Sarkar et al. 2016; Kathayat et al. 2017). While richer countries can adapt to their cities' heat waves (Vautard et al. 2019), India is unlikely to fall into this category. Indian cities will struggle to handle heat waves which can lead to the death of many of its citizens. Even if wealth increases, India has severe economic inequalities, which means that there will still be large numbers of vulnerable people who are unable to adapt through accommodations such as air-conditioning. In urban areas, it is the poorest and most vulnerable who are more likely to perish from a heat wave. While the links between climate change, migration, and conflict are complex, the effects of climate change on subsistence farmers could produce waves of climate migrants from India that would dwarf the flows seen thus far from Syria and Latin America, since their crops would fail and they would be forced off their land (Brzoska and Fröhlich 2016; Reuveny 2007). Thus, the consequences will be felt beyond India.

In Russia, forest fires in boreal forests are likely to increase dramatically, with far-reaching ecological and socioeconomic consequences (Kelly et al. 2013; WMO, 2019; RFERL 2019; NASA, 2019). Increased air pollution, combined with rising alcoholism and suicide rates, could reduce life expectancy in Russia's population (Burke et al. 2018; Razvodovsky 2015). The boreal forest fires also increase global climate risk by destroying an important carbon sink and increasing Russia's emissions.

Brazil's status as an agricultural powerhouse will decline as the effects of climate change increase; the destruction of the Amazon is likely to accelerate that process (USAID 2018; Economist 2019; NASA 2019). There is a risk that the ongoing destruction of the Amazon will pass a point of no return, in which the transition from rainforest to dry tropical forest or savannah becomes unstoppable. This threshold could be as low as 20% of the Amazon. Already, 17% has been destroyed (Temple 2019). Thus, as is the case with Russia, the destruction of the Amazon increases economic risk to Brazil and global climate risk, by destroying an important carbon sink and increasing emissions.

Science can observe the effects of catastrophic climate events, such as droughts and floods. Climate change threatens the four pillars of food security: availability (yield and production), access (prices and ability to obtain food), utilization (nutrition and cooking), and stability (disruptions to availability) (IPCC 2019). Human innovations can move the dial, for example, with crops genetically modified to withstand drought or with improved irrigation systems, both of which are relevant to crop insurance. If technology develops effective approaches to mitigation and adaptation, we might experience less than the worst-case scenario. Insurance policies implement incentives to create and adopt these technologies, as we discuss below.

We are facing an existential threat to civilization and our survival as a species (Spratt and Dunlop 2019). Climate change is difficult to address as every country has its own vulnerabilities and inequalities. Political responses to climate change, such as catastrophic crop failures and the related issue of mass migration of refugees, will have to take multiple insurance issues into account. Crop insurance can help farmers manage the risk of crop failures, but food shortages have consequences on human health, which has implications for health insurance. The mass migration of refugees also has serious implications for health insurance, particularly in countries with already overburdened public health insurance schemes. The effects of the climate crisis will only accelerate from this point on, increasing such politically destabilizing consequences, such as opposition to trade and migration.

As a result of the ever-shifting range of possible climate change scenarios, the time frame for climate change predictions is not precise. Science can show us how to mitigate climate change, how to adapt to climate change, and what the factors are that make one country, or one population, more vulnerable than another. However, the degree of climate change and the speed with which it takes place will depend on political will and technological developments, as well as the unforeseeable magnitude of shifts in the climate system. A climate-induced financial crisis would further complicate efforts to address the climate crisis (Rudebusch 2019; Andreas et al. 2019).

## The Markets for Pollution Permits

Financial and insurance markets can play critical roles in mitigating emissions and adapting to the effects of climate change. The financial industry can contribute to mitigation through cap-and-trade markets. As we shall see in this chapter, these markets reduce the growth of new emissions, by capping emissions, distributing emissions permits, and allowing polluters to trade emissions permits in a market. They also encourage better mitigation strategies for countries because they create incentives for innovations in the polluting industries that lower the costs of emissions below the cost of the emissions permits. The insurance industry can contribute to both mitigation and adaptation. Insurance and reinsurance companies naturally take a long-term view of the types of risks associated with climate change because the entire business of insurance is based on pricing risks. For example, rising seas and more intense hurricanes will bring more flooding to coastal communities. Insurance and reinsurance companies can measure those risks and price insurance policies on buildings and municipal governments accordingly. They can create incentives for their clients to mitigate and adapt to those risks. For example, they can encourage municipalities to refuse building permits on flood plains and discourage homeowners from rebuilding a home that was destroyed by floods. When a flood destroys a home, if the insurance company refuses to insure the municipality against lawsuits for having issued a building permit for a new one or refuses to insure the new home against flood risks, the owner is unlikely to invest in rebuilding the flooded home.

In this section, we first analyze how the lessons learned from sulfur dioxide ($SO_2$) markets in the United States can be applied to $CO_2$ markets. Then, we discuss two $CO_2$ markets—one compulsory and one voluntary. In the following section, we discuss the role of insurance and reinsurance markets in the context of adaptation and mitigation strategies for climate change.

### *Mitigation Lessons from $SO_2$ Market*

The traditional approach to reduce pollution was a "command and control" regulation, until the $SO_2$ market came along. In the command and control method, a government determines a pollution target and decides by how much each polluting agent has to reduce pollution (EPA 2017). This is usually done by setting a uniform emissions rate for a class of emitters (such as a fixed rate for electric utility company per ton of coal used) or by mandating a specific type of pollution-control equipment (such as a scrubber, regardless of the technology being used). This "one size fits all" approach ignores the heterogeneity of types of technologies that exist in the industry. As a result, the cost of compliance varies considerably across plants of different vintages.

Why did the Environmental Protection Agency (EPA) target the electric utilities for their $SO_2$ emissions? Electric utilities accounted for about 70% of $SO_2$ emissions in 1990. Coal-fired electric generation units accounted for 96% of this total, and oil-fired units accounted for the remainder. The other 30% of emissions were accounted for by a wide variety of industrial/commercial/residential boilers, smelters, paper mills, and other process-oriented sources (EPA 2019).

The $SO_2$ market, operating in the United States since 1995, became the first cap-and-trade market in the world to operate successfully. There are lessons to be learned from that for the $CO_2$ market. Therefore, we take a closer look at the $SO_2$ market.

In 1990, the Clean Air Act Amendments established the Title IV Acid Rain Program (ARP). The amendment (in the Title IV) of the Clean Air Act mandated requirements for the control of acid deposition—also known as acid rain. The Clean Air Act Amendments of 1990 set a goal of reducing annual $SO_2$ emissions by 10 million tons below 1980 levels. To achieve these reductions, the law required a two-phase tightening of the restrictions placed on fossil fuel-fired power plants.

*How Does One Go About Creating Such Markets?*

First, to set the parameters, the legislators have to come together to pass certain laws. The political economy of such rule-making is messy (Joskow and Schmalensee 1998). Any new legislation produces winners, who benefit economically from the new laws, and losers, who suffer economically. New legislation can have differing effects as it is difficult to benefit everyone affected by the legislative change. In the case of $SO_2$ it was no different. There were states that produced coal and were net exporters to other states. Some states produced and used coal for power generation but did not export either to other states. In addition, there were states that did neither but were affected by acid rain for being located in the neighborhood. In the United States every state is different in its production and export markets; therefore the $SO_2$ regulations affected some positively and some negatively. As a large producer of coal, West Virginia was a clear loser because the $SO_2$ regulations made coal a less profitable energy source for electricity generation companies to use.

We note that this problem looms larger in the case of $CO_2$ because the inequality between states in the United States is much smaller than the inequality that exists between countries. Therefore, any practical solution to the $CO_2$ problem must address the problem of political economy inherent in these issues. Otherwise, proposed solutions are doomed to fail as was demonstrated clearly by the failure of the Kyoto Protocol (Kutney 2014).

Second, regulators have to set up regulatory parameters based on the laws enacted. They must anticipate whether such regulations would produce perverse reactions or unintended negative consequences somewhere else. Essentially, they have to produce regulation to properly internalize the externality created by $CO_2$ emissions that leads to market failure.

Third, once the regulation is set forth, institutions have to be built for permit exchange. There has to be constant vigilance to prevent fraudulent activities. Additional legal institutions might be necessary for such new activities to take place.

Finally, a new legion of traders has to be trained and the buyers and the sellers of the permits have to be educated. At every stage, a number of lawyers will have to be involved to make sure all the transactions are admissible.

For the $SO_2$ market, Phase I of the process began operating in 1995. It was targeted to 263 units at 110 coal-burning electric utility plants located in 21 Eastern and Midwestern states of the United States. An additional 182 units were added to the Phase I of the program as substitution or compensating units, bringing the total of affected units to 445 in Phase I.

The idea of the market was simple. The EPA would auction permits (each representing one ton of pollution). Then, private companies would trade these permits in a specially created product at the Chicago Board of Trade. Once the permits were auctioned, they were resold in the private market. The price was determined by demand and supply, not just in the spot market, but also by the expected future value of each permit. Thus, expectation plays a vital role in the market for permits (see Fig. 12.1 for the market prices).

In the first 12–18-month period, there were a handful of traders. The price was in the US$250–300 per ton range. By the end of 1994, the price had dropped below US$150 per ton, and the volume of private trades exceeded the volume offered in the EPA auction (see Fig. 12.1). The prices had fallen to about US$100 per ton by 1998, and private trading of allowances for more than 5 million tons per year that had eclipsed the EPA auction by a factor of 15 to 1. The costs of trading allowances were 2% of the prevailing price (see Fig. 12.1).

The prices of traded permits were very close to one another. For example, the spread between average bids and lowest winning bids at EPA auctions was 1–3% (of the price) and trading in the private market appeared to be similarly concentrated around a single price. The $SO_2$ program spurred innovation in the technology of power plants because compliance would reduce the cost of operation. All the new plants installed scrubbers to reduce $SO_2$ emissions.

The technology also had a spillover effect. It reduced other harmful emissions such as NOx, mercury, lead, and microscopic particles because the process of $SO_2$ reduction not only reduces $SO_2$ but also reduces other microscopic particles (Advanced Technologies for the Control of Sulfur Dioxide Emissions from Coal-Fired Boilers 1999). Another innovation

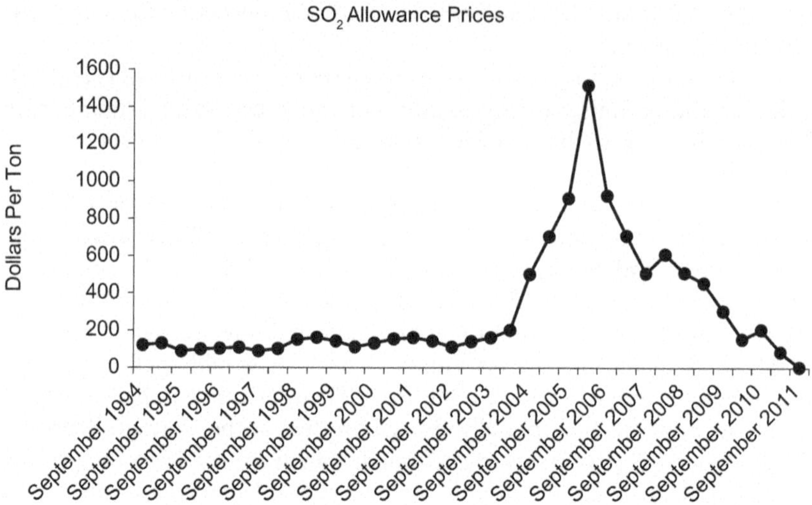


**Fig. 12.1** Prices of the traded permits in $SO_2$ market 1994–2012. Source: EPA (2019). Compilation by the authors

was in the mining techniques for extracting lower-sulfur coal seams. These were known methods in the coal industry, but they were not in wide use because there was no incentive for this method. Another benefit from the $SO_2$ program was the re-examination of the old industry standards to find low-cost modifications to reduce $SO_2$. One example of this was the blending of low-sulfur and high-sulfur coal (Chen et al. 2012). The industry standard did not allow large-scale blending for it was believed that the boilers would not function correctly. That belief turned out to be wrong. A change in the mentality of the industry and the reincorporation of large-scale blending allowed the combination of low- and high-sulfur coast blending without costly modifications to the equipment (Paul 2004).

The Acid Rain Program (ARP) also generated innovations in the management practices of the utilities (EPA 1995). It encouraged the utilities to seek to streamline the fluctuation in the input cost through activities in the futures markets for coal and oil as uncertainty in cost increases the cost of production. As a result, the power generating utility companies were able to reduce their overall cost of production.

Phase II began in 2000 with more stringent annual emissions limits imposed on large, higher emitting plants (in 1995, 263 generating units at 110 mostly coal-burning electric utility plants located in 21 Eastern and Midwestern US states were identified as "large, higher emitting plants"). It also set restrictions on smaller, cleaner plants fired by coal, oil, and gas, encompassing over 2000 power generating units in total. The program incorporated existing utility units serving generators with an output capacity of greater than 25 megawatts and all new utility units.

In Table 12.1, we reproduce the winners of the permits auctioned by the EPA in 1995. There are names that we expect for such bids, such as Duke Power and Virginia Power. They are companies that were buying

**Table 12.1** Winning bidders for the 1995 $SO_2$ permits

| *Bidder's name* | *Quantity* | *Percent of total* | *Cost* |
|---|---|---|---|
| Duke Power Company | 17,750 | 35.1% | $2,332,500 |
| PECO Energy Company | 8000 | 15.8% | $1,061,000 |
| Cantor Fitzgerald Brokerage, L.P. | 8000 | 15.8% | $1,058,000 |
| Virginia Power | 6000 | 11.9% | $800,000 |
| Canterbury Coal Company | 4000 | 7.9% | $520,000 |
| Detroit Edison Company | 2952 | 5.8% | $386,712 |
| Allowance Holdings Corporation | 2160 | 4.3% | $280,800 |
| Hoosier Energy REC, Inc. Ratts Unit 2SG1 | 500 | 1.0% | $68,000 |
| Marine Coal Sales Company | 500 | 1.0% | $67,500 |
| National Healthy Air License Exchange | 135 | 0.3% | $18,350 |
| Sam Peltzman Revocable Trust | 50 | 0.1% | $7050 |
| INHALE/Glens Falls, NY Middle School | 21 | <0.1% | $3171 |
| CATEX Vitol Electric Inc. | 12 | <0.1% | $1584 |
| University of Michigan Environmental Law Society | 5 | <0.1% | $1000 |
| Environment Law Students Association | 2 | <0.1% | $410 |
| Hamline University School of Law | 2 | <0.1% | $350 |
| New England School of Law | 1 | <0.1% | $350 |
| Electric Software Products David Gloski | 1 | 0.01% | $300 |
| Electric Software Products Alexander Long | 1 | 0.01% | $300 |
| Thomas M. Cooley Environment Law Society | 1 | <0.1% | $200 |
| Duke University School of the Environment | 1 | <0.1% | $176 |
| Michael S. Hamilton | 1 | <0.1% | $170 |
| Pollution Retirement Center | 1 | <0.1% | $160 |
| L.J. O'Callaghan, Sr. | 1 | <0.1% | $153 |
| University of Maryland School of Law | 1 | <0.1% | $150 |
| Total | 50,600 | 100.0% | $6,676,386 |

Source: EPA (2019). Compilation by the authors

permits for their own use. However, some buyers didn't intend to purchase these permits for profit or speculation. These nonspeculative, nonprofit-maximizing buyers included several law schools and societies, as well as the Pollution Retirement Center. They were buying these permits not only for profit or speculation but to participate in the market for the explicit purpose of reducing the number of permits that the other market players could have, so that in the aggregate there would be less pollution. In the end, they were very minor players and they did not affect the market price or quantity in any significant way. Ultimately, they did not make much of a difference in the market. However, this practice highlights the possibility that in other circumstance, other entities can enter the market and change the market dynamics.

In 2003, following the success of $SO_2$ trading, the NOx Budget Trading Program (NBP) started in nine states. The NBP was a cap-and-trade program that required emissions reductions from power plants and industrial plants in the Eastern United States during the summer months. The program was to last until 2008. Meanwhile, the Bush administration tried but failed to tighten the $SO_2$ emissions through the Clear Skies Act. It died at the committee level in the Congress (Chen et al. 2012).

The Bush administration then came up with the Clean Air Interstate Rule (CAIR) in 2005. The purpose was to lower the $SO_2$ emissions to a level 70% below the 2003 level (McLean 2008). CAIR tried to achieve this by reducing the cap by two-thirds in some of the states that were not part of the original ARP—it intended to include 28 Eastern states plus the District of Columbia by replacing the entire ARP with CAIR. The aim was to reduce interstate transport of pollution from upwind states to downwind states. This action had a clear impact on the $SO_2$ price in the market. It shot up nearly threefold. However, the entire structure of the CAIR was based on the so-called good neighbor policy interpretation of the Clean Air Act Clause §110(a)(2)(D)(i)(I) (McLean 2008).

Not surprisingly, various states (principally Michigan, Minnesota, and North Carolina) were opposed to the CAIR. In July 2008, the US Court of Appeals for the District of Columbia Circuit declared that the CAIR cap-and-trade method was fundamentally flawed, concluding that the EPA focused on region-wide emission reductions and did not adequately factor in each state's significant contribution to air pollution issues. It declared that the methods for determining $SO_2$ and NOx pollution were not objective. The court held that the EPA lacked authority to remove the Acid Rain Program allowances through CAIR (Chen et al. 2012).

To salvage the situation, the EPA finalized the Cross-State Air Pollution Rule (CSAPR) to replace CAIR. This rule responded to the court's concerns and fulfilled the "good neighbor" provision of the Clean Air Act by addressing the problem of air pollution that is transported across state borders. The "good neighbor" provision means one state must be a "good neighbor" by not polluting a neighboring state with its emissions of $SO_2$. The court decision of 2008 and the subsequent maneuver by the EPA to resurrect the $SO_2$ market through other mechanisms failed. Predictably, the price of $SO_2$ permits went down to virtually zero. The introduction of the CSAPR did not fare much better. In another lawsuit, the CSAPR was also struck down in August 2012. The courts decided that the EPA failed to show that the "downwind states" are different from "upwind states." In addition, the EPA did not give the affected states enough time to come up with their own solution (EME Homer City v. EPA 2012).

In spite of the litigation setbacks suffered by the EPA with respect to $SO_2$ emissions, there is no doubt about the overall success of the program. We will discuss three dimensions of success.

First, the program managed to reduce the $SO_2$ emissions much faster than what was originally stipulated by the EPA. This dimension is illustrated in Fig. 12.2. Overall $SO_2$ emissions were reduced from about 23,000 tons per year in 1990 to less than 7000 tons per year in 2011. One common criticism of this reduction examines the reduction in emissions between 1970 and 1990. During that period too, there was a reduction in $SO_2$ emissions. Therefore, it is argued that the reductions during the two decades after 1990 were going to happen with or without the ARP.

To understand the impact of the ARP, we need to examine exactly from where such a reduction in $SO_2$ emissions came. Recall that ARP was directed squarely at the power utilities. In Fig. 12.2 we examine two separate sources—the utilities and others. In 1990, the utilities accounted for two-thirds of all the $SO_2$ emissions. The electric utilities were the principal source of reductions during the following two decades. The rest did not have much of a reduction. This evidence gives us a clear indication that the $SO_2$ reduction was not simply a "natural" reduction with better technologies from all sources. The ARP was indeed the catalyst for such a change.

Second, the EPA has documented the dramatic changes in geographical distribution of sulfate deposition in the United States between 1989 and 2011. From Illinois, Indiana, Ohio, and Pennsylvania to all the way up to Maine, the sulfate deposit has been reduced at least by half in most states. In some states, the reduction has been over 70%. There is no doubt that

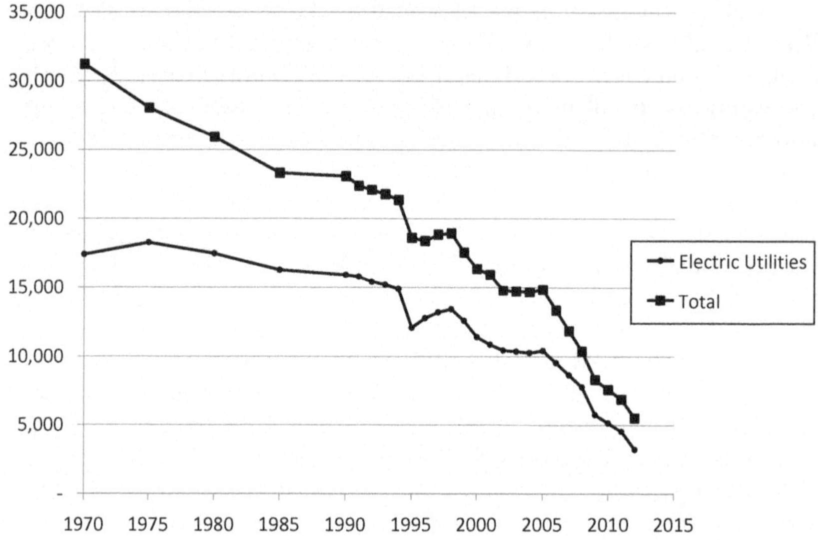


**Fig. 12.2** Thousands of tons of $SO_2$ emitted in 1970–2012. Source: EPA (2019). Compilation by the authors

this reduction was largely caused by the Acid Rain Program because, in the previous decade, the reduction was about 5%.

Third, as a consequence of the reduction in pollution in the Midwestern and Northeastern states of the United States, where nearly 40% of the US population lives, large benefits have been accruing due to (1) health impact, (2) improved land value for agriculture, and (3) ecological impact. The value of such benefits has been calculated by the EPA. We demonstrate the impact in Fig. 12.3.

Figure 12.3 shows the monetized value of cumulative benefits coming from the $SO_2$ reduction program. The value is measured in terms of reduction of lost lives, reduction of respiratory diseases, improved recreational facilities, and ecological improvement, among other things. Estimated median value of such gains for 2000 was US$700 billion, rising to US$1300 billion in 2010 and to US$2000 billion in 2020. The EPA also estimated the minimum and maximum gains for each of those years as we illustrate in Fig. 12.3. These are extremely large gains. To get an idea of

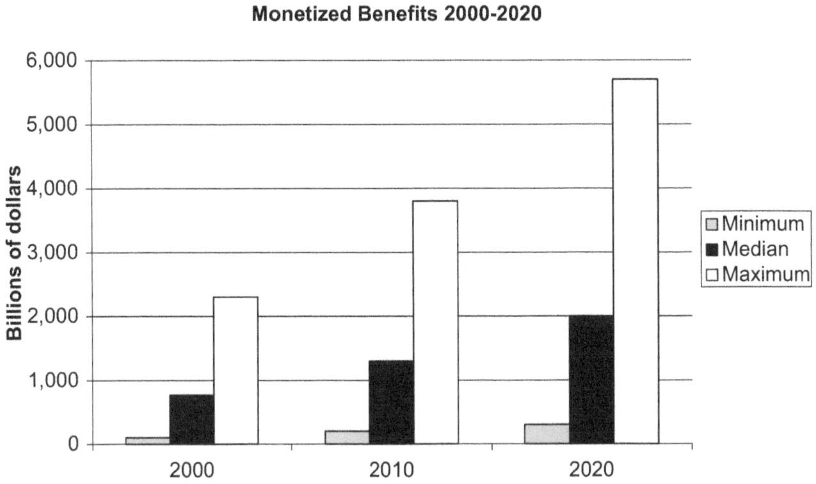


**Fig. 12.3** Monetized benefits 2000–2020. Source: Author calculation based on EPA (2009)

the magnitude, the US GDP for the year 2011 was estimated at US$15,000 billion.

The $SO_2$ experiment shows that cap-and-trade can actually work in real life. While the gains in terms of morbidity and mortality were not well understood at the time when the plan was implemented, it became clear later. These additional benefits of reduced mortality eclipsed the original benefits of reduced morbidity posited when the implementation was being debated in the US Congress.

### *$CO_2$ Markets*

This discussion about $SO_2$ brings us to the question of $CO_2$ emissions and cap-and-trade markets for $CO_2$. The first serious stab at reducing $CO_2$ emissions came with the Kyoto Protocol. The Kyoto Protocol set binding targets for 37 industrialized countries and the European Community for reducing GHG emissions. The goal was to reduce the GHG emissions of these countries in 2008–2012 to a level of 5% below the level of emissions of 1990. The detailed rules for the implementation of the Protocol were adopted at the 2001 Conference of Parties (COP 7) in Marrakesh and came into effect on February 16, 2005 (UNFCCC 2019). Under the

United Nations Framework Convention on Climate Change (UNFCCC), the countries needed to meet the emissions standards with national measures. However, the Protocol created flexibility. It allowed each country to meet the targets with additional measures: (1) cap-and-trade, (2) Clean Development Mechanism (CDM), and (3) Joint Implementation (JI). Below we briefly discuss the CDM and the JI. The most important element of the Kyoto Protocol, the cap-and-trade markets, is discussed in greater detail at the end.

Under the CDM, emissions-reduction projects in developing countries can earn certified emission reduction credits. Industries in the developed countries can use these saleable credits to meet a limited part of their emissions-reduction targets under the Kyoto Protocol.

One key element of the CDM is the mechanism for verifying compliance of whether the proposed reduction in emission has been achieved. Some are easy to verify. For example, one of the projects funded for the CDM was the Delhi Metro (CDM 2019). It was fairly easy to calculate the benefits of $CO_2$ accrued due to the project. Similarly, another project funded was the 2012 extension of the Mexico City Metro. For these kinds of projects, compliance was not a problem.

There are, however, potential problems with the CDM. It has been argued by some advocates of small-scale developments that the CDM would allow large companies in developed countries to impose projects that are not in the best interests of host countries (UNEP 2019). The CDM now requires that host countries verify that CDM projects contribute to their own sustainable development. Such certification processes are also not without problems. Since developing country government officials are often susceptible to bribes, it is possible that such processes can be corrupted easily (Olken and Pande 2012).

Joint Implementation (the third measure) means one country in Annex I can implement a project in another country in Annex I to reduce $CO_2$ emissions to earn credits for reducing emissions. The aim of JI is to encourage clean energy technology use in the so-called transition economies—the countries of the former "Eastern Bloc" (countries such as the Russian Federation and Ukraine that lack modern technology for power generation and other areas).

The logic behind the Kyoto Protocol can be illustrated by the following (see Fig. 12.4). In 2010, total emissions in the world were about 43 gigatons of $CO_2$. By 2050, they are slated to grow to over 70 gigatons per year

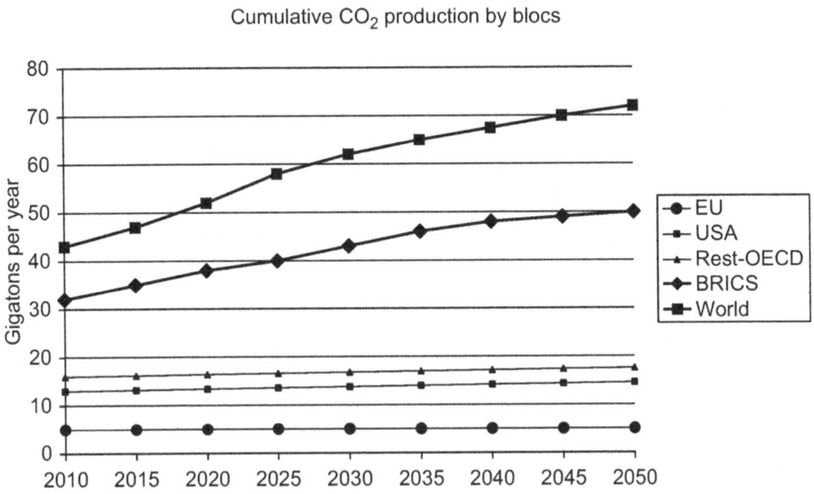


**Fig. 12.4** $CO_2$ emissions up to 2050 by blocks of countries. Source: Author calculations based on various IPCC reports

if nothing is done. The emissions would not change much in the European Union over the next 40 years. They would go up marginally in the United States and the rest of the Organisation for Economic Co-operation and Development. However, the main growth of the emissions would come from Brazil, Russia, India, China, and South Africa and from the rest of the world if nothing is done. Therefore, to make any headway into a possible future reduction, two things have to happen. First, there has to be an absolute reduction in emissions in the developed world, which accounts for nearly 40% of the emissions today but contains less than 20% of the world's population (see Fig. 12.4). Second, the developing countries need to have the technology of the developed world today in order to reduce their emissions.

### *Compulsory and Voluntary Markets for $CO_2$*

In this section, we discuss two separate markets: one compulsory (European Union Emissions Trading System [EU ETS]) and one voluntary (Chicago Carbon Exchange [CCX]).

*Compulsory Market: EU ETS*

As a direct result of signing the Kyoto Protocol, the European Union set up the EU ETS emissions trading system for 11,300 energy-intensive installations across the 27 Member States. In the Kyoto Protocol, the EU set its emissions-reduction target to 8% by 2012 compared with the level observed in 1990. This goal was modified into emissions-reduction objectives at the Member State level following the so-called Burden Sharing Agreements. In 2003, Directive 2003/87/EC established a scheme for greenhouse gas emission allowance trading within the community and amending Council Directive 96/61/EC, creating the EU ETS. It explicitly recognized the following six gases as greenhouse gases: carbon dioxide, methane (CH4), nitrous oxide (N2O), hydrofluorocarbons (HFCs), perfluorocarbons (PFCs), and sulfur hexafluoride (SF6). The scheme covered about half of all GHGs at the EU level.

There were four phases of the market envisioned in the plan (EU ETS 2019).

Phase I went from 2005 to 2007—the so-called warm-up period prior to the introduction of the Kyoto Protocol. Phase II went from 2008 to 2012. It is concomitant to the Kyoto Protocol. Phase III went into effect from 2013 to 2020. Phase III corresponds to the objectives of the EU "Energy-Climate Package" introduced in January 2008 to reduce emissions by 20% by 2020 along with increasing energy efficiency by 20% and increasing the share of renewable resources in the energy mix to 20%. This plan became known as the "20-20-20 target." Phase IV envisions full implementation of the Paris Agreement target by 2030.

The allowance for one contract exchanged on the EU ETS corresponds to one ton of $CO_2$ released into the atmosphere. It is called a European Union Allowance (EUA). For the Phase I, 2.2 billion allowances per year were distributed (2005–2007). During the Phase II (2008–2012), 2.08 billion allowances per year were distributed.

Figure 12.5 displays the movement of daily EUA prices between 2005 and 2008 for the contracts expiring in 2007 and 2008. The first notable feature of the prices is that they were volatile. It covered an enormous range over a relatively short period of time.

The second feature is that the EUA 2007 and EUA 2008 prices moved in tandem and close to each other over a year before the dramatic fall of the EUA 2007 price. Since EUA 2007 contracts did not have much value after 2007, it was expected that the prices would diverge at the end. But when they were both valuable, both the prices were close. In economic

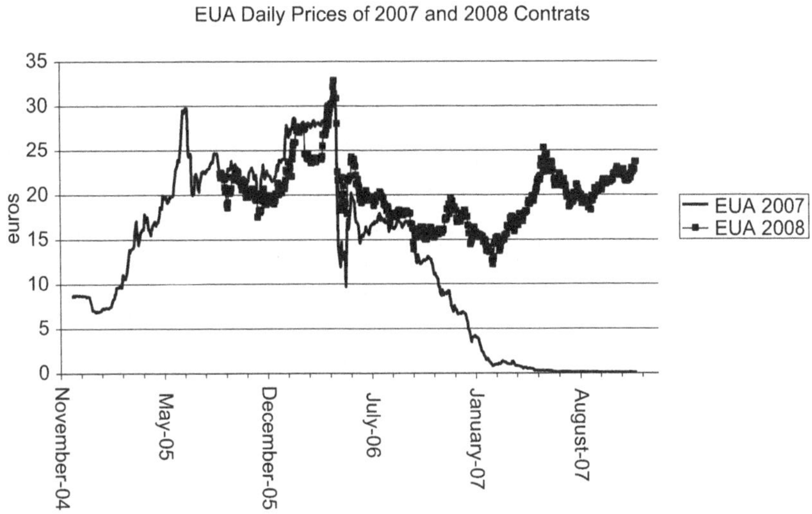


**Fig. 12.5** EUA 2007 and EUA 2008 prices in the EU ETA market. Source: EU ETS (2019) data extracted and graphed by the authors

terms, these products were close substitutes for a while and therefore had very similar prices. This phenomenon is called the "law of one price" in economics. It is often used as an acid test for understanding the pricing of a product. As we will see below, the price in other parts of the world for one ton of carbon has not been the same. This illustrates that the price is critically dependent not just on the current laws governing the market but also on future expectations about the legal status of the market. For example, we saw how the successful challenge of CAIR in the courts caused the collapse of the $SO_2$ market in the United States (Chen et al. 2012).

Each year, the EU ETS issued more permits with expiry dates and then they were traded in the markets. In Fig. 12.6, we examine the co-movement of three such contracts over time: EUA 2008, EUA 2009, and EUA 2010. Once again, the prices show closeness which demonstrates that they were being treated very similarly in the marketplace.

In addition, we performed correlation analysis between the EUA 2009 and EUA 2010 prices. It shows that the correlation between the prices is 0.9988, which can also be seen when we plot these two prices together in Fig. 12.7.

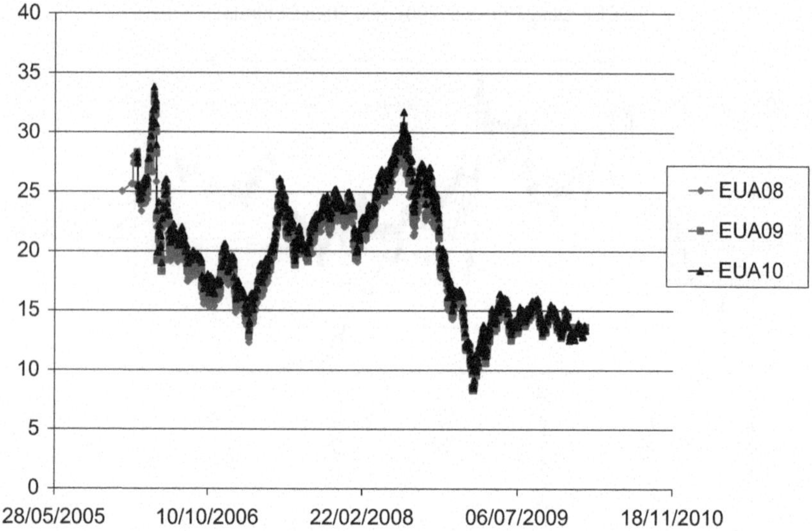


**Fig. 12.6** Co-movement prices of different contracts in the EU ETA market. Source: EU ETS (2019) data extracted and graphed by the authors

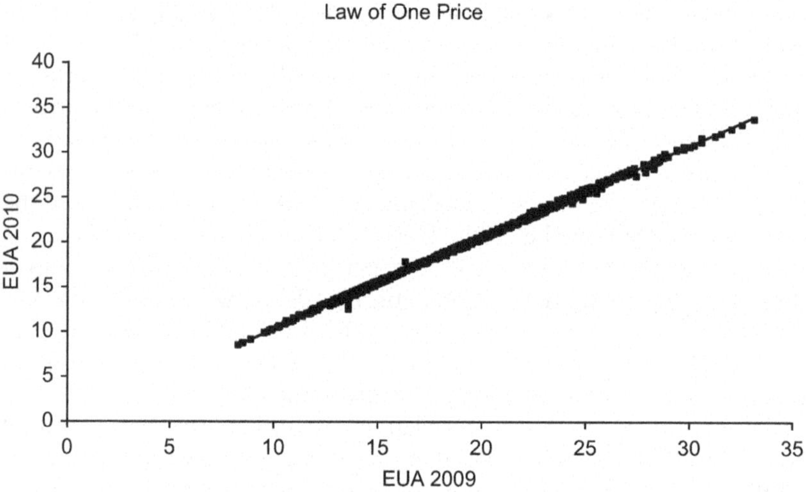


**Fig. 12.7** Law of one price in EU ETA. Source: EU ETS (2019) data extracted and graphed by the authors

The EU ETS market was a compulsory market—the companies in the EU were forced to participate. In this regard, it stands in contrast to the voluntary market that we talk about in the next section.

*Voluntary Market: Chicago Carbon Exchange*

In addition, in the United States, another experiment was conducted by a voluntary market called the Chicago Carbon Exchange. This was the brainchild of Robert Sandor (Sandor 2012). He took his cue from an observation of the economist Ronald Coase, who noticed that while economists have argued that economic agents would not pay for public goods with positive externalities (such as the maintenance of a lighthouse), the Trinity House, a private consortium, had been building lighthouses in England for five centuries and making profits (Sandor 2012).

While this was a voluntary market, over time it managed to capture 17% of the value of the companies listed in the Dow Jones Index (Sandor 2012). It represented 25% of the power industry, and during the peak year, it managed to reduce more $CO_2$ than France did (which operated under the compulsory market of the EU ETS). The CCX not only managed to do business in the US market, but it also helped to generate $CO_2$ reductions in far-flung places like Kerala, India, by getting payment for producing biogas (Kurian 2008).

In a number of villages in Andhra Pradesh and Kerala, the CCX helped develop collection of waste from cows. The cow waste was used to capture methane, which was to be used for cooking (Sandor 2012). Families received a financial incentive of about US$2 per month for collecting cow waste. As a result, the amount of GHG reduced more than offset the "cost" of carbon captured by other means, as wood burning became unnecessary. It also generated a bonus. In those villages, small school-age girls were used to fetching wood and sticks to burn for cooking. Their time was freed up, allowing them to attend school. Moreover, the use of methane burning stoves reduced the air pollution inside the huts, improving the health of those villagers (Sandor 2012).

Sandor (2012) sets out the requisites for a successful launch of financial products. First, the financial products have to be traded in a well-defined exchange. Second, the trades have to be completely transparent to all the market participants. Third, they have to be regulated. Here, he noted that it does not have to be regulated by the government. The exchange can be self-regulated (such as the lighthouses in England where a charity organization called the Trinity House runs all the lighthouses with a Royal

Charter from 1514). Finally, there should be a central clearing system in the market to minimize counterparty risk. He notes that these conditions are sufficient for a market to work, but all conditions are not necessary. Products such as interest-rate and foreign-exchange swaps are not centrally cleared, but they work well. He also insists that there has to be a standard product for the market to work well. Without a well-defined product, the market would collapse. There is also a need for evidence of ownership of the product. If property rights are not well established, the market will not work.

Sandor explains why a volunteer market like the CCX would work. There is not a single reason why all the parties came to trade. Some companies traded because they had business to conduct in the EU. That was the case with the Ford Motor Company. Baxter Laboratories traded in the market because they wanted to create goodwill. They wanted to be part of the green market. As Sandor (2012, p. 379) notes: "Baxter Laboratories was a leader in the health-care industry. Although the company's emissions were negligible, its commitment to sustainability and the public relations benefits from joining the exchange were obvious." Other companies came in because they anticipated that sooner or later the market would be implemented across the entire nation, therefore they wanted to have a practice run. In Fig. 12.8, we display the entire experiment between 2003 and 2011 with volumes that were traded in the CCX, along with the prices at which they were traded.

The Regional Greenhouse Gas Initiative (RGGI) is another mandatory program to reduce greenhouse gas emissions in the United States. The RGGI is a cooperative effort among nine Eastern states of the United States: Connecticut, Delaware, Maine, Maryland, Massachusetts, New Hampshire, New York, Rhode Island, and Vermont. Together, these states have capped and reduced $CO_2$ emissions from the power sector by about 50% between 2005 and 2018. Originally, New Jersey was also part of the RGGI. In 2012, New Jersey pulled out of the program after the governor argued that it was not an effective way of capping emissions.

In our discussion above, we observe that the price of carbon differs in different countries. The law of one price does not seem to hold, and there is a clear reason for it. The future viability of carbon markets is not clear in many places. There are potentially fatal lawsuits challenging the legality of making the trade mandatory that could invalidate the operations in some markets (such as California).

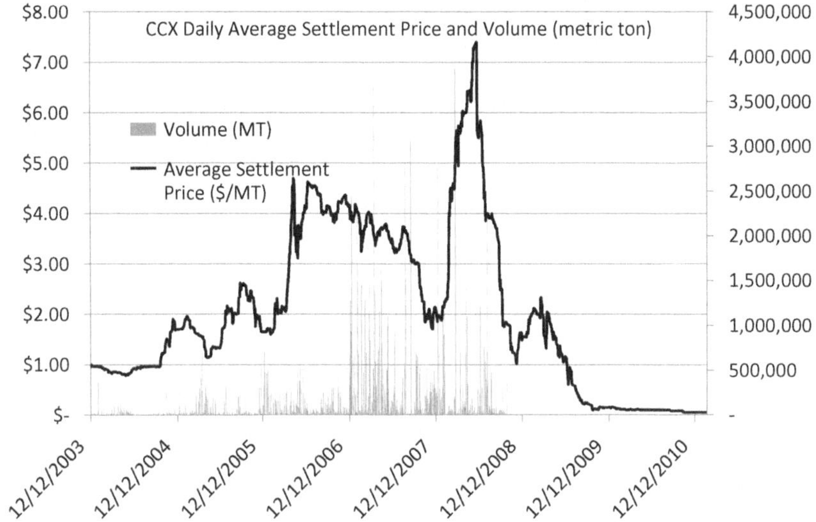


**Fig. 12.8** Chicago Climate Exchange market price and volume. Source: Data supplied personally by Richard Sandor and on file with the authors

Progress in multilateral treaty negotiations is also doubtful, with only EU countries agreeing to extend their participation in the Kyoto Protocol and the announced withdrawal of the United States from the Paris Agreement. While the 2018 Conference of Parties (COP 24) led to an agreement on implementing the Paris Agreement (the Katowice Climate Package of December 15, 2018), there will be no new targets until the COP in 2020. All of this legal uncertainty makes the same ton of $CO_2$ emissions different in various jurisdictions. On one hand, the price in the voluntary Chicago market never went above US$10 per ton. On the other hand, in the EUA markets, the prices were well above that for a period of time. This explains why prices are not (yet) equalized across countries and regions.

China has become the largest producer of $CO_2$ in the world by producing double the amount of the second biggest producer, the United States (UCS 2018). Pollution in China has become a big problem, killing more than a million persons a year and with an estimated cost of US$38 billion a year (Gu et al. 2018).

Not surprisingly, China has proposed pilot programs of cap-and-trade in five provinces and two cities for 2013: Beijing, Shanghai, Tianjin, Chongqing, Shenzhen, Guangdong, and Hubei. Some of them are cities with large industries and others are states with large industrial hubs. The markets are expected to begin trading in 2020 (Hua 2019).

Ironically, the cap-and-trade model seems especially well suited to address the problem of climate change, in that emitted GHGs are evenly distributed throughout the world's atmosphere. Emissions reductions anywhere make identical contributions to help alleviate the problem, and there are no pollutant concentration hot spots. The number and variety of GHG emissions sources increase the practical difficulty of developing a comprehensive and effective command-and-control approach. Additionally, it magnifies the cost savings that could be achieved by enlisting the market to find the least costly abatement options.

As we saw earlier in our discussion of the $SO_2$ market, the "one size fits all" approach of mandatory pollution controls ignores the heterogeneity of types of technologies that exist in a particular industry, such as electricity generation plants. As a result, the cost of compliance would vary considerably across plants of different vintages, depending on their technological starting point, making this type of environmental regulation less cost-efficient than cap-and-trade. This is because a cap-and-trade program imposes an overall pollution limit for the emissions, distributes permits up to that limit, and then allows the plants to buy and sell pollution permits. Plants that can reduce emissions more cheaply than the cost of permits do so and sell their permits to plants for which reductions are more costly than the cost of buying pollution permits. In this way, emissions reductions occur first where they are least costly to achieve. Over time, the cap-and-trade program reduces the overall pollution limit for the emissions for the industry as a whole.

It is difficult to achieve an international agreement to limit GHG emissions, however, for precisely the same reasons, many countries, hosting many emissions sources, must agree to take action. Given the complexities of either developing a domestic US cap-and-trade system for GHGs or obtaining congressional approval for an international system in which the United States participates, it is likely that at least as much bipartisan (between the Democrats and the Republicans parties) collaboration would be required as was evident in the process to enact the Clean Air Act Amendments that established the Acid Rain Program. Instead, we have much less. This is because of the concerns regarding the effects of mandatory GHG emissions reductions on the competitiveness and profitability of the affected industries.

If one country requires its industry to reduce emissions, this implies higher compliance costs for that industry. If other countries do not require emissions reductions, their industry will not face the same additional costs. This would give the nonregulated country's industry a competitive advantage over the regulated country's industry. Domestically, the regulated industry resists regulation that would increase its production costs and impair profits. The regulated industry also resists regulation that would increase its production costs, impair profits, and shift production to competitors in other countries that face less regulatory costs. In international negotiations, countries seek advantages for their own industries by arguing that they should face less strict requirements, for example, because they are *developing* countries or because *developed* countries have more historical responsibility for climate change than more recently industrialized countries. The result of domestic industry lobbying politicians thus plays out in domestic negotiations over the appropriate emissions regulation and in international negotiations over which countries industry will bear the greatest cost of emissions reductions.

The stakes for a broad-based GHG policy—economic, political, and environmental—are much higher than they were for $SO_2$ policy in 1990 because the effects are global. While the debate over federal policy to address climate change in the United States is currently in hiatus, due to the Trump administration's refusal to address climate change, the lessons of the $SO_2$ allowance-trading program will prove useful and relevant to future deliberations about climate change policy when the time arrives for serious reflection. As the effects of climate change multiply, governments will come under increasing pressure to act, for example, by creating $CO_2$ cap-and-trade programs that are capable of repeating the local success of the US $SO_2$ cap-and-trade program on a global level for $CO_2$. Since the effects of $CO_2$ and climate change are global, regardless of the source of the emissions, the largest $CO_2$ emitters must create cap-and-trade programs both domestically and internationally if the planet is to have any hope of containing the serious risks that climate change poses to human, animal and plant life, and health around the globe.

If the fragmented $CO_2$ markets of China, Australia, the EU, RGGI, and California band together, they can produce a vast market for $CO_2$. In that market, they would compete for clean energy technology and buy up permits to drive up the demand for clean air technology. The experience with the $SO_2$ market in the United States suggests that such an approach would be an effective means to achieve emissions reductions and clean energy technology dissemination and adoption. It would be even more effective with more players. Indeed, if the countries that account for the majority of GHG emissions could negotiate such an agreement, it would represent a big step forward.

## Adaptation, Mitigation, and Insurance

In our discussions so far, we have had very little to say about adaptation strategies. For the governments of many countries, so far, adaptation strategies are nonexistent (Mertz et al. 2009). This state of affairs is not just for the developing countries. For example, in the "Status of State Climate Adaptation Plans" in the United States, most of the states have no plans at all (GlobalChange.gov 2019). This is the status in a *developed* country. Not surprisingly, in the developing countries, adaptation is not even on the radar of the policymakers.

In summary, there is very little that is being done either at the level of international institutions or at the state and local government levels. This is one area where private insurance and reinsurance companies can make a substantial contribution by teaming up with governments by developing risk mitigation and adaptation activities or offering products (such as Cat Re bonds). Most individuals and companies avoid risks. Insurance companies, however, create business by accepting risks.

The US$5 trillion insurance industry is at the vanguard of climate change. Many risks that insurance and reinsurance companies cover are related to weather. Flood insurance, hurricane insurance, windstorm damage insurance, and crop insurance (along with more recent synthetic insurance policies with features of put options) are staples of the insurance and the reinsurance business. At least half of the world's population lives in regions highly exposed to natural disasters, but only a small fraction of them are insured. Insured losses alone from weather-related disasters have jumped from US$5 billion per year in the period between 1970 and 1989 to US$27 billion annually over the last three decades. Events such as Hurricane Katrina pushed the annual cost of catastrophes to over US$100 billion in 2005. While the actual losses from Katrina were over US$113 billion, less than half of it was insured. In 2017, losses from Harvey rivaled that of Katrina.

In theory, any risk whose probability distribution and loss magnitude can be quantified can be priced and insured. Therefore, it is possible to insure against natural catastrophic losses. Such risks are changing over time and the volatility of such risks is rising, which makes forecasting future losses a challenge. Many such risks are insured on a year-by-year basis. But if the underlying variability of such risks changes, that is, events that were once in 100 years become once in 30, it may take the insurers a long time to find that out. When they do find out, it may make them insolvent.

Consider crop and flood insurance products. They are related to the amount and the variability of rainfall. Over time, rainfall in a given area is changing. It is not a simple matter of more or less rain; the entire distribution of rainfall is moving in unexpected ways.

Most of these extreme events are not insured by ordinary insurance companies but by reinsurance companies because reinsurance companies are mainly in the large risk/low probability markets. Naturally, large global reinsurance companies like Munich Re and Swiss Re have taken great interest in this field. They take the IPCC reports very seriously. The companies provide a market test: they have a financial stake in climate change in the long run. Thus, they take climate change more seriously than politicians, many of whom, by the nature of their business, have very short-term interests.

Specific actions have been suggested by many governments. For example, the October 2010 report on climate change from the White House suggests that the government needs to "facilitate the incorporation of climate change into insurance mechanisms." Particularly, insurance markets may have insufficient capital to cover increasing catastrophic losses, especially if rates cannot track climate risks. It also encourages public-private partnerships to produce an open-source risk assessment model. However, in the Fourth National Climate Assessment for 2018, the report notes that coastal property owners depend on private or public insurance policies to recover losses from the coastal effects of climate change, but there are few private flood insurance policies. Mortgage holders within a federally designated Special Flood Hazard Area are required to purchase flood insurance, which almost always comes from the National Flood Insurance Program, generating losses and creating substantial financial risk for the US federal government and taxpayers (U.S. Global Change Research Program 2019).

For the developing countries, the stakes are higher. For some countries, like the small island nations around the globe (the Maldives, Micronesia, and Polynesian island countries among the most affected ones), rising sea water levels will critically affect their survival as low-lying countries will have higher likelihood of floods. But island countries will not be the only ones affected, other countries will face challenges as well. For example, many large cities in Latin America where there is urban poverty and precarious living conditions have grown without any plan. As we saw in the first section, climate change will cause rising sea levels, more violent storms, flooding, and extreme temperatures. There will be problems of water supply, food scarcity, and threats to health and sanitation.

The lack of maturity of capital markets brings additional challenges for the developing countries. Routine synthetic financial products (such as rainfall insurance) are simply not available in most developing countries. This is where international multilateral organizations such as the World Bank, International Monetary Fund, Inter-American Development Bank, and Asian Development Bank can play an important role in providing private–public partnerships in the form of microinsurance and other innovative products that are normally not available in such markets.

There are many ways that insurance companies can help to address climate change.

First, insurance companies can help with the understanding of the climate change problem. Insurers are beginning to share their expertise in data collection, catastrophe modeling, and risk analysis to track trends in weather-related data. These activities can be used to address problems posed by climate change. Insurers are building forward-looking risk models that take climate change into account. For example, the movement of the rainfall index over the past century can be used to create a rainfall index for the future. For planning and for insurance, such modeling will not generate unexpected losses in the long run. Such modeling is essential for the survival of the insurance industry itself. If a 100-year flood becomes a 10-year flood, insurance companies will have insufficient capital to confront such risks in the long run.

Second, insurance can promote loss prevention through risk mitigation. Managing risks and controlling losses is central to any insurance business. The insurance industry has been setting up fire departments and advocating building codes for natural and man-made hazards for a long time. For example, after the Great Fire of London in 1666, Nicholas Barbon started an insurance company to offer protection against fire

(Sheldon 2019). He did two other innovative things: (1) he started differential rates for different building material used—2% of the rent if the houses were made of bricks and 5% of the rent if they were made of wood—and (2) he also hired the watermen from the river Thames to work as part-time firefighters.

The first of these acts encouraged the building of brick houses in London. The second act created an eventual fire department for the city. More recently, insurance companies have been giving rebates for households with fire insurance if they do not use halogen lamps. For insurance companies, it reduces the fire hazards and for households it reduces the use of electricity, thereby reducing GHG emissions. This is a simple example of how spillover effect from fire hazard to lower GHG gas emission is facilitated by insurance companies.

Third, insurance companies can encourage risk reducing behavior. Insurance contracts can design policy exclusions to instill behaviors that reduce greenhouse gas emissions and seek the appropriate efforts to prepare for the impacts. For example, the so-called pay-as-you-drive insurance products are offered by insurers that recognize the link between accident risk and the distance driven. In this case, the insurance company can do this cost effectively with today's technology. It can use the car's GPS to monitor activities with very little cost. It encourages people to drive less. This, in turn, co-benefits the environment.

Fourth, insurance companies are promoting innovative products. Insurance companies are offering special rates for "green buildings" and products that cover risks associated with energy efficiency or renewable energy projects (III 2019). This encourages the construction of more efficient buildings in the future as well as retrofitting old buildings to become more energy efficient.

Fifth, insurance companies are offering climate protection improvements. Insurance companies that also have banking operations are engaged in financing projects that (1) improve resilience to the impacts of climate change and (2) contribute to reducing emissions. Several companies are providing preferential mortgage rates for energy efficient appliances and home upgrades. Some companies are offering "Clean Car Credit" financing for low-emissions vehicles (Mills 2009).

Sixth, the so-called carbon risk disclosure requirement is being encouraged by insurance companies that insure business entities. The carbon risk disclosure requires a company to disclose information related to risk factors and calls for management discussion and analysis (Mills 2009). This issue got a boost with the 2009 position paper of the Securities and Exchange Commission, which states that businesses "should consider the impact of existing climate change legislation and regulation, international accords or treaties on climate change, indirect consequences of regulation or business trends, for example new risks for the company created by legal, technical, political and scientific developments, and the physical impacts of climate change" (SEC 2010). Canada has had similar requirements since 2008. In addition, in the near future, Canada will make such disclosures obligatory rather than voluntary (Council of Canadian Academies 2019).

## Conclusion

Global warming poses risk management challenges for the financial sector in two principal ways: (1) extreme weather events (such as floods, droughts, hurricanes, blizzards, and wildfires) and (2) health (such as diseases, pandemics, and food shortages). These two categories are not mutually exclusive. For example, extreme weather events can cause food shortages and spread diseases. However, reducing emissions reduces air pollution, which in turn reduces associated health risks. Climate change also presents opportunities for the financial sector.

The experience with $SO_2$ markets demonstrates the potential benefits of a similar mitigation strategy for $CO_2$ markets. The Acid Rain Program reduced $SO_2$ emissions from about 23,000 tons per year in 1990 to less than 7000 tons per year in 2011. This demonstrates that a cap-and-trade program for $CO_2$ emissions could be effective in rapidly reducing emissions. While we cannot say that the success of the $SO_2$ markets would be duplicated in the $CO_2$ markets, it does indicate just how effective such an emissions-reduction approach can be.

The lessons of the $SO_2$ markets go beyond mere reductions in emissions. In the Midwestern and Northeastern states of the United States, where nearly 40% of the US population lives, the reduction in $SO_2$ pollution has had big benefits due to (1) health impact, (2) improved land value for agriculture, and (3) ecological impact. The EPA calculated the monetized value of these benefits, including the reduction of lost lives, reduction of respiratory diseases, improved recreational facilities, and ecological improvement. The estimated median value of such gains for 2000 was US$700 billion, rising to US$1300 billion in 2010, and to US$2000 billion in 2020. These are extremely large gains. To get an idea of the magnitude, the US GDP for the year 2011 was estimated at US$15,000 billion (see Fig. 12.3). The $SO_2$ experiment shows that cap-and-trade can also produce gains in terms of morbidity and mortality (Laden et al. 2006). These lessons have important implications for selling $CO_2$ reductions to politicians and voters based on the immediately foreseeable benefits to public health and economic gains, in addition to longer-term environmental benefits and risk reductions.

There is a strong connection between the role of cap-and-trade markets and insurance markets. First, the emissions reductions that cap-and-trade markets achieve will benefit the insurance industry by reducing economic risks from damage to infrastructure and the economies that depend on that infrastructure, health risks from air pollution and the spread of disease, and risks of catastrophic financial losses from extreme weather events such as hurricanes, floods, and droughts. Second, the incentives that the insurance industry creates to reduce emissions can act in a synergistic way with the incentives created by cap-and-trade markets. The effectiveness of cap-and-trade markets increases with insurance incentives to reduce emissions, and the insurance markets reap risk reduction benefits from incentives in the cap-and-trade markets to reduce emissions. Finally, the reductions in economic, health, and catastrophic risks also reduce the financial risks from the investment portfolios of insurance companies. The success of cap-and-trade markets is thus closely tied to the success of insurance markets.

Financial and insurance markets can play a critical role in reducing emissions and promoting adaptation. The principal contribution the financial industry can have to mitigation is through cap-and-trade markets. These markets can reduce the growth of new emissions, encourage better mitigation strategies, and bring innovations to the targeted industries that are not related to the emissions themselves. The insurance industry can contribute to both mitigation and adaptation. Insurance and reinsurance companies take a long-term view of the types of risks associated with climate change, can measure those risks, and can create incentives for their clients to mitigate and adapt to those risks.

The financial industry has a critical role to play in addressing climate change. Limiting climate change is also critical to the future of the financial industry–in particular, for insurance business which is a lifeline for reducing business risks.

## References

Advanced Technologies for the Control of Sulfur Dioxide Emissions from Coal-Fired Boilers. (1999). Topical report. Retrieved from https://pdfs.semanticscholar.org/4196/36dada5f3d2a235b99b834ebefb5a2f01d4a.pdf.

Andreas, D. et al. (2019). *Regulating LIBRA: The transformative potential of Facebook's Cryptocurrency and possible regulatory responses.* European Banking Institute Working Paper Series 2019/44; University of New South Wales Law Research Series UNSWLRS 19–47. Retrieved from SSRN: https://ssrn.com/abstract=3414401.

Bamber, J. L., et al. (2019). Ice sheet contributions to future sea-level rise from structured expert judgment. *PNAS – Proceedings of the National Academy of Sciences, 116*(23), 11195–11200.

Brzoska, M., & Fröhlich, C. (2016). Climate change, migration and violent conflict: Vulnerabilities, pathways and adaptation strategies. *Migration and Development, 5*, 190–210.

Burke, M., et al. (2018). Higher temperatures increase suicide rates in the United States and Mexico. *Nature Climate Change, 8*(8), 723.

CDM – Climate Development Mechanism. (2019). Project 4463: Metro Delhi, India. Retrieved from https://cdm.unfccc.int/Projects/DB/SQS1297089762.41/view.

Chen, G. et al. (2012). *The SO2 allowance trading system and the Clean Air Act Amendments of 1990: Reflections on twenty years of policy innovation.* M-RCBG Faculty Working Paper No. 2012-01. Mossavar-Rahmani Center for Business and Government. Harvard University.

Collins, M., et al. (2013). Long-term climate change: Projections, commitments and irreversibility. In T. F. Stocker et al. (Eds.), *Climate change 2013: The physical science basis. Contribution of Working Group I to the fifth assessment report of the intergovernmental panel on climate change.* Cambridge, UK and New York, NY: Cambridge University Press.

Council of Canadian Academies. (2019). *Canada's top climate change risks.* Ottawa, ON: The Expert Panel on Climate Change Risks. Retrieved from https://cca-reports.ca/wp-content/uploads/2019/07/Report-Canada-top-climate-change-risks.pdf.

CRP – Climate Reality Project. (2019, May 31). How the climate crisis is driving Central American migration. Retrieved from https://www.climaterealityproject.org/blog/how-climate-crisis-driving-central-american-migration.

De Châtel, F. (2014). The role of drought and climate change in the Syrian uprising: Untangling the triggers of the revolution. *Middle Eastern Studies, 50*, 521–535.

Diffenbaugh, N. S., & Burke, M. (2019). Global warming has increased global economic inequality. *PNAS – Proceedings of the National Academy of Sciences, 116*(20), 9808–9813. Retrieved from https://www.pnas.org/content/116/20/9808.

Dumitru, O. A., et al. (2019, August). Constraints on global mean sea level during Pliocene warmth. *Nature*. Retrieved from https://www.nature.com/articles/s41586-019-1543-2.

Economist. (2019, August 1). The Amazon is approaching an irreversible tipping point. *Economist*. Retrieved from https://www.economist.com/briefing/2019/08/01/the-amazon-is-approaching-an-irreversible-tipping-point.

EME Homer City v. EPA. (2012). 11-1302. U.S. App. D.C. Retrieved from http://www.cadc.uscourts.gov/internet/opinions.nsf/19346B280C78405C85257A61004DC0E5/$file/11-1302-1390314.pdf.

Englander, J. (2019, February). *Rising sea level: The crisis on our doorstep*. The Royal Institution, London. Retrieved from https://www.johnenglander.net/sea-level-rise-blog/my-royal-institution-video-goes-viral/.

EPA – Environmental Protection Agency. (1995). *Acid rain program: Technology and innovation*. Washington, DC.

EPA – Environmental Protection Agency. (2009). Benefits analysis approach and results. Retrieved from https://www3.epa.gov/ttn/ecas/regdata/RIAs/pso2ch5_11-16-09.pdf.

EPA – Environmental Protection Agency. (2017). Regulatory and non-regulatory approaches to pollution control. Retrieved from https://www.epa.gov/sites/production/files/2017-09/documents/ee-0568-04.pdf.

EPA – Environmental Protection Agency. (2019). Air markets program data. Retrieved January 12, 2019, from https://ampd.epa.gov/ampd/.

EU ETS – EU Emissions Trading System. (2019). EU Emissions Trading System (EU ETS). Retrieved from https://ec.europa.eu/clima/policies/ets_en.

Globalchange.gov. (2019). Status of state climate adaptation plans. Retrieved from https://www.globalchange.gov/browse/multimedia/status-state-climate-adaptation-plans.

Grant, W. (2019, June 8). US-Mexico talks: Trump hails deal on migrants to avoid tariffs. Retrieved from www.bbc.com; https://www.bbc.com/news/world-us-canada-48568389.

Gu, Y., et al. (2018). Impacts of sectoral emissions in China and the implications: Air quality, public health, crop production, and economic costs. *Environmental Research Letters*. https://doi.org/10.1088/1748-9326/aad138.

Holland, P. R., et al. (2019). West Antarctic ice loss influenced by internal climate variability and anthropogenic forcing. *Nature Geoscience*. https://doi.org/10.1038/s41561-019-0420-9.

Hua, Y. (2019). China's carbon market development and carbon market connection: A literature review. *Energies, 12*. https://doi.org/10.3390/en12091663.

III – Insurance Information Institute. (2019). Green insurance. Retrieved from https://www.iii.org/article/green-insurance.

IPCC – Intergovernmental Panel on Climate Change. (2019, September 25). Special report on the ocean and cryosphere in a changing climate (SROCC). Retrieved from https://www.ipcc.ch/srocc/download-report/.

Joskow, P. L., & Schmalensee, R. (1998). The political economy of market-based environmental policy: The U.S. acid rain program. *Journal of Law and Economics, 41*, 37–84.

Kabat, P. et al. (2019). High-level synthesis report of latest climate science information convened by the Science Advisory Group of the UN Climate Action Summit 2019. World Meteorological Organization/Science Advisory Group of the UN Climate Action Summit 2019. Retrieved from https://wedocs.unep.org/bitstream/handle/20.500.11822/30023/climsci.pdf?sequence=1&isAllowed=y.

Kahn, M. E. et al. (2019, August). *Long-term macroeconomic effects of climate change: A cross-country analysis.* NBER Working Paper 26167. Retrieved from http://www.nber.org/papers/w26167.

Kathayat, G. et al. (2017, December). The Indian monsoon variability and civilization changes in the Indian subcontinent. *Science Advances, 3*(12), e1701296. Retrieved from https://advances.sciencemag.org/content/3/12/e1701296.

Kelly, R., et al. (2013). Recent burning of boreal forests exceeds fire regime limits of the past 10,000 years. *PNAS – Proceedings of the National Academy of Sciences.* https://doi.org/10.1073/pnas.1305069110.

Kelley, C. P., et al. (2015). Climate change in the Fertile Crescent and implications of the recent Syrian drought. *PNAS – Proceedings of the National Academy of Sciences, 112*, 3241–3246.

Kuil, L. et al. (2016). Conceptualizing socio-hydrological drought processes: The case of the Maya NCAR – National Center for Atmospheric Research/ University Corporation for Atmospheric Research. (2019) Predictions of Future Global Climate. Retrieved from https://scied.ucar.edu/longcontent/predictions-future-global-climate.

Kurian, J. (2008, May 14). *Kerala farmers enter carbon trading. Hindustan Times.*

Kutney, G. (2014). *Carbon politics and the failure of the Kyoto protocol.* Abingdon, Oxon: Routledge Explorations in Environmental Studies.

Laden, F., et al. (2006). Reduction in fine particulate air pollution and mortality. *American Journal of Respiratory and Critical Care Medicine, 173*, 667–672.

McLean, B. (2008, July 29). Testimony of Brian McLean Director, Office of Atmospheric Programs Office of Air And Radiation US Environmental Protection Agency before the Committee on Environment and Public Works Subcommittee on Clean Air and Nuclear Safety United States Senate in the US Senate.

Mertz, O., et al. (2009). Adaptation to climate change in developing countries. *Environmental Management, 43*(5), 743–752. https://doi.org/10.1007/s00267-008-9259-3.

Mills, E. (2009). *Insurer responses to climate change.* Ceres Report. Retrieved from http://insurance.lbl.gov/opportunities/risk-to-opportunity-2008.pdf.

NASA – National Aeronautics and Space Administration. (2019, August 21). Boreal forest fires could release deep soil carbon. Retrieved from https://www.nasa.gov/feature/goddard/2019/boreal-forest-fires-could-release-deep-soil-carbon.

Olken, D., & Pande, R. (2012). *Corruption in developing countries.* Working Paper, MIT, Cambridge, MA.

Paul, E. (2004). *Handbook of industrial mixing.* Hoboken, NJ: Wiley.

Razvodovsky, Y. E. (2015). Suicides in Russia and Belarus: A comparative analysis of trends. *Acta Psychopathologica, 1*, 22. Retrieved from http://psychopathology.imedpub.com/suicides-in-russia-and-belarus-a-comparative-analysis-of-trends.php?aid=7536.

Reuveny, R. (2007). Climate change-induced migration and violent conflict. *Political Geography, 26*, 656–673.

Revill, C. et al. (2017). The climate turning point. Retrieved from http://www.mission2020.global/climate-turning-point/.

RFERL – Radio Free Europe/Radio Liberty. (2019, August 12). Siberian wildfires set to break land area record. Retrieved from https://www.rferl.org/a/siberian-wildfires-set-to-break-land-area-record/30106388.html.

Ricke, K. et al. (2018). Country-level social cost of carbon. *Nature Climate Change, 8*, 895–900. Retrieved from https://coalitionclimatmtl.org/wp-content/uploads/Country-level-social-cost-of-carbon-Ricke_et_al_2018.pdf.

Rudebusch, G. D. (2019, March 25). Climate change and the Federal Reserve. FRBSF Economic Letter 2019-09. Retrieved from https://www.frbsf.org/economic-research/publications/economic-letter/2019/march/climate-change-and-federal-reserve/.

Sandor, R. (2012). *Good derivatives.* Hoboken, NJ: Wiley.

Sarkar, A., et al. (2016). Oxygen isotope in archaeological bioapatites from India: Implications to climate change and decline of Bronze Age Harappan civilization. *Scientific Reports, 6*(26555), 2016. https://doi.org/10.1038/srep26555.

SEC – Securities Exchange Commission. (2010, January 27). SEC issues interpretive guidance on disclosure related to business or legal developments regarding climate change. Retrieved from https://www.sec.gov/news/press/2010/2010-15.htm.

Selby, J., et al. (2017). Climate change and the Syrian civil war revisited. *Political Geography, 60*, 232–244.

Sheldon, R. (2019). Nicholas Barbon. Oxford Dictionary of National Biography. https://doi.org/10.1093/ref:odnb/1334.

Spratt, D. & Dunlop, I. (2019). Existential climate-related security risk: A scenario approach. Breakthrough – National Centre for Climate Restoration. breakthroughonline.org.au, May. Retrieved from https://docs.wixstatic.com/ugd/148cb0_a1406e0143ac4c469196d3003bc1e687.pdf.

Temple, J. (2019). We aren't terrified enough about losing the Amazon. *MIT Technology Review.* Retrieved from https://www.technologyreview.com/s/614222/we-arent-terrified-enough-about-losing-the-amazon/.

U.S. Global Change Research Program. (2019). Fourth national climate assessment. Retrieved September 27, 2019, from https://nca2018.globalchange.gov/chapter/8/.

UCS – Union of Concerned Scientists. (2018). Each country's share of CO2 emissions. Retrieved from https://www.ucsusa.org/global-warming/science-and-impacts/science/each-countrys-share-of-co2.html.

UNEP – United Nations Environmental Program. (2019). The Clean Development Mechanism (CDM). Retrieved September 27, 2019, from https://unfccc.int/files/cooperation_and_support/capacity_building/application/pdf/unepcdmintro.pdf.

UNFCCC – United Nations Framework Convention on Climate Change. (2019). What is the Kyoto Protocol? Retrieved September 27, 2019, from https://unfccc.int/kyoto_protocol.

USAID – United States Agency for International Development. (2018). Climate risk profile Brazil. Retrieved from https://www.climatelinks.org/sites/default/files/asset/document/2018-April-30_USAID_CadmusCISF_Climate-Risk-Profile-Brazil.pdf.

Vautard, R. et al. (2019). Human contribution to the record-breaking July 2019 heatwave in Western Europe. Retrieved from https://www.worldweatherattribution.org/wp-content/uploads/July2019heatwave.pdf.

Wang, H., et al. (2019). China's CO2 peak before 2030 implied from characteristics and growth of cities. *Nature Sustainability*. https://doi.org/10.1038/s41893-019-0339-6.

WMO – World Meteorological Organization. (2019). Unprecedented wildfires in the Arctic. Retrieved from https://public.wmo.int/en/media/news/unprecedented-wildfires-arctic.

PART III

# Technological Risks

CHAPTER 13

# An Incentives-Based Mechanism for Corporate Cyber Governance Enforcement and Regulation

*Shaen Corbet and Constantin Gurdgiev*

## Introduction

Asymmetric information in international financial markets is defined as the environment in which one party in the transaction has superior, private information relevant to the transaction relative to other parties. One such example of asymmetric information importance to the financial services links technological innovation with the need for protecting consumer

*JEL classifications: G15, G32, G38*
*We wish to extend our gratitude to Erwin L. Alberty and Asmita Jain of Middlebury Institute of International Studies at Monterey, CA, USA for their helpful comments on this paper.*

S. Corbet • C. Gurdgiev (✉)
DCU Business School, Dublin City University, Dublin, Ireland

Trinity Business School, Trinity College, Dublin, Ireland
e-mail: shaen.corbet@dcu.ie; gurdgic@tcd.ie



T. Walker et al. (eds.), *Ecological, Societal, and Technological Risks and the Financial Sector*, Palgrave Studies in Sustainable Business In Association with Future Earth, https://doi.org/10.1007/978-3-030-38858-4_13

data. It is a relationship mostly based on trust between consumers and the service provider, backed by reputational signals concerning the provider's trustworthiness. Corporate reputational damage risks and potential breach-related legal judgements and awards, thus, can be seen as key deterrent against cybersecurity strategies and practices that can lead to a breach. Unfortunately, as shown in Corbet and Gurdgiev (2017a, 2019), as well as in the regulatory literature surveyed below, these strategies may not be enough as the rate of cybersecurity attacks, their adverse impact, and complexity continue to grow.

In this chapter, we first summarize the current state of evidence for the unexpected transmission of cybercrime shocks via equity markets valuations during the period of 2005–2015. We show that these transmissions are beyond those which would occur through the known spill-over channels between stock prices of companies subjected to cybercrime in a variety of jurisdictions. In fact, equity trading and portfolio links as well as institutional structures such as international subsidiaries and intermediaries all help propagate risk contagion effects, creating systemic cybersecurity risk spill-over channels. The systemic risk contagion channel transmits cybersecurity risk from one company's share price to other sectoral and market-related companies.

As we show, on the regulatory side of the financial markets, the Committee on Payments and Market Infrastructures (CPMI) of the International Organization of Securities Commissions (IOSCO) warns financial and monetary institutions (FMIs) about the potential for cybersecurity to become systemic through contagion effects. As the result, the IOSCO and other regulatory agencies have been calling for pre-emptive testing of FMI systems as 'an integral component of any cyber resilience framework', stating that 'all elements of a cyber-resilience framework should be rigorously tested to determine their overall effectiveness before being deployed within an FMI, and regularly thereafter' (CPMI-IOSCO 2016, p. 18). Similarly, Dahlgren (2015) warns that cyber threats pose a potentially systemic risk to financial stability through the disruption or corruption of critical payment, clearing and settlement systems, and related data. A glaring and obvious omission in this literature is a failure to include other potential channels for systemic risk transmissions, including exchanges and over-the-counter markets. Another omission is the fact that none of the aforementioned sources provide empirical evidence to support the hypothesis of systemic nature of cybersecurity risks. Corbet and Gurdgiev's (2019) study corrected for both omissions.

Beyond the systemic nature of the threat, the magnitude of costs and disruptions imposed onto the economies by cyber-attacks is growing. According to the EU authorities, as reported by Stearns (2016), 'network security incidents resulting from human error, technical failures or cyber-attacks cause annual losses of 260 billion euros ($288 billion) to 340 billion euros'. And despite the common perception that cybersecurity vulnerabilities apply primarily to private sector companies, evidence is mounting that central banks and regulators themselves are not immune to cybercrime.

As the best practice for cybersecurity implementation, CPMI-IOSCO (2016, p. 18) suggests the need for penetration testing of FMI systems:

> FMIs should carry out penetration tests to identify vulnerabilities that may affect their systems, networks, people or processes. To provide an in-depth evaluation of the security of FMIs' systems, those tests should simulate actual attacks on the systems. Penetration tests on internet-facing systems should be conducted regularly and whenever systems are updated or deployed. Where applicable, the tests could include other internal and external stakeholders, ... as well as third parties.

To carry out such testing, it is proposed that FMIs need to 'challenge their own organisations and ecosystems through the use of so-called red teams to introduce an adversary perspective in a controlled setting'. Furthermore, CPMI-IOSCO also suggests that 'a red team may consist of an FMI's own employees and/or outside experts, who are in either case independent of the function being tested' (CPMI-IOSCO 2016, p. 19). In more common parlance, such 'red teams' are known in the industry as 'white knights' or 'white hats', representing teams of experts in cybersecurity hired by companies on a fee-for-service basis to provide audits and test the company's own cybersecurity systems.

On foot of these regulatory discussions and the empirical findings presented in Corbet and Gurdgiev (2019), this chapter proposes a novel regulatory mechanism for identification, prevention, and mitigation of cybersecurity risks in financial markets. We build on the idea of active deployment of the white knights teams, while aiming to expand the potential technical capabilities of such teams and the scope of incentives for these teams to aggressively pursue their test targets. We further propose putting these teams outside direct reporting to the companies tested to reduce potential conflicts of interest and agency problems that may arise from close proximity between the white knights and their target companies. Our proposal is to deploy the power and the capabilities of the hacktivists to provide regulatory and enforcement supports. The idea of drawing on hacking community resources to combat cybercrime may initially appear counter-intuitive, but it is anchored in the already evolving markets for hacktivist services in detecting and preventing potential weaknesses in corporate cybersecurity infrastructure. It is also linked to the existent and successfully growing systems of using whistle-blowers and independent reporters to detect and punish corporate financial/accounting irregularities and crimes.[1]

The ethical dilemma implied by this proposal is addressed throughout this chapter. In our opinion, hacktivists (or hackers that are at least marginally committed to illicit hacking), if appropriately remunerated and monitored, could provide the necessary skill set and offer benefits to regulatory agencies and companies in the form of identifying structural cybersecurity weaknesses.[2] Such a skill set is currently lacking in the regulatory and enforcement community for a variety of reasons, including the lack of aligned incentives for hacktivists to join regulatory and enforcement institutions. Our proposal counters this problem by creating a functional set of incentives and rewards, aligned with key performance indicators, for hacktivists' participation in legal and supervised tests of the firms' security systems.

Of course, the data breaches, when supervised, must not lead to the resultant or potential future damage to consumers. Our proposal addresses these potential problems by offering a staggered system of reimbursement for hacktivists, linked to the success of the cybersecurity tests conducted by them over time.

[1] Evidence for the potential efficacy of such a mechanism may be presented in the attempted start-up of a hedge fund 'TRO LLC'. This hedge fund idea was developed by Mr. Andrew Auernheimer (a hacker also known as 'WEEV'). The main issue with this hedge fund idea is that at its core is the promotion of hacking or identity theft for financial gain. As a result, Mr. Auernheimer has proposed that the fund will not be directly for hack companies but will 'probe the public surface of a company' and 'actually watch hackers' (CNBC interview, 28 April 2014).

[2] This view is broadly consistent with the existent literature and practices on the use of whistle-blowers (internal and external to the company) in detecting other potential breaches and violations, as discussed in Dahlgren (2015) and referenced by the RICO system, discussed below.

Overall, the identification of the weakness can provide a deterrent based on a threat of reputational damage to the company through regulatory disclosure in cases where structural data security weaknesses have been identified, and if the mitigation of discovered breaches is lagging. Public disclosure in this scenario may in fact be more beneficial as a punishment alongside regulatory fines, as shown by the evidence on the abnormal negative returns resulting from voluntary and involuntary disclosures, presented in Corbet and Gurdgiev (2019) and summarized in Fig. 13.1.

The evidence concerning an increasing frequency and severity of cybersecurity breaches over time leads to another view of problems addressed by the proposed mechanism, where regulatory authorities can maintain their current technological capabilities as the hackers' skill sets and tools develop in real time. Direct engagement with hacktivists can provide invaluable access to the skills and tools that regulatory authorities often lack. Hackers and hacktivists learn by doing. In traditional sequencing of events, hackers first breach a company's or an organization's data systems and cause financial and reputational damage to it, thereby imposing severe costs on consumers and other companies (through the systemic contagion

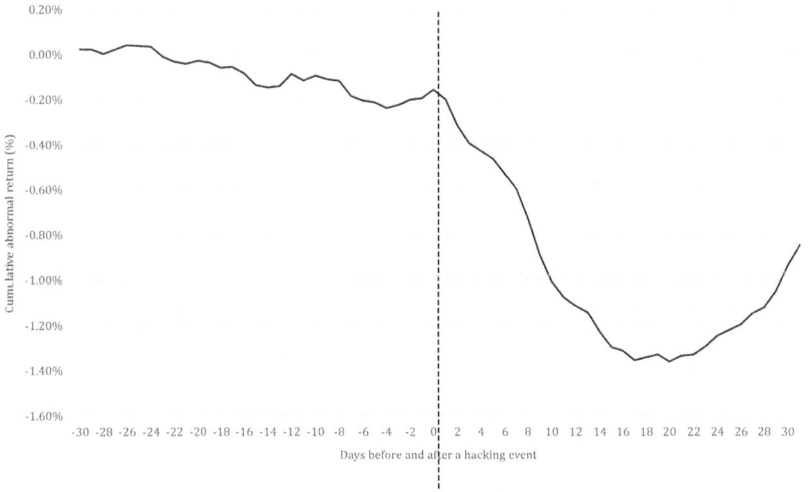


**Fig. 13.1** Cumulative abnormal returns associated with investigated hacking events. Source: Authors own data extraction from the LexisNexis database, see Corbet and Gurdgiev (2019)

channels). Subsequent to this, regulatory authorities spend time and resources identifying who has caused the breach, mitigating the breach costs, and pursuing prosecution of those responsible. In this process, authorities and companies also discover and address the causes of the vulnerability exposed by the hackers. Our proposal establishes a transmission channel for skills from the hackers to the regulators who supervise actual live hacks ex ante illegal breaches occurring.

Put in simpler terms, in the current environment, regulators chase hackers after the damage is done, while companies remedy the cost of breaches through insurance and by ex post systems upgrades.[3] In our proposed preventative channel, hacktivists and regulatory authorities can work together under a model of effective monitoring and remuneration, instead of opposing each other. Currently, U.S. Government agencies (outside security institutions, for which data is not available[4]) operate on the basis of hiring former hackers and hacktivists, and employing contractors who use former hackers in formal employment. Larger U.S. corporations do the same. This employment situation presents a set of problems associated with broader 'agency issues'. Firstly, hacktivists available for hire are self-selected to be older, a more mature generation of hackers who are moving to become white knights. Their skill sets can be outdated relative to the younger generations of hackers still operating in the grey or black markets. Secondly, once in employment, white knights can be subject to contractual and career pressures to act in the interest of the employers and managers, as opposed to the interest of the firm owners. Thirdly, white knights are usually hired on the basis of exploiting a known vulnerability, as opposed to proactively testing all systems.

[3] Data on the frequency of cybercrime on publicly traded companies covering the period from 2005 through early 2015 shows that one specific form of cybercrime becoming ever more prevalent is a breach of the company's firewall to steal client data which can be used for a host of illegal activities.

[4] While U.S. Security Agencies are reported to have engaged white knights and current hacktivists, these engagements are structured on selecting known hacktivists and using them as agents working for the agency. This is distinct from the mechanism we propose in a fundamental way. Our proposal involves voluntary self-selection of hacktivists to participate in a reward-for-breach testing 'tournament', as opposed to cooption of a selected hacktivist for cooperation with an agency. As a result, our mechanism is designed to address the core issue of economic agency problems that arise from direct or indirect employment of hacktivists by the contracting entity.

In an environment where the size and technical complexity of data breaches are becoming more advanced and sophisticated, more pressure must be placed on corporate mechanisms to protect consumers' data across all sectors.[5,6]

We propose a fine-sharing model for rewarding hacktivists who successfully breach tested companies' cybersecurity under regulatory and enforcement bodies' supervision. Such a system would price hacktivists' efforts based on imposing a regulatory cost of cyber risk discovery onto companies directly responsible for maintaining cybersecurity in the first place. In economic policy terms, this mechanism qualifies as satisfying 'user-payer' principle of efficiency in enforcement, as such fines would directly target those corporate counterparties and markets participant that are most directly responsible for potential failures of cybersecurity.

In general, the reputational damage from the disclosure of a successful cybercrime event should be reflected through the influence of the efficient market hypothesis into stock prices.[7] Partially, as our discussion below indicates, this reflection is true. Examples of negative reputational costs to companies due to cybersecurity attacks abound and include the world's largest shipping company, AP Moller-Maersk, which suffered a loss of US$300 million in a 2017 cyber-attack, leading to a reputationally costly profit guidance revision and share price loss of 7 percent (Novet 2017).

[5] Notably, in a range of sectors, although not yet widely in finance, the use of 'white hat' or 'white knight' hackers is growing in both frequency and scope. Some industry-level examples are discussed in Kelly (2013). The lack of similar approaches in financial regulation was recently discussed in McKendry and Macheel (2015). Our proposal builds on this momentum and extends the system of cooperative engagement between regulators, companies, and white knight hacktivists to a mechanism that would create functional incentives for hacktivists' participation in the regulatory prevention of the cybersecurity risks. Such a mechanism is currently lacking in the industry.

[6] Those hackers or hacktivists possessing the best technological talent are more likely to be swayed by the financial returns of private practice. In simple terms, there is an argument in favour of a learning-by-doing second order effect of such a system of enforcement based on repeated interactions with leading experts in cybersecurity who represent the front end of the knowledge curve, as opposed to the past 'dark hat' hackers who may or may not be leaders in their field at the moment of their engagement by the firms and regulators as 'red teams' or white knights.

[7] Corbet and Gurdgiev (2019) document the evidence on the negative abnormal returns experienced by the companies following cybersecurity breaches. This evidence is summarized below and in Fig. 13.1. Some examples of reputational damages sustained by companies following the attacks is discussed and summarized in Alva Group (2016), Tiedemann-Nkabinde and Davydoff (2019), and Spam Titan (2019), amongst others.

The Moller-Maersk hack was part of a much wider ranging NotPetya DNS (Domain Name System) attack that impacted thousands of businesses and public agencies around the world. As per Security Magazine (2019): 'No sector was spared, leaving organizations open to a range of advanced effects from compromised brand reputation to losing business. … The top impacts of DNS attacks—damaged reputation, business continuity and finances' with reported 26 percent of businesses experiencing 'lost brand equity due to DNS attacks'. Another example of reputational damages arising from cybersecurity breaches is the case of the Equifax data breach of 2017 which exposed sensitive data of more than 145 million people worldwide. In the wake of the public disclosure of the attack, Equifax shares dropped 13 percent in one day, and the company is currently dealing with numerous lawsuits resulting from the breach. Shell (2017) reported, in the wake of the Equifax breach disclosure, that the company sustained significant brand damages as the result of the hack. According to Shell (2017), the second-worst breach-related impact 'was a drop of 10 points suffered by eBay in the 10 days after its May 2014 hack. Other high-profile breaches, such as one at Anthem Blue Cross in February 2015 and Home Depot in September 2014, did not cause as big a hit to those brands'. Furthermore, as Shell (2017) notes, 'Equifax's initial hit to its reputation is bigger than the 23-point decline in Chipotle Mexican Grill's Buzz score decline in October 2015 after its E. coli crisis began'. Notably, Ponemon (2018b) shows that in 2017–2018, the direct costs of data breaches were smaller than the indirect costs, which include reputational losses in every country and region covered in their study. Overall, The Council of Economic Advisers (2018, p. 6) shows that reputational damages from cyberattacks rank 6th in magnitude of associated costs after losses of intellectual property, increases in cost of financial capital, losses of strategic information, data and equipment, and court settlement costs. This rank puts reputational damages and costs ahead, in magnitude, of losses of revenues, costs of breach notifications, costs of cybersecurity improvements and consumer protection improvements, and regulatory fines and penalties. The latter rank the lowest in terms of their cost impact to companies experiencing a cybersecurity breach, providing further evidence of the ineffectiveness of current regulatory and enforcement regimes in providing preventative deterrence.

Given the continuous growth in cybersecurity threats and the success rates with which cyber criminals can penetrate corporate security systems, this reputational cost is not sufficient to create functional incentives for the firms to take corrective actions to prevent hacking threat from materializing. Under our proposed mechanism, this reputational cost would be augmented by the threat of more effective fines and would provide financial support for hacktivists' engagement with the authorities. The onus of corporate responsibility would therefore shift back to the target company, forcing the company to proactively improve its internal infrastructure, or face a repeat attack and regulatory disclosure of potential risks to the public and the markets. In time, the constant threat of data breaches could be reduced from the technological advancements of both the company and the regulatory/supervisory authorities, making consumer data more protected and the companies operating within a regulated regime more trustworthy.

The remainder of the chapter is organized as follows. Section "Cybercrime and Financial Markets" discusses the related, previous literature on the influence of cybercrime on financial markets and the systemic nature of the risks presented by such attacks to the international financial markets. Section "White Knights and Proactive Risk Mitigation" proposes a brief outline of the regulatory/supervisory mechanism that uses white knight hackers and hacktivists as regulatory and enforcement agents. Section "Concluding Remarks" concludes.

## Cybercrime and Financial Markets

To date, the only study that focuses specifically on the interlinkages between the differing types of cybercrime and financial market volatility or systemic stability risks within the financial markets is provided by Corbet and Gurdgiev (2019) (see McKendry and Macheel 2015).

In this section, we first summarize the existent research on cybercrime impact in the financial markets and the economy in general, followed by a review of the classification of the cybercrime events. We conclude this section by summarizing the findings from Corbet and Gurdgiev (2017a, b, 2019) that establish the systemic nature of the cybersecurity risks in financial industry.

### *Cybercrime and Financial Risks: The State of [Regulatory] Play*

In the early literature, Rollins and Wilson (2007) found that although the U.S. and international community have taken some steps to coordinate laws to prevent cybercrime, computer attacks will continue to become more numerous, faster, and more sophisticated, leading to the situation where the U.S. Government agencies may not, in the future, be able to respond effectively to such attacks. Rollins and Wilson's (2007) view is confirmed by UN (2011) and DHS (2018), amongst others.

Amplifying the predictions of Rollins and Wilson (2007) concerning the evolution of the cyber threats, Ionescu et al. (2011) find that the Global Financial Crisis led to an exponential growth in cybercrime in the period 2007 to 2011. This growth has been only partially matched by improvements in the knowledge and technological abilities of computer specialists who are acting to prevent or restrict cybercrime expansion. Ionescu et al. (2011) argue that the rate of growth in cyber threats is unlikely to fall, a sentiment also echoed by Ponemon's (2018a, b) reports.

An added threat, subject to the even greater potential costs, risks, systemic uncertainty and enforcement problems, is the evolution of the Artificial Intelligence (AI) (Yampolskiy 2016), where 'the potential that a super-intelligence may be capable of inventing dangers we are not capable of predicting'. Quite naturally, in an environment of malicious AI deployment, the robustness of cybersecurity systems will have to be tested live, in real time, and not ex post as today's best practices imply.[8] This view of evolutionary dynamics in cybersecurity threats within the financial sector is mirrored in the findings concerning the general trend toward an ever-increasing degree of automation/computerization and the pursuit of speed of information processing in financial services. For example, MacKenzie (2018) clearly states that today, financial markets are already operating at speeds as fast as within 50 microseconds of the speed of light. This increase in speed of data transmission and processing, associated with the rise in algorithmic trading, puts ever more pressure on existent regulatory and enforcement structures designed to prevent, mitigate, and punish cybercrime as it relates to the financial markets. An additional and related dimension is the evolution of quantum computing, which brings higher degrees of uncertainty and complexity to the analysis of the future evolution of cyber threats (Keplinger 2018).

[8] These tests will have to involve not only the best human hacktivist talent, but also preventative AI. Reactionary responses to cybersecurity breaches in the age of AI will be too little, too late to mitigate extensive damages that can be inflicted by information systems moving closer to the speeds of light, as opposed to human-led attacks by modern day hacktivists.

One startling observation throughout numerous research papers identifies the ease with which stolen data can be purchased and sold through a network of illicit, secretive, and publicly available mechanisms. Holt and Lampke (2010) examine the nature of the market for stolen data based on the analysis of six web forums run by data thieves. All manner of personal and financial data can be obtained at a fraction of their true value, with inefficient regulation and numerous legal issues enhancing the ease at which these hackers can operate. In 2016, cybersecurity firm Kaspersky Labs uncovered an online marketplace for trading illegally obtained data and sales of access to more than 70,000 hacked corporate and government servers for as little as US$6 each, according to Khrennikov (2016). The evolutionary development of illicit markets for trading in stolen data is also highlighted in Beckert and Dewey (2017).

Kraemer-Mbula et al. (2013) examine the effects of globalization on growth in sophistication of financial cybercrime. One of the key findings of the paper is the need to further develop policy makers', law enforcement's, and security firms' capacity to identify trends and concentrate preventative resources, as well as to increase knowledge of how cybercrime operates.

If proactive testing of corporate systems by hackers can be deployed to increase the publicly visible probability of detecting cybersecurity systems flaws, such tests can act not only as an enforcement mechanism, but also as a regulatory deterrence. Kremer (2014) asks how the perceptions of security and threats in cyberspace play an important role in justifying the means and measures employed by different security agencies. Security mind-sets in this sense are differentiated between a national security mind-set, concerned with military and strategic considerations of national security, and a liberal mind-set which perceives security together with individual rights. Summers (2015) states that one of the biggest challenges that remains for the regulation of information and communication technology is that the global information space does not respect national boundaries and that any regulatory approach can call for some degree of cooperation between countries. Eric S. Rosengren from the Federal Reserve Bank of Boston echoes Summers' conclusions in his April 2016 speech (Rosengren 2016, p. 2), stating that 'Cyber criminals are looking for the targets of opportunity without regard to geographic location, and the existence of a global population of potential attackers looking for softer targets means increased risks'.[9]

[9] Another example of the lagging nature of legal and enforcement frameworks relating to cybercrime is presented by the relatively frequent hacking events involving cryptocurrencies exchanges. According to Chen and Yuji Nakamura (2016), lack of legal frameworks operat-

In a forward step in terms of international coordination of cybersecurity enforcement, the European Union approved the first set of joint rules aimed at preventing cyber-attacks, including rules requiring companies to improve defensive systems and to disclose such attacks. As reported by Stearns (2016), the EU legislation '...will impose security and reporting obligations on service operators in industries such as banking, energy, transport and health and on digital operators like search engines and online marketplaces. The law ... also requires EU national governments to cooperate among themselves in the field of network security'. Unfortunately, the European Union initiatives in this area continue to rely on the company's and regulators' internal resources and systems to detect threat vulnerabilities and address cyber risks. Once again, as with the U.S. regulators' approach, the European regulatory bodies continue to use response-based systems for managing cybersecurity, instead of adopting a proactive preventative approach. As noted by numerous reports, an added dimension to this approach is posited by the predominance of the 'insure and forget' model of corporate responses to cyber threats (Egan 2014 and PWC 2014).

Meanwhile, the impact of data security breaches on financial bottom line is growing. The Ponemon (2015, 2018a, b) studies find that the total cost of data breaches across corporate sectors rose 23 percent year-on-year in 2014, with cyberattacks now accounting for 47 percent of all data-breach cases in 2015, up from 37 percent in 2013. In 2018, the comparable figure was 56 percent. In 2016, Russian hackers stole the account data of some 76 million clients from a global banking institution. As claimed by the FBI, nearly 519 million financial records have been stolen from U.S. companies by hackers within the period of 12 months prior to October 2014. In one incident, Russian hackers allegedly acquired more than 150,000 press releases from Wall Street publications in August 2015 and used them to gain a trade advantage, worth US$100 million (Riley et al. 2015). As revealed in an indictment unsealed in 2016, a group of Iranian-sponsored hackers launched attacks against 46 Wall Street institutions in 2011, including the New York Stock Exchange and NASDAQ (Larson et al. 2016). The presence of big data-based FinTech services providers and other non-banks offering e-banking-related products complicates the picture, as recently noted by Packin and Aretz (2016). As

ing in the relation to cybersecurity is illustrated by the August 2016 attack on Hong Kong-based bitcoin exchange Bitfinex.

stated by Robert Anderson, executive assistant director of the FBI's Criminal, Cyber, Response, and Services Branch, 'We're in a day when a person can commit about 15,000 bank robberies sitting in their basement' (Anderson et al. 2013).

As argued in Corbet and Gurdgiev (2017b), despite the executives' rhetoric about the urgency of preparing traditional banks and MFIs for cybersecurity challenges, banking institutions continue to treat cybersecurity as a non-strategic matter. Three major cybersecurity exercises carried out in recent years in the U.S., U.K., and Canada, such as SFIMA-organized Quantum Dawn, CBEST, and IIROC (Investment Industry Regulatory Organization of Canada), through which scenarios testing exposed significant areas of concern when it comes to the financial sector's ability to counter systemic risks associated with cybercrime. More ominously, the results also indicate that at the organizational level, major banks and MFIs continue to treat cybersecurity as a technical challenge, to be handled by the IT departments, rather than a strategic threat to be prioritized across the entire organizational structure through fully integrated enterprise risk management systems.

### *Cybercrime Events and Their Impact*

Both Egan (2014) and PWC (2014) suggest that the prevalent view in the business and regulatory community is that cybersecurity breaches can pose a systemic threat to the financial sector as a whole or to the financial markets at large. However, empirically mainstream literature on the subject still lacks evidence to prove such a hypothesis.

Corbet and Gurdgiev (2019) look at 819 cybercrime events with sufficient disclosure identified between January 1, 2005, and April 30, 2015, which are divided into the following categories: data breaches caused by an employee release, data breaches caused by an external data breach or hack, data breaches caused by a lost, stolen, or discarded internal data device, and data breaches caused by unintentional disclosure. The data is taken from the systemic analysis of the LexisNexis database, using methodologies described in Corbet and Gurdgiev (2019). Our analysis and data collection cover the publicly listed companies regulated by the U.S. Securities and Exchange Commission, which represents a wide range of multinational, globally trading companies, as well as all foreign-registered companies trading on the U.S. exchanges. As a result, our data represents the entire population of all publicly disclosed breaches involving U.S. regulated companies.

Figure 13.1 shows the evidence for Cumulative Abnormal Returns (CAR) relating to hacking events.[10] The data clearly indicates that financial markets are becoming more aware of the negative sentiment contained within these events and are punishing the companies involved. This analysis was confirmed by an investigation of company media coverage in the days following the identified cybercrime events.

In Table 13.1 we display the annual summary statistics relating to announced hacking events on publicly traded companies. In total, 1.9 billion individual records were exposed throughout the 2005–2015 period, with 230 severe hacking events announced and admitted by the

**Table 13.1** Annual summary statistics of the included cybercrime events (2005–2015)

| *Year* | *Total number of events* | *Clients records exposed* | *Average of CAR* | *Total number of hacking events* | *Clients records exposed in hacking events* | *Average of CAR to a hacking event* |
|---|---|---|---|---|---|---|
| 2005 | 30 | 677,314,000 | −1.59 | 4 | 36,480,000 | −1.34 |
| 2006 | 108 | 498,330,900 | −2.46 | 15 | 27,402,500 | −3.25 |
| 2007 | 85 | 408,197,900 | −1.51 | 19 | 18,690,700 | −2.68 |
| 2008 | 45 | 326,522,000 | −1.76 | 8 | 128,056,800 | −0.87 |
| 2009 | 44 | 238,973,800 | −2.67 | 13 | 54,655,000 | −4.97 |
| 2010 | 134 | 573,785,700 | −3.29 | 29 | 242,697,200 | −5.12 |
| 2011 | 126 | 1,008,086,300 | −2.63 | 34 | 409,421,900 | −6.20 |
| 2012 | 104 | 264,776,600 | −4.36 | 33 | 217,769,000 | −8.40 |
| 2013 | 62 | 430,011,700 | −4.78 | 20 | 190,794,800 | −6.39 |
| 2014 | 56 | 644,055,000 | −6.48 | 37 | 559,620,000 | −10.56 |
| *2015*[a] | *25* | *120,671,600* | −6.19 | *18* | *57,186,600* | −10.15 |

Source: Authors' own data extraction from the LexisNexis database, see Corbet and Gurdgiev (2019)

Note: The above events are compiled after a thorough search of company announcements relating to cybercrime and a thorough media investigation using the LexisNexis database. The number of clients records exposed is reported based on the estimates released in company statements after the cybercrime events. The average CAR is calculated based on the ten-day period following the denoted cybercrime

[a]2015 data covered in the study implies annualized, seasonally adjusted rate of 93 total cybercrime events, and 48 hacking events implying a reversal in the 2013–2014 dynamics

[10] CAR methodology for assessing financial markets penalty for cybersecurity breach is consistent with that used in The Council of Economic Advisers (2018).

companies involved. The frequency of these events is of primary concern. On one hand, numerous hacks may indeed be kept as private as possible due to the reputational damage and other associated concerns attached. On the other hand, the proliferation of social and media fora creates an environment where such concealment is harder to execute. More disturbingly, there has been a dramatic rise in the number of hackers and hacking organizations that 'take responsibility' for their actions, further fuelling the debate about the lack of legal scope and punishment against such actions.

Hacking has become more prevalent and more costly to targeted firms since 2010. CAR analysis presents evidence that the average stock market reaction in the ten days following the hacking event has become increasingly negative as one would expect. Whereas, between 2005 and 2008, the average CAR fell by 3 percent, the same abnormal returns have fallen over 5 percent since 2010, with 2014 and 2015 presenting the largest average falls of over 10 percent associated with hacks. In fact, since 2010, the minimum of the ten-day post-CAR, reflective of the worst-case scenario for the investigated companies, indicates that post-hack share price falls in excess of 45 percent.[11] This share price behaviour presents evidence that stock markets attempt to price the specific risk associated with such hacks, representing the perceived reputational, legal, and regulatory costs associated with a breach in regulatory platforms. This result agrees with the findings in Table 13.1, where we identify an increasingly negative sentiment pertained in the CARs associated with hacking events over time, with the trend peaking at over 10 percent in 2014 and 2015.

Analysing the summary statistics for all events presents evidence that, as a proportion of total cybercrime, hacking is now the most dominant form and has grown substantially throughout the period. This result validates the scope of this chapter that hacking is a concern that is simply not disappearing and requires a proactive, pre-emptive, and preventative approach to enforcement.

The ease of sale of stolen data appears to be incentivizing hackers to further the scale and sophistication of their attacks, particularly with lucrative profits correlated to the number of individual records that can be

[11] Data on other cyber-risk events, including accidental disclosure of data, and theft of data and devices is available in Corbet and Gurdgiev (2019).

obtained (Ablon et al. 2014; Townsend 2014; Boes and Leukfeldt 2016).[12] This phenomenon increases the scope of issues for companies and regulators alike.[13]

The above evidence is in line with the findings reported in more current studies. For example, Ponemon (2018b) shows significant increases in the cost of cybersecurity breaches in 2017–2018. According to the author, the average total cost of a data breach rose 6.4 percent in 2018 to reach US$3.86 million per company impacted by the breach. In contrast, in 2014, the average total cost of data breaches was US$3.5 million. The severity of the breaches rose as well: the average cost for each lost record rose to US$148, an increase of 4.8 percent. Meanwhile, the average size of the data breach is up 2.2 percent. Per Ponemon (2018b, p. 3), 'the average global probability of a material breach in the next 24 months is 27.9 percent, an increase over last year's 27.7 percent'. In 2014, the first year covered by the annual Ponemon reports, the same probability was 22.2 percent. Confirming our findings above, Ponemon (2018b) also shows that malicious or criminal cyberattacks took longer to identify and detect in 2018 than in 2017. Overall, The Council of Economic Advisers (2018, p. 1) estimates that 'malicious cyber activity cost the U.S. economy between $57 billion and $109 billion in 2016'. Finally, Accenture (2019, p. 14) reports estimates of the value of economic activity at risk from cybersecurity events:

> globally, we found that the total value at risk from cybercrime is US$5.2 trillion over the next five years. ... [and] the size of opportunity varies by industry, with High tech subject to the greatest value at risk—US$753 billion—over the next five years, followed by US$642 billion for Life Sciences and US$505 billion for the Automotive industry.

This statement supports our assertion that cybercrime impacts are widely distributed across the globe and economic sectors.

[12] The extent of markets development for transactions in illicit data is exemplified by the fact that today, data obtained from cybercrime activities represent a de facto self-sustained industry supported by back office and supply chain services, as described, for example in Levchenko et al. (2011) for the case of spam activities.

[13] A substantive discussion of legal and enforcement challenges relating to development and implementation of cybercrime combatting legal frameworks and operational enforcement systems is discussed in Kramer et al. (2009) and Wilson (2014).

### *Systemic Risk Spill-Overs from Hacking Events*

Corbet and Gurdgiev (2019) present the evidence for stock price volatility and contagion for all companies above US$1 billion market capitalization based on the results of the individual EGARCH analysis of hacking events between 2005 and the end of April 2015 across the differing cybercrime types, defined in Sect. "Cybercrime Events and Their Impact" above. Almost every company's stock price in the sample has a statistically significant and positive systematic co-movement with the global stock markets, indicating exposure to global systematic risk.

We note the presence of heteroscedasticity and volatility persistence in our returns data. When testing for contagion and volatility spill-overs, methods which do not correct for heteroscedasticity are found to be biased. Such tests overstate any increases in market volatility and the magnitude of cross-market relationships. As such, non-heteroskedastic adjusting tests may incorrectly suggest that volatility spill-overs have occurred. To account for this, we implement a variation of the generalized autoregressive conditional heteroscedasticity (GARCH) based approach. Specifically, we use the exponential generalized autoregressive conditional heteroscedasticity (EGARCH) model, as it allows for asymmetric effects between positive and negative returns. After completing the standard robustness tests, the EGARCH (1,1) methodology, for the most part, was selected as the appropriate model to test for changes in volatility. We also considered the use of GARCH, Threshold GARCH (TGARCH), and GJR-GARCH, but EGARCH was found to outperform each methodology. An intercept and a deterministic trend were included in the Augmented Dickey Fuller (ADF) and Phillips Perron (PP) models. The trend was included to capture the reduction in average volatility that took place during the period under investigation. The ADF model tests, whether the equity series, contain a unit root in order to correct for serial correlation. PP tests employ a non-parametric estimator of the variance-covariance matrix with d truncation lags. The models test down by sequentially removing the last lag until a significant lag is reached. This gives the order of augmentation for the ADF test that minimized the Akaike information criterion. The results rejected the null-unit root hypotheses at a minimum of the 5 percent level. Models that incorporate volatility asymmetries, or negative correlations between returns and volatility innovations, generally outperform models that do not. Further, the EGARCH methodology exploits information contained in realized measures of volatility while providing a flexible leverage function that accounts for return-volatility dependence and remaining in a GARCH-like modelling framework and estimation convenience. The model allows independent return and volatility shock, and this dual shock nature leaves a room for the establishment of a variance risk premium.

Focusing on hacking events, Corbet and Gurdgiev (2019) note that hacking events are predominantly targeted at higher value publicly listed companies (in this case: over US$1 billion in market capitalization). This finding indicates that some of these companies may have superior physical security systems in place to mitigate other cybercrime events, such as physical theft and insider release, but the increased sophistication of hacking appears to affect larger companies just as effectively as the smaller ones.

Of the 29 reported large hacks that occurred between 2005 and 2011, eight events had no contagion effects on the domestic exchange in which the stock trades. Two events instigated systematic contagion effects, whereas seven generated idiosyncratic contagion. The remaining 12 events generated contagion through a combination of all drivers. Hacking events taking place between 2012 and 2015 included 34 large-scale events. Of these, nine hacks resulted in no contagion and only one event resulted in systematic contagion, five hacks resulted in idiosyncratic contagion, whereas the remaining 19 events were a result of a combination of the contagion channels.

Segregating the differing types of contagion stemming from cybercrime over time presents interesting observations based on stock market behaviour. Figure 13.2 documents the rise of systematic contagion since early 2014.

In 2014 over 12 percent of cybercrime events resulted in systematic contagion to the wider national stock exchange. This key finding can be explained through the increased sophistication of such cyber-attacks which has been shown to have caused increased abnormal cumulative losses to the targeted company and a significant rise in the number of client's records that have been illegally exposed. One explanation for such a shift in contagion dynamics is the rise of the Darknet/web, which acts as an international market platform in which this data can be readily sold.

The marked increase in hacking events and their associated negative CARs in 2014 and 2015 (over 10%) appear to be directly responsible for the rise in systematic contagion. Investors also appear to recognize that the successful targeting of one company may in fact represent a wider

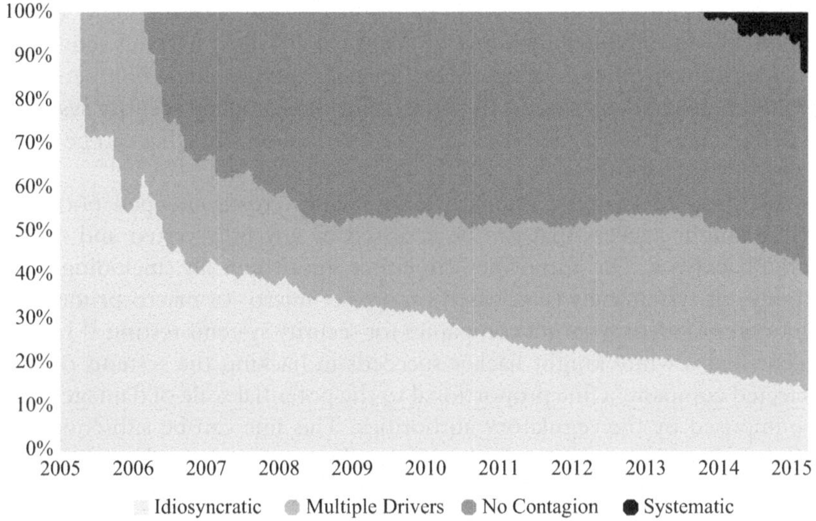


**Fig. 13.2** EGARCH calculated contagion type stemming from cybercrime event (2005–2015). Source: Corbet and Gurdgiev (2019)

threat to the technological structures of domestic publicly traded companies, therefore resulting in such systematic contagion. The results provided in Corbet and Gurdgiev (2019) continue to present evidence of continuing advancements in contagion resulting from a variety of cybercrime, but none more so than hacking.

We must ask what actions can be taken to mitigate the effects of such events, particularly in an environment that is continuing to develop and damage at such increased speed.

## White Knights and Proactive Risk Mitigation

The increasingly systemic nature of risks involved in cybersecurity attacks requires more than an amplification of the currently prevalent means for preventing and mitigating the damages inflicted onto companies, exchanges, and economic systems by such adverse events. In line with the empirical findings in Corbet and Gurdgiev (2019), we propose that the regulatory authorities interested in developing preventative approaches to cybersecurity introduce a more structured relationship with hacktivists and the 'white knights' in order to dis-incentivize 'black knight' cyber attackers and to reduce the flows of talent toward illicit hacking activities.

This objective can be achieved via formally establishing a link between white knight hackers success in penetrating the company security systems based on a fully supervised hack and the financial rewards that can be generated by such a success.

We propose that the regulatory authorities create an open pool for white knight hackers that can be accessed by any fully vetted and registered hacktivist. The authorities can either algorithmically (including randomly) or systemically (e.g. based on pre-set micro- or macro-prudential risk criteria) identify target companies for security systems testing.[14] In the event that a white knight hacker succeeds in hacking the systems of the selected company, a fine proportional to the potential scale of damages can be imposed by the regulatory authorities. This fine can be subsequently co-shared with white knight hacktivists instrumental to detecting the vulnerability.

To reduce incentives to 'double dip'—an activity whereby a white knight hacktivist first penetrates the company cybersecurity systems for the purpose of gaining the regulatory reward, and then subsequently uses/resells access software to collect information illicitly, the pay-outs from the winners' pool should be staggered over time (e.g. 3–5 years), conditional on no repeat security breaches of the tested company. As a second order effect, such time lock-in can also nudge greater degree of commitment by the hacktivists to assisting regulators and enforcement agencies over time, following their first successful contest.

The key regulatory and enforcement objective of the white knight contest would be to identify the unexposed liabilities of a company and deploy regulatory enforcement based on such a discovery. A mechanism for this cooperative interaction can be glimpsed from the Federal statutes and practices relating to the Racketeer Influenced and Corrupt Organizations Act, RICO,[15] and the Dodd-Frank Act[16] recovery approaches, in which a percentage of fines secured against the corporate misbehaviour is allocated

[14] This mixed approach is consistent with the selection mechanisms currently used by the tax authorities in identifying target companies and individuals for conduct of audits.

[15] See https://www.justice.gov/sites/default/files/usao/legacy/2012/10/31/usab6006.pdf for some details on RICO cases rewards.

[16] See http://www.kmblegal.com/practice-areas/whistleblower-law/dodd-frank-act-whistleblower-incentives for some details on Dodd-Frank Act and associated whistleblower rewards system.

to the entities (including for-profit organizations) and/or individuals (especially, whistle-blowers) that help to proactively expose corporate malfeasance.[17]

Beyond the above mechanism, owing to the highly uncertain nature of the size and the likelihood of the payoff for individual hacktivists, we propose that the regulatory authorities provide a notional reward to the top five or even the top ten of the white knight hacktivists who take part in the hacking contest.

This payment, alongside the staggered payout, are two crucial modalities to our proposal because they ensure that hacking contests would remain active and well-resourced, even in the event where a small group of hackers comes to dominate the market in any period of time, capturing the top rewards repeatedly. Recently, Brown (2015) modelled the decision of a profit-motivated hacker to choose the life of a malicious hacker, a 'black hat', or to provide cybersecurity services as a 'white hat' hacktivist. Brown (2015, p. 1) notes that 'a key component of the model is the contest between white and black hats for some part of firm output that is vulnerable to attack. White and black hat earnings are increasing, nonlinear functions of the proportion of black hats'. In the context of our structuring of approved white knight contests, the regulatory and supervisory authorities need to include in the white knight enforcement system design an explicit incentive for non-winning hackers to remain in the white knights pool. As per Brown (2015, p. 3), 'assuming that hackers prefer to work in the industry with the highest returns, when white hat wages fall below the amount that could be made working as a black hat, hackers will switch to black hat work.

Fortunately, although displaying a general lack of consensus within the profession itself, many individual regulators and regulatory analysts are increasingly converging on the view that in relation to cybersecurity risks, threat intelligence is the key to more proactive management of the cybersecurity (Dahlgren 2015; Rosengren 2016; DHS 2018). Our proposal is in line with this evolving approach to structuring preventative systems for enhancing cybersecurity.

[17] Dahlgren (2015) argument can be seen as supportive of the idea that regulatory and supervisory fines should apply more broadly to the cases of cybersecurity breaches. She states: 'I fear that until we can assign financial consequences to cyber risks, and ensure staff are taking that into account when making decisions, we will not get the commitment needed from every level of the organization to adequately address the problem. As long as decisions are made and actions are taken without this type of assessment, we are going to see more and more of these weaknesses exposed.'

## Concluding Remarks

To understand the nature and extent of cybersecurity risks contagion across the financial markets, Corbet and Gurdgiev (2019) have implemented an EGARCH-based modelling framework that encapsulates several channels of contagion and relates them to 819 observed incidents of cybercrime between 2005 and 2015. The authors find that hacking was the most prevalent source of cybercrime, with incidents becoming more frequent and sophisticated since 2012. This increase has resulted in wider transmission of systematic and idiosyncratic contagion to the domestic stock exchange in which the companies' stock trades. Two key findings from Corbet and Gurdgiev (2019) are of significant interest to regulatory authorities in shaping the future institutional structures for addressing rapidly evolving cybersecurity risks. Firstly, stock market volatility was found to be strongly positively correlated to both the size of the company and the number of client's records that have been obtained through the cybercrime incident. Secondly, the changing nature of contagion from cybersecurity events to the broader financial markets: between 2005 and 2012, almost 50 percent of all contagion could be denoted as either idiosyncratic or a combination of idiosyncratic and systematic contagion. Since 2014, systematic contagion has grown rapidly, to the extent that over 10 percent of such contagion to the wider stock exchange originates from cybercrime events.

In response to these findings, the present chapter stresses the need for an immediate and robust regulatory intervention to mitigate the potential disastrous effects of cybercrime. The timeliness of such intervention is ever more important given the growth of cybercrime in recent years, their complexity, their use for commercial and political purposes, and the development of AI. Cybercriminals currently appear to be more advanced in a host of key areas than those whose role is to monitor and regulate. Therefore, it is of vital importance that urgent action is taken. A novel alternative and regulatory strategy for combatting cybercrime, as discussed in this paper, includes formally integrating 'white knights' hacktivists into regulatory institutions of risk prevention, mitigation, and regulatory enforcement. We propose that the regulatory authorities interested in developing preventative approaches to cybersecurity introduce a more structured relationship with white knight hackers. These structured relationships should aim to dis-incentivize black knight cybersecurity attackers and to reduce the flows of talent toward illicit hacking activities, while simultaneously increasing the rate and the robustness of cybersecurity risk tests imposed onto publicly listed companies.

## References

Ablon, L., Libicki, M. C., & Golay, A. A. (2014). Markets for cybercrime tools and stolen data. *Rand National Security Division*. Retrieved from https://www.rand.org/content/dam/rand/pubs/research_reports/RR600/RR610/RAND_RR610.pdf.

Accenture. (2019). The cost of cybercrime. Retrieved from https://www.accenture.com/_acnmedia/PDF-96/Accenture-2019-Cost-of-Cybercrime-Study-Final.pdf.

Alva Group. (2016, November 10). What is the long-term impact of a cybersecurity breach on corporate reputation? *Alva*. Retrieved from https://www.alva-group.com/case-studies/what-is-the-long-term-impact-of-a-cybersecurity-breach-on-corporate-reputation/.

Anderson, R., Barton, C., Böhme, R., Clayton, R., van Eaton, M. J. G., Levi, M., Moore, T., & Savage, S. (2013). Measuring the cost of cybercrime. *The Economics of Information Security and Privacy, 1*(4), 265–300.

Beckert, J., & Dewey, M. (2017). The architecture of illegal markets: Towards an economic sociology of illegality in the economy. *Oxford Scholarship Online*: August 2017. https://doi.org/10.1093/oso/9780198794974.001.0001.

Boes, S., & Leukfeldt, E. R. (2016). Fighting cybercrime: A joint effort. In R. M. Clark & S. Hakim (Eds.), *Cyber-physical security: Protecting critical infrastructure at the state and local level*. Springer.

Brown, C. (2015). *White or black hat? An economic analysis of computer hacking* (working paper). Retrieved from the Economics Department of Georgetown University.

Chen, L. Y., & Yuji Nakamura, Y. (2016, August 5). Hacked bitcoin exchange says users may share $68 million loss, *Bloomberg*. Retrieved from https://www.bloomberg.com/news/articles/2016-08-05/hacked-bitcoin-exchange-says-it-will-spread-losses-among-users.

Corbet, S., & Gurdgiev, C. (2017a). Hacking the market: Systemic contagion from cybersecurity breaches, LSE Business Review, Retrieved November, 2017, from http://eprints.lse.ac.uk/86064/.

Corbet, S., & Gurdgiev, C. (2017b). Financial disrupters: Is the rise of financial disruptors knocking traditional banks off their track? *Journal of Terrorism and Cyber Insurance, 1*(2), 58–62.

Corbet, S., & Gurdgiev, C. (2019). What the hack: Systematic risk contagion from cyber event. *International Review of Financial Analysis, 65*, 101386.
CPMI-IOSCO. (2016). *Guidance on cyber resilience for financial market infrastructures*. Retrieved from BIS: https://www.bis.org/cpmi/publ/d146.pdf.
Dahlgren, S. (2015, March 24). The importance of addressing cybersecurity risks in the financial sector. *Federal Reserve Bank of New York*. Retrieved from https://www.newyorkfed.org/newsevents/speeches/2015/dah150324.
DHS. (2018). *Cybersecurity strategy*. Department of Homeland Security. Retrieved from https://www.dhs.gov/sites/default/files/publications/DHS-Cybersecurity-Strategy_1.pdf.
Egan, M. (2014, March 20). Companies turn to cyber insurance as hacker threats mount. *Fox Business*. Retrieved from http://www.foxbusiness.com/features/2014/03/20/companies-turn-to-cyber-insurance-as-hacker-threat-mounts.html.
Finkle, J., & Spicer, J. (2016, June 7). U.S. warns banks on cyber threat after Bangladesh heist. *Reuters*. Retrieved from http://www.reuters.com/article/us-cyber-heist-regulator-idUSKCN0YT25H.
Greenfield, D. (2014). Social media in financial markets: The coming of age..., [GNIP White Paper]. Retrieved from https://s3.amazonaws.com/st-research/social-media-and-markets-the-coming-of-age.pdf.
Holt, T. J., & Lampke, E. (2010). Exploring stolen data markets online: Products and market forces. *Criminal Justice Studies: A Critical Journal of Crime, Law and Society, 23*(1), 33–50.
Ionescu, L., Mirea, V., & Blăjan, A. (2011). Fraud, corruption and cybercrime in a global digital network. *Economics, Management and Financial Markets, 6*(2), 373–380.
Kelly, M. (2013, November 8). From dark days to white knights: 5 bad hackers gone good. *Venture Beat*. Retrieved from http://venturebeat.com/2013/11/08/black-to-white-hat/.
Keplinger, K. (2018). Is quantum computing becoming relevant to cyber-security? *Network Security, 2018*(9), 16–19.
Khrennikov, I. (2016, June 15). Hackers found selling access to 70,000 company computer systems. *Bloomberg*. Retrieved from https://www.bloomberg.com/news/articles/2016-06-15/your-company-s-servers-now-on-sale-for-just-6.
Kraemer-Mbula, E., Tang, P., & Rush, H. (2013). The cybercrime ecosystem: Online innovation in the shadows? *Technological Forecasting and Social Change, 80*(3), 541–555.
Kramer, F. D., Starr, S. H., & Wentz, L. K. (2009, April). *Cyberpower and national security*. Center for Technology and National Security Policy, National Defense University, Washington DC. Retrieved from http://ctnsp.dodlive.mil/2009/04/01/cyberpower-and-national-security/.

Kremer, J. (2014). Policing cybercrime or militarizing cybersecurity? Security mind-sets and the regulation of threats from cyberspace. *Information and Communications Technology Law, 23*(3), 220–237.

Larson, E., Hurtado, P., & Strohm, C. (2016, March 24). Iranians hacked from Wall Street to New York dam, US says. *Bloomberg*. Retrieved from https://www.bloomberg.com/news/articles/2016-03-24/u-s-charges-iranian-hackers-in-wall-street-cyberattacks-im6b43tt.

Levchenko, K., Pitsillidis, A., Chachra, N., Enright, B., Felegyheazi, M., Grier, C., ... Savage, S. (2011). Click trajectories: End-to-end analysis of the spam value chain. *2011 IEEE Symposium on Security and Privacy*, pp. 431–446. Retrieved from http://www.ieee-security.org/TC/SP2011/PAPERS/2011/paper027.pdf.

MacKenzie, D. (2018). Material signals: A historical sociology of high-frequency trading. *American Journal of Sociology, 123*(6), 1635–1683.

McKendry, I., & Macheel, T. (2015, July 28). Regulators to step up cybersecurity activity: Lawsky. *American Banker*. Retieved from http://www.americanbanker.com/news/bank-technology/regulators-to-step-up-cybersecurity-activity-lawsky-1075715-1.html.

Novet, J. (2017, August 16). Shipping company Maersk says June cyberattack could cost it up to $300 million. *CNBC*. Retrieved from https://www.cnbc.com/2017/08/16/maersk-says-notpetya-cyberattack-could-cost-300-million.html.

Packin, N. G., & Aretz, Y. L. (2016). Big data and social netbanks: Are you ready to replace your bank? *Houston Law Review, 53*(5), May 11, 2016.

Ponemon Institute. (2015). 2015 Cost of data breach study: Global. Retrieved from http://ibm.co/1FStqBu.

Ponemon Institute. (2018a). DNS cybersecurity & protection. Retrieved from https://www.onserve.ca/ponemon-institute-2018-cybersecurity-report-information/

Ponemon Institute. (2018b). 2018 Cost of data breach study: Global. Retrieved from https://www.ibm.com/downloads/cas/861MNWN2.

PWC. (2014, June). Managing cyber risks with insurance: Key factors to consider when evaluating how cyber insurance can enhance your security program. Retrieved from https://www.pwc.com/us/en/increasing-it-effectiveness/publications/assets/pwc-managing-cyber-risks-with-insurance.pdf.

Riley, M., Robertson, J., & Geiger, K. (2015, October 17). Russian hackers of Dow Jones said to have sought trading tips. *Bloomberg*. Retrieved from https://www.bloomberg.com/news/articles/2015-10-16/russian-hackers-of-dow-jones-said-to-have-sought-trading-tips.

Rollins, J., & Wilson, C. (2007). *Terrorist capabilities for cyberattack: Overview and policy issues* (Congressional Research Service (CRS) Report for Congress,

Order Code RL33123), The Library of Congress, updated January 22, 2007, pp. 43–63.

Rosengren, E. S. (2016). Perspectives on risks – Both economic and cyber: Remarks at the Federal Reserve Bank of Boston's 2016 Cybersecurity Conference. *Federal Reserve Bank of Boston*. Retrieved from https://www.bostonfed.org/news-and-events/speeches/2016/perspectives-on-risks-both-economic-and-cyber.aspx.

Security Magazine. (2019, June 20). Domain name system attack cost rises 49 percent to $1,070,000. Retrieved from https://www.securitymagazine.com/articles/90400-domain-name-system-attack-cost-rises-49-percent-to-1070000.

Shell, A. (2017, September 17). Equifax image is battered by data breach as consumers feel violated. *USA Today*. Retrieved from https://www.usatoday.com/story/money/2017/09/18/equifax-image-battered-data-breach-consumers-feel-violated/677908001/.

Spam Titan. (2019, January 25). New research reveals extent of reputation loss after a cyberattack. Retrieved from https://www.spamtitan.com/web-filtering/new-research-reveals-extent-of-reputation-loss-after-a-cyberattack/

Stearns, J. (2016, July 6). European Union's first cybersecurity law gets green light. *Bloomberg*. Retrieved from https://www.bloomberg.com/news/articles/2016-07-06/european-union-s-first-cybersecurity-law-gets-green-light.

Summers, S. (2015). EU criminal law and the regulation of information and communication technology. *Bergen Journal of Criminal Law and Criminal Justice, 3*(1), 48–60.

The Council of Economic Advisers. (2018). The cost of malicious cyber activity to the U.S. economy. *The Council of Economic Advisers*. Retrieved from https://www.whitehouse.gov/wp-content/uploads/2018/03/The-Cost-of-Malicious-Cyber-Activity-to-the-U.S.-Economy.pdf.

Tiedemann-Nkabinde, R., & Davydoff, D. (2019, March 4). Why reputational risk is a security risk and what to do about it. *Security Magazine*. Retrieved from https://www.securitymagazine.com/articles/89908-why-reputational-risk-is-a-security-risk-and-what-to-do-about-it.

Townsend, K. (2014, September). Cybercrime and punishment. *InfoSecurity*. Retrieved from http://www.infosecurity-magazine.com/magazine-features/cybercrime-and-punishment/.

UN. (2011). Cybersecurity: A global issue demanding a global approach. Retrieved from http://www.un.org/en/development/desa/news/ecosoc/cybersecurity-demands-global-approach.html.

Wilson, C. (2014). Cyber Crime. In F. D., Kramer, S. H., Starr, & L. K. Wentz (Eds.), *Cyberpower and national security* (Chapter 18). Center for Technology and National Security Policy, National Defense University, Washington DC, April 2009. Chapter 18 updated version from March 2014. Retrieved from http://ctnsp.dodlive.mil/files/2014/03/Cyberpower-I-Chap-18.pdf.

Yampolskiy, R. V. (2016, June 13). Fighting malevolent AI: Artificial intelligence, meet cybersecurity. *The Conversation*. Retrieved from https://theconversation.com/fighting-malevolent-ai-artificial-intelligence-meet-cybersecurity-60361.

CHAPTER 14

# FinTech for Consumers and Retail Investors: Opportunities and Risks of Digital Payment and Investment Services

*Matthias Horn, Andreas Oehler, and Stefan Wendt*

## Introduction

The link between finance and technology dates back to the nineteenth century when the transatlantic cable enabled the first wave of financial globalization, in which new communication technologies such as the telegraph made possible the rapid transmission of financial information across borders. Since then, the financial services sector has been continuously developing new technical solutions to provide cheaper and more convenient services, such as the automated teller machine in 1967, and to make its business processes more efficient by introducing digital payment and settlement systems, such as SWIFT in 1973 (Arner et al. 2016).

M. Horn (✉) • A. Oehler
Department of Finance, Bamberg University, Bamberg, Germany
e-mail: Matthias.horn@uni-bamberg.de

S. Wendt
The Department of Business Administration, Reykjavik University, Reykjavik, Iceland



T. Walker et al. (eds.), *Ecological, Societal, and Technological Risks and the Financial Sector*, Palgrave Studies in Sustainable Business In Association with Future Earth, https://doi.org/10.1007/978-3-030-38858-4_14

Developing and using new, faster, and more efficient information technology is inherently connected to the financial sector, because business models in financial services are heavily based on gathering, processing, and providing information (see, e.g., Oehler 1990, 1992 and Oehler et al. 2018a).

The newest developments in information technologies, including digitalization, enable financial market participants on the supply side and on the demand side of money to directly enter into contracts with each other, without involving financial institutions. In this sense, digitalization appears to unwind the need for financial intermediaries. However, retail investors still need financial service providers, which help them enter into contracts by providing coordination via online platform solutions, advice or brokerage, and payment services. This change means that—as a result of digitalization—universal banks enter into fewer transactions in their own name and focus more on brokerage instead. In this sense, FinTech (a contraction of Financial Services & Technology) does not necessarily lead to disintermediation, but to a shift from intermediation, where financial service providers *enter into contracts* with consumers on the demand side and on the supply side, to intermediation, where financial service providers *facilitate contractual agreements* between consumers on the demand side and on the supply side. It also means that FinTech is not limited to start-ups in financial markets (Oehler et al. 2016b). Instead, global players, such as Alibaba, Amazon, Apple, and Google, also provide FinTech.

Due to the critical role of investment services and payments in a society, the evolution of FinTech and corresponding innovations pose challenges in balancing the potential benefits of FinTech with its potential risks (Arner et al. 2016). This chapter analyzes the opportunities as well as the ecological, societal, and technological risks of FinTech from consumer and retail investor perspectives in two major financial service sectors: digital payments and investment services. We follow Bitz (1993) by defining risk as the threat or danger as result of uncertainty that a variable deviates negatively from the corresponding target (see also Oehler et al. 2015). Ecological, societal, and technological risks in this context differ regarding their negative effects, which may, among others, include an excess amount of carbon dioxide emissions (ecological), welfare loss for the group of consumers in a society (societal), and down time of a digital service or number of data breaches (technological). However, ecological, societal, and technological risks are not disjunct. Instead, they may overlap or the incidence of one risk can trigger another, for instance, when criminals use data from a cyber attack to blackmail consumers.

This chapter is structured as follows. Section "Digital Payments" describes and analyzes examples of recent innovations that focus on digital payments. More specifically, we focus on mobile payments and cryptocurrencies. In Section "Investment Services", the investment services are subdivided in investment brokerage, investment advice, and portfolio management. As examples, the business models of crowdinvesting platforms (investment brokerage), robo advisors (investment advice), and social trading platforms (portfolio management) are outlined and analyzed. Section "Conclusions" concludes the chapter.

## Digital Payments

### *Mobile Payments*

Raina (2014) describes mobile payment services as services that make mobile devices, for example smartphones and mobile phones, act as business tools, thus replacing banks, ATMs, and credit cards. Slade et al. (2015) add that mobile payments combine payment systems with mobile devices and services to provide users with the ability to initiate, authorize, and complete a financial transaction via mobile network or wireless communication technologies. The definition of mobile payments by Oehler et al. (2016b) includes only those mobile payments that are personally initiated via mobile devices and transferred via mobile communication networks to the payment service provider. The definition by Oehler et al. (2016b) is narrower than the definitions by Raina (2014) and Slade et al. (2015) as it does not consider payments as mobile payments when they are either based on credit or debit cards applications or when a transaction is only initiated via smartphone but takes place via original internet services such as banking apps. The overall process, however, is largely similar in the context of all three definitions. When a consumer pays a seller or service provider, both parties contact the mobile payment service provider (MPSP) as the trusted third party to authenticate the users and the amount of purchase. As the authentication happens almost instantaneously, this type of payment methods is also referred to as instant payments or real-time payments.[1] The MPSP settles the funds via the consumer's bank account,[2] phone bill, or credit card (Raina 2014).

The opportunities of mobile payment services for consumers are threefold.[3] First, mobile payment services have the potential to make checkout in shops and e-commerce retailers easier and faster—and even more so when the payment services are combined with self-service checkout (see Taylor 2016). Second, some MPSPs also offer loyalty programs which can help consumers save money through discounts or provide offers for products and services that may be of interest to the consumer. Third, the fees charged by MPSPs are in some cases lower than the fees charged for other digital payment services, for instance for transactions in foreign currencies, so consumers do not face the costs of searching and going to an ATM to retrieve cash (see Oehler et al. 2016b). As the highest adoption rate of mobile payment services can be observed in quick-service-oriented industries, such as public transportation, service stations, and fast-food and beverage vendors (see Taylor 2016), it seems that consumers particularly perceive the faster and easier payment process as the major advantage of mobile payment services.

However, using smartphones and mobile phones for payments and sharing transaction data with a MPSP as the institution in addition to the consumer's bank and/or credit card company comes with additional risks. Similar to other technical devices that employ software, smartphones and mobiles are potential targets for cyber criminals and are under permanent attack (see Wang et al. 2012). Malware that compromises a mobile payment account can cause both a financial loss and privacy exposure which

[1] However, not all instant or real time payments are necessarily mobile payments.

[2] In the European Economic Area, the Payment Services Directive 2 (PSD 2) allows payment service providers other than banks since 2018 to get access to bank accounts when the account holder gives permission, which enables consumers to initiate payments without the need to additionally log in to their online banking accounts (see https://www.bundesbank.de/en/tasks/payment-systems/psd2/psd2-775954). The concept of providing access to bank accounts is called *open banking*. A similar regulation to foster open banking in the US is not yet on the way (see https://www.forbes.com/sites/ronshevlin/2019/04/15/open-banking-wont-work-in-us/#754f70691e52).

[3] The analysis in this chapter focuses on consumers in developed countries. Particularly in some developing countries with a weak infrastructure of bank branches and stationary internet, mobile payments and mobile banking solutions are the only possibility for consumers to participate in the financial system. This is, of course, an enormous opportunity for these previously unbanked people. However, as they do not have an alternative when they want to participate in the financial system, the analysis in this chapter hardly applies to their situation.

can—in an extreme case—lead to identity theft (see Wang et al. 2012). In addition, either the electronic devices of the seller or the consumer may run out of electric power or be unable to connect to the internet or a wireless network, which would make a transaction impossible.

The need to own suitable technical devices to be able to participate in the payment network can be considered an individual risk, but also a societal risk. As some consumers might be unable to use smartphones, they are locked out from the network and may suffer from this inability to use the mobile payment service (see Oehler and Stellpflug 2015; Oehler 2017). Another societal risk of mobile payment services arises from the so-called *lock-in effects* and a monopoly resulting in welfare losses for consumers. Potential lock-in effects and a monopolistic structure arise because the consumers' utility of a payment service depends on the acceptance rate of the payment service, that is, the size of the payment service network (see Fischer et al. 2019). Furthermore, the willingness of consumers to switch to smaller payment networks decreases when consumers get acquainted with a service through repetitive uses, for example, because transferring personal data, such as bank account information, can cause high perceived switching costs.

Consequently, consumers lock themselves in the service of the largest network that they are used to (see Directorate General for Internal Policies 2015, p. 33). History shows that comparable markets tend to have one network (and thus one provider) that sooner or later unites all users, or at least the vast majority of them, in a "the winner takes all" manner; for example, social networks: Facebook; online retailers: Amazon; search engines: Google (Directorate General for Internal Policies 2015, p. 8). This result can be problematic when the lock-in effect leads to a monopoly, since the service provider then can use its market power to introduce mechanisms of price differentiation or even price discrimination, which lead to welfare losses for consumers (see Oehler 2015; Oehler et al. 2016b). Furthermore, the presence of a monopolistic market structure increases barriers to entry for competitors and might hamper innovation that could be beneficial for consumers.

### *Cryptocurrencies*

Comparable to mobile payment networks, cryptocurrency networks are designed for the settlement of payment transactions. However, when consumers want to use a cryptocurrency network, they have to make their transaction in units of the cryptocurrency and not in fiat money. Cryptocurrencies only exist as electronic signals and records that provide information about processed transactions in the corresponding cryptocurrency, and they are generally based on decentralized computer networks (see Smith and Kumar 2018).[4] This means that no central institution, such as a central bank or a payment service provider, can intervene in the settlement of transactions or the production of currency units (see Hameed and Farooq 2016). Because of the exclusion of central institutions that generally act as regulators, cryptocurrencies are—by definition—not currencies in the sense of a classic monetary system, but rather an asset comparable to commodities.[5]

Cryptocurrencies have benefits for consumers when it comes to fast transaction settlement, which is comparable to the speed of instant payment services. For transaction settlements, cryptocurrency networks use distributed ledger technology, which can be described as a system that is "a record of data that allows verifying and certifying who is the final and definitive owner of a certain value or asset. Unlike traditional payment schemes, distributed ledgers do not have a central administrator or a central data storage" (Scardovi 2016, p. 36). The records of the payees' or payers' transactions are linked to their so-called *wallet*, also referred to as *e-wallet* or *cryptocurrency wallet*, used to determine the units of a cryptocurrency that users have available (see Smith and Kumar 2018; Swammy et al. 2018). The owners of a wallet do not have to specify their real name and can use a pseudonym.[6] Hence, cryptocurrencies are designed to meet the demands of certain users who require a payment system that allows pseudonymous/anonymous transactions between two parties without an intermediary (see Chaum 1983; May 1994; Dai 1998; Nakamoto 2008). The pseudonymity, however, only applies to transactions within the network. When consumers exchange fiat currency into cryptocurrencies, or

[4] Cryptocurrencies can be subdivided into different types based on the underlying distributed ledger/blockchain technology (see Hasanova et al. 2019). The details of the corresponding technological differences are of minor relevance to the considerations in this chapter.

[5] See Johnson and Pomorski (2014), Thiele and Diehl (2017), Yermack (2014), https://www.ccn.com/finland-decides-treat-bitcoin-as-a-commodity. The German Central Bank uses the term crypto token (see Thiele 2018).

[6] See Böhme et al. (2015). Contrary to the popular belief, transactions in cryptocurrency are, therefore, not really anonymous but pseudonymous.

vice versa, it might, depending on the interface, be possible to identify the consumer behind the pseudonym.

The risks of cryptocurrencies—beyond fluctuations in the value of the cryptocurrency itself—arise as a consequence of distributed data storage and the pseudonymity in the cryptocurrency network. Ecological risks of cryptocurrencies result from a high energy demand of their networks. Since no central authority proves the validity of a transaction, the majority of the participating computers in the distributed cryptocurrency network have to reach consensus that a transaction is valid for a transaction settlement. This consensus is achieved via a computing-intensive verification procedure, performed by so-called miners. These miners help run the cryptocurrency network and receive units of the cryptocurrency as reward (see BaFin 2016; Brühl 2017). Due to the high demand of computing power (and, hence, electric power), mining companies started to operate their mining data centers in countries with low energy prices, such as Iceland[7] or China.[8] The energy consumption of mining companies in Iceland is so enormous that it exceeds the total energy consumption of all private households in the country.[9] While the ecological risks related to energy consumption might be relatively small as long as renewable energy sources are used—although even in these cases, the construction of additional power plants will have an impact on the environment—they might become very high when fossil fuels or nuclear power are used, as risks for these methods include, respectively, $CO_2$ emissions and pollutants, and risks related to radiation and final storage. This possibility is particularly alarming considering that cryptocurrencies are not yet widely spread in society.[10] If cryptocurrencies gain more users, operating the cryptocurrency network will be even more energy demanding.

It can be problematic for a society that the pure digital and distributed nature of cryptocurrencies restrains the possibility of assigning

[7] https://www.ccn.com/crypto-cooldown-icelands-bitcoin-miners-turn-to-blockchain-enterprise.

[8] https://www.howtogeek.com/349033/why-it%E2%80%99s-nearly-impossible-to-make-money-mining-bitcoin/.

[9] https://www.theguardian.com/world/2018/feb/13/how-iceland-became-the-bitcoin-miners-paradise.

[10] E.g., less than 400,000 transactions are settled in the Bitcoin network per day (see https://www.blockchain.com/de/charts/n-transactions). The number of daily transactions via electronic channels is higher than 270 million in the European Union alone (see ECB (2015)).

cryptocurrencies to a jurisdiction (see Lerch 2015). In this sense, the high degree of anonymity in the cryptocurrency network and the lack of centralized supervision can provide an ideal playing field for criminal activities, such as money laundering and tax evasion, that threaten the consumers' and the entire society's welfare (see FATF 2014; Keatinge et al. 2018; Lerch 2015; Xu 2016). In addition, the high energy demand of the cryptocurrency network may have negative effects when the use of cryptocurrencies increases further. First, energy prices might rise because of high demand. Thus, less wealthy consumers could no longer afford a sufficient amount of energy. Second, if it is more profitable for privately owned utility companies to deliver electricity to mining companies, these energy suppliers may delay investments in the infrastructures that deliver electricity to private households and, consequently, decrease the security of uninterrupted supply in the long run.

Comparable to the technological risks of digital payment services discussed above, a disadvantage of cryptocurrencies compared to cash is that they can be used only when the technical infrastructure is working (electricity, internet access, etc.). Furthermore, e-wallets are a worthwhile target for hackers. When hackers manage to transfer units of a cryptocurrency from one e-wallet to another, these units are irretrievably lost to the owner of the e-wallet (see Ali et al. 2015; Münzer 2014; Smith and Kumar 2018). In addition, entire cryptocurrency networks can be targets of hacker attacks. Prominent examples are the DAO hack in the Ethereum network[11] and the 51 percent attack on Bitcoin Gold.[12] Even Bitcoin was in danger of 51 percent attack in 2014 (see Böhme et al. 2015). These, among further technical vulnerabilities,[13] can result in large financial losses because of cyber theft or a collapse of the entire network which—when cryptocurrencies were more widespread—can also lead to further societal risks. Even though recently launched cryptocurrencies employ newer generations of distributed ledger technology that fix some of the security issues of the first generations (see Hasanova et al. 2019), the technical security of cryptocurrencies remains an arms race between hackers and the developers of the cryptocurrency network.

[11] https://www.heise.de/newsticker/meldung/Kryptowaehrung-Ethereum-Crowdfunding-Projekt-DAO-um-Millionen-beraubt-3240675.html.

[12] https://www.heise.de/select/ct/2018/14/1530921921642329.

[13] For an overview see e.g., Hasanova et al. (2019).

## Investment Services[14]

### *Crowdinvesting*[15]

Crowdinvesting services enable retail investors to invest jointly with other retail investors (the "crowd") and potentially also institutional investors in a project company—usually a start-up (see Oehler 2016a). The investment brokerage takes place via an online crowdinvesting platform.

The business model of crowdinvesting platforms is based on an extension of the investment opportunities available to retail investors, and likewise an extension of the group of potential investors for companies in need of capital. More specifically, crowdinvesting platforms provide retail investors access to the market segment of early-stage company financing, which was hardly available to retail investors before.[16] For this purpose, crowdinvesting platforms, as intermediaries, provide project companies with an infrastructure to present their ideas to retail investors and consumers. If retail investors decide to invest in a project—for instance, by buying shares or, in most cases, partial subordinated loans—the retail investor and the project company enter into a contract via the crowdinvesting platform. Usually, consumers must invest a minimum amount set by the crowdinvesting platform—some platforms already allow investments of five dollars. In some countries, also an upper limit for investments is set by regulators.[17] The crowdinvesting platform subsequently receives a commission—often as a proportion of the mediated investment—from the project company for successful intermediation. In return for their investment, retail investors either receive a share of the future profits of the funded project or a right to fixed compensation via debt instruments (see BaFin 2017a).

By extending the investment universe, crowdinvesting platforms theoretically provide retail investors with the opportunity to enhance the risk-return position of their portfolio. The first empirical studies about the returns of crowdinvesting projects, however, indicate that retail investors

[14] For the following see Oehler et al. (2016b); see also Oehler et al. (2018a) and Oehler and Wendt (2018).

[15] For the following see Oehler et al. (2016a); see also Wendt (2016) for a more detailed analysis of crowdfunding also covering crowdlending in addition to crowdinvesting.

[16] One exception may be bonds of SMEs that are tradable over exchanges.

[17] E.g., in Germany investments are limited to a maximum of 10,000 Euros per retail investor and crowdinvesting project.

hardly benefit from crowdinvestments due to the insolvencies of project companies and associated negative returns (see Hornuf and Schmitt 2016). Although a total loss can be very challenging for individual retail investors, the average negative returns of crowdinvesting projects are hardly economically significant for whole societies at the moment. The global crowdinvesting market is estimated to have had a transaction volume of only 5.3 billion US dollars (see Statista 2019) in 2018, compared to a market capitalization of almost 69 trillion US dollars for companies listed on global stock markets that same year.[18]

The technological risks for retail investors are comparable to the risks of e-commerce services and mainly concern the risk of data loss and leakages. In the ecological domain, crowdinvesting seems to provide more opportunities than risks. While running a crowdinvesting platform does not expend more ecological resources than any other e-commerce platform, crowdinvesting became a popular instrument to finance ecologically sustainable projects such as solar or wind parks. Some crowdinvesting platforms even advertise how they exclusively offer ecologically sustainable investments.[19]

### *Robo Advisors*

Robo advisors are online services that provide retail investors with automated investment advice. More specifically, retail investors receive an investment suggestion or sample portfolio based on a simple investor profile, consisting of characteristics such as age, income, investable financial wealth, and risk tolerance, as previously identified on the robo advice platform (see BaFin 2017b; Oehler et al. 2016c). The suggested portfolio usually consists of exchange-traded funds (ETFs) invested in stocks and bonds. Most robo advisors additionally offer continuous asset management with an automated rebalancing service, meaning the robo advisor keeps the relative portfolio weights of different asset classes stable over time using calendar-based and threshold-based rebalancing strategies. The latter service, however, is not further considered in this chapter as it

[18] https://data.worldbank.org/indicator/CM.MKT.LCAP.CD.

[19] See Oehler et al. (2018b) for an assessment regarding sustainable investments.

represents automated financial portfolio management rather than automated investment.[20]

For retail investors, the advantages of robo advice compared to analog investment advice include the 24/7 availability and therefore the increased flexibility of the consultation, as well as the lower consultation costs. However, far-reaching standardization of the consultation process is necessary to offer automated advice. This standardization leads to the possible disadvantage that the functionality of robo advisors is limited to the specifications decided on by the platform's investment committee and IT department. Usually only a predetermined amount of ETFs can be subject to investment advice (see Oehler et al. 2016c). In addition, retail investors can only choose to follow the robo advisor and invest in the suggested portfolio or not. A multi-stage adjustment process of the investor profile and the suggested portfolio or individual portfolio components is not intended by most robo-advisors (see Wendt et al. 2018). As the counseling process hardly offers the potential for further inquiries to verify whether investors have understood the provided information, robo advisors cannot ensure that an investor fully grasps the risks associated with an investment and whether the suggested investments actually fit their needs (see Oehler et al. 2016c). Moreover, only some robo advisors offer the possibility to directly call a human financial advisor as complement, making it even more important for retail investors to re-examine their own financial needs before making the investment.

Robo advisors per se are not a source of ecological risks. Instead, some robo advisors such as Sustainfolio, Swell Investing, and Earthfolio solely offer investments in ecologically sustainable indices. Further, robo advisors such as Betterment provide the option to only recommend investments in ecologically sustainable indices.

As changes in public and private pension systems make personal financial and retirement planning more essential (see Oehler et al. 2018c), unintended negative effects of robo advice for consumers and the financial system can become societal risks. Such unintended effects may arise from solely recommending ETFs. As Ben-David et al. (2018) show, stocks with higher ETF ownership display significantly higher volatility. In bullish markets, retail investors are compensated for the higher volatility with a

[20] For a more detailed analysis of the automated rebalancing services, see Horn and Oehler (2019). They find that automated rebalancing is hardly beneficial for retail investors; these results support the findings of Hilliard and Hilliard (2018).

monthly risk premium of up to 56 basis points (see Ben-David et al. 2018). However, it is unclear whether retail investors are aware "that ETFs are a new source of systematic risk" (Ben-David et al. 2018, p. 2474) which are nondiversifiable. This risk means that ETF investors—consumers using robo advisors and shareholders of stocks that are also held by ETFs—could be negatively affected by the increasing spread of ETFs as investment vehicles, which is catalyzed by robo advisors.

### *Social Trading*

Social trading is based on the concept that a social trading platform provides retail investors, often referred to as *followers*, the possibility to automatically replicate the trading signals of other allegedly successful market participants, so-called *traders* or *signal providers*, in real time (see Oehler 2016b; Oehler et al. 2016a). Hence, social trading is a form of copy trading in which followers copy the trades of signal providers (see Wendt 2016, p. 11). Since retail investors delegate investment decisions to a third party, social trading is a new form of portfolio management. In comparison to investments in actively managed mutual funds, social trading offers retail investors more transparency regarding the trades and portfolios of the portfolio managers, as the previous investment decisions of signal providers are saved in a transaction history on the platform and new transactions are added in real time. In contrast to investments in mutual funds, retail investors, however, do not transfer their invested capital to the signal provider but instead only copy the transactions (see Oehler et al. 2016a; Wendt 2016). As compensation for sharing their investment decisions, signal providers receive a fee that, depending on the social trading platform, consists of either a performance fee based on the investment success, a fixed management fee computed as a share of the capital that followers invest by replicating the strategy of the signal provider, or a fee based on the number of followers.

Hence, social trading platforms generally have the potential to be beneficial for both retail investors as signal providers and as followers. However, it is unlikely that followers earn positive abnormal returns by investing in social trading. Instead, after controlling for fees and transaction costs, investments in social trading, on average, underperform in broadly diversified market indices (see Oehler et al. 2016a; Dorfleitner et al. 2018). This result may be a reason for the low market penetration of social trading platforms, in terms of assets under management (see

Dorfleitner and Hornuf 2016). Due to the rather marginal assets under management, the absolute amount of fees that the signal providers receive should also be negligible. Similar to the crowdinvestment market, the risk of financial loss is hardly economically significant for a whole society, but can be substantial for individual retail investors.

Relevant ecological risks resulting from social trading are unknown. Technological risks also play a minor role; however, they may become more severe when social trading is more often combined with algorithmic trading. The necessary infrastructure for this combination is already available, for instance with the MetaTrader platform by MetaQuotes.[21] The platform allows individuals to share trading algorithms with other users of the platform. Followers subscribe to the provided algorithms and—when applicable—pay a monthly fee, comparable to a license fee, to the programmer of the trading algorithm. Since even algorithms of established Wall Street market makers and traders are not always free from errors,[22] it is unlikely that all algorithms programmed by signal providers are infallible.

## Conclusions

The analysis of FinTech innovations shows that they generally provide consumers new opportunities compared to older analogue or digital services, but that these opportunities also come with new risks. Mobile payment services and cryptocurrencies could allow consumers to pay faster, with lower fees, and be more convenient for products and services at digital and analogue points of sale. However, when consumers use mobile payment services, they involve an additional party to which they make their data available. Consequently, consumers are subject to new risks that arise from a potentially detrimental use of their data. Cryptocurrencies supposedly tackle these risks by enabling a degree of anonymity close to that of cash transactions. However, cryptocurrency networks are highly energy demanding and by using them, consumers lose some of the protective functions of a central-bank-monitored monetary system and the legal system they live under.

It is initially positive for consumers that new investment services expand the range of investable financial products. Corresponding diversification

[21] See https://www.metatrader5.com/en/terminal/help/signals.

[22] E.g., Knight Capital in 2012 or the Flash Crash of the Dow Jones in 2010 (see, e.g., https://www.bbc.com/news/magazine-19214294).

effects have the potential to enhance the risk-return position of consumers' portfolios. Moreover, the high availability of the digital services and the respective information at the disposal of the consumers can reduce their information and transaction costs. However, responsibility rests with the consumers to assess the trustworthiness of the service provider and the counterparties—signal providers in social trading, or project companies in crowdinvesting—on these platforms.

From a consumer perspective, information asymmetries considerably hamper the possibility to assess the direct risks of the investment services and cryptocurrencies. Additionally, the presentation of rather irrelevant information can have a negative influence on consumers' economic decisions (see, e.g., Oehler et al. 2019). However, each consumer's direct, maximum financial risk is limited to their invested wealth. In contrast, the risks for consumers and societies that arise from decreasing trust in financial services and the financial system is hardly assessable, but they are assumed to be much higher than the direct financial risk. The same applies to data abuse in mobile payment networks, price discrimination, and the withholding of certain services, products, or assets.

Ecological risks are primarily identified for cryptocurrencies due to their enormous energy demands. Investment services committed to providing ecological and sustainable products can be beneficial for consumers and decrease the ecological risk exposure of their portfolios.

All payment and investment services analyzed in this chapter are subject to technological risks. Besides problems that may arise when consumers do not have access to the internet or run out of electric power for the necessary devices, the most severe risk in the digital world is that either service providers or hackers use the consumers' data against them through price discrimination or identity theft. While the risk of a hacker attack is inherent to digital services, governments can address the risk of price discrimination by facilitating competition among market participants and—when necessary—break up monopolistic structures.

## References

Ali, S. T., Clarke, D., & McCorry, P. (2015). Bitcoin: Perils of an unregulated global P2P currency. In *Revised Selected Papers of the 23rd International Workshop on Security Protocols XXIII, Vol. 9379* (pp. 283–293). New York: Springer.

Arner, D., Barberis, J., & Buckley, R. (2016). *The Evolution of Fintech: A New Post-Crisis Paradigm?* University of Hong Kong, Faculty of Law Research Paper No. 2015/047, UNSW Law Research Paper No. 2016/62.

BaFin. (2016). *Die Technologie hinter den virtuellen Währungen am Beispiel der Blockchain* [Distributed ledger: The technology behind virtual currencies using the example of blockchain]. Retrieved May 8, 2019, from https://www.bafin.de/SharedDocs/Veroeffentlichungen/DE/Fachartikel/2016/fa_bj_1602_blockchain.html.

BaFin. (2017a). Crowdinvesting. Retrieved from https://www.bafin.de/DE/Aufsicht/FinTech/Crowdfunding/Crowdinvesting/crowdinvesting_node.html.

BaFin. (2017b). Robo-Advice und Auto-Trading – Plattformen zur automatisierten Anlageberatung und automatischem Trading. Retrieved from https://www.bafin.de/DE/Aufsicht/FinTech/Anlageberatung/anlageberatung_node.html.

Ben-David, I., Franzoni, F., & Moussawi, R. (2018). Do ETFs Increase Volatility? *Journal of Finance, 73*(6), 2471–2535.

Bitz, M. (1993). Grundlagen des finanzwirtschaftlich orientierten Risikomanagements [Fundamentals of financial risk management]. In G. Gebhard, W. Gerke, & M. Steiner (Eds.), *Handbuch des Finanzmanagements – Instrumente und Märkte der Unternehmensfinanzierung* (pp. 641–668). Munich: Beck.

Böhme, R., Christin, N., Edelman, B., & Moore, T. (2015). Bitcoin: Economics, technology, and governance. *Journal of Economic Perspectives, 29*(2), 213–238.

Brühl, V. (2017). Bitcoins, Blockchain und Distributed Ledgers: Funktionsweise, Marktentwicklungen und Zukunftsperspektiven [Bitcoins, Blockchain and Distributed Ledgers]. *Wirtschaftsdienst, 97*(2), 135–142.

Chaum, D. (1983). Blind signatures for untraceable payments. In D. Chaum, R. L. Rivest, & A. T. Sherman (Eds.), *Advances in cryptology: Proceedings of Crypto 82* (pp. 199–203). New York: Plenum Press.

Dai, W. (1998). B-money. Retrieved April 5, 2019, from http://www.weidai.com/bmoney.txt.

Directorate General for Internal Policies. (2015). *Challenges for competition policy in a digitalised economy*. Study for the ECON Committee.

Dorfleitner, G., Fischer, L., Lung, C., Willmertinger, P., Stang, N., & Dietrich, N. (2018). To follow or not to follow – An empirical analysis of the returns of actors on social trading platforms. *Quarterly Review of Economics and Finance, 70*, 160–171.

Dorfleitner, G., & Hornuf, L. (2016). The Fintech market in Germany. Retrieved June 18, 2019, from http://www.bundesfinanzministerium.de/Content/EN/Standardartikel/Topics/International_affairs/Articles/2016-12-13-study-fintech-market-in-germany.pdf?__blob=publicationFile&v=2.

ECB. (2015). *Virtual currencies – A further analysis*. Frankfurt am Main: European Central Bank.

FATF. (2014). Virtual currencies: Key definitions and potential AML/CFT risks. Retrieved April 11, 2019, from https://www.fatf-gafi.org/media/fatf/documents/reports/Virtual-currency-key-definitions-and-potential-aml-cft-risks.pdf.

Fischer, R., Öztürk, G., Weimert, M., & Lammer, D. (2019). Mobile Payment in Deutschland – Letzte Chance für Banken, ihre strategischen Fehler der Vergangenheit zu korrigieren [Mobile payment in Germany – Last chance for banks to correct their strategic mistakes of the past]. Retrieved June 18, 2019, from https://www.oliverwyman.de/content/dam/oliver-wyman/v2-de/publications/2019/mai/20190509_OliverWyman_POV_Mobile_Payment.pdf.

Hameed, S., & Farooq, S. (2016). The art of cryptocurrencies. *International Journal of Advanced Computer Science and Applications, 7*(12), 426–435.

Hasanova, H., Baek, U., Shin, M., Cho, K., & Kim, M. (2019). A survey on blockchain cybersecurity vulnerabilities and possible countermeasures. *International Journal of Network Management, 29*(2), 1–36.

Hilliard, J., & Hilliard, J. (2018). Rebalancing versus Buy and Hold: Theory, simulation and empirical analysis. *Review of Quantitative Finance and Accounting, 50*(1), 1–32.

Horn, M., & Oehler, A. (2019). *Automated portfolio rebalancing: Automatic erosion of investment performance?* Working Paper, Bamberg, presented at 88th International Atlantic Economic Conference, Miami, October 17–20, 2019; 2019 Annual Meeting of the Academy of Financial Services, Minneapolis, October 15–16, 2019; 30th European Conference on Operational Research, Dublin, June 23–26, 2019; 2019 European Conference of FMA, Glasgow, June 12–14, 2019.

Hornuf, L., & Schmitt, M. (2016). Success and failure in equity crowdfunding. In CESifo DICE Report 2/2016, pp. 16–22.

Johnson, G. and Pomorski, L. Briefing on digital currencies. Briefing to the Senate of Canada, Ontario: Bank of Canada, (2014, April).

Keatinge, T., Carlisle, D., & Keen, F. (2018). Virtual currencies and terrorist financing: Assessing the risks and evaluating responses. Retrieved April 11, 2019, from http://www.europarl.europa.eu/RegData/etudes/STUD/2018/604970/IPOL_STU(2018)604970_EN.pdf.

Lerch, M. (2015). Bitcoin als Evolution des Geldes: Herausforderungen, Risiken und Regulierungsfragen [Bitcoin as evolution of money: Challenges, risks and regulatory issues]. *Journal of Banking Law and Banking, 3*, 190–204.

May, T. (1994). Cyphernomicon. Retrieved April 5, 2019, from http://www.cypherpunks.to/faq/cyphernomicron/cyphernomicon.html.

Münzer, J. (2014). Bitcoins: Aufsichtliche Bewertung und Risiken für Nutzer [Bitcoins: Supervisory assessment and risks for users]. BaFin. Retrieved April 11, 2019, from https://www.bafin.de/SharedDocs/Veroeffentlichungen/DE/Fachartikel/2014/fa_bj_1401_bitcoins.html.

Nakamoto, S. (2008). Bitcoin: A Peer-to-Peer Electronic Cash System. Retrieved April 11, 2019, from https://bitcoin.org/bitcoin.pdf.

Oehler, A. (1990). Konsequenzen der Selbstbedienung für die Vertriebspolitik [Consequences of self-service for sales policy]. *geldinstitute 1*(2), 4–12.

Oehler, A. (1992). POS-Banking. *Südwestfälische Wirtschaft, 3*, 32–34.

Oehler, A. (2015). Alles digital? Innovative Geschäftsmodelle im digitalen Zahlungsverkehr und Verbraucherpolitik [All digital? Innovative business models for digital payment and consumer policy]. *Wirtschaftsdienst, 95*(12), 817–821.

Oehler, A. (2016a). Digitale Welt und Finanzen. Formen des Crowdfunding: Handlungsbedarf für die Verbraucherpolitik? [The digital world and finance. Types of crowdfunding: Do consumer policy makers need to act?] Veröffentlichungen des Sachverständigenrats für Verbraucherfragen, Berlin 2016.

Oehler, A. (2016b). Digitale Welt und Finanzen. Zahlungsdienste und Finanzberatung unter einer Digitalen Agenda [The digital world and finance. Payment services and financial advisory under a digital agenda]. Veröffentlichungen des Sachverständigenrats für Verbraucherfragen, Berlin 2016.

Oehler, A. (2017). Der technologische Wandel: Herausforderungen in der Digitalen Welt [The technological change: Challenges in the digital world]. In P. Kenning, A. Oehler, L. Reisch, & C. Grugel (Eds.), *Verbraucherwissenschaften – Rahmenbedingungen, Forschungsfelder und Institutionen* (pp. 69–80). Wiesbaden: Springer.

Oehler, A., Herberger, T., Höfer, A., & Wendt, S. (2015). Risk assessment and risk management in economics. In H.-W. Micklitz & T. Tridimas (Eds.), *Risk and the EU law* (pp. 33–48). Cheltenham: Elgar.

Oehler, A., Horn, M., & Wendt, S. (2016a). Benefits from social trading? Empirical evidence for certificates on wikifolios. *International Review of Financial Analysis, 46*, 202–210.

Oehler, A., Horn, M., & Wendt, S. (2016b). Digitale Zahlungsdienste: Chinese Walls 2.0 oder Trennung? [Digital payment services: Chinese Walls 2.0 or separation?] *DIVSI Magazin*, pp. 23–25.

Oehler, A., Horn, M., & Wendt, S. (2016c). [Was taugt die Finanzberatung durch Robo-Advisors wirklich?] What are the real benefits of Robo-Advice? *Der Neue Finanzberater, 2016*(2), 28–29.

Oehler, A., Horn, M., & Wendt, S. (2018a). Neue Geschäftsmodelle durch Digitalisierung? Eine Analyse aktueller Entwicklungen bei Finanzdienstleistungen [New business models as result of digitalization? An analysis of current developments in financial services]. In F. Keuper, M. Schomann, L. I. Sikora, & R. Wassef (Eds.), *Disruption and transformation management* (pp. 325–341). Wiesbaden: Springer.

Oehler, A., Horn, M., & Wendt, S. (2018b). Why self-commitment is not enough: On a regulated minimum standard for ecologically and socially responsible financial products and services. In T. Walker, S. Kibsey, & R. Crichton (Eds.), *Designing a sustainable financial system: Development goals and socio-ecological responsibility* (pp. 405–421). Cham: Palgrave Macmillan.

Oehler, A., Horn, M., Wendt, S., Reisch, L. A., & Walker, T. J. (2018c). Young adults and their finances: An international comparative study on applied financial literacy. *Economic Notes, 47*(2–3), 305–330.

Oehler, A., Horn, M., & Wendt, S. (2019). Information illusion: Placebic information and stock price estimates. Conference Paper presented at 88th International Atlantic Economic Conference, Miami, October 17–20, 2019; 2019 Annual Meeting of the Academy of Financial Services, Minneapolis, October 15–16, 2019; 2019 IAREP/SABE Conference, Dublin, September 1–4, 2019; 2019 Behavioural Finance Working Group Conference, London, 6–7 June 2019.

Oehler, A., & Stellpflug, J. (2015). Daseinsvorsorge in der Digitalen Welt: Der Staat für alle oder jeder für sich? [Services of public interest in the digital world: Should the state do it for everyone or everyone on his or her own?] Stellungnahme der Verbraucherkommission Baden-Württemberg, 41. Stuttgart.

Oehler, A., & Wendt, S. (2018). Trust and financial services: The impact of increasing digitalisation and the financial crisis. In T. O. Sigurjonsson, D. L. Schwarzkopf, & M. Bryant (Eds.), *The Return of Trust?* (pp. 195–211). Bingley: Emerald.

Raina, V. (2014). Overview of mobile payment: technologies and security. In F. Liebana, F. Munoz-Leiva, & J. Sanchez-Fernandez (Eds.), *Electronic payment systems for competative advantage in E-Commerce* (pp. 186–222). IGI Global.

Scardovi, C. (2016). Fin Tech innovation and the disruption of the global financial system. In C. Scardovi (Ed.), *Restructuring and innovation in banking* (pp. 21–49). Cham: Springer.

Smith, C., & Kumar, A. (2018). Crypto-currencies – An introduction to not-so-funny moneys. *Journal of Economic Surveys, 32*(5), 1531–1559.

Slade, E., Williams, M., Dwivedi, Y., & Piercy, N. (2015). Exploring consumer adoption of proximity mobile payments. *Journal of Strategic Marketing, 23*(3), 209–223.

Statista. (2019). FinTech report 2019 – Alternative financing. Retrieved June 18, 2019, from https://de.statista.com/statistik/studie/id/47351/dokument/fintech-report-alternative-financing/

Swammy, S., Thompson, R., & Loh, M. (2018). Creation of a distributed ledger. In S. Swammy, R. Thompson, & M. Loh (Eds.), *Crypto uncovered* (pp. 133–148). Cham: Palgrave Macmillan.

Taylor, E. (2016). Mobile payment technologies in retail: A review of potential benefits and Risks. *International Journal of Retail & Distribution Management, 44*(2), 159–177.

Thiele, C.-L. (2018). Digitales Geld – Gefahr oder Chance? [Digital money – Threat or Opportunity?] Retrieved April 11, 2019, from https://www.bundesbank.de/de/presse/reden/digitales-geld-gefahr-oder-chance—724694.

Thiele, C.-L., & Diehl, M. (2017). Kryptowährung Bitcoin: Währungswettbewerb oder Spekulationsobjekt: Welche Konsequenzen sind für das aktuelle Geldsystem zu erwarten? [Cryptocurrency bitcoin: Currency competition or speculative asset: Which consequences can be expected for the current monetary system?] Ifo Schnelldienst 22, pp. 3–6.

Wang, Y., Streff, K., & Raman, S. (2012). Smartphone security challenges. *Computer, 45*(12), 52–58.

Wendt, S. (2016). Geld anlegen mit und im Schwarm – Chancen und Risiken für Verbraucherinnen und Verbraucher [Invest with and within the crowd – Opportunities and risks for consumers]; in: Studien und Gutachten im Auftrag des Sachverständigenrats für Verbraucherfragen, Berlin 2016.

Wendt, S., Horn, M., & Oehler, A. (2018). Robo-Advisors: The future of financial advice? *Tölvumál, 2018*, 20–21.

Xu, J. (2016). Are blockchains immune to all malicious attacks? *Financial Innovation, 2*(1), Article 25.

Yermack, D. (2014). Is Bitcoin a real currency? An economic appraisal. In S. Chuen (Ed.), *Handbook of digital currency* (pp. 31–43). London: Elsevier.

CHAPTER 15

# Empirical Modelling of Man-made Disaster Scenarios

*Melanie Windirsch*

## Introduction

Natural catastrophes may make the headlines, but man-made perils can be equally destructive (Zurich Insurance Group 2017). In 2017, out of the 301 disaster events worldwide, 118 were man-made, resulting in USD 6 billion insured losses (Swiss Re Institute 2018c, pp. 2–4). Man-made disasters have the potential to jeopardise an individual insurer's solvency position if the risk is not properly managed. Furthermore, these catastrophes may trigger market shocks and subsequent economic downturns, like it happened in 2008s subprime financial crisis, because these events are highly destructive and result in the destruction of billions of physical property and infrastructure and affect millions of people and multiple

The views expressed in this paper are those of the author, and not necessarily those of Allianz.

M. Windirsch (✉)
Chicago, IL, USA
e-mail: melanie.windirsch@aol.com



T. Walker et al. (eds.), *Ecological, Societal, and Technological Risks and the Financial Sector*, Palgrave Studies in Sustainable Business In Association with Future Earth, https://doi.org/10.1007/978-3-030-38858-4_15

companies across different industries (e.g., banks, industrial companies). This kind of disaster leads to a disruption of business activities across regions (due to globalisation and high interconnectivity of business) and halts the economic output, taking several years to recover. These spill-over effects result in consequential amplifiers of this shock throughout the global economy and have an impact on both sides of an insurer's balance sheet—the losses that would be paid out in claims and the devaluation and reduction in returns in relation to the financial assets. Due to multiple insurers as well as other parties being affected by such market events, those losses may ultimately remove billions of anticipated Gross Domestic Product (GDP) from economies across the world (Cambridge Centre for Risk Studies 2018).

Due to an increase in frequency, duration, and magnitude of man-made disasters, the need for a comprehensive approach to identify, assess, transfer, and mitigate the risks arises today even more than in the past. Therefore, a proper estimation of their extent (frequency and severity) is important for the healthiness and future existence of insurance companies as well as the stability of the financial market.

Natural catastrophes are well understood. But unlike with natural hazards and their sophisticated risk models, the empirical modelling of man-made disaster scenarios is very challenging (Clark et al. 2015, p. 5-2) and mainly results from two facts:

1. Variety of loss triggers: The variety of loss triggers, such as explosions, collisions, human errors, leads to an even more unpredictable set of possible catastrophic risks.
2. Low frequency: It is often the case that sufficient historical claims data do not exist for man-made catastrophes (low frequency) to model those properly.

Nonetheless and especially because of their severity, there is a need to evaluate these risks, not only due to regulatory requirements, such as Solvency II, but also for internal purposes (e.g., planning or cost allocation) (Brüske et al. 2010, p. 134).

Due to the lack of empirical modelling approaches for man-made disaster scenarios, the insurance industry uses expert-based approaches to assess the frequency and severity of man-made catastrophes. In many cases, a group of experts estimates the frequency and severity of specific predefined scenarios based on experience. Combined with the potential loss volume (derived from the analysis of internal portfolio data), an overall assessment of these scenarios can ultimately be conducted. Expert assessments are subjective views that result in relatively high uncertainties. This peculiarity is addressed as part of this research.

The ultimate goal of this research is to determine how the frequency and severity of tail events can be evaluated and modelled based on empirical data. Because of the variety of triggers that require separate modelling approaches, this research is focused on man-made fire/explosion disasters since recent events, such as the Tianjin harbor explosion,[1] have shown the significance of this disaster type and their impact on the insurance industry. Hence, empirical modelling shall be applied to develop a loss curve to ultimately reflect man-made fire/explosion disasters properly.

For this purpose, man-made disaster scenarios are defined and characterised first. Then, the main section focuses on the modelling of man-made disaster scenarios based on historical claims data. Once the data collection and preparation are explained, different methods for developing appropriate frequency and severity curves for man-made fire/explosion catastrophes are explored by fitting and validating different potential distributions. Ultimately, an aggregate loss distribution is derived, illustrating the probability for man-made fire/explosion catastrophes. A conclusion closes the research work.

## Definition and Characteristics of Man-made Disasters and Their Distinction to Natural Hazards

Broadly, catastrophes (or so-called disasters/tail events) describe extremely negative but very rare events resulting in a sudden and massive destruction of property, lives, environment, and/or economy. Thus, disasters are characterised with high severity, but low frequency. They can either be caused by natural hazards or man-made events. Natural catastrophes refer to an event induced by natural forces (weather- or geological-related events) such as tropical cyclones, floods, tornadoes, hailstorms, wildfires,

[1] Tianjin harbor explosion is one of the largest global insurance losses in the history of man-made disasters. Current estimates assume insurance losses around USD 3.5 billion. In 2015, a hazardous chemical explosion occurred at a warehouse storing dangerous and flammable materials in the Port of Tianjin. The explosion caused enormous economic and human losses for enterprises and society. The review and analysis of the causes and effects of the explosion has triggered a wider discussion about risk management and the impact of man-made disasters (Swiss Re 2016, p. 1).

blizzards, earthquakes, tsunamis, volcanic eruptions, mudslides, or avalanches. Conversely, man-made catastrophes refer to accidental or intentional human actions. Hence, man-made disaster scenarios represent losses from single man-made catastrophic events that are deemed extreme and atypical but realistic (Banks 2009, pp. 17–22; Clark et al. 2015, p. 5-2).

Man-made disasters are characterised by various aspects that need to be taken into consideration (Thornton 2016, pp. 2–3):

- Variability: Man-made disasters can originate from various, very heterogeneous perils that show significant differing characteristics and treatment requirements. Hence, there is a broad variety of triggers.
- Geographical location: Some of the man-made disasters don't have geographical boundaries. Hence, accumulations cannot be defined in terms of the location of the insured parties, as for example in the case of cyberattacks.
- Sparse Data: Due to the low frequency of man-made disasters, there is limited historical data available used to perform risk assessments.
- Constant Evolution: Because of the nature of man-made disasters being affected by people and behaviour, they constantly evolve which deteriorates the data reliability topic as past performances cannot be used as a guarantee for future results.
- Prevention: Other than natural catastrophes, man-made disasters can theoretically be stopped or even prevented.

Man-made disaster scenarios can be divided into different clusters because they show similar characteristics. Cluster groups can mainly be structured according to the trigger that is causing a man-made disaster; for example, fire/explosion or collision (Lloyd's 2018). This contribution focuses on man-made fire/explosion disasters only as this particular man-made disaster cluster is of high importance, not only for insurance companies, but also for its significance and huge impact on the market.

## Data Collection, Preparation, and Analysis

### *Data Collection and Preparation*

Different external data sources that are used to build up a loss database for man-made fire/explosion disasters are first presented. To explicitly capture man-made fire/explosion disasters, only the events that outline fire/explosion as triggers are considered for this exercise.

Reinsurance companies, acting as protectors for multiple insurance companies with regards to catastrophic risks, and similar reinsurance brokers, acting as intermediaries in this context, as well as marketplaces like Lloyd's, have access to a great variety of historical loss data due to their large portfolios. Therefore, the main reinsurance companies and brokers have been contacted to access their historical loss data for man-made fire/explosion disasters. In addition, the internet is screened for publicly available data on man-made catastrophes; a Google research is carried out to further identify large fire/explosion losses. For instance, Marsh regularly publishes an official report about the 100 largest property losses—current data is available for the time period 1974–2017 (Marsh 2016, 2018). Furthermore, Marsh also presents reports with information about historical loss experiences that have affected the power generation industry in recent years (Marsh 2014; Marsh 2012). Reuters, for example, provides an overview of the world's worst industrial accidents in the last 20 years (Cutler 2013). Additional insights are obtained through the list of historical explosions collected by the organisation Explosion Hazards Ltd. (ATEX Explosion Hazards Ltd. 2018). The database is built based on the various sources mentioned above.

Finally, it should be noted that it is quite challenging to access valuable data about historical fire/explosion catastrophe losses, especially for losses that occurred far in the past. Hence, it is almost impossible to build a complete database for large man-made fire/explosion losses worldwide. Nonetheless, the collected data as described above can be considered representative since various data sources are combined.

First, the historical losses that would no longer occur under current conditions, for example, due to a change in production mode, are removed from the list of historical industry loss data for man-made fire/explosion catastrophes.

Second, some events did not have the insured loss amount on record and only the total economic loss. Thus, the insured loss amount has to be derived thereof, since the total economic loss also includes the uninsured loss portion. To achieve this, the insured loss share of the total economic loss is to be identified by using the time-series comparison 'Insured vs Uninsured Losses 1970–2016' from Swiss Re's sigma 1/2018 report as a basis (Swiss Re Institute 2018b). For every particular year, the insured loss share is calculated by dividing the man-made Insured Loss by the man-made Total Economic Loss. Whereas the annual Insured Loss is specifically available for man-made catastrophes, the Total Economic Loss figure also includes Natural Catastrophes (NatCat). Hence, the annual Total Economic Loss for man-made catastrophes is to be calculated by deducting the NatCat portion from the overall figure. For the year 2001, the Insured Loss Share is calculated without consideration of the World Trade Center catastrophe as its inclusion would distort the results because of the extreme severity of this event. This calculation results in an average man-made Insured Loss Share of 63.14% for the time period 1970–2016. A correlation factor of 0.93 confirms the significance of the linkage between the Total Economic Loss and the Insured Loss per year. Depending on the event year, the respective Insured Loss Share for this particular year is to be multiplied with the Total Economic Loss figure to estimate the Insured Loss amount for the single event.

The collected historical loss data are further prepared to accurately reflect the changing environment. First, the inflation measured by the consumer price index (2010 base year) needs to be taken into account to adjust past loss amounts for the current living standards. Consumer Price Index (CPI) is defined as the period-to-period proportional change in the prices of a basket of goods and services that are purchased by the reference population (OECD 2019). As the CPI for USD is available for a longer time period, the adjustment for inflation is to be rendered in USD. Hence, the USD loss amount values are extrapolated using the US CPI to give the current (2017) values. The World Bank Group is used as a reasonable source for this purpose (The World Bank Group 2019). To adjust the losses per event for inflation, an individual inflation factor per event year is calculated by dividing the level of CPI 2017 by the level of CPI for the particular event year. To derive the adjusted loss values for inflation to 2017, the inflation factor is multiplied with the respective Gross Exposure value in USD (Swiss Re Institute 2018a).

In addition, different currencies also need to be converted to one central currency for further processing. All data available are converted into EUR by using a fixed exchange rate, that is 31.03.2018 (date of conversion) in this particular case.

Finally, all loss data from the different data sources are merged to a single overall fire/explosion loss database. To focus on catastrophic losses, all losses with a gross exposure/insured loss amount less than EUR 100 million (inflated amount) are removed and will no longer be considered for the following analysis.

### *Data Analysis*

The overall man-made fire/explosion disaster loss database shows 114 fire/explosion losses with a gross exposure exceeding EUR 100 million for the time period 1974–2017.

Table 15.1 shows the major five man-made fire/explosion catastrophes.

The annual number of claims ranges from 0 to 7. The summarised measures for the 44-year sample of loss history of claim numbers are as follows (Gray and Pitts 2012, pp. 58–61):

mean 2.59, variance 3.83, standard deviation 1.96, min 0.00, max 7.00.

The average number of large fire/explosion losses is at 2.59 per year, but a negative trend can be observed, which predicts an average number of annual large fire/explosion losses between 3 and 4 at least for the next five years.

The size of claims ranges from EUR 101.29 million to EUR 2522.92 million. The summary measures per single event for the 44-year sample of loss history of claim sizes (in million EUR) are as follows (Gray and Pitts 2012, pp. 58–61):

mean 315.87, variance 111,624.8, standard deviation 334.10, min 101.29, max 2522.92.

The total loss amount for large fire/explosion losses for the time period 1974–2017 is roughly at EUR 36 billion. This leads to an average loss amount of EUR 316 million per event. The picture with regards to the annual loss amounts is very volatile with peaks in 1989 and 2011, which is illustrated in Fig. 15.1.

Large parts of the volatility can be explained by the differences regarding the number of events per year as the average loss amount per event is quite stable.

**Table 15.1** Major five man-made fire/explosion catastrophes

| *Event year* | *Location* | *Event* | *Gross insured loss in mn EUR* |
|---|---|---|---|
| 2011 | Cyprus | Vasilikos Power Station (Explosion) | 2523 |
| 1988 | North Sea | Piper Alpha (Fire/Explosion) | 1433 |
| 1989 | Texas | Polyolefin Plant Pasadena (Vapor Cloud Explosion) | 1405 |
| 2017 | Abu Dhabi | Ruwais Refinery (Fire) | 1379 |
| 2015 | Hertfortshire | Buncefield Oil Storage Depot (Fire) | 1085 |

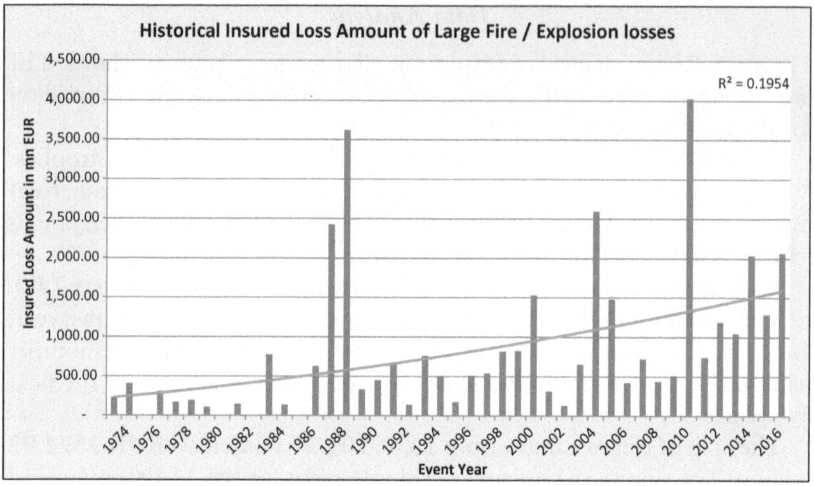


**Fig. 15.1** Gross large fire/explosion loss amounts in mn EUR

The predicted future large fire/explosion loss amounts result in an average annual fire/explosion loss amount between EUR 1.5 billion and EUR 2 billion at least for the next five years. Linking these results to the predicted average number of events per year, an average loss amount of EUR 500 million per event may be assumed.

Overall a negative trend, in frequency and severity, is observable that shall be considered during the risk modelling process.

## Developing a Loss Curve for Man-made Fire/Explosion Disasters based on Historical Industry Loss Data

### *Frequency Distribution*

The **Poisson distribution** is the most commonly used distribution to model the frequency within a catastrophe model by giving the probability of a number of independent events occurring in a specific time frame (Mitchell-Wallace et al. 2017, p. 40; Wälder and Wälder 2017, p. 60). The Poisson family of distributions has a single parameter, called $\lambda$, which represents the mean of the distribution (Gray and Pitts 2012, p. 13).

The random variable *X* has a Poisson distribution $Pr(x)$ for $x = 0, 1, 2\ldots$ and parameter $\lambda > 0$, if the following applies (Forbes et al. 2011, pp. 152–156; Mitchell-Wallace et al. 2017, p. 40):

$$\Pr(x) = \frac{e^{-\lambda}\lambda^{x}}{x!} \tag{15.1}$$

$$E[X] = Var[X] = \lambda \tag{15.2}$$

The **negative binomial distribution** is used when a dependence between events is known. As in the case of this research, independence between the events of the underlying data set may be assumed due to the nature and type of the risk (man-made catastrophe), only the Poisson distribution shall be used for modelling the frequency (Mitchell-Wallace et al. 2017, p. 41).

To fit the Poisson distribution $Poi(\lambda)$, parameter $\lambda$ is to be estimated first. For this purpose, the claims data for the time period 1974–2017 is classified according to the number of claims per year exceeding the threshold of EUR 100 million. This is illustrated in Table 15.2.

Independent whether the Method of Moments or the Method of Maximum Likelihood is used, parameter $\lambda$ can be derived by calculating the sample mean $E[X]$ from the existing data set. The calculation can be summarised as follows:

$$\text{Sample Mean} = E[X] = \overline{x} = \frac{1}{44}\sum_{j=0}^{7} r\, f_r = 2.5909 = \lambda$$

**Table 15.2** Number of claims per year

| *Number of claims per year r* | *Frequency (number of years affected)* $f_r$ |
|---|---|
| 0 | 4 |
| 1 | 13 |
| 2 | 8 |
| 3 | 6 |
| 4 | 5 |
| 5 | 3 |
| 6 | 3 |
| 7 | 2 |
| >7 | 0 |

The fitted distribution is then calculated using the fitted frequency for $r$ claims, $\hat{f}_r = 44 * \Pr(X = r)$, where $X \sim Poi(2.5909)$. Hence, the fitted claims frequency is calculated by applying $\hat{f}_r = 44 * \Pr(x) = 44 * \frac{e^{-2.5909} 2.5909^x}{x!}$ to the respective annual number of claims (Gray and Pitts 2012, pp. 60–61).

Table 15.3 compares the observed with the fitted claims frequency for the 44-year sample period.

Based on the elaboration above, the following frequency distribution is used to describe the annual number of claims exceeding EUR 100 million:

$$\Pr(x) = \frac{e^{-2.5909} 2.5909^x}{x!}$$

This is ultimately resulting in the graph as per Fig. 15.2.

Now, the goodness of fit of this distribution is assessed by using informative visual displays and appropriate test statistics to evaluate the adequacy of the Poisson distribution.

A visual inspection is used to evaluate the quality of the frequency distribution (Forbes et al. 2011, pp. 69–73). For this purpose, the observed and expected frequency values are compared in Fig. 15.3.

The graph shows a quite harmonised course of both curves, even though the peak for the observed frequency curve is at one claim per year, while the fitted frequency has its peak at two claims per year. In addition, the upper tail of the observed frequency is heavier than the fitted frequency tail. Nonetheless, the flow of both curves overall fits. Hence from a visualisation point of view, the fitted frequency may be deemed appropriate.

**Table 15.3** Observed versus fitted (Poisson distribution) frequency of claims

| *Number of claims* | *Observed frequency* | *Poisson fitted claims frequency* |
|---|---|---|
| 0 | 4 | 3.2979 |
| 1 | 13 | 8.5445 |
| 2 | 8 | 11.0690 |
| 3 | 6 | 9.5596 |
| 4 | 5 | 6.1920 |
| 5 | 3 | 3.2086 |
| 6 | 3 | 1.3855 |
| 7 | 2 | 0.5128 |
| >7 | 0 | 0.0 |

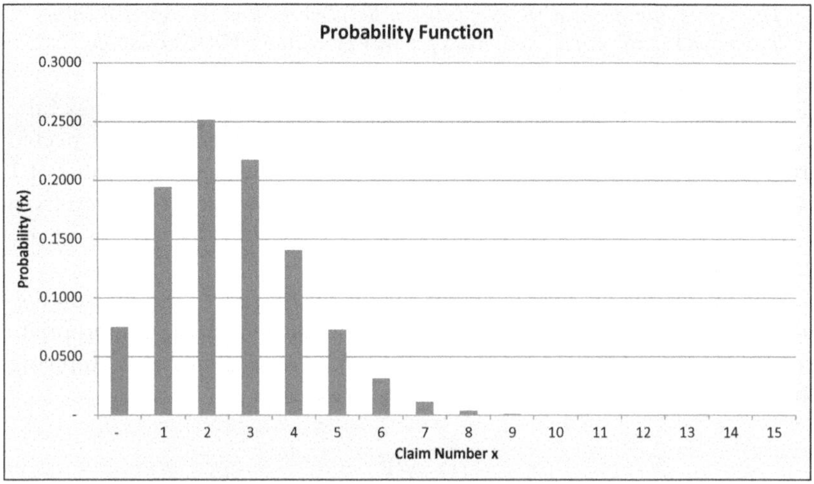


**Fig. 15.2** Claim number probability function (Poisson distribution)

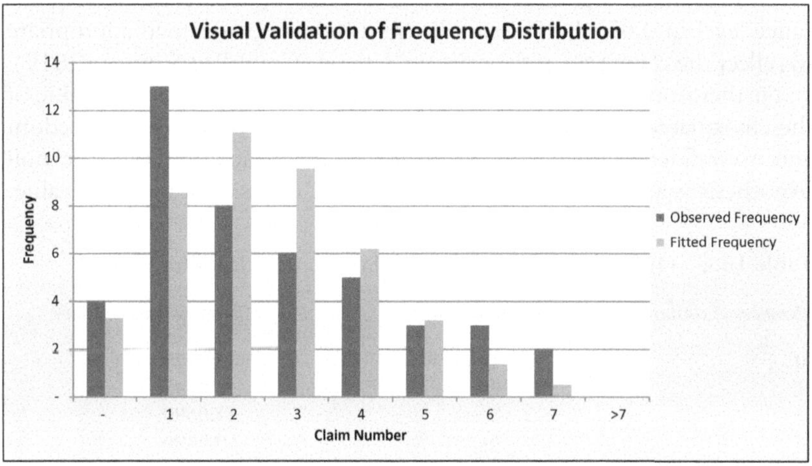


**Fig. 15.3** Visualisation observed versus fitted frequency

As a second and even more important approach, an appropriate test statistic is used to evaluate the quality of the frequency distribution. To perform the Pearson chi-square goodness-of-fit test, the null hypothesis regarding the frequency distribution is to be formulated first (Forbes et al. 2011, pp. 69–73):

*There is no significant difference between the observed and the expected values with respect to the number of claims per year exceeding EUR 100 million.*

To fulfil the minimum requirements in terms of fitted frequency,[2] the cells for six and seven claims per year need to be combined as the expected frequency for seven or more losses per year does not exceed the value of 1 (Gray and Pitts 2012, pp. 63–65). This combination leads to the results in Table 15.4 that can now be used to perform the Pearson chi-square goodness-of-fit test.

As one parameter is estimated in the fitting process of the Poisson distribution and as seven cells are used during calculation, the appropriate chi-squared distribution has parameter $a = 5$, degrees of freedom. Applying the outlined formula, the calculation looks as follows:

$$X^2 = \sum \frac{(O-E)^2}{E} = 9.9598$$

This results in a p-value of 0.0764. As this value exceeds the significance level of 0.05, the Poisson distribution may be deemed appropriate to reflect the claim size of the existing data set (GraphPad Software 2019).

Furthermore, comparing the calculated $X^2$ value with the table value of the chi-squared distribution, that is, 11.07 for $a = 5$ degrees of freedom and a confidence level of 95%, results in the conclusion that the null hypothesis is accepted, as the calculated value is less than the table value.

**Table 15.4** Observed frequency versus adjusted fitted claims frequency

| *Number of claims* | *Observed frequency* | *Poisson fitted claims frequency* |
|---|---|---|
| 0 | 4 | 3.2979 |
| 1 | 13 | 8.5445 |
| 2 | 8 | 11.0690 |
| 3 | 6 | 9.5596 |
| 4 | 5 | 6.1920 |
| 5 | 3 | 3.2086 |
| ≥6 | 5 | 1.8984 |

[2] A cell is only deemed usable if the expected frequency is not too small, meaning all cells need to reach $E \geq 1$, and not more than 20% of the cells should have $E < 5$. If the frequencies are too low, neighbouring cells are combined.

Therefore, it can be concluded that there is no significant difference between the observed and expected values.

To summarise, it can be observed empirically that the fit of the Poisson distribution is considered good as the frequencies expected under the fitted model are not far away from the observed frequencies; in particular, the Poisson model is also capable of reproducing the tail of the observed data. The observed data shows 5 out of 44 years with six or more large fire/explosion losses exceeding EUR 100 million, while the Poisson fit manages an expected frequency of about 1.9—the tail of the fitted Poisson is slightly too light but still appropriate. Since the Poisson distribution is a member of a single-parameter family, its distribution is not very flexible, and its ability to fit an observed frequency distribution is restricted. Nevertheless for this purpose, the selected distribution seems to reflect the data set accordingly. Formally, the hypothesis that the number of claims follows a Poisson distribution is confirmed (Gray and Pitts 2012, pp. 63–65).

### *Severity Distribution*

With respect to modelling the severity, Pareto, Weibull, or lognormal distributions are often used (Embrechts and Schmidli 1994, pp. 7–10).

To identify which of these distributions are worth modelling, the mean-excess function is considered because it describes the distribution in the tail quite good. As the area around the large quantiles is extremely risk relevant, it is important to determine a distribution that is close to the empirical distribution in this area. The mean excess function $e(t)$ of a random variable $X$ with $X \geq 0$ describes the expected exceedance of a given threshold and is defined as follows:

$$e(u) := E\left(X - u \middle| X > u\right) = \frac{\int_u^{\infty} (t-u) f(t)\,dt}{P(X > u)}$$

For the empirical case with $x_1, \leq \ldots \leq x_n$ large losses, the following applies:

$$e_n(u) = \frac{\sum_{i=1}^{n} x_i 1_{x_i} > u}{\sum_{i=1}^{n} 1x_i > u} - u$$

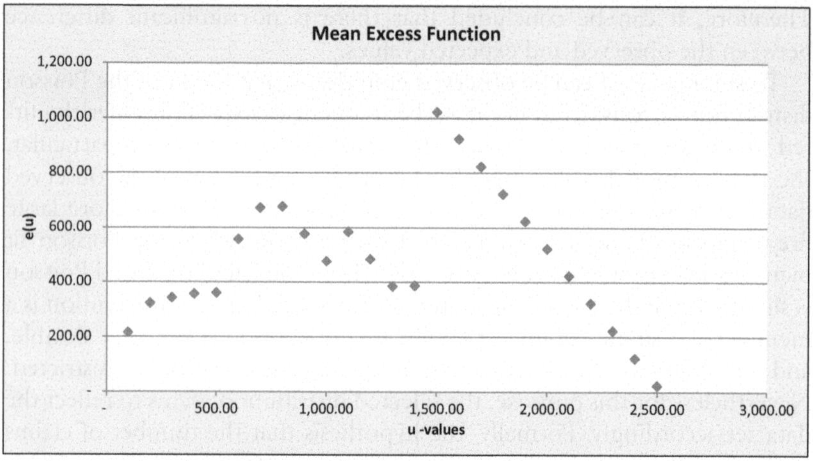


**Fig. 15.4** Mean excess function (empirical data)

with $1_{x>u}$ being the indicator function that equals the value 1 for $x > u$ and 0 in any other case (Brüske et al. 2010, pp. 137–138; Embrechts et al. 2003, pp. 294–297; Embrechts and Schmidli 1994, p. 11).

For the existing data set, the mean excess function for different thresholds $t$ results in the graph as per Fig. 15.4.

Comparing this figure to the graphs of the mean excess function $e(u)$ of some standard distributions indicates that all distributions as outlined above might potentially be capable of reflecting the empirical data accordingly.

First, the Pareto distribution will be considered, including two types: the one parameter Pareto and the three parameter Generalized Pareto distribution.

Due to their characterisation as heavy-tailed distributions, **Pareto distributions** are appropriate for modelling the severity of catastrophe losses (Brüske et al. 2010, pp. 137–138; Wälder and Wälder 2017, pp. 51–52). There are different types of Pareto distributions. The **one parameter Pareto distribution** is often used in catastrophe pricing. In general, the distribution has two parameters, although one is not a free parameter as it is defined upfront by the threshold $t$ beyond which the distribution applies. For threshold >0, $x > t$ and parameter $a > 0$, the one parameter Pareto distribution is given as follows:

$$f(x) = \frac{at^a}{x^{a+1}}$$

$$F(x) = 1 - \left(\frac{t}{x}\right)^a$$

$$E[X] = \frac{at}{a-1}$$

$$\text{Var}[X] = \frac{at^2}{(a-1)^2(a-2)}$$

If the mean can be calculated based on the existing data set, parameter *a* is estimated using the following formula (Forbes et al. 2011, pp. 149–151; Mitchell-Wallace et al. 2017, p. 43):

$$a = \frac{E[X]}{E[X]-t}$$

To fit the **one parameter Pareto distribution** *Par*(*a*, *t*), threshold *t* and parameter *a* are to be defined. Threshold *t* reflects the amount beyond which the distribution applies. As the existing data set only considers losses exceeding EUR 100 million, threshold *t* is defined as $t = 100$. To finally fit the one parameter Pareto distribution, parameter *a* is estimated. For this purpose, the sample mean is calculated as follows:

$$\text{Sample Mean} = E[X] = \overline{x} = \frac{1}{114}\sum_{n=1}^{114} X_n = 315.87$$

Based on the sample mean $E[X] = 315.87$ and threshold $t = 100$, parameter *a* is calculated as follows:

$$a = \frac{E[X]}{E[X]-t} = \frac{315.87}{315.87-100} = 1.4632$$

Applying the parameter as defined above, the following severity distribution is used to describe the claim size exceeding EUR 100 million:

$$f(x) = \frac{1.4632 * 100^{1.4632}}{x^{2.4632}}$$

The cumulative distribution function is then determined as follows (Forbes et al. 2011, pp. 149–151; Mitchell-Wallace et al. 2017, p. 43):

$$F(x) = 1 - \left(\frac{100}{x}\right)^{1.4632}$$

This is ultimately resulting in the graphs as per Figs. 15.5 and 15.6.

To model a specific claim size section beyond a particular threshold, the **three parameter Generalized Pareto distribution** is commonly considered (Peng and Welsh 2001, pp. 53–54). For parameters $k$ (shape parameter) with $k \in R$, $\sigma$ (scale parameter) with $\sigma > 0$, and $\xi$ (location parameter) with $\xi \in R$, the Generalized Pareto distribution is given as follows (Zea Bermudez and Kotz 2010, p. 1354):

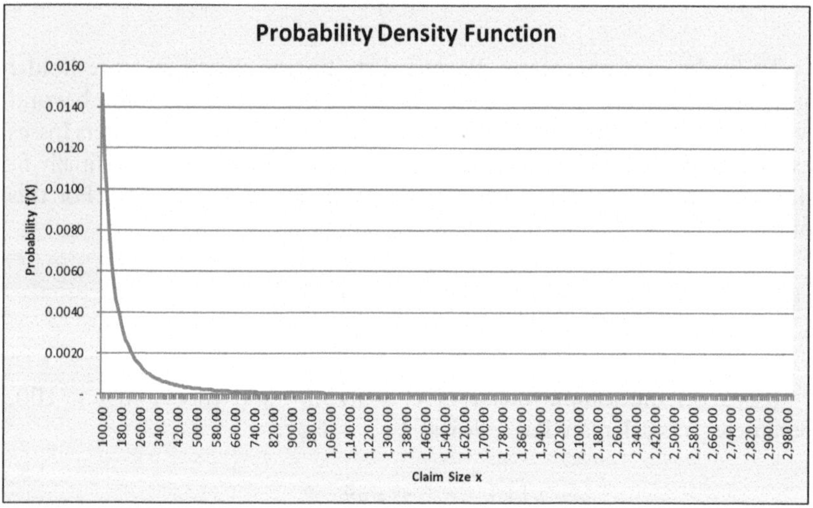


**Fig. 15.5** Claim size probability density function (one parameter Pareto distribution)

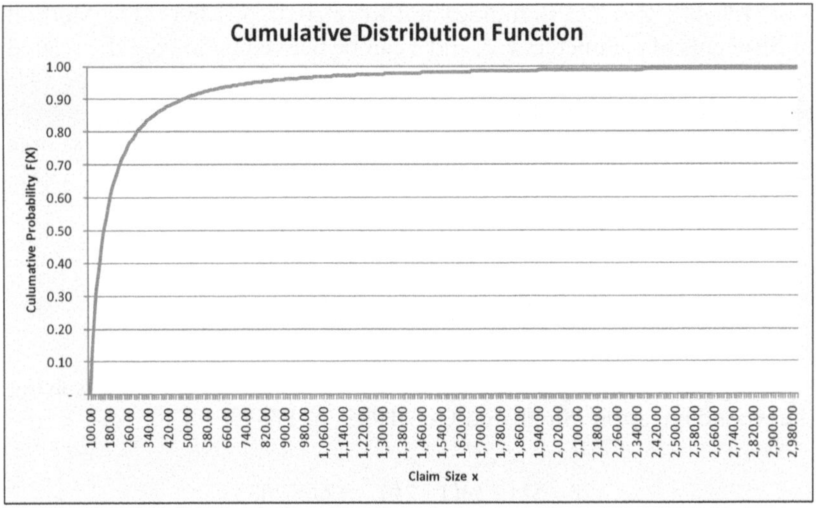


**Fig. 15.6** Claim size cumulative distribution function (one parameter Pareto distribution)

$$f(x) = \begin{cases} \frac{1}{\sigma}\left(1 - k\frac{x-\xi}{\sigma}\right)^{\frac{1}{k}} & for\, k \neq 0 \\ \frac{1}{\sigma} e - \frac{x-\xi}{\sigma} & for\, k = 0 \end{cases}$$

$$F(x) = \begin{cases} 1 - \left[1 - \frac{k}{\sigma}(x-\xi)\right]^{\frac{1}{k}} & for\, k \neq 0 \\ 1 - e - \frac{x-\xi}{\sigma} & for\, k = 0 \end{cases}$$

To fit the **three parameter Generalized Pareto distribution** ($k$, $\xi$, $\sigma$), parameters $k$, $\xi$ and $\sigma$ are to be defined first. Several methods exist in literature to estimate these parameters, but the Method of Maximum Likelihood is mostly used (Zea Bermudez and Kotz 2010, p. 1354). One of the major prerequisites to achieve reliable results through its application is a minimum size sample of 500 data points. For smaller samples (like in the case of this research), estimators derived from the Method of Moments are more reliable (Zea Zea Bermudez and Kotz 2010, p. 1354). The Method of Moments of parameters $k$, $\xi$, and $\sigma$ can be derived by solving the related equations for the moment estimators (Hosking and Wallis 1987, p. 341; Singh and Guo 1995, p. 174):

First, the moment estimates of $k$ is obtained by determining the sample skewness and solving the third equation (Hosking and Wallis 1987, p. 341):

$$\hat{k} = \frac{1}{2}\left(\frac{\overline{x}^2}{s^2 - 1}\right) = 0.4469$$

Using parameter $k$ = 0.4469, parameter $\sigma$ can be calculated by solving the second equation (Singh and Guo 1995, p. 174):

$$\sigma = S(1+k)(1+2k)^{0.5} = 665.2683$$

Using parameters $k$ = 0.4469 and $\sigma$ = 665.2683, parameter $\xi$ can be calculated by solving the third equation:

$$\xi = \overline{x} - \frac{\sigma}{\sigma + k} = 314.8708$$

Applying the parameters defined above, the following severity distribution may be used to describe the claim size exceeding EUR 100 million (as $k \neq 0$ applies) (Zea Bermudez and Kotz 2010, p. 1354):

$$f(x) = \frac{1}{665.2683}\left(1 - 0.4469\frac{x - 314.8708}{665.2683}\right)^{\frac{1}{0.4469}}$$

The cumulative distribution function is then determined as follows (as $k \neq 0$ applies):

$$F(x) = 1 - \left[1 - \frac{0.4469}{665.2683}(x - 314.8708)\right]^{\frac{1}{0.4469}}$$

As for catastrophic risks, extreme value distributions are often used and thus the **Weibull distribution** is next considered. The random variable $X$ has a Weibull distribution for $0 \leq x < \infty$ and parameters $a > 0$ and $\beta > 0$, if the following applies (Forbes et al. 2011, pp. 193–201):

$$f(x) = \frac{\beta x^{\beta-1}}{a^{\beta}} e - \left(\frac{x}{a}\right)^{\beta}$$

$$F(x) = 1 - e - \left(\frac{x}{a}\right)^{\beta}$$

$$E[X] = a\Gamma\left(\frac{\beta+1}{\beta}\right)$$

$$\mathrm{Var}[X] = a^2\Gamma\left(\frac{\beta+2}{\beta}\right) - \left[\Gamma\left(\frac{\beta+2}{\beta}\right)\right]^2$$

To fit the **Weibull distribution** $Wei(a, \beta)$, parameters $a$ (shape parameter) and $\beta$ (scale parameter) are to be defined first. Applying the Method of Maximum Likelihood requires the application of a numerical method as both parameters are unknown (Gray and Pitts 2012, p. 60). The log-likelihood function is given by:

$$l_n(a,\beta) = n \log a - n \log \beta + (a-1)\Sigma \log\left(\frac{x_i}{\beta}\right)\Sigma\left(\frac{x_i}{\beta}\right)^a$$

To maximise the log-likelihood function, an iterative procedure is used. The Newton-Raphson method is one common option to be applied (Nwobi and Ugomma 2014, p. 69; Pobočíková and Sedliačková 2014, p. 4141). The method starts with a function $h$ defined over the sample data set $n$ with values $x_i$, the function's derivative $h'$ and an initial guess $\beta_0$ for the value of $\beta$. To define a new estimate for the value of $\beta$, i.e. $\beta_{k+1}$, the following calculation is performed:

$$\beta_{k+1} = 1 - \frac{h(\beta_k)}{h'(\beta_k)} \text{ with } h(\beta) = \frac{1}{\beta} + \frac{u}{n} - \frac{w}{v} \text{ and } h'(\beta) = -\frac{1}{\beta^2} + \frac{w^2}{v^2} - \frac{s}{v},$$

The calculation is repeated until the value of $\beta_k$ converges, meaning that $h(\beta_k)$ becomes close to zero. Based on parameter $\hat{\beta}$, parameter $\hat{\alpha}$ can be calculated using the following formula (Zaiontz 2019):

$$a = \left(\frac{v}{n}\right)^{\frac{1}{\beta}}$$

Applying the described methodology to the underlying data set results in the following parameter estimates:

$$\hat{a} = 342.3824$$

$$\hat{\beta} = 1.2269$$

Applying the parameter as defined above, the following severity distribution may be used to describe the claim size exceeding EUR 100 million (Forbes et al. 2011, pp. 193–201):

$$f(x) = \frac{1.2269x^{0.2269}}{342.3824^{1.2269}} e - \left(\frac{x}{342.3824}\right)^{1.2269}$$

The cumulative distribution function is then determined as follows:

$$F(x) = 1 - e - \left(\frac{x}{342.3824}\right)^{1.2269}$$

ultimately resulting in the graphs as per Figs. 15.7 and 15.8.

Conditional distributions may be considered to model the probability of a claim size exceeding a particular threshold. For this purpose, the **log-normal distribution** is considered to reflect the conditional tail probability. The random variable $X$ has a lognormal distribution for $x > 0$ and the two parameters, $\mu$ and $\sigma$, if the following applies (Gray and Pitts 2012, pp. 23–36; Wälder and Wälder 2017, p. 50):

$$f(x) = \frac{1}{\sigma\sqrt{2\pi}} \frac{1}{x} e^{-\frac{1}{2}\left(\frac{\log x - \mu}{\sigma}\right)^2}$$

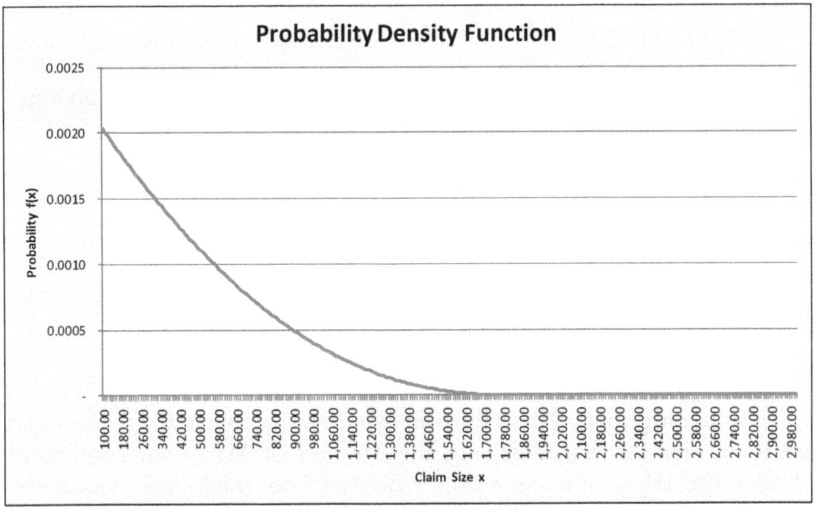


Fig. 15.7 Claim size probability (Weibull distribution)

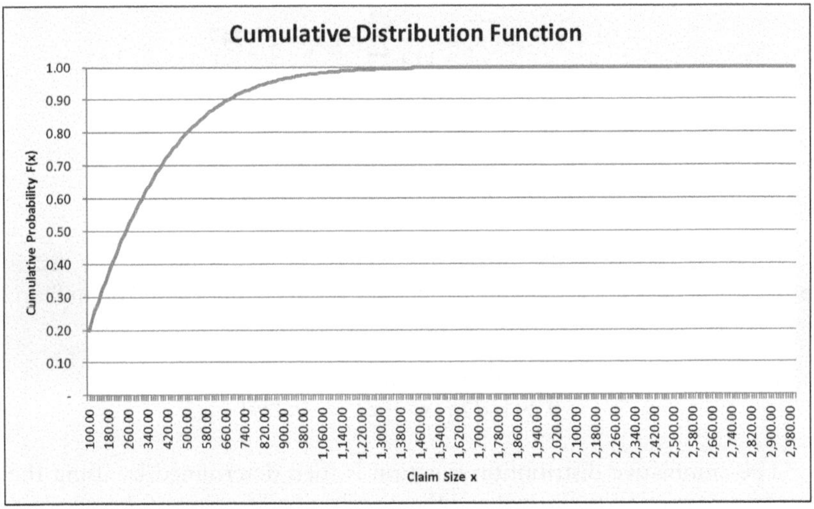


Fig. 15.8 Claim size cumulative distribution function (Weibull distribution)

(1) $F(x) = \Pr\left(Z < \frac{\log x - \mu}{\sigma}\right)$, the distribution function is determined by using the log transformation to normal and the distribution function of the standard normal distribution $Z \sim N(0, 1)$.

$$E[X] = e^{\mu + \frac{1}{2}\sigma^2}$$

$$\text{Var}[X] = e^{(2\mu + \sigma^2)\left(e^{\sigma^2} - 1\right)}$$

To fit the **lognormal distribution** *lognormal*($\mu$, $\sigma$), parameters $\mu$ and $\sigma$ are to be defined first. Applying the Method of Maximum Likelihood (MLE), the MLEs of $\mu$ and $\sigma$ can be derived from the logged data as the sample mean and standard deviation of the log($x_i$) values. Their calculations can be summarised as follows (Gray and Pitts 2012, p. 36):

$$\hat{\mu} = \overline{y} = \overline{\log x_i} = \frac{1}{114}\sum_{n=1}^{114} \log x_i = 2.3747$$

$$\hat{\sigma} = \left(\frac{1}{114}\sum_{114}^{i=1}(y_i - \overline{y})^2\right)^{\frac{1}{2}} = 0.2941$$

Applying the parameter as defined above, the following severity distribution may be used to describe the claim size exceeding EUR 100 million:

$$f(x) = \frac{1}{0.2941\sqrt{2\pi}}\frac{1}{x}e - \frac{1}{2}\left(\frac{\log x - 2.3747}{0.2941}\right)^2$$

The cumulative distribution function is then determined by using the log transformation to normal and the distribution function of the standard normal distribution $Z \sim N(0, 1)$:

$$F(x) = \Pr\left(Z < \frac{\log x - 2.3747}{0.2941}\right)$$

Although the normal, exponential, and gamma distributions are widely used to model the severity of insurance losses, they will not be considered due to their thin-tailed characteristics.

Now, the goodness of fit of these distributions is assessed by using informative visual displays and appropriate test statistics to finally decide which distributions are selected for further processing.

A visual inspection is first used to evaluate the quality by comparing the empirical cumulative distribution function with the various fitted cumulative distribution functions. For independent and identically distributed random variables $X_1$, $X_2$, …, $X_n$ the empirical cumulative distribution function is defined as

$$F_n(x) = \frac{1}{n}\sum_{i=1}^{n} 1(X_i \leq x)$$

with $1(X_i \leq x)$ being the indicator function that equals the value 1 for $X_i \leq x$ and 0 in any other case (Gray and Pitts 2012, pp. 63–65). The result is shown in Fig. 15.9.

The graph shows a quite harmonised course of the empirical cumulative distribution function and the **one parameter Pareto distribution**

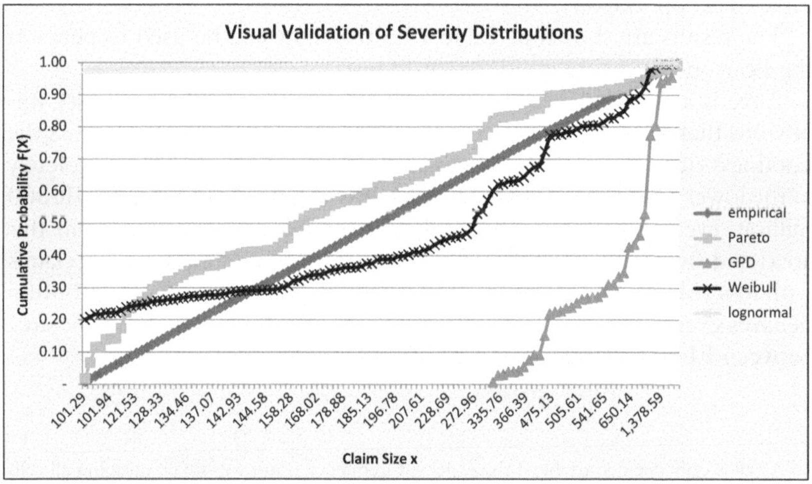


**Fig. 15.9** Visualisation empirical versus fitted distribution functions

function; however, the **Weibull distribution** function seems to be quite adequate too, even though it seems to overemphasise the lower tail. The graph already outlines that the **Generalized Pareto** and the **lognormal distribution** do not reflect the empirical data at all. From a visualisation point of view, the one parameter Pareto distribution may be deemed the most appropriate one, but as this is not completely clear, further tests are carried out.

Therefore, as a second and even more important approach, an appropriate test statistic is used to evaluate the quality of the severity distributions. To perform the Pearson chi-square goodness-of-fit test, the null hypothesis regarding the severity distribution is to be formulated first (Forbes et al. 2011, pp. 69–73):

> *There is no significant difference between the observed and the expected values with respect to the size of a single claim exceeding EUR 100 million.*

The chi-squared test divides the observed claim sizes into $k$ intervals and compares the observed counts (number of data values observed in interval $i$) to the number expected given the fitted distribution (number of data values expected in interval $i$) (Packová and Brebera 2015, p. 18). To fulfil the minimum requirements in terms of fitted frequency,[3] the observed claim sizes need to be combined to specific categories (Gray and Pitts 2012, pp. 63–65).

The results are shown in Table 15.5 that now can be used to perform the Pearson chi-square goodness-of-fit test.

Already at a first glance (and hence similar to the visualisation test), it is obvious that only two distribution functions have the potential to pass the goodness-of-fit test. The Generalized Pareto Distribution fails completely in the lower tail (no claims expected for loss volumes lower than EUR 300 million, even though the observed data show a major frequency in this area) and overemphasises the upper tail with a huge frequency for claims with loss volumes greater than EUR 1 billion. The lognormal distribution behaves even worse as it only covers claims with loss volumes in the area between EUR 100 million and EUR 150 million.

[3] A cell is only deemed usable if the expected frequency is not too small, meaning all cells need to reach $E \geq 1$, and not more than 20% of the cells should have $E < 5$. If the frequencies are too low, neighbouring cells are combined.

**Table 15.5** Observed versus expected frequency for different claim size categories

| *Claims interval* | *Observed frequency* | *Expected frequency Pareto* | *Expected frequency GPD* | *Expected frequency Weibull* | *Expected frequency Lognormal* |
|---|---|---|---|---|---|
| 100–150 | 39 | 51.0145 | | 34.7268 | 112.3157 |
| 150–200 | 24 | 21.6403 | | 11.2988 | 0.4650 |
| 200–250 | 12 | 11.5173 | | 10.2141 | 0.2794 |
| 250–300 | 3 | 6.9845 | | 9.0512 | 0.1848 |
| 300–350 | 6 | 4.6128 | 5.9320 | 7.9029 | 0.1304 |
| 350–400 | 4 | 3.2357 | 8.1419 | 6.8200 | 0.0964 |
| 400–450 | 1 | 2.3739 | 7.7907 | 5.8291 | 0.0737 |
| 450–500 | 6 | 1.8032 | 7.4425 | 4.9413 | 0.0580 |
| 500–750 | 8 | 4.8410 | 32.1014 | 14.8917 | 0.1662 |
| 750–1000 | 0 | 2.0535 | 23.9067 | 5.5745 | 0.0764 |
| 1000–1250 | 2 | 1.0929 | 16.2274 | 1.8987 | 0.0424 |
| >1250 | 4 | 2.8305 | 12.4575 | 0.8509 | 0.1115 |

Therefore, only the one parameter Pareto as well as the Weibull distribution function will be considered for further analysis.

As for the one parameter Pareto distribution, only one parameter is estimated in the fitting process, and 12 categories are used during calculation, the appropriate chi-squared distribution has parameter $a = 10$ degrees of freedom. Applying the above outlined formula, the calculation looks as follows:

$$X^2 = \sum \frac{(O - E)^2}{E} = 33.5817$$

This formula results in a p-value of 0.0002. As this value by far falls below the significance level of 0.05, the one parameter Pareto distribution may not be deemed appropriate to reflect the claim size of the existing data set (GraphPad Software 2019).

Furthermore, comparing the calculated $X^2$ value with the table value of the chi-squared distribution, that is 3.940 for $a = 10$ degrees of freedom and a confidence level of 95%, results in the conclusion that the null hypothesis is denied, as the calculated value is higher than the table value. Hence, it can be concluded that there is a significant difference between the observed and expected values.

As for the Weibull distribution, two parameters are estimated in the fitting process and 12 categories are used during calculation, the appropriate chi-squared distribution has parameter $a = 9$ degrees of freedom. Applying the outlined formula, the calculation looks as follows:

$$X^2 = \sum \frac{(O - E)^2}{E} = 42.4882$$

This formula results in a p-value of 0.0001. As this value by far falls below the significance level of 0.05, the Weibull distribution may not be deemed appropriate to reflect the claim size of the existing data set (GraphPad Software 2019).

Furthermore, comparing the calculated $X^2$ value with the table value of the chi-squared distribution, that is 3.325 for $a = 9$ degrees of freedom and a confidence level of 95%, results in the conclusion that the null hypothesis is denied, as the calculated value is higher than the table value. Hence, it can be concluded that there is an extremely significant difference between the observed and expected value.

To summarise, it can be observed empirically that the fit of none of the reviewed severity distributions is good because the expected frequencies for particular claim size intervals under the fitted model in some parts are far away from the observed frequencies; in particular, these distributions are not capable of reproducing the tail of the observed data. Formally, the hypotheses that the size of claims has a one parameter Pareto or Generalized Pareto or Weibull or lognormal distribution is to be denied. The conclusion is that none of these distributions provides an adequate description of the variation in the claim sizes that has been observed.

Even though none of the distribution properly fits, the one parameter Pareto distribution, providing the best fit, will be considered going forward to allow the development of an approximation of the aggregate loss distribution for large fire/explosion catastrophes.

### *Aggregate Loss Distribution*

The aggregate loss distribution is determined by the frequency and severity distribution and describes the probability of the annual expected total loss resulting from large fire/explosion losses with individual loss volumes exceeding EUR 100 million (Cottin and Döhler 2013, p. 27). Both distributions have been modelled on an individual basis and now need to be combined through an approximation method (Gondring 2015, p. 539). As both, claim size and claim number, are random variables expressed by a distribution, the collective model of risk aggregation is to be applied (Cottin and Döhler 2013, pp. 88–92). For the following, it is worth highlighting that claim size and claim number will be deemed independent. For the purpose of aggregation, compound distributions may be considered. For a known claim number distribution function $p_N(t)$ and a known claim size distribution function $F(x)$, the aggregate loss distribution is given as:

$$G(x,t) = p_0(t) + \sum_{\infty}^{v=1} p_v(t) * F^{*v}(x)$$

with $F^{*v}(x)$ being the v-fold convolution of the distribution function $F(x)$ that is calculated as follows:

$$F^{*1}(x) = F(x), F^{*k}(x) = \left(F^{*(k-1)} * F\right)(x) \text{ for } K > 1$$

Determining the aggregate loss distribution is quite challenging as the simplified approximation method via Panjer recursion cannot be used: The main prerequisite that the claim size $X$ can only have values 0, $h$, $2h$, $3h$, …, does not apply for the existing data set. This challenge can only be solved with the support of statistical applications, such as Matlab or Solver. Using the command 'PsiPareto(1.4632, 100, PsiCompound(PsiPoisson(2.5909)))' the graphs of the aggregate loss distribution can be derived.

Because an explicit calculation of the aggregate loss distribution is not available for the distributions used, Monte Carlo simulation is an acceptable alternative to derive the aggregate loss distribution (Betram and Feilmeier. 1987; Mikosch 2009). For this, a series of incidental claim numbers $N_1$, $N_2$, $N_3$, … is to be created based on the predefined claim number distribution, that is, $\Pr(x) = \frac{e^{-2.5909} 2.5909^x}{x!}$. Then, for every claim number $N_i (i = 1, 2, 3\ldots)$, a series of incidental claim size values $X_1^{(i)}, X_2^{(i)}, X_3^{(i)}, \ldots$ is to be assigned based on the predefined claim size distribution, that is, $F(x) = 1 - \left(\frac{100}{x}\right)^{1.4632}$.

For every $i = 1, 2, \ldots, n$ the annual aggregate loss $S^{(i)}$ is calculated as follows:

$$S^{(i)} = \sum_{j}^{N_i} X_j^{(i)}$$

This formula results in the following aggregate loss distribution function:

$F_s(x) \approx \frac{m(x)}{n}$ with $m(x)$ being the number of all $S^{(i)}$.

If simulating in Excel, the inverse of the respective cumulative distribution functions is to be determined to define the incidental values for both, claim number and claim size. Based on the simulated annual aggregate losses, the aggregate loss distribution can be derived through applying the fitting process. Due to the permanent changing values in Excel, only a snapshot can be discussed in the following by using the particular values from one simulation cycle as a basis to fit the distribution (Wälder and Wälder 2017, pp. 83–85). Due to limited computer capacity, a simulated sample of size 1000 is considered appropriate. When analysing the simulated data, it is quite obvious that the Exponential distribution might be a good fit.

To fit the **Exponential distribution** $Exp(\lambda)$, parameter $\lambda$ is estimated. For this, the sample mean is calculated (Gray and Pitts 2012, pp. 25–26). The calculation can be summarised as follows:

$$\text{Sample Mean} = E[X] = \bar{x} = \frac{1}{1000}\sum_{n=1}^{1000} X_n = 787.2676$$

Based on the sample mean $E[X] = 787.2676$ parameter, $\lambda$ can be calculated as follows:

$$\lambda = \frac{1}{E[X]} = \frac{1}{787.2676} = 0.0013$$

Applying the parameter as defined above, the following aggregate loss distribution is used to describe the annual aggregated loss volume for large fire/explosion losses exceeding EUR 100 million:

$$f(x) = \lambda e^{-\lambda x} = 0.0013e^{-0.0013x}$$

The cumulative distribution function for $x > 0$ is then determined as follows:

$$F(x) = 1 - e^{-\lambda x} = 1 - e^{-0.0013x}$$

This formula is ultimately resulting in the graphs as per Figs. 15.10 and 15.11.

To confirm the validation of the developed aggregate loss distribution, a visual inspection is used by comparing the empirical with the fitted cumulative distribution function (Gray and Pitts 2012, pp. 65–67). The results are shown in Fig. 15.12.

The graph shows a quite harmonised course of the empirical cumulative distribution function and the exponential distribution function, although it seems to underestimate the upper tail. From a visualisation point of view, the exponential distribution may be deemed appropriate.

To confirm the visual fit, an appropriate test statistic is used to evaluate the quality of the aggregate loss distribution.

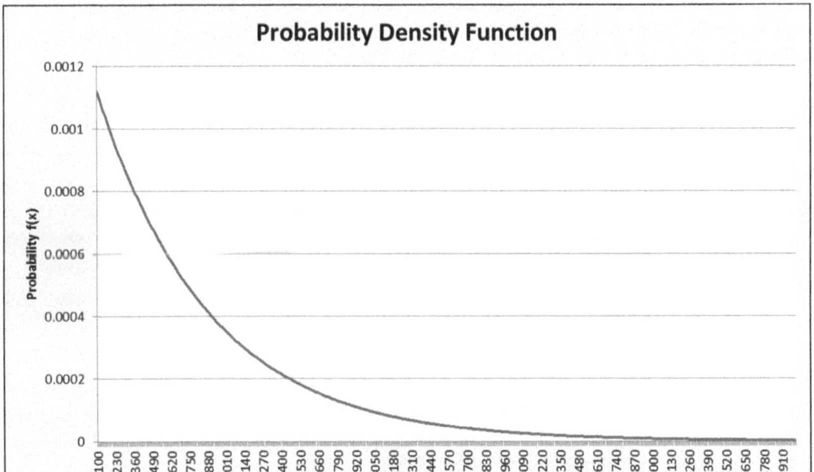


**Fig. 15.10** Aggregate loss probability density function (Exponential distribution)

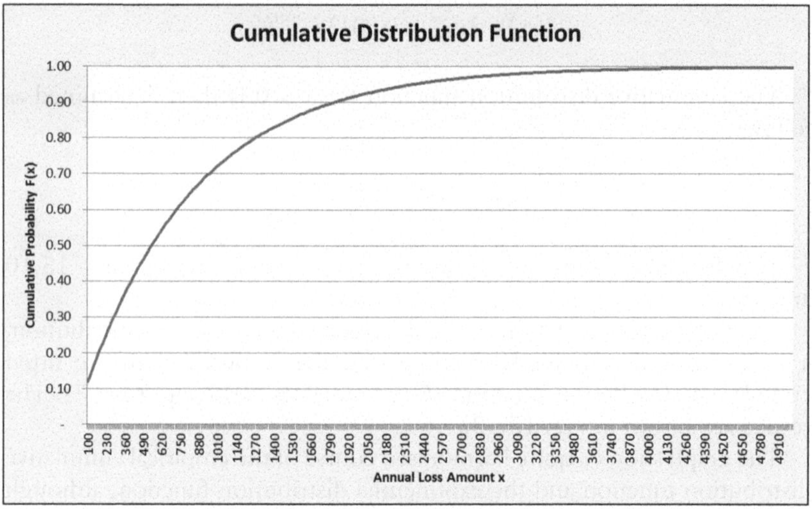


**Fig. 15.11** Aggregate loss cumulative distribution function (Exponential distribution)

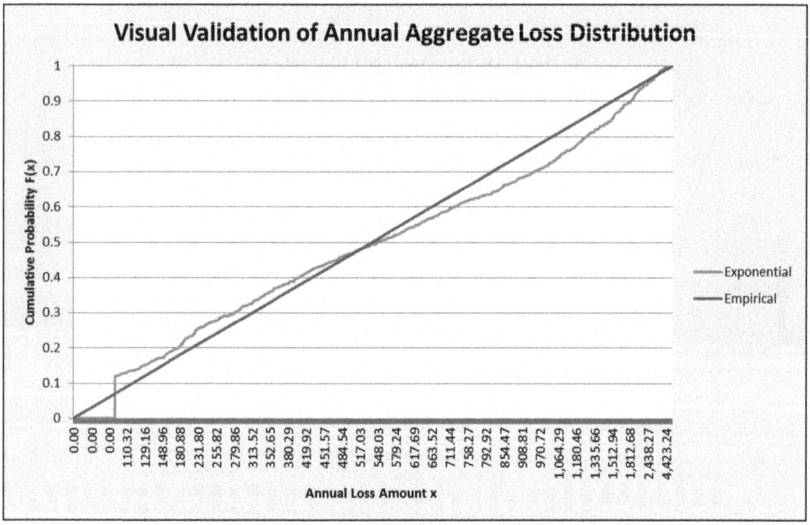


**Fig. 15.12** Visualisation empirical versus fitted aggregate loss distribution function

The chi-squared test divides the observed annual aggregate losses into $k$ intervals and compares the observed counts (number of data values observed in interval $i$) to the number expected given the fitted distribution (number of data values expected in interval $i$) (Packová and Brebera 2015, p. 18). To fulfill the minimum requirements in terms of fitted frequency,[4] the observed annual aggregate losses need to be associated to specific categories (Gray and Pitts 2012, pp. 63–65).

As for the exponential distribution, only one parameter is estimated in the fitting process and 36 categories are used during calculations, the appropriate chi-squared distribution has parameter $a = 34$ degrees of freedom. Applying the previously outlined formula, the calculation is rendered as follows:

$$X^2 = \sum \frac{(O - E)^2}{E} = 136.3417$$

This results in a p-value lower than 0.00001. As this value by far falls below the significance level of 0.05, the exponential distribution may not be deemed appropriate to reflect the aggregate loss distribution of the existing data set (GraphPad Software. 2019).

Furthermore, comparing the calculated $X^2$ value with the table value of the chi-squared distribution, that is between 18.493 for $a = 30$ degrees of freedom and 26.509 for $a = 40$ degrees of freedom for a confidence level of 95%, results in the conclusion that the null hypothesis is denied, as the calculated value is higher than the table value. Hence, it can be concluded that there is an extremely significant difference between the observed and expected values. This result is not surprising since the underlying claim size distribution also failed the goodness-of-fit test, but was still used for further processing in the Monte Carlo simulation because it still reflects parts appropriately.

To summarise, it can be observed empirically that the fit of the created distribution is not good; in particular, this distribution is not capable of reproducing the tail of the observed data. Formally, the hypothesis that the aggregate loss distribution has an exponential distribution is to be

[4] A cell is only deemed usable if the expected frequency is not too small, meaning all cells need to reach $E \geq 1$, and not more than 20% of the cells should have $E < 5$. If the frequencies are too low, neighbouring cells are combined.

denied. The conclusion is that this distribution does not provide an adequate description of the variation in the annual aggregate loss volumes that has been observed.

Although there seems to be no appropriate loss curve reflecting the severity and frequency for man-made fire/explosion disasters based on a historical data set, the developed loss curves (frequency—Poisson distribution/severity—one parameter Pareto distribution) may still be useful to the insurance industry. They can be integrated into the existing expert-based assessment processes for man-made disaster scenarios as they at least fit for specific sections and may support the estimation process from a quantitative/scientific perspective.

## Conclusion

Due to the potential of man-made disasters to not only jeopardise an individual insurer's solvency position if the risk is not properly managed, but also to trigger market shocks and subsequent economic downturns, the need for a comprehensive approach to identify, assess, transfer, and mitigate the risk arises today even more than in the past. The objective of this research was to determine how the frequency and severity of such tail events can be evaluated and modelled based on empirical data. Due to the variety of triggers that require separate modelling approaches, this research was focused on man-made fire/explosion disasters since recent events, such as Tianjin harbor explosion, have shown the significance of this disaster type and their impact on the insurance industry and other markets.

In a broader perspective, it can be confirmed that the empirical modelling of man-made disaster scenarios remains very challenging since limited historical claims data exist (although different data sources were combined and a historical large fire/explosion loss database was developed) to model man-made catastrophes properly. For the time period 1974–2017, 114 large fire/explosion losses with a loss volume exceeding EUR 100 million were identified with an overall loss volume of EUR 36 billion. Based on the loss data, frequency, and severity, distributions were modelled on an individual basis and then combined through a Monte Carlo simulation to derive an aggregate loss distribution reflecting the industry loss data (collective risk model). For both, typical distribution types that are commonly used in the large/catastrophic loss modelling space were considered. In terms of the claim number, the Poisson distribution was fitted and a positive goodness-of-fit test was performed. In terms of the claim size, various distributions—one parameter Pareto, Generalized Pareto, Weibull, and lognormal distribution were fitted, but for all of these distributions the goodness-of-fit test was negative. Thus, although an appropriate distribution for the claim number was identified, no proper distribution could be created in terms of claim size, which mainly refers to the significant standard deviation with regards to the loss volume.

Therefore, it is not surprising that the aggregate loss distribution, for which an exponential distribution was used, fails in the goodness-of-fit test as well. This result emphasises the challenges outlined at the beginning of this contribution and furthermore confirms that an assessment of man-made catastrophes is currently not possible if this is purely based on empirical modelling techniques by using historical loss data. Thus, the developed catastrophe loss curves should not be regarded as a stand-alone solution to the problem of quantifying tail events, but may be used as an additional tool for assessing man-made catastrophes since they provide an indication of the estimated loss potential. Accordingly, the quantitative outcome of this research should be integrated in the existing expert-based assessment approaches to ultimately create a more powerful and sophisticated methodology for evaluating man-made catastrophes. Since modelling approaches evolve, especially in times of predictive analytics, research on modelling man-made disasters should be continued and alternative approaches should be further explored.

## References


ATEX Explosion Hazards Ltd. (2018). *List of historic explosions (Dust, vapour and gas)*. Source. Retrieved January 5, 2019, from http://www.explosionhazards.co.uk/list-of-historic-explosions/.

Banks, E. (2009). *Risk and financial catastrophe*. Hampshire: Palgrave Macmillan.

Brüske, S., Cottin, C., Hiebing, A., & Hille, B. (2010). Die stochastische Modellierung von Großschäden für den Einsatz in internen Risikomodellen der Schadenversicherung. *ZVersWiss, 99*(2), 133–154.

Cambridge Centre for Risk Studies (2018, March). *Impact of severe Natural Catastrophes on Financial Markets*.

Clark, K., Chang, H., & Manghnani, V., (2015). Chapter 5 – Catastrophe risk. In IAA/AAI (Ed.), *IAA risk book: Governance, regulation and management of insurance operations*. n.p. n.p.

Cottin, C., & Döhler, S. (2013). *Risikoanalyse: Modellierung, Beurteilung und Management von Risiken mit Praxisbeispielen*. Wiesbaden: Springer Verlag.

Cutler, D. (2013). *Factbox: Industrial accidents in the last two decades*. Retrieved January 5, 2019, from https://www.reuters.com/article/us-usa-explosion-texas-accidents/factbox-industrial-accidents-in-the-last-two-decades-idUSBRE93H1EM20130418.

Embrechts, P., & Schmidli, H. (1994). Modelling of extremal events in insurance and finance. *Zeitschrift für Operations Research, 39*(1), 1–34.

Embrechts, P., Klüppelberg, C., & Mikosch, T. (2003). *Modelling extremal events for insurance and finance*. Berlin and Heidelberg: Springer Verlag.

Forbes, C., Evans, M., Hastings, N., & Peacock, B. (2011). *Statistical distributions*. New Jersey: John Wiley & Sons.

Gondring, H. (2015). *Versicherungswirtschaft: Handbuch für Studium und Praxis*. München: Franz Vahlen Verlag.

GraphPad Software (2019). *P value calculator*. Retrieved February 3, 2019, from https://www.graphpad.com/quickcalcs/pvalue1.cfm.

Gray, R., & Pitts, S. (2012). *Risk modelling in general insurance: From principles to practice*. Cambridge: Cambridge University Press.

Hosking, J., & Wallis, J. (1987). Parameter and Quantile estimation for the generalized Pareto distribution. *Technometrics, 29*(3), 339–349.

Lloyd's. (2018). *Realistic disaster scenarios: Scenario specification*. Retrieved January 3, 2019, from https://www.lloyds.com/market-resources/underwriting/realistic-disaster-scenarios-rds.

Marsh. (2012). *Marsh insights: Property*. Retrieved January 10, 2019, from https://www.marsh.com/content/dam/marsh/Documents/PDF/US-en/Marsh-Insights-Property-Fall-2012.pdf.

Marsh. (2014). *Historical loss experiences in the global power industry*. Retrieved January 5, 2019, from http://www.oliverwyman.com/content/dam/marsh/Documents/PDF/UK-en/Historical%20Loss%20Experiences%20in%20the%20Global%20Power%20Industry-08-2014.pdf.

Marsh. (2016). *The 100 largest losses 1974–2015: Large property damage losses in the hydrocarbon industry – 24th edition*. Retrieved December 28, 2018, from https://www.marsh.com/content/dam/marsh/Documents/PDF/UK-en/100%20largest%20losses%201974%20to%202015-03-2016.pdf.

Marsh. (2018). *The 100 largest losses 1978–2017: Large property damage losses in the hydrocarbon industry – 25th edition*. Retrieved December 28, 2018, from https://www.marsh.com/content/dam/marsh/Documents/PDF/UK-en/100-largest-losses.pdf.

Mikosch, T. (2009). *Non-life insurance mathematics: An introduction with the Poisson Process*. Berlin and Heidelberg: Springer Verlag.

Mitchell-Wallace, K., Foote, M., Hilier, J., & Jones, M. (2017). *Natural catastrophe risk management and modelling: A practitioner's guide*. Chichester: John Wiley & Sons.

Nwobi, F., & Ugomma, C. (2014). A comparison of methods for the estimation of weibull distribution parameters. *Metodološki zvezki, 11*(1), 65–78.

OECD. (2019). *Inflation*. Retrieved January 21, 2019, from https://data.oecd.org/price/inflation-cpi.htm.

Packová, V., & Brebera, D. (2015). *Loss distributions in insurance risk management*. Retrieved January 21, 2019, from http://www.inase.org/library/2015/barcelona/bypaper/ECBAS/ECBAS-03.pdf.

Peng, L., & Welsh, A. (2001). Robust estimation of the generalized Pareto distribution. *Extremes, 4*(1), 54–65.

Pobočíková, I., & Sedliačková, Z. (2014). Comparison of four methods for estimating the Weibull distribution parameters. *Applied Mathematical Sciences, 8*(83), 4137–4149.

Singh, V., & Guo, H. (1995). Parameter estimation for 3-parameter generalized pareto distribution by the principle of maximum entropy (POME). *Hydrological Sciences Journal, 40*(2), 165–181.

Swiss Re (2016). *Analysis of Tianjin port explosion: Risk management is the key*. Retrieved August 17, 2019, from https://www.swissre.com/china/Analysis_of_Tianjin_Port_Explosion.html.

Swiss Re Institute (2018a). Information and methodology of sigma explorer data. Retrieved December 28, 2018, from http://www.sigma-explorer.com/documentation/Methodology_sigma-explorer.com.pdf.

Swiss Re Institute. (2018b). *sigma 1/2018: Natural catastrophes and man-made disasters in 2017: A year of record-breaking losses*. Retrieved January 15, 2019, from http://institute.swissre.com/research/overview/sigma/1_2018.html#tab_2.

Swiss Re Institute. (2018c). *Natural catastrophes and man-made disasters in 2017: A year of record-breaking losses*. Retrieved January 3, 2019, from http://media.swissre.com/documents/sigma1_2018_en.pdf.

The World Bank Group. (2019). *Consumer price index (2010 = 100)*. Retrieved January 28, 2019, from https://data.worldbank.org/indicator/FP.CPI.TOTL.

Thornton, R. (2016). *Man-made catastrophes: A perpetual emerging risk*. Retrieved January 28, 2019, from https://www.globalreinsurance.com/man-made-catastrophes-a-perpetual-emerging-risk/1419434.article.

Wälder, K., & Wälder, O. (2017). *Methoden zur Risikomodellierung und des Risikomanagements*. Wiesbaden: Springer Verlag.

Zaiontz, C. (2019). *Fitting Weibull parameters using MLE and Newton's method*. Retrieved January 17, 2019, from http://www.real-statistics.com/distribution-fitting/distribution-fitting-via-maximum-likelihood/fitting-weibull-parameters-mle-newtons-method/.

Zea Bermudez, P., & Kotz, S. (2010). Parameter estimation of the generalized Pareto distribution – Part I. *Journal of Statistical Planning and Inference, 140*(6), 1353–1373.

Zurich Insurance Group. (2017). *Assessing man-made catastrophes*. Retrieved December 3, 2018, from https://www.zurich.com/en/knowledge/articles/2017/03/assessing-man-made-catastrophes.

CHAPTER 16

# Changing Dynamics of Financial Risk Related to Investments in Low Carbon Technologies

*Mohd Hafdzuan Bin Adzmi, Huiying Cai, and Masachika Suzuki*

## Introduction

The international discourse on climate change has thus far placed greater emphasis on each nation's best effort to mitigate and adapt to the effects of climate change. A synthesis of the Nationally Determined Contributions (NDC) submitted by signatory countries to the Paris Agreement indicates that, for developing countries, financing is still a key issue that impedes the diffusion of climate change responses (Zhang and Pan 2016). In mitigating climate change, the focus has been on increasing low carbon energy sources while reducing the negative contribution of fossil fuels in the atmosphere. Low carbon technologies are commonly referred to as technologies that release a low amount of greenhouse gas (GHG) emissions,

M. H. B. Adzmi (✉) • H. Cai • M. Suzuki
Graduate School of Global Environmental Studies, Sophia University, Tokyo, Japan
e-mail: hafdzuan@eagle.sophia.ac.jp; caihuiying@eagle.sophia.ac.jp; msuzuki@sophia.ac.jp



T. Walker et al. (eds.), *Ecological, Societal, and Technological Risks and the Financial Sector*, Palgrave Studies in Sustainable Business In Association with Future Earth, https://doi.org/10.1007/978-3-030-38858-4_16

with renewable energy (RE) technologies being the most common as they derive from natural sources such as the sun (solar), biomass, biogas, rivers (hydro), and wind. In contrast, high carbon technologies derive from fossil fuels/conventional fuels and use resources such as coal, natural gas, and oil. Nuclear technology, with plutonium or uranium as feedstock, is also considered low carbon as it emits close to zero carbon dioxide. However, due to its operational complexity and scale, it is usually analyzed separately from renewable energy (Edenhofer 2014; Grubler et al. 2012).

The first part of this chapter briefly looks at the effect of divesting investment from fossil fuels such as coal to low carbon (Section "Climate Change Investment Landscape") and the risks associated with climate change for coal technology and low carbon technologies (Section "Climate Change and Financial Risks"). Despite a growing interest in low carbon technologies (RE specifically), financing still remains an issue. As such, this part discusses how policies help to alleviate some of the investment risks in renewable energy while also highlighting how increased interest in low carbon policies has led financial institutions to view fossil fuel investment as increasing in risks with investors potentially facing "stranded assets" issues.

The second part of this chapter reviews measures taken by regulatory and institutional bodies to accompany the shift into the low carbon era (Section "Shifting to Low Carbon Technologies") before discussing a variety of measures and instruments employed by financial institutions to cope with these risks and avoid stranded assets issues. These measures and instruments are taken by international financial institutions, including banks, credit agencies, development finance institutions, and private financial institutions. In addition, this part discusses potential measures to reduce risks in the implementation of low carbon technologies.

The changing dynamics of policies is addressed next with a focus on how the development of low carbon technologies impacts the coal industry and how companies can manage these risks (Section "Opportunities for the Financial Sector and the Management of Low Carbon Technologies Risks"). Despite the existence of various mechanisms aiming to address market failures, unfavorable views due to the perceived risks associated with low carbon technologies remain in many countries. In addition, limited evaluating capabilities by financial institutions also act as a barrier. Low carbon policies provide the opportunity to reduce investment risks, but in turn it could increase risks for coal technology in the form of reduced development of coal mines and increasing pressures from investors to divest from fossil fuels. Both these issues have increasingly contributed to "stranded assets" that may lead to disastrous consequences and potential asset misallocation for the financial sector in the future. In addition, the depreciating coal prices and increasing competitiveness of renewable energy are presently making many coal and coal-related industries struggle financially. From the perspectives of financial institutions, diversifying their portfolios by turning their attention to low carbon technologies might prove to alleviate some of the effects of what is projected to be less support for fossil fuels (especially coal).

## Climate Change Investment Landscape

As humankind develops, more energy sources are burned resulting in increased greenhouse gas (GHG) concentration in the atmosphere. Scientific studies have shown that the concentration of GHG, especially carbon dioxide, has resulted in heat being trapped in the atmosphere and to an increase in the average global temperature as seen in Fig. 16.1 (NASA's GISS 2018). Increased average global temperatures are known to alter the climate, which presents various types of risk to human beings and to the natural ecosystem.

Although emissions are released locally, climate change transcends geographical boundaries, requiring global efforts to combat its effect. The scientific community and policymakers are aware of this fact, but coming

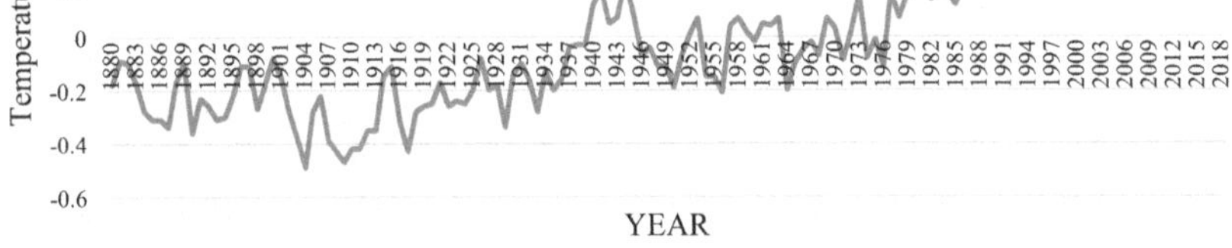


**Fig. 16.1** Global land-ocean temperature index (Adapted from NASA's Goddard Institute for Space Studies (GISS) 2018)

to an agreement on the mechanics to reduce GHG emissions has seen decades of disappointments. At the 21st Conference of Parties (COP 21) held in Paris in 2015, a significant step was finally made to limit global average temperature increase below 2 °C with the burden of responsibility shifting from developed countries to all countries (UNFCCC 2016).

To attain this target, the focus is to limit GHG emissions and transition to clean energy. To limit GHG, and in particular carbon dioxide emissions, scientists have calculated the carbon budget which specifies the amount of anthropogenic carbon dioxide that can be released into the atmosphere to keep the global average temperature below 2 °C. The calculations reveal that 65 per cent, or 1900 $GTCO_2$, of the "budget" has been utilized in the period from 1870 to 2011, with 35 per cent, or 1000 $GTCO_2$, still remaining underground (IPCC 2014).

The disconnect between the value of energy firms and their commercialization rests within this concept of "unburnable carbon" (the portion of fossil fuel that must be left underground to stay within the carbon budget) (Carbon Tracker Initiative 2011). According to the United Nations Environment Report ( 2018), at least three-quarters of existing reserves must remain underground.

The emphasis to move away from carbon-intensive technologies is partially one aspect of mitigation. To complement this measure, the increased use of low carbon technologies to curb emissions while meeting the growing energy demand is needed. Herein lies the problem: despite this fact and various efforts to reduce emissions, $CO_2$ emissions from burning fossil fuel has dramatically increased as shown in Fig. 16.2 (Carbon Dioxide Information Analysis Center 2012). Coal is currently the main source of $CO_2$ emissions, accounting for 42 per cent of global $CO_2$ emissions, followed by oil (33 per cent), and natural gases (19 per cent) (Buckley 2019). With the demand for power is expected to increase, low carbon technologies are important elements to reduce the effect of climate change. Yet, most developing countries argue that a lack of resources to counter social, economic, and environmental issues limits the investment in low carbon technologies. In general, the cost to produce a unit of electricity from low carbon technologies is relatively higher compared to a unit of electricity from conventional fossil fuel power plants such as coal. Although the production cost for certain technologies, such as solar energy, has drastically decreased, overall costs still remain the main barrier for widespread deployment of these technologies (Edenhofer 2014).

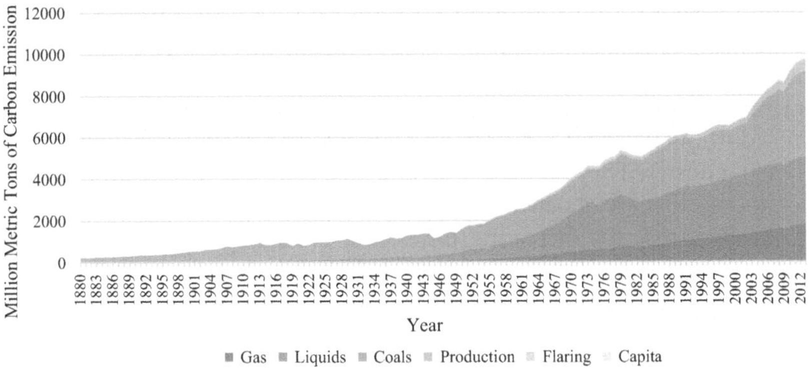


**Fig. 16.2** $CO_2$ emission from fossil fuel consumptions (Adapted from: Carbon Dioxide Information Analysis Center 2012)

Selecting fossil fuels reveal the necessity for cost-effective energy supply and presents a challenge for low carbon technologies. Financing issues are expressed as a major hindrance to promote renewable energy by many developing countries (Zhang and Pan 2016). Globally, US$343 to 385 billion was estimated to have been invested in GHG reduction initiatives per year for 2010/2011. From the figure, however, public financing for developing countries constituted only US$35 to 49 billion from 2011 to 2012, highlighting the importance of private financing (Edenhofer 2014).

From the financial institution's point of view, uncertainties regarding the technologies and a lack of information give rise to multiple risks. Therefore, policy interventions reducing uncertainties and risks can be effective in attracting private financial institutions (Polzin et al. 2019). With more constrained policies to curb $CO_2$ emissions, especially in the power sector, large capital inflows to fund low carbon technologies and renewable resources are making a significant impact in curtailing $CO_2$ emissions. In 2017 alone, US$ 279.8 billion was invested in new renewables projects globally (REN21 2018).

With the push for low carbon technologies, conventional technologies such as coal are facing a different kind of challenge. Some developers would still opt to invest in a fossil fuel power plant with relatively lesser carbon emissions (such as natural gas) instead of coal or renewables (REN21 2018). Thus, coal technology is now facing "stranded assets" issues, which have become one of the heated research topics in the energy realm. Stranded assets are assets suffering a sudden change in valuation under certain situations, such as a change in regulations and/or policies or unexpected disasters. When stranded assets occur, they negatively impact investors' portfolios (Silver 2017). Scholars argue that unburnable carbon will contribute to stranded assets and threaten the development of the fossil fuel industry. They may also lead to a financial crisis that could threaten economies that are dependent on it (Silver 2017).

As discussed, the increasing physical and financial impacts of climate changes pose immediate and unexpected threats that are likely to affect the whole economic cycle. Therefore, without an accurate understanding of risks related to climate change, making strategic investments for either technology will become increasingly difficult.

## Climate Change and Financial Risks

To understand how the financial sector reacts to the current regulations and policies toward conventional and low carbon technologies, this chapter first addresses the broad implications of risks on these technologies and the financial sector.

### *Climate Change Risks Associated with Coal Technology*

At present, many economic activities are increasingly impacted by extreme weather events due to climate change. For example, Honda incurred a total loss of 150,000 car units when one of its automobile manufacturing plants was severely affected by the Thai floods of 2011. Financially, the floods have caused Honda losses in term of net profits amounting to approximately US$12 million (Haraguchi and Lall 2015). Huge financial losses because of natural disasters brought about unexpected negative consequences for firms and institutions. Therefore, climate risks need to be integrated into the overall risks management of the manufacturing sectors as well as the financial sector.

Financially, investors assess their capital holding and make predictions on their future returns while taking into account the risks taken. Identifying and recognizing potential risks is perhaps one of the key functions of the financial market. Although the concept of climate risks is clear from the scientific perspective, the deliberation on climate risks in financial terms is considered at its infancy. The Task Force on Climate-related Financial Disclosures (TFCD), aiming at helping policymakers and the financial industry to identify all forms of risks, divided climate risks into three categories: physical risk, transition risk, and liability risk. Their brief descriptions are as follows (TCFD 2017):

*Physical Risk* is defined as risks related to climate change, which impact the valuations of financial assets. This category includes extreme weather that damage properties and could even affect employment opportunities.

*Transition Risk* is a type of financial risk that occurs during the passage to a low carbon economy. The key element of transition risks is stranded assets, which mainly affect fossil fuel industries. The issues of stranded assets can be viewed in the following context:

- Prospective companies interested in investing in fossil-related business need to consider current fossil fuel reserves and the company's future valuations in view of the transition taking place;
- Even though numerous researches have revealed the loss of value as a result of the transition, capital that has already been invested into fossil-related businesses can still be salvaged as fossil fuel remains the preferred option and the main economic driver of the world.

*Liability Risks* refer to negative outcomes that arise as a result of mismanagement of climate risks. For example, exposure to liability rests on insurance companies or manufacturers who fail to ensure that the infrastructures could perform or withstand extreme weather.

Despite these risks, coal technology still has its importance in the world and divesting from it would require serious analysis to assess its cost and benefit. Indeed, approximately 1.2 billion people still lack access to electricity in the world (Roberts 2017), and coal could be one solution to reduce this number because of its relatively cheap price and availability. Coal is still the most popular energy source in the world, and it is unsurprising that 30 per cent of the world's primary energy, 40 per cent of global electricity, and 68 per cent of steel is provided by coal (Standard and Poor's 2015). In fact, various top commercial banks continue to invest by lending and underwriting service to companies planning to establish new coal power plants in some developing countries (Banktrack 2018a). Over the last three years, seven banks in China and Japan have provided half of their funding to the coal power plant business (Banktrack 2018a).

However, a shift in investment also seems to be taking place. Although some top banks such as the Royal Bank of Canada, JP Morgan Chase,

Toronto-Dominion Bank, and HSBC have increased their funds in the fossil fuel industries, other banks that finance fossil fuels, including tar sands oil, ultra-deepwater oil, LNG, coal mining, and coal-fired power, chose to decrease their funding for fossil fuels in order to achieve one of the goals of the Paris Agreement—"*making finance flows consistent with a pathway towards low greenhouse gas emissions and climate-resilient development*" (Article 2,1.(c) in UNFCCC 2015, p. 3). This goal includes China Construction Bank, ranked first in the list of funders for extreme fossil fuels (2015 to 2017) with funding reduced from US$10.3 billion in 2015 to US$6.9 billion in 2017 (Banktrack 2018a). Other notable banks to complete the ranks include the Industrial and Commercial Bank of China, the Bank of China, the Agricultural Bank of China, the Citi Group, and the Bank of America (Banktrack 2018a).

As such, banks can be forced to base their investing decisions on tightened carbon regulations and could advance their financial decisions for non-fossil fuel-based energy. Allocating capital could present a challenge with the apparent enthusiasm in fossil fuel from the industry.

### *Financial Risks Associated with Low Carbon Technologies*

Although low carbon technologies are perceived as the energy source of the future, many risks still plague their development. Risks associated with low carbon technologies are largely due to uncertainties especially the "randomness, volatility and intermittency" of the technology and its resource (Liu and Zeng 2017). Uncertainties can also be extended to their acceptance in society, business model, and market behaviour. They not only affect the overall implementation of a project, but also result in a longer return on investments, uncertain future profits, and possible losses due to unforeseen changes in policy. To convince financial institutions, companies need to demonstrate a strong capability to execute the project, possess a viable business model, and create a realistic project design (Liu and Zeng 2017). With renewable energy as an example, these uncertainties are briefly described below:

*Maturity of technology and industry.* The infrastructure for fossil fuel technologies is better developed compared to low carbon technologies. Since revenue depends on the reliability of the chosen technology, the maturity of the technology and the industry for low carbon technologies are regarded as ones of the main risks in the project development (Liu and Zeng 2017). Technology risks include the possibility of being outdated and whether it could adapt to local conditions (Liu and Zeng 2017). Apart from operational reliability, the maturity and availability of various support services (maintenance, spare parts, etc.) would not only ensure smooth operation, but also provide prompt action in case of unplanned stoppages (Gatzert and Kosub 2016). With unique technology requiring special parts and components, the ability to access these items should also be included as a risk (Gatzert and Kosub 2016; Liu and Zeng 2017). The upstream component of the industry also presents various uncertainties for technology that requires procuring or harvesting feedstock from a third party, such as from biomass-based power plants. A special agreement should be in place to avoid feedstock shortages (MEGTW 2009).

*Power Purchase Agreement (PPA).* The off-taker for the electricity generated from conventional power plants or RE plants is typically the grid operator. The grid operator refers to the entities responsible in distributing electricity and commonly maintaining the grid infrastructure such as transmission and distribution lines. The grid operator also purchases the electricity generated before distributing it to consumers at a tariff (price) according to consumption. For renewable energy, a willing buyer-willing seller concept could most likely favor grid operators if negotiations on power purchase agreement (PPA) are left ungoverned or without any oversight, especially in a relatively new investing environment (MEGTW 2009). Delay tactics could also be employed to pressure investors into agreeing on the terms of the PPA. With a lack of proper governance structure, investors are left with no choice but to absorb the increased cost or withdraw from the agreement (MEGTW 2009). In a fairly new industry, poor information dissemination and a lack of experience result in the unwillingness of financial institutions to provide financing due to the many uncertainties associated with new technology like renewable energy. Financial risk issues might include grid operators intentionally offering a price that does not commensurate with the cost of production, demanding stringent non-negotiable technical requirement and including unrealistic performance clauses (MEGTW 2009). Financing issues could also be related to the poor terms spelled out in the PPA and the viability of the renewable energy industry as a whole (Sovacool and Drupady 2011).

*Project Design.* Karneyeva and Wüstenhagen (2017) highlight the issue of scale, which depends on the investor's business model and technical design. Larger-scale installations typically adopt a high capital model, with higher installed capacity and reliance on electricity sales as revenue. This model is typically adopted by fossil power plants. Smaller-scale projects usually refer to installations with relatively lower capital and installed capacity, such as rooftop solar panels that also rely on electricity sales as revenue. Another business model for smaller-scale installations involves off-setting the electricity produced with the electricity purchased from electricity utility companies to save electricity bill. Either business model could be adopted depending on the existing policy, the costs, and the complexity of exchanges with the grid operator (Karneyeva and Wüstenhagen 2017). However, some projects require an economy of scale to be viable. Capacity caps imposed by an authority or geographical limitation threaten investors to commit to a suboptimum scaled project, making it not worthwhile to be developed and presenting a greater risk if pursued (Karneyeva and Wüstenhagen 2017; Gatzert and Kosub 2016). A grid operator's reaction to oversupply and mandated caps by authorities should also be considered well ahead to account for its impact.

*Project Logistics.* Some installations are situated in remote areas with a difficult access to the site. This situation increases risks during the construction phase and poses problems for suppliers or service providers to access the project site, hence causing delays and ultimately increasing the cost for repairs and maintenance (Gatzert and Kosub 2016). Some sites with vast potential could also contain natural or technical features that are incompatible with the technology proposed. These site-specific projects may be located away from the grid interconnection point which makes transmitting power to these points difficult (Sovacool and Drupady 2011). Some technologies, such as solar rooftops, do well in this area, though they present new problems for grid operators to plan their operation. Solar panels can be installed modularly, thus making the presence of cumulative renewable energy installations in the grid relatively quicker (similar with wind technology) compared to a single conventional power plant, which can take years and more careful planning to build (Gatzert and Kosub 2016). Concentrated installations around areas with low demand would require operators to limit access to renewable energy installations to avoid oversupply (Gatzert and Kosub 2016). This effect is uncertain, and risks can only be seen over time as the industry develops.

*Operational Uncertainties.* Revenue could also vary as some renewable energy technology depends on nature as its feedstock (e.g., solar, wind, hydro), which is somewhat difficult to accurately predict. In view of these variations, adopting measures to ensure a stable revenue should be considered even in the planning stages (Gatzert and Kosub 2016). Operational uncertainties include frequent natural events such as extreme weather and harsh conditions, which pose access issues to staff and service providers (Gatzert and Kosub 2016). During construction, some of the concerns involve delay risks like getting the necessary permits (Gatzert and Kosub 2016; Liu and Zeng 2017) and damage risks to goods during the installation or construction (Gatzert and Kosub 2016). By far, the most important stage of the development are the testing and commissioning stage. In this stage, investors and grid operators verify that the electricity production and connection to the grid adhere to agreed specifications. Unplanned delays and unforeseen technical issues due to poor planning between both parties would present a risk of delay (Gatzert and Kosub 2016). Typically, investors are already expected to service their debt in this phase, and delays would only increase financial burden. On top of the aforementioned issues, new technologies could result in unexpected component failures and produce unreliable performance (Gatzert and Kosub 2016; Liu and Zeng 2017). Although issues such as component wear and tear could be managed, operational uncertainties as described still loom.

*Policy Uncertainties.* There is little doubt that the drivers for renewable energy growth have been through policy intervention to provide incentives and relevant regulatory measure (Edenhofer 2014). Financially, revenue stability hinges on policy decisions, and investors may find that profitability can be negatively affected when policy risks are taken into account (Karneyeva and Wüstenhagen 2017). Therefore, investors need to be aware of political stability, which could result in support being scaled down, changed, or removed altogether due to cost issues, pressure from the public, or even political instability (war, etc.) (Gatzert and Kosub 2016; Liu and Zeng 2017). Policy risks also encompass caps on installation capacity or access to the grid, administrative delays, and the determination of the length of the PPA (Karneyeva and Wüstenhagen 2017). With developing countries implementing various policies to spur the development of renewable energy, investors need to be aware that new policies take time, as some cannot be easily adapted to local conditions. Governance structure and other local conditions can also impact policy decisions and need to be carefully assessed as part of the overall risk components (Gatzert and Kosub 2016; Liu and Zeng 2017). As such, controversy, perception of the public, or unknown reasons could alter decisions and favor certain technologies (Sovacool and Drupady 2011). In some instances where permit or license authority deals with policy formulation, approval issues due to political reasons could arise (Liu and Zeng 2017).

## Shifting to Low Carbon Technologies

Shifting to low carbon usually involves a shift in a low carbon power supply by introducing a mix of regulatory measures and incentives. Some of the main policy instruments include (REN21 2018):

- *Feed-in tariff.* A system where renewable energy companies generate revenue through the premium price for each unit of electricity generated. The price is usually higher (premium) than the price to supply a unit of electricity from fossil sources.
- *Tenders.* A similar process to procure bids for conventional (fossil) power plants. It is typically reserved for large scale projects where a tender is opened for bids by interested companies and projects are awarded to the successful bidder. Bids that fulfill the project's technical requirement and can do so at a lower cost compared to other bidders are usually selected.
- *Net metering.* The electricity consumed from the grid is being offset with self-generated electricity produced from renewable energy sources.
- *Renewable Portfolio Standards.* A mandate by authorities for the grid operator to distribute a certain share of electricity from renewables.

In 2017, 179 countries had set a renewable target with most focusing on the power sector with 113 countries favouring feed-in tariff as the mechanism to realize this target (REN21 2018). Low carbon policies, such as the feed-in tariff, can be expected to solve the economic issues related to the technology. In addition, policies could also address institutional issues that hinders the promotion of renewable energy. The introduction of multiple instruments, especially laws, generally produces the intended results mainly due to its "instrumentality" and "coercive effect." It also significantly reduces the cost of exchange for all parties by providing information and obligations that are clearly specified and enforceable by law (North 1990).

With regulatory measures and various instruments working together, compliance can be directed at various players in the energy market and is achieved through provisions on enforcement and penalties that when executed, negate problematic behavior (North 1990; Scott 2008).

Apart from providing economic incentives, government institutions also play a vital role in formulating and executing instruments that facilitate low carbon development through regulations, rules, and guidelines. The benefit of having an instrument coercive by nature is that it reduces policy risks by providing financial institutions with the element of certainty. With the Malaysian feed-in tariff, for example, negotiation time is reduced with the introduction of a Standardized Renewable Energy Power Purchase Agreement (REPPA), which standardizes key negotiation terms such as price, duration, and access to the grid (MEGTW 2009). Other instruments that facilitate the growth of renewable energy include:

*The certainty of the source to finance incentives.* Typically, the feed-in tariff system needs to be simultaneously established with a funding mechanism because the system subsidizes the cost of distributing the relatively more expensive renewable energy which the grid operator would otherwise not incur by distributing fossil fuel-based electricity. Funds to subsidize this cost are sourced from a levy on consumer's electricity bill or any other source deemed suitable by the government (MEGTW 2009).

*Information and guidelines.* Connecting various independent installations to the main electricity grid could pose problems. Therefore, safeguarding the grid's assets is a legitimate concern raised by grid operators. Though valid, it can sometimes be taken to extremes by placing stringent requirements to protect the grid and thus incurring unnecessary costs to companies (MEGTW 2009). The availability of these types of information beforehand would enable every player in the industry, especially investors, to perform a different type of risk assessment since information on payments, approval time, technical and license requirement would be clearly spelled out.

In certain situations, any attempt on the part of the companies to contest or independently assess the situation can be futile as the information pertaining to the grid is within the grid operator's rights and control. Having this information also means that the grid operator has the upper hand during negotiations (MEGTW 2009). Thus, transparent technical requirements and an opportunity for the companies to perform their own connection check can greatly reduce asymmetrical information by both parties (North 1990).

*Due Diligence.* Irregular supply poses concerns to financial institutions and the grid operator. It is difficult, especially for financial institutions, to ascertain whether these irregularities could affect the performance of the plant. These difficulties are down to their own logical determination of the project's credibility (Karneyeva and Wüstenhagen 2017) compounded by a lack of any credible certification (MEGTW 2009). With a system like the feed-in tariff, fulfilling some minimal requirement is required and can serve as due diligence to financial institutions.

With various policies and instruments promoting low carbon technologies as described above, the global coal mining industry could face pressures from analysts and researchers to restructure its business model. China and EU countries, for example, plan to become coal-free. South Korea, the fourth largest coal importer in the world, claims to have reduced its coal power in 2017, which illustrates that the coal mining industry could go into a much more critical situation (Banktrack 2018a). This trend has led investors to reallocate their capitals to renewable resources.

In some developing countries such as India and China, solar and wind technologies are economically competitive to the extent that governments had to cancel plans to develop a new coal power project and shift to renewable energy sources. China leads the world in renewable energy capacity with 334 Gigawatts installed in 2017. For comparison, the total installed capacity for the entire world, BRICS countries (Brazil, Russia, India, China, and South Africa) and the 28 European Union countries (EU-28) was 1,081, 429, and 320 Gigawatts respectively (REN21 2018).

Another factor affecting the global coal industry is the widespread divestment campaigns in Europe and Australia. People are calling for a "non-coal world," which contributes to the surge of restructuring and bankruptcies of coal miners. With the tightening of coal regulations in recent years, banks are forced to reconsider and change their strategies for the coal mining sector. As millions of dollars are collected through general corporate finance, reducing corporate finance for coal mining companies is emerging as one of the key agendas for the banking sector.

The impacts of these changes to coal mining and the coal power industry have already been felt. Since the Paris Agreement in 2015, the UNEP has called for the closure of the new coal power plants and a fastened retirement of current plants to achieve the goals of the agreement. A U.K. and Canada-leading organization, the Powering Past Coal Alliance, also established a union encompassing more than 50 countries, regions, and businesses that have declared their restrictions on financing for coal power.

Concerned about financial risks, several institutional investors are divesting from fossil fuel companies. Large sums have been invested in renewable resources instead of fossil fuel industries. This energy transformation has significant implications for the fossil fuel industry. During

COP21 in Paris, research revealed that more than US$3.4 trillion has been diverted away from fossil fuels (Schueneman 2015). As such, the coal industry is expected to experience the greatest reduction in financial returns. According to the report from the Institute for Energy Economics and Financial Analysis (IEEFA), over 100 financial institutions in the world have already restricted and/or divested from coal in response to the carbon reduction targets as envisaged under the Paris Agreement (Buckley 2019).

## Opportunities for the Financial Sector and the Management of Low Carbon Technologies Risks

Climate change has been addressed from the scientific and political fronts and has seen many developments. Yet, the financial sector is still considerably behind in recognizing the link between climate change and its impacts on the wider economy, or the potential risks associated with financial returns on investment. Until recently, the financial world was still outside of the discussions and decisions made by UNFCCC (Miller and Swann 2016).

The next section describes how financial institutions, especially in the banking and insurance sectors, view fossil fuel–related policy goals, guidance, and instruments to overcome the increased investment risk or stranded assets for investors. It also addresses ways to manage financial risks for low carbon projects.

### *Insurance Companies*

Due to the unpredictability of extreme weather events, the rapid increase in global economic losses results in insurers viewing climate change as a threat rather than an opportunity. In a major disaster, evidence reveals that countries with lower levels of insurance coverage record more fiscal losses (Golnaraghi 2018). The rapid increase in global economic losses from extreme weather events has become the impetus for government investments to reduce existing risks and prevent new ones. Impacts of climate change on the insurance sector can be deep and broad, affecting insurers' profits and investments. The impacts can extend to other insurance products such as life insurance and health insurance.

To date, property insurers do not have a full understanding of how extreme weather events will drive higher claims, and what kind of unexpected risks should be deemed uninsurable. At present, in response to concerns over climate change and fossil fuel investments, insurance companies are trying to integrate climate change scenarios into their models, but this effort is still in its early stage.

As one of the largest institutional investors in the world, insurance companies manage more than US$31 trillion (Simons and De Wilde 2017) and take essential roles as underwriters in coal projects. Without the necessary coverage of these projects' risks, major coal mines or plants would not be funded, built, or operated. By continuously underwriting and investing in the coal industry, the business models of the insurance companies are indirectly contributing to climate change, and their roles are expected to be highlighted when the Paris Agreement is operationalized.

A recent Standard and Poor's Rating Services report (2015) summarizes climate change as a greater threat to insurers than has been previously recognized. The rating agency believes that insurers' earnings would be affected by weather-related losses and lower investment returns. Therefore, as part of their efforts to work on the Paris Agreement, insurance companies have begun to invest in renewable energy. According to research conducted by CERES, if 55 insurers in the U.S. hypothetically shifted US$590 billion holdings in fossil fuel to renewable energy, investments in renewable resources would triple (Mchale and Spivey 2016). Allianz, the largest insurance company in the world, became one of the first insurers to divest from the coal industry (accounting for 30 per cent of its revenue) in 2015 (CERES 2016). Also, in 2017, AXA became the first major insurer to discontinue underwriting for coal companies (CERES 2016). It is becoming a trend for top insurance companies to divest from the fossil fuel industry with most of them having done so in the late 2017 or 2018 (Buckley 2019). As data shows, shifting to renewable resources is one method to reduce financial risk for insurance companies.

Simultaneously, insurance companies have conducted research to develop insurance products and instruments for the low carbon market to complement the method mentioned above. For example, to satisfy investors' demand for risk-mitigating tools, Austrian Garant Insurance, French Global Sustainable Development Project (GSDP), and Swiss Re Greenhouse Gas Risk Solution launched the Carbon Delivery Guarantee (CDG) insurance, an insurance for which the insurer acts as the guarantor for future carbon credit delivery to sell the unused carbon credits to the businesses that need more carbon credits. The insurance covers all carbon delivery guarantee, political risk insurance, and business interruption (Carney 2015).

### *Banking Sector*

In adjusting to climate change, banks play a very important role in the financial sector through financing and investing. By closing the finance supply and demand gap, banks do not only ensure financing for the whole economic activity, but also play a role in managing risks. The banking sector involves a wide range of financing and investment activities through capital allocations, such as mortgage lending, business lending, project finance, assets management, and investment banking. These activities span to all aspects of the society, including climate change, thereby becoming an indispensable part in adjusting to the effects of climate change.

Policies to reduce GHG emissions and the uncertainty of future weather patterns may transfer new liabilities and produce new business risks to the economy. In view of climate change issues, credit risks are the main risks presently for banks. Under the European Union Emissions Trading Scheme (EU ETS) and Kyoto Protocol, the policy regarding risks was to transfer liabilities risks or other new business risks to banks ( Allianz Group and WWF 2005). These risks are likely to influence the credit quality of borrowers and therefore increase risks for banks. The ETS is one of the examples that have increased the cost of compliance on the industry sectors covered by the EU ETS.

In view of the current development in the international climate policy arena, the EU ETS and Kyoto Protocol could be modelled for future global climate policies, which has deep implications for banks. The following chart (Miller and Swann 2016) summarizes the current risks and opportunities for banks (Table 16.1).

Despite the number of new coal plants across the world being halved between 2015 to 2016, data from the Global Coal Plant Tracker shows that there are still over 1600 coal plants under construction, predominantly in developing countries (Banktrack 2018b). If these plants materialize, the power capacity would expand by more than 40 per cent (Banktrack 2018b). These plants will pose a serious threat in achieving the goals set under the Paris Agreement and various international conferences. As seen from Fig. 16.3 (Banktrack 2018b), banks in Asian countries, especially in China, are the big sponsors of coal plant developers.

**Table 16.1** Potential risks and new opportunities for banks (Adapted from: Miller and Swann 2016)

| *Banking types* | *Risks* | *Opportunities* |
|---|---|---|
| Corporate banking | • Increasing costs for consumers<br>• Losing competitiveness in carbon-intensive industries<br>• Price uncertainty toward carbon prices<br>• Reputational risks | • Enhancing the services toward risk management, carbon trust, and carbon projects |
| Investment banking | • Immature technologies<br>• Increasing insurance costs for unexpected weather | • Chances to establish the carbon funds<br>• Offering high-leverage products such as financial derivatives |
| Retail banking | • Financial losses<br>• Uncertain policies risks | • Microfinance for climate-friendly activities<br>• Advisory services |

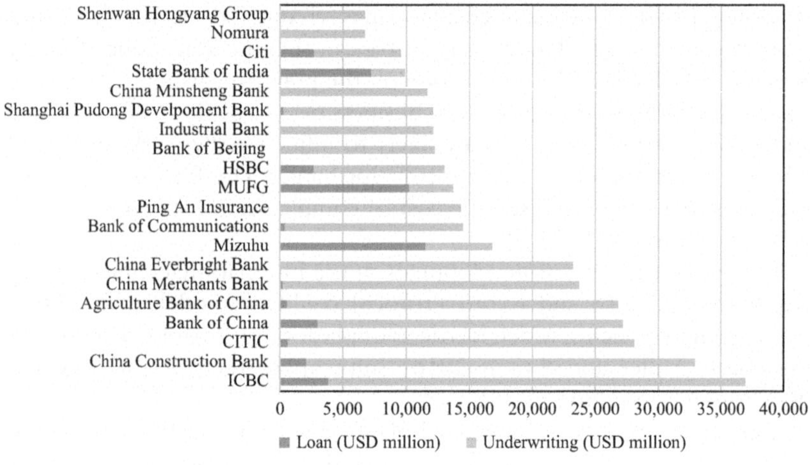


**Fig. 16.3** Top 20 banks for coal plant developing banks (Data Period: 2014–2017) (Reprinted from: Banktrack 2018b)

### *Management of Risks by Renewable Energy Companies*

A company's financial strength and competency to execute a project are assessed by its current financial situation, its access to funds, and its track record (Liu and Zeng 2017). However, uncertainties generate serious questions outside of the company's financial capability, especially issues on policy risks, the viability of the low carbon industry, and the multitude of factors that could influence revenue. Companies could address these uncertainties by taking proactive measures, though policy intervention would eventually be required to significantly address these risks in the final analysis. Nevertheless, there are some measures that the investors and the company could adopt to mitigate these risks. They are briefly explained below:

*Identification of Risks.* Liu and Zeng (2017) list "policy, technology, economic, security and market" as some of the risk sources, but their study focuses on policy, technology, and market risks as they are considered significant in a renewable energy project. An honest attempt to identify all the risks and their consequences in the planning stages is therefore crucial in ensuring a successful renewable project (Gatzert and Kosub 2016). The main purpose is essentially to allow investors to identify risks involved during the planning stages and facilitate informed decision making at all stages of the project lifetime (Liu and Zeng 2017).

*Risk Assessment.* In assessing the risks involved in an offshore wind project, Gatzert and Kosub (2016) list "strategic/business, transport, operation and maintenance, liability/legal, market and sales, counterparty, political and regulatory" as their risks assessment typology. Liu and Zeng (2017) highlight that risks should not be assessed independently as they are interlinked and contain unique feedback that influences the impact of these risks. Risks also change over time and may not be relevant until it reaches a certain stage of the project development. The authors propose an assessment method which involves identifying risks, their consequences, and attaching a score to quantify the impact of those risks. The quantification can be modelled and simulated to determine how the system will behave, the significant effect of the risks involved, and the financial returns across various scenarios. The authors also highlight that most evaluation methods are qualitative in nature, which implies that risks are determined without some relevant form of measurement to indicate the severity of the impact (Liu and Zeng 2017).

*Risk Management.* Gatzert and Kosub (2016) categorize risk management instruments into three categories: risk transfer, mitigation, and avoidance. Insurance is the main instrument to transfer risks while diversification can be useful to transfer risks. Diversification involves relying on various technologies to normalize revenue over time, subscribing to various insurances covering different risks, applying various government support schemes, and having multiple service providers. Mitigation of risks involve:

a. Forecasting resources availability, political stability, curtailment, natural hazards, etc.;
b. Monitoring of various technical components of the project;
c. Incorporating a minimum or fixed revenue clause, longer-term contracts, maintenance needs in contracts, etc.

Risk mitigation methods can be reflected through guarantees and warranties specified in contracts between investors and service providers. In terms of avoidance, investing in proven technology or existing facility could alleviate some of the risks discussed above (Gatzert and Kosub 2016).

## Conclusion

The definitions of climate risks are more complex than expected, and yet extremely important for investors and business managers. There is a need for further understanding of what climate risks mean in investments (Miller and Swann 2016). In December 2016, the TFCD elaborated on the climate change risks in its report (TCFD 2017):

> *There is a growing demand for decision-useful, climate-related information by a range of participants in the financial markets. Creditors and investors are increasingly demanding access to risk information that is consistent, comparable, reliable, and clear. There has also been increased focus, especially since the financial crisis of 2007–2008, on the negative impact that weak corporate governance can have on shareholder value, resulting in increased demand for transparency from organizations on their risks and risk management practices, including those related to climate change.*

The need to take climate risks into account in the decision-making process is vital in ensuring informed decisions based on recent and relevant issues. This, along with the focus to strengthen governance and transparency in climate risks, may facilitate in avoiding the negative impacts of the shareholder's value.

The TFCD also states in the report that institutions should disclose climate-related risks and potential opportunities in their public report, especially in the financial sector and more specifically for banks, insurance companies, and private institutions (TCFD 2017). In addition, the organization notes that revealing information associated with climate change could improve the investors' ability to identify and price climate risks and future opportunities properly (TCFD 2017).

For low carbon technologies, the absence of clear information has created a lot of uncertainties. Policies are important to establish and maintain a growing industry but as illustrated, implementation can be far more effective with specific instruments. These instruments are interlinked to provide clear specific information, a structure for players to perform exchanges, create level-playing field, and provide a governance structure to achieve the intended outcome. For low carbon technologies, as the industry grows, feedback from understanding the mechanics and structure of the RE industry can help financial institutions to better perform risk assessments. With these instruments in place providing knowledge and certainty, financial institutions are expected to further grow and provide financing products/packages that are attractive and conducive for the benefit of the low carbon technologies.

The feed-in tariff (FIT) system and other various instruments have the potential to increase the number of renewable energy projects. The FIT essentially allows independent renewable power producers to sell the electricity produced to the grid at a specified rate (tariff). However, the FIT system was mostly developed with the assumption that the cost of production for renewable energy would be on par with that of fossil fuel. Consequently, the government could decide to withdraw or adjust the feed-in tariff system to match the current market situation. Although the cost of production for both types of resource could match or reach "grid parity" (Karneyeva and Wüstenhagen 2017), institutional issues could still raise concerns and uncertainties. Policies address institutional issues by shaping the behaviour and driving the exchanges of all parties involved, including the financial sector. As such, the need for policy support to reduce risks should remain in place until renewable energy competes with fossil fuel and reaches widespread diffusion (Karneyeva and Wüstenhagen 2017).

The interests of stakeholders in society have influenced investments in both the industries promoting low carbon technologies and the coal and coal-related industries. In particular, the investments in low carbon technologies highlight shifting trends of the interests among various stakeholders toward a low carbon society. They illustrate how the financial decisions among financial institutions are being shaped differently over time under different sets of opportunities, norms, and regulative pressures in society (Scott 2008; North 1990). Despite coal technology's proven track record, investment in low carbon technologies addresses opportunities to generate income while fulfilling environmental and social obligations for developing countries. However, it could come at the expense of coal technology.

## References


Allianz Group and WWF. (2005). Climate change and the financial sector: An agenda for action. Foreword. Retrieved from http://citeseerx.ist.psu.edu/viewdoc/summary?doi=10.1.1.410.5914

Banktrack. (2018a). Banking on climate change: Fossil fuel finance report card 2018. Retrieved from https://www.banktrack.org/download/banking_on_climate_change_2018_fossil_fuel_finance_report_card/banking_on_climate_change_2018_web_final_1.pdf.

Banktrack. (2018b). Banks VS Paris agreement: Who's still financing coal plant development? Retrieved from https://www.banktrack.org/coaldevelopers/.

Buckley, T. (2019). Over 100 global financial institutions are exiting coal, with more to come. Retrieved from http://ieefa.org/wp-content/uploads/2019/02/IEEFA-Report_100-and-counting_Coal-Exit_Feb-2019.pdf.

Carbon Dioxide Information Analysis Center. (2012). Fossil-fuel CO2 emissions. Retrieved April 18, 2019, from https://cdiac.ess-dive.lbl.gov/trends/emis/meth_reg.html.

Carbon Tracker Initiative. (2011). Unburnable Carbon-Are the world's financial markets carrying a carbon bubble? Retrieved from https://www.banktrack.org/download/unburnable_carbon/unburnablecarbonfullrev2.pdf

Carney, M. (2015). Breaking the Tragedy of the Horizon-climate change and financial stability. Retrieved from http://www.icpmnetwork.com/wp-content/uploads/2016/05/The-Impact-of-Climate-Change-Risk-on-the-Balance-Sheet_Required-Reading.pdf

CERES. (2016). Assets or Liabilities? Fossil Fuel Investments of Leading U.S. Insurers Ceres. Retrieved from https://www.ceres.org/resources/reports/assets-or-liabilities-fossil-fuel-investments-leading-us-insurers

Edenhofer, O. (2014). IPCC WG3 AR5 summary for policymakers. Retrieved from https://www.ipcc.ch/site/assets/uploads/2018/02/ipcc_wg3_ar5_summary-for-policymakers.pdf.

Gatzert, N., & Kosub, T. (2016). Risks and risk management of renewable energy projects: The case of onshore and offshore wind parks. *Renewable and Sustainable Energy Reviews, 60*, 982–998. https://doi.org/10.1016/j.rser.2016.01.103.

Golnaraghi, M. (2018). Climate change and the insurance industry: Taking action as risk managers and investors. Perspectives from C-level executives in the insurance industry. Retrieved from www.genevaassociation.org.

Grubler, A., Johansson, T. B., Mundaca, L., Nakicenovic, N., Pachauri, S., Riahi, K., ... Strupeit, L. (2012). Chapter 1 – Energy Primer. In *Global Energy Assessment – Toward a Sustainable Future* (pp. 99–150). Cambridge University Press, Cambridge, UK and New York, NY, USA and the International Institute for Applied Systems Analysis, Laxenburg, Austria.

Haraguchi, M., & Lall, U. (2015). Flood risks and impacts: A case study of Thailand's floods in 2011 and research questions for supply chain decision making. *International Journal of Disaster Risk Reduction, 14*, 256–272. https://doi.org/10.1016/j.ijdrr.2014.09.005.

IPCC, Intergovernmental Panel on Climate Change. (2014). AR5 synthesis report: Summary for policymakers. Retrieved from https://www.ipcc.ch/site/assets/uploads/2018/02/AR5_SYR_FINAL_SPM.pdf.

Karneyeva, Y., & Wüstenhagen, R. (2017). Solar feed-in tariffs in a post-grid parity world: The role of risk, investor diversity and business models. *Energy Policy, 106*, 445–456. https://doi.org/10.1016/j.enpol.2017.04.005.

Liu, X., & Zeng, M. (2017). Renewable energy investment risk evaluation model based on system dynamics. *Renewable and Sustainable Energy Reviews, 73*, 782–788. https://doi.org/10.1016/j.rser.2017.02.019.

Mchale, C., & Spivey, R. (2016). Assets or liability: Fossil fuel investments of leading U.S. Insurers. Retrieved from www.mercer.com.

MEGTW, Ministry of Energy, Green Technology and Water. (2009). *National renewable energy policy and action plan.* Putrajaya: Ministry of Energy Green Technology and Water. Retrieved from http://seda.gov.my/?omaneg=00010100000001010101000100001000000000000000000000&s=31.

Miller, A., & Swann, S. (2016). Climate change and the financial sector: A time of risk and opportunity. Retrieved from https://papers.ssrn.com/sol3/papers.cfm?abstract_id=2865250.

NASA's Goddard Institute for Space Studies (GISS). (2018). Global surface temperature change. Retrieved from https://data.giss.nasa.gov/gistemp/.

North, D. C. (1990). *Institutions, institutional change, and economic performance/ Douglass C. North.* Cambridge and New York: Cambridge University Press.

Polzin, F., Egli, F., Steffen, B., & Schmidt, T. S. (2019). How do policies mobilize private finance for renewable energy? – A systematic review with an investor perspective. *Applied Energy, 236*, 1249–1268. https://doi.org/10.1016/j.apenergy.2018.11.098.

REN21, Renewables Energy Policy Network for the 21st Century. (2018). *Renewables 2018 global status report*. Paris: REN21 secretariat. Retrieved from http://www.ren21.net/gsr_2018_full_report_en.

Roberts, D. (2017). Energy poverty is a real problem. Coal is a bogus solution. – Vox. Retrieved February 25, 2019, from https://www.vox.com/2016/10/25/13309076/energy-poverty-coal.

Schueneman, T. (2015). Record $3.4 trillion committed to fossil fuel divestment. Retrieved March 29, 2019, from http://www.triplepundit.com/story/2015/record-34-trillion-committed-fossil-fuel-divestment/30096.

Scott, W. R. (2008). *Institutions and organizations: Ideas and interests/W. Richard Scott* (3rd ed. Thousand Oaks, CA: Sage Publications.

Silver, N. (2017). Blindness to risk: Why institutional investors ignore the risk of stranded assets. *Journal of Sustainable Finance and Investment, 7*(1), 99–113. https://doi.org/10.1080/20430795.2016.1207996.

Simons, M., & De Wilde, J. (2017). *The involvement of European insurance groups in the fossil fuels sector*. Profundo.

Sovacool, B. K., & Drupady, I. M. (2011). Examining the Small Renewable Energy Power (SREP) program in Malaysia. *Energy Policy, 39*(11), 7244–7256. https://doi.org/10.1016/j.enpol.2011.08.045.

Standard and Poor's. (2015). Climate risk: Rising tides raise the stakes.Retrieved from http://www.watergas.it/grk_files/uploads/redazione_commedia/news/climate_risk_rising_tides_rais/downloads/climate_change_book_climate_risk__rising_tides_1_12_2015.pdf.

TCFD, Task Force on Climate-related Financial Disclosures. (2017). Recommendations of the Task Force on climate-related financial disclosures. Retrieved from https://www.fsb-tcfd.org/wp-content/uploads/2016/12/TCFD-Recommendations-Report-A4-14-Dec-2016.pdf.

UN Environment. (2018). Emissions gap report 2018. Retrieved from http://www.un.org/Depts/Cartographic/english/htmain.htm.

UNFCCC, United Nations Framework Convention on Climate Change. (2015). The Paris agreement. Retrieved from https://unfccc.int/sites/default/files/english_paris_agreement.pdf

UNFCCC, United Nations Framework Convention on Climate Change. (2016). Report of the Conference of the parties on its twenty-first session, held in Paris from 30 November to 13 December 2015. Addendum. Part two: Action taken by the Conference of the Parties at its twenty-first session. Retrieved from https://unfccc.int/documents/9097.

Zhang, W., & Pan, X. (2016). Study on the demand of climate finance for developing countries based on submitted INDC. *Advances in Climate Change Research, 7*(1), 99–104. https://doi.org/10.1016/j.accre.2016.05.00.

CHAPTER 17

# A New Era in the Risk Management of Financial Firms

*Sureyya Burcu Avci*

## Introduction

Emerging new technologies are disruptive by nature, even though they are considered to provide more benefits than harms overall (Arner et al. 2016; Alt et al. 2018; WEF 2018). Emerging technologies in financial transactions facilitate new business interactions and personal transactions; they give users greater satisfaction and make them more productive. For example, many people use e-banking almost every day, without having to visit neither the bank branch nor the post office, allowing the customer to save valuable time and costs such as transportation costs, wage disruption, and so on. For the bank it allows them to reduce their employment costs for physical employees at the branch, as some of the customer needs are dealt with through online automatic services, such as depositing, transmitting, and investing funds. At the same time, online banking destroys traditional branch banking and brick-and-mortar retail, while creating new

S. B. Avci (✉)
School of Management, Sabanci University, Istanbul, Turkey
e-mail: avcis@sabanciuniv.edu



T. Walker et al. (eds.), *Ecological, Societal, and Technological Risks and the Financial Sector*, Palgrave Studies in Sustainable Business In Association with Future Earth, https://doi.org/10.1007/978-3-030-38858-4_17

opportunities for e-commerce (WEF n.d.). This convenience comes at a cost to the customers as well as their passwords and identity can become vulnerable to theft. These costs fall on the financial institutions as well as their customers. Users can try to control some of these risks by not sharing passwords with third parties and using reliable virus programs on computers. Nevertheless, many risks remain beyond users' personal control. Besides, dealing with traditional risks of financial services, risk managers must now take care of these new costs and risks that emerging new technologies generate BIS (2003b).

Due to changes in technological conditions, the world is shifting to a new paradigm. Technological changes create new threats and opportunities for financial companies (BIS 2006). Since the 2000s, companies in the finance sector have become web-based operating companies (Arner et al. 2016). As technology facilitates new forms of financial businesses, financial companies can obtain numerous new customers via the use of internet marketing, promotion, and ease of access. Companies now run transactions not only in their domestic country but also overseas. Several financial transactions have become convenient, available, or cheaper for domestic and international customers.

With the rise of digitalization, the definition of financial companies broadens to include FinTechs. FinTechs are startups which offer financial services that once were almost exclusively the business of banks (Mead 2016). These activities include online payments and e-banking activities, e-wallets, digital investments, digital currencies, and many more financial activities some of which did not exist before the improvement of FinTechs (Nienaber 2016). Even though FinTechs are an emerging type of financial organization, they are different from traditional financial companies in the eye of regulators. FinTechs are not subject to supervision and regulation of financial authorities unless they apply for financial certifications to become a financial company as a whole or in part. Conclusively, risk management processes of FinTechs can be different from those of traditional finance companies. This chapter focuses on the risk management of traditional financial companies.

Ultimately, digitalization, provides many positive effects to financial firms such as a lower cost of business, international coverage, ease of acquiring customers, between others. Yet, financial firms also suffer various negative effects from emergence of new technologies. In addition to the traditional risks originating from the nature of the business, financial companies must now deal with risks emerging from digitalization such as e-financing risks, cyber security risks, and outsourcing risks.

According to a recent survey on financial services industry (Proviti and North Carolina State University's ERM Initiative Survey 2017), top risks are categorized as follows: rapid speed of disruptive innovations and new technologies within the finance industry; cyber threats that can disrupt core operations and damage brand value; confidentiality of privacy, information security, systems protection; and regulatory changes and heightened scrutiny that would affect the format of service delivery.

The goal of risk management is to ensure business continuity and prosperity under different economic and environmental conditions. Basic principles of risk management remain the same while tactics to ensure business continuity can vary as business risks change. How can risk managers distinguish and classify new risks and continue operations without disruptions in the ongoing business? How can these risks deteriorate financial business? Why should risk managers consider managing risk? These are the new challenges to be answered by risk managers.

The first step for managing these risks is to define all the players and their tools in the new environment. Financial companies are defined as financial institutions or other organizations that would buy and sell financial claims, which can be financial contracts, such as deposits and loans; and financial assets, such as stocks and bonds (Freixas and Rochet 2008, p. 15). Financial companies are subject to regulation and supervision by at least one financial authority. Commercial banks, investment banks, insurance companies, and investment companies such as mutual funds, securities firms, stock exchanges, operators of payments, and settlement systems including central banks, and messaging service providers, such as SWIFT, are examples of financial organizations (BIS 2006).

Risk management aims to reduce the expected costs of risks. Traditionally, financial companies' risk management departments focus on risk silos (Bascand 2014; Deloitte 2017) such as interest rate risk, market risk, liquidity risk, and credit risk. Each risk type is measured individually using econometric models and some of the risks are hedged by using appropriate tools and instruments. While keeping traditional risks under control, companies should identify new risk sources and adjust risk management practices accordingly. Hereby, the assumption is that innovations in finance do not principally change the risk management tools; yet they expand their coverage by increasing operational, reputational, strategic, and legal risks (BIS 2006). New technologies increase especially operational risks, and it is hard to hedge operational risks with financial tools.

Companies must use insurance and business continuity management tools to tackle these operational risks.

If a disruption takes place in operations, business continuity management minimizes its visible effects for customers. As a result, business continuity management gained importance in the new digitalized era. This chapter reviews High Level Principles for Financial Firms (BIS 2006) in order to emphasize the importance of these principles in the risk management applications in the finance industry.

This chapter is organized as follows: Section "Traditional Risks of Financial Companies" reviews the traditional risks that financial companies face. These risks are still valid, and they are expected to increase in importance as new technologies develop. Section "Business Continuity Principles for Financial Companies" summarizes business continuity principles recommended for financial companies. Section "New Outlook of the Finance Industry" introduces the new outlook of the finance industry with technological innovations, especially after the emergence of FinTechs. Section "Taxonomy of Digital Finance Business Functions" presents a taxonomy of digital finance business to display how financial operations are changing and how they can be classified. Section "Risks and Risk Management of Financial Companies in the Digitalization Era" introduces new risks to the finance industry emerging with high technology use. These risks are e-financing risks (Section "E-Financing"), outsourcing risks (Section "Outsourcing"), and cyber security risks (Section "Cyber Security"). E-financing risks are mostly comprised of e-banking risks, and as a result, the related subsection focuses on e-banking risks. Section "Conclusion" concludes and discusses the necessity of a holistic risk management approach.

## Traditional Risks of Financial Companies

Financial sector regulators are concerned with financial risks not only because they disrupt the financial system, but also because they disrupt the economic system. The mischannelling of funds from efficient investment opportunities to less efficient ones can ultimately disrupt the whole economy (Mishkin 1992). The purpose of financial regulation is to minimize this inefficiency by protecting the solvency of financial institutions, in turn protecting the welfare of citizens and taxpayers (Ely n.d.). Financial company risks can be classified under the following categories (Christoffersen 2012, p. 6).

*Credit risk* is perceived as the most important financial risk for a company. If credit repayments are delayed or cancelled, either in part or completely, it can cause systemic cash flow problems and endanger bank liquidity (Van Greuning and Bratanovic 2000, p. 125). Commercial banks are exposed to a large amount of credit risk because their core business is credit intermediation. Credit risk is also typical for other financial companies; however, it can be hedged fully as long as the core business of the financial company is not credit provision (Christoffersen 2012, p. 7).

*Liquidity risk* refers to the facilitation of transactions. When market liquidity is low, possibly due to some crisis, financial firms can meet their liquidity risks either from the asset side (by selling assets) or the liability side (raising new funds) (Christoffersen 2012, p. 6). Banks are expected to have sufficient liquid assets to compensate cash needs of depositors and loan holders (Tursoy 2018). Low liquidity causes low trading volume, and lower profitability from trading. Moreover, trade takes longer time than usual, and asset prices may be below their fundamental values. Liquidity risk draws financial companies into funding problems, and financial companies may have difficulties to fulfill their obligations (Christoffersen 2012, p. 6).

*Market risk* arises from decreases in asset prices, such as equity and bonds. Financial companies typically have assets that have positive exposures to market prices. For example, if a financial company offers loans that perform better in up-markets, then it will have market risk since credit risk ascends in down markets (Christoffersen 2012, p. 6). Alternative hedging strategies should be adopted to harvest profits in up-markets and to protect from damages of reduction in asset prices during down-markets.

*Operational risk* is the risk of loss due to an error, fraud, or failure in the ongoing operations; physical catastrophes; and technical failures. Unlike market risk, operational risk does not yield any benefits to companies. Thus, firms do not manage operational risks actively; they try to minimize it. It is hard to hedge operational risks from asset markets, and the best way to deal with operational risks is to insure against risks (Christoffersen 2012, p. 7).

*Business risk* is an integral part of the core business operations and cannot be hedged. For example, financial crises, changes in competition, technology, and demand may destroy the business plan of financial companies, but all these factors are in the very nature of financial businesses. Business risk is a type of risk that companies must take on to be in the business (Christoffersen 2012, p. 7).

There are other risks of secondary importance for financial companies. The most important risks of this group include interest rate risk, reputational risk, legal risk, concentration risk, insurance risk, political risk, and country risk. Risk management departments of financial companies use several techniques such as Value-at-Risk, expected shortfall, back testing, stress testing, simulation, and model building approaches to quantify risks; and other techniques such as credit rationing, insurance, hedging, and risk aggregation to keep risks at a manageable level (Hull 2015, p. 17). These traditional risk management techniques are still very much in use after the introduction of new technologies. However, new technologies can dramatically increase contagion risk and thus the probability of adverse incidents (BIS 2006). As a result, business continuity management gains importance within the risk management programs in the digitalization era.

## Business Continuity Principles for Financial Companies

Aiming to mitigate all business disruptions to an unperceivable level by external parties, business continuity planning is a very important component of operational risk management. While risk management identifies, analyzes, ranks, and minimizes probability and destruction of risks before a major disruption occurs, business continuity management ensures that operations are maintained or recovered within an acceptable time frame once an incident occurs (BIS 2006). In other words, business continuity management steps in to fix the defects in operations despite all precautions to reduce failures. Therefore, risk management and business continuity management go together to mitigate the impact of negative events. The Joint Forum of Basel Committee on Banking Supervision provides a framework of business continuity principles for financial companies (BIS 2006). These principles can be summarized as follows.

*Principle 1*: Financial companies and financial authorities are ultimately responsible for business continuity. It is the board of director's/senior management's responsibility within an organization to make sure that the financial company is applying business continuity practices, standards, and principles and communicating effectively with financial authorities.

*Principle 2*: Financial authorities should be in compliance with financial regulations. Recovery levels and durations should be identified, and system efficiency should be tested for fast recovery. These objectives are vital for sole suppliers of crucial services, such as payment and settlement system operators or central banks, which cannot be provided by other financial institutions rapidly.

*Principle 4*: In the case of a major financial disruption, financial companies should prepare communication protocols that include responsible personnel for communication, contact information of relevant parties, and call schedules. Moreover, alternate communication systems should be defined, and communication protocols should be regularly updated as preparation for incidents.

*Principle 5*: Because many financial companies have cross-border exposures, a major disruption in a country would affect cross-border businesses. To be on the secure side, financial companies should develop communication protocols, including responsible personnel, contact information of relevant parties, and call schedules with international parties.

*Principle 6*: Financial companies and financial authorities should collaborate to regularly test and evaluate the effectiveness of business continuity plans, and update if appropriate.

*Principle 7*: Financial authorities should review business continuity plans of financial companies. Financial authorities should assess and evaluate the practices as a supervisory body. Communication protocols and recovery objectives should be supervised and assessed if the objectives and protocols provide adequate assurance for their business processes to be recovered in case of emergencies.

## New Outlook of the Finance Industry

Digitalization is the integration of social life domains with digital communication and media infrastructures (Brennen and Kreiss 2016). Digitalization of financial services replaced delivery and access to a broad range of traditional financial services including payments, credits, savings, and insurances via computers and mobile phones (DFS 2016). Digitalization is introduced to the finance industry by three means.

First, traditional finance companies enlarge their IT departments to provide a wide range of high-technology activities. This trend became widespread after the 1960s (Alt et al. 2018). Traditional finance companies focus on the core finance business, such as pooling and moving funds, managing risks, providing information for decision makers and addressing asymmetric information problems (Merton 1992). These activities are naturally complex and require high level of security-related actions because of regulations. As a result, financial companies have historically made large expenditures on digitalization and other IT-related activities (Scott et al. 2017). Finance is the first industry to adopt computers and technology-driven activities (Franke 1987). Starting from the establishment of ATMs in the 1960s, banks have reached a level where they operate core business activities, such as lending, borrowing, and wire transfers, through digital systems (Millo et al. 2005; Alt et al. 2018).

Contrary to the rising trend in the last 50 years, today the share of bank expenditures dedicated to IT-related investments dropped to a historical minimum (Scott et al. 2017). Instead of bearing high switching costs to invest in new technologies, banks downsize their IT departments and collaborate with FinTechs that provide more efficient technology solutions. Today, banks spend a substantial share of their resources to fulfill the regulatory requirements to continue core operations (Brandl and Hornuf 2017). It is expected that a number of banks will fail in the coming years, and FinTechs will replace many of the smaller banks (Finextra 2015).

Second, FinTechs use of digitalization could allow them to replace traditional financial companies. FinTechs are innovative firms that use digital technologies to enable, innovate, and disrupt financial services (Gimpel et al. 2018). FinTechs have been offering new technologies for financial solutions since approximately 2008 (Alt et al. 2018). It is important to note that founders of FinTechs come from a business background rather than an IT background, they know the deficiencies of the financial system. Their management abilities allow them to work closely with the IT experts to provide user-friendly and innovative solutions to customers (Brandl and Hornuf 2017). Not only do FinTechs provide more efficient B2C business models, they also provide more efficient B2B models for traditional finance companies. They usually create a network of specialized partners to distribute tasks in order to obtain solutions more efficiently. Such a business model would expedite processes, reduce margins, respond quickly to regulatory requirements, and satisfy customers and regulators (Alt et al. 2018). The growing number of FinTechs and their enlarging coverage in the financial sector erode the market shares of traditional finance companies in some service areas (Mead 2016). Despite their efficient models, the majority of financial services companies compete with FinTechs. It is unknown which direction the financial market will take; however, the early signs show that FinTechs can ultimately replace banks (Menat 2016; Van der Kleij 2016; Beck 2001, p. 7).

Third, digitalization can be introduced by traditional finance and FinTechs collaborations. Brick-and-mortar banks are struggling to serve today's digitally savvy customers, they are losing market shares to FinTechs. Even then, banks are the cornerstones of the economy, therefore, they will not completely vanish in the foreseeable future. Banks provide the primary means of financing (Merton 1992). FinTechs usually focus on one service area, such as digital payments, and they do not compete with banks for all other service areas. The FinTechs that compete with banks have to receive banking licenses like Solaris Bank in Germany (Brandl and Hornuf 2017). As a result, collaborations among banks and FinTechs would provide benefits to both parties: banks would have more efficient service deliveries while FinTechs would benefit from the banks' large customer database and the additional services such as lending, financing, and so on that banks offer. (Nienaber 2016). BIS (2003b) suggests that collaborations can be in the form of partnerships, alliances, and outsourcing services. Brandl and Hornuf (2017) present a network analysis of the strategic partnerships among banks and FinTechs as well as among FinTechs and FinTechs. The results are remarkably cost efficient as both banks and FinTechs start strategic partnerships with FinTechs to integrate new technology by using the software of a FinTech for transaction-based fees. Banks do not have to invest on expensive IT structures, rather they concentrate on their core business and save from capital and labor by depending on the IT structures of FinTechs.

## Taxonomy of Digital Finance Business Functions

It would be helpful to provide details about the digital finance business in order to understand the risks that arise from digitalization. Even though it is possible to classify digital finance business by many ways, we follow the taxonomy of Gomber et al. (2017) due to its large coverage and simplicity. Gomber et al. (2017) group digital finance business functions in six categories: digital financing, digital investments, digital money, digital payments, digital insurances, and digital financial advice. After reviewing each category briefly, we will focus on the changing risks associated with the digitalization of these activities.

*Digital financing (fund-raising)*: All types of digital fund-raising activities, such as online lending, crowdfunding, leasing, invoicing, and factoring, are categorized under this umbrella. Traditional fund-raising is the task of banks, venture capitals, angel investors, and/or some government organizations (Kloehn and Hornuf 2012) along with exchange markets and financial institutions working with exchange markets. Crowdfunding is a new financing method introduced with financial digitalization, it is not offered by financial companies. Other types of digital fund-raising activities can be realized through the digital platforms of traditional financial institutions and of FinTechs.

Yet, what about the risks arising from crowdfunding or from other digital financing activities realized by FinTechs? FinTechs are not regulated by authorities; as a result, investments through these companies are not under the supervision of governmental bodies. There is evidence that more than 2 percent of successfully funded crowdfunding projects are fraudulent and more than half of the projects deliver rewards with delays (Mollick 2014). As of now there is no academic research about the payment performance of other FinTech activities.

Other important questions arise: what is the difference between customers that fund their projects by traditional finance companies and the customers that fund their projects from alternate funding methods, such as crowdfunding? Are the latter the people who cannot get credit from financial institutions for they are not credible or are they eligible for bank credit but do not want to apply for a bank loan? How many customers banks have lost because of these new financing platforms? Has the credibility of customers changed after these digital platforms started operating? These questions have two dimensions: 1) FinTechs can reduce market shares and profits for traditional finance companies, and 2) those customers would be rendered by credit rationing mechanisms if they applied for bank financing, and their choice of financing does not affect the market shares and profits of traditional finance companies. These questions have not yet been subject to academic research.

*Digital investments*: Mobile trading, social trading, online brokerage, high-frequency and algorithmic trading can be categorized as digital investments. Digital investments include trading and engaging in brokerage activities without the need to meet an advisor/broker face to face. As a result, investors do not have to work with a single advisor/broker, they can minimize transaction costs by doing self-directed trading. Such a system can cause investors to be over-confident in their personal abilities and competence (Barber and Odean 2001; Barber and Odean 2002). From a risk management point of view, digital investments do not impose new risks on financial companies, but they increase the existing risks.

Among all, only social trading is the only digital investment that does not need the contribution of a financial institution. Mobile trading, online brokerage, high-frequency and algorithmic trading are offered by financial institutions. Social trading is a new internet phenomenon that involves securities trading via digital platforms. It combines investment activities with social media networks. These platforms offer investment products such as stocks, bonds, foreign exchange, and commodities. Moreover, they connect the investor to some social networks where investors can search and share investment advice (Doering et al. 2015).

*Digital money*: Digital money or digital currency is a computerized representation of value. It owns all the functions of real money, such as being a medium of exchange, and a unit of account, and storing of value. It can be digitally traded but does not have a legal tender status (FATF 2014). Traditional currencies are issued and regulated by central banks whereas digital money is decentralized and created via crypto technologies. It operates without a mediating institution such as a central bank or international organization (Nakamoto 2008). Its value is determined on supply and demand conditions.

Cryptocurrencies are not yet accepted as means of payment by traditional finance companies and central banks. As a result, it is too early to describe digital currencies as a reliable payment and investment tool. There is evidence showing their performance and increasing roles in portfolios (Bouri et al. 2017; Gangwal 2016; Baur et al. 2017). There is partial evidence showing that the efficiency of the digital currency market increases with more participants (Mensi et al. 2019). Another risk of digital currencies is that no central bank regulates, supervises, or backs them. (ECB 2012).

*Digital payments*: Electronic payments, mobile payments, peer-to-peer payments, and digital wallets can be categorized as digital payments. Financial organizations and e-business companies provide digital payment platforms for money transmitting and return for a good or service (Contini et al. 2011). In less developed countries where the reliability of banks is questionable, digital payment platforms and mobile banking provide a more feasible and promising alternative to traditional banking (Contini et al. 2011; Merritt 2010).

Peer-to-peer (P2P) payments are payments without the use of a bank, like PayPal. The customer gives the bank account information to PayPal and PayPal realizes the payment. It provides a higher security level than sharing bank account or credit card information to unknown third parties. There are other types of P2P payment systems that include a bank account or a credit card in payments (Bradford and Keeton 2012). As long as banks take necessary precautions to protect account and credit information, these activities do not pose new challenges on the risk management of banks.

Digital wallets are digital storages for identity, bank, and credit card information, and temporary tokens like bus tickets. A digital wallet is an online substitute for a physical wallet (Ebringer et al. 2000). As long as digital wallet owners keep products of financial institutions, such as credit cards and account information in their digital wallet, identity and personal information protection is important for the financial institutions offering these products.

*Digital insurances*: Insurance companies provide platform-based insurance services to their customers, which do not require additional risk management measures to take for insurance companies. In addition to conventional risk management practices, they require to secure customer information and money transfers. As usual, each insurance company should make a thorough risk analysis and perform customized risk management systems based on needs.

There are different digital insurance systems, such as family or friends-insurance. In such systems, participants ally to reduce insurance payments. Part of monetary payments are made to the insurance company and the rest is kept within the group. In case of small insurance instances, the remedy is paid by the stored amount within the group; in case of big insurance instances, participants apply for the insurance company. This system facilitates obtaining lower insurance premiums for participants (Arumugam and Cusick 2008; Moenninghoff and Wieandt 2013; Gomber et al. 2017). Such platforms do not pose new challenges on insurance companies in terms of risk management.

*Digital financial advice*: Digital financial advice has long been provided by financial companies to customers. Digitalization of the services does not impose new risks on financial advisers. Financial advisory is a license-required business, and as a result, investors are taking on individual risks if they trust unlicensed organizations or people.

## Risks and Risk Management of Financial Companies in the Digitalization Era

The digitalization of traditional finance businesses does not impose new types of risks to financial companies per se; rather, they increase and modify the strategic, operational, legal, and reputational risks of financial companies. Thus, financial companies should not only continue applying the existing risk management activities, if not, they should also tailor, adapt, and expand these risk management activities to address evolving risk management challenges. Rapidly improving technological innovation would leave existing risk management principles outdated soon, the board of directors/senior management should overview financial companies' current risk management policies and practices and tailor them if necessary (BIS 2003b).

The new risks to finance industry can be categorized as e-financing risks, outsourcing risks, and cyber security risks. Challenges and required risk management principles are discussed below.

### *E-Financing*

*Challenges of E-Financing*

Expedited competition and financial innovation among finance companies have resulted in new assets and tools to serve customers. Both individual and institutional customers can enjoy almost all conventional banking, insurance, and investment services online. Electronic fund transfers, card payments, account management, investments, insurance claims, and many other services are presented to customers by financial institutions via electronic services. The rapid development of e-finance activities provides new business opportunities, at the same time, it does pose some risks on financial companies.

BIS (2003b) describes four challenges to financial companies in terms of e-banking activities: the speed of new technologies, the dependence on computerized systems, the operational security issues, and the data protection issues. These risks apply for other e-financing businesses because the nature of business is the same for all e-financing activities.

The first challenge is the speed of technology. Traditionally, financial companies, especially banks, adopted new technologies over a longer time horizon and after several in-depth tests. Today financial companies are under competitive pressure to adopt new technologies quicker. As regulated entities, financial companies must ensure adequate strategic assessment and risk analysis in this short few months' time frame.

Second, financial companies rely on computer systems to operate online activities. On one hand, these computer systems reduce human error and fraud; on the other hand, financial companies become dependent on those computer systems because they cannot continue digital operations without them.

Third, dependence on information technology increases security issues, and consequently, operational risks. The collaboration between traditional finance companies and FinTechs paves the way for new business models. FinTechs are unregulated by financial authorities, and traditional finance companies must deal with the risk management responsibilities of new business models.

Last, financial companies are subject to risks of identity theft and other data protection issues. As a result, they must enhance customer privacy standards, data protection methods, security controls, and audit trail procedures.

*Risk Management Principles for E-Financing Activities*

BIS (2003a, b) recommend three categories of risk management of e-commerce activities for financial companies: board and management oversight (Principles 1–3), security controls (Principles 4–10), and legal and reputational risk management (Principles 11–14). These principles are explained in this section.

*Principle 1*: Because the delivery channel is out of the financial companies' direct control, the internet adds additional risks to traditional financial activities. The internet enables and expedites delivery of services across borders. It is a board of directors'/senior management's duty to effectively oversee risks over e-finance activities. The technical experience of the board of directors/senior management is usually not enough to assess internet activities. A mismeasurement of risks may put banks under risk of underestimating costs of disruptions. This underestimation may cause reputational damage and financial losses. E-financing policies and procedures should be consistent with the overall strategy of the financial company. The board of directors/senior management is responsible for establishing accountability, policies, and controls to manage electronic risks and must pay special attention to data privacy and identity security. They should ensure due diligence in risk analysis in cross-border e-financing activities. Cross-border financing activities pose legal, regulatory, and country risks on financial companies as they must comply with the host country's legal requirements.

*Principle 2*: Key aspects security controls of the financial institution should be reviewed and approved by the board of directors/senior management. Safeguarding assets, including e-financing systems and data, is one of the main duties of the board of directors/senior management. To achieve this goal, the board of directors/senior management must provide comprehensive security systems, appropriate policies, and procedures. An effective e-financing security process includes personnel responsibilities for oversight, enough physical controls, and prevents unauthorized access to the IT environment.

*Principle 3*: To manage the financial companies' outsourcing processes, the board of directors/senior management has to establish comprehensive and continuous oversight and due diligence. Rapidly evolving e-financing activities made outsourcing a necessity for financial companies. Historically, one outsourcing service provider was enough; today, multiple outsource providers work on the same project. Similarly, a limited number of outsourcing service providers may provide services to multiple financial companies. All the outsourcing activities pose new threats on financial companies. To handle these risks, financial companies should understand the risks associated with outsourcing, apply due diligence in the selection process of the outsourcing service providers for e-financing activities, and define the requirements and responsibilities for each party in the agreement with the outsourcing provider. The outsource service providers must agree to comply with the financial company's security standards and privacy policies. They must also agree to be monitored and audited by the financial company. Appropriate contingency plans should exist for e-financing activities.

*Principle 4*: Customer verification reduces the risk of identity theft, fraudulent account applications, and money laundering. Failure in customer verification may cause financial loss and reputational damage to the financial company. Financial companies must have formal policies and procedures for identity authentication and customer authorization. Identity authentication and authorization are especially important in cross-border e-banking activities.

*Principle 5*: Financial companies should design e-finance systems that reduce the likelihood of unauthorized users and transactions; ensure that customers understand the risks of unauthorized access to systems; maintain authentication controls and data protection methods.

*Principle 6*: Appropriate measures should be taken to promote segregation of duties within e-finance systems, databases, and applications. Segregation of duties is traditionally used to mitigate fraudulent activities. E-financing activities imperatively need segregation of duties because identities can be easily disguised in electronic systems. Financial companies should ensure that transaction processes are designed so that unauthorized people cannot be granted access.

*Principle 7*: E-finance systems, databases, and applications should be protected by proper authorization controls and access privileges. Financial companies should strictly control authorization and access privileges to keep databases away from unauthorized access and enable segregation of duties.

*Principle 8*: Appropriate measures should be taken to protect the data integrity of e-finance transactions and records. Data integrity refers to the security of information in-transit or in storage. If data is accessed or obtained by unauthorized parties, financial losses and reputational damages are inevitable.

*Principle 9*: Clear audit trails should be ensured for all e-financing transactions. E-financing activities intensify the audit processes. Opening, modifying, or closing customer accounts; making any financial transaction; making any transaction exceeding customer limits; and any granting, modifying, or revoking of system access rights or privileges should be audited.

*Principle 10*: Appropriate measures to keep the confidentiality of key e-finance information need to be preserved. The degree of measures to be taken to preserve the data should be determined by the sensitivity of the information in the databases. Only authorized parties should access confidential data, unauthorized visualization and modification of confidential data should be prohibited, and data confidentiality rules should strictly apply to outsource service providers.

*Principle 11*: Before starting an e-financing transaction, potential customers should be informed about the financial companies' identity and regulatory status. To inform the customers the financial company should create or use their existing website. The website should include the name of the financial company and the location of the head office; the financial company's primary supervisory authorities; the contact information of the customer service, ombudsman, and other departments to contact in case of a problem; and the contact information of or the link to other important institutions to customers, such as deposit and insurance institutions, or compensation services.

*Principle 12*: Appropriate measures should be taken to ensure that the customer privacy requirements comply with regulations in all of the countries where the financial company serves. Customers should also be informed about the financial company's privacy policy so that they may decline to share their data with third parties.

*Principle 13*: Financial companies should ensure the availability of e-financing systems via capacity, business continuity and contingency planning processes. Acceptance level of e-commerce and e-banking should be analyzed to determine the capacity and future scalability. Stress tests, periodic reviews, and contingency plans should be applied to e-banking activities.

*Principle 14*: Appropriate incident response plans should be prepared and adopted to tackle problems arising from unexpected events regarding e-finance services. Incident response plans are elements of scenario analysis that address the recovery of e-banking systems and services under various locations and businesses. The risk likelihood and impact should be included in incident response plans. Plans should include incident response teams and a protocol about how to cope with the issue when it arises.

## *Outsourcing*

### *Challenges of Outsourcing*

Outsourcing risks arise from the collaborations of financial companies with FinTechs. Because FinTechs are not regulated, financial companies must ensure that their collaborators comply with financial regulations so that outsourced services will not pose any regulatory risks on financial companies. Risks associated with outsourcing activities are reported in the "Outsourcing in Financial Services" report of the BIS. These risks can be summarized as follows (BIS 2005):

*Strategic risk*: If the strategic goals of the financial company and those of the outsourcing service provider do not fit, the strategic risks of the financial company increase. A FinTech associated with money laundering activities would shrink the market share of a financial company if they collaborate. Thus, failure to oversee strategies and activities of the outsource service provider, either because of inadequate expertise or because of other reasons, would pose strategic risks on financial companies.

*Reputational risk*: Poor service, inadequate customer communications, and service practices of outsource service providers could increase reputational risks of financial companies. End users receive the service from the financial company, and they will blame the financial company if dissatisfied by the low service quality.

*Compliance risk*: If the outsourcing service provider has inadequate control systems to comply with prudential and customer laws and/or regulations, financial companies will be negatively affected. All activities of financial companies, including outsourced services, should comply with regulations. Otherwise, financial companies might have to bear legal consequences. The board of directors/senior management of financial companies should find a way to guarantee that the outsourcing service providers comply with financial regulations.

*Operational risk*: Inadequate financial and technical capacity to fulfill obligations or provide remedies, fraud or error, technology failure as well as inadequate monitoring, supervision, and inspection of the outsourcing service provider, can increase the operational risks of the financial company. Outsourcing activities require several special operational risk management practices. For example, the outsourcing of e-banking activities requires risk management of e-banking, customer privacy security, response plans, data integrity management, and other risk management specialties, such as capacity, business continuity and contingency planning (BIS 2003b, 2005).

*Exit strategy risk*: If appropriate exit strategies cannot be applied in a timely fashion, the exit strategy risk arises. Over-reliance on one outsource provider can compel a financial company to collaborate with the same provider. The financial company's loss of relevant skills to bring the outsourced activity in-house can compel the financial company to outsource the activity in every situation, even if it is too costly or unnecessary. Contracting is an important task that financial companies should develop while working with outsourcing service providers. Contracting can help financial companies overcome the speedy exit problem.

*Counterparty risk*: The risk of having the outsourcing service provider default. If a collaborator defaults, the financial company's business can be negatively affected: credit ratings, equity prices, and the quality of receivables can decline. Reputational costs can increase.

*Country risk*: The political, legal, and social climate of the outsourcing service provider's country may add additional risks to financial companies and make business continuity plans more complex to establish and implement. High risk-prone countries or unstable political climates can increase country risk for the financial company.

*Contractual risk*: The ability to enforce the contract may be a problem due to contract-related issues. If the finance company and the outsource provider are located in different jurisdictions, the law of enforcement should be pre-determined. Additionally, contracts should be prepared carefully for foreseeable risks prior to outsourcing agreements.

*Access risk*: The outsourcing agreement may add a layer of difficulty for regulators to understand the activities of the financial company. It may also delay the arrival of timely data and other information to the financial authorities. Understandable, clear, and timely data should be delivered to financial authorities. It is also important to provide data to financial authorities in all jurisdictions where the financial company is active.

*Concentration and systematic risk*: This risk arises if the overall industry has a significant exposure to certain outsource service providers. The individual firms' lack of control over the provider, and the systematic risk to the industry can be diversified by employing several outsource service providers, which have various features and business concentrations.

### *Risk Management Principles for Outsourcing*

The BIS' "Outsourcing in Financial Services" report documents the guiding principles for risk management. These principles can be summarized as follows (BIS 2005):

Principle 1—Outsourcing policy: Once a financial company decides to outsource a service, it should prepare comprehensive policies and evaluation criteria to guide the outsourcing process. The benefits and costs of outsourcing should be listed, and an acceptable level of risk should be determined. The financial company should ensure that it can oversee the activities of the outsourcing service provider. To do that, the financial company should prepare a governance structure that defines the roles and responsibilities of the outsource service provider. The engagement process and responsibilities of the outsourcing service provider should be clearly processed.

The financial company must ensure that outsourcing activities will not negatively affect the compliance with legal and regulatory requirements of the financial company both at home and in foreign countries. Outsourcing activities should be cancelled if they impair the financial authorities' right and ability to assess the business.

Principle 2—Risk management: The financial company should establish an outsourcing risk management program for the outsourcing activities. The risk management program should account for the operational, reputational, legal, and financial impact of a failure of the outsourcing service provider, the potential losses to customers and other counterparties in case of a failure by the outsourcing service provider; the costs of the agreement; the regulatory status of the outsourcing service provider; the time and effort required to alternate outsource service provider or to bring the activity in-house if necessary; and the complexity of the outsourcing agreement.

Principle 3—Regulatory obligations: The financial company should ensure that outsourcing arrangements do not hamper to fulfill its obligations to customers or regulators. It should also not impede effective supervision by regulators.

Principle 4—Due diligence: The financial company should conduct appropriate due diligence in selecting outsourcing service providers. The financial company must assess the quality of outsourced services effectively. To do that, the financial company should select qualified, high quality, and financially sound outsource service providers that can understand and meet the objectives of the financial company.

If the outsourcing service provider fails to perform the outsourced activity, it would be more costly to switch to a new provider than to bring the activity in-house and eliminate the negative publicity from the financial company.

Principle 5—Contracting: Outsourcing agreements should clearly describe all material aspects, such as rights, obligations, and expectations from all parties. The written agreement should include what activities will be outsourced and to what extent; the qualitative and quantitative statements of outsourcing service provider's requirements and responsibilities; the regulatory obligations born from the agreement; the accessibility of the financial company to outsource service provider's records, books, and other documents; the termination terms and provisions; the location of the service/production activities, choice of law, agreement and jurisdictional covenants. If necessary, it should also include the subcontracting conditions if the outsource service provider is to subcontract a third party and the transfer policy to switch to a new outsourcing service provider to an in-house provider.

Principle 6—Contingency plans: The financial company and the outsourcing service provider should maintain periodic testing of backup facilities; have contingency plans, and disaster recovery plans. Even though the financial company has global contingency plans, it should make separate contingency plans for each of its outsourcing service providers. The plan should include appropriate steps to assess the processes and address the potential consequences of possible business disruptions. Robust information is a necessity for financial activities, and the financial company must make sure that it has adequate IT capacity to perform operations. Possible financial, legal, and reputational costs should be determined.

Principle 7—Data protection: The financial company is responsible for data and identity protection of customers and related third parties. Data protection provisions should be added to outsourcing agreements. Misappropriation and misuse of customer data by the outsourcing service provider should be prevented.

Principle 8—Regulatory coverage: Outsourcing activities should be an integral part of the ongoing assessment of financial companies. Regulators should supervise and take appropriate measures if there is a problem in the performance or compliance of the outsourcing service provider.

Principle 9—Concentration risk: When a limited number of outsourcing service providers serve more than one company, concentration risks and the probability of systematic breakdowns increase. Financial regulators should understand the potential risks and take precautions such as continuous monitoring and awareness programs, risk assessments, and contingency planning to curb the risks.

## *Cyber Security*

### *Challenges of Cyber Security*

Cyber security protects users' assets from unauthorized access or attacks (Von Solms and van Niekerk 2013). Security risks can be in the form of digital attacks, which usually attempt to access and change sensitive information, extort money from users, and interrupt normal businesses activities (Cisco 2019). Because financial companies are internationally interconnected, a cyber risk to an institution threatens other institutions and financial systems. As a result, all cyber risks are relevant for all financial companies and financial regulatory bodies. To establish and achieve a successful risk management system against cyber risks, financial companies should work in collaboration with regulatory and supervisory bodies. Individual and collective strategic planning are necessary. Financial companies should tailor their strategy and frameworks based on nature, size, scope, risk profile, and culture. Standards on business continuity planning, outsourcing, and e-financing are relevant to cyber security risk management principles. Moreover, country governing bodies should collaborate with financial companies to establish sector-wide cyber security strategies that draw the line for collaborations among institutions (BIS 2018).

Cyberattacks are dynamic and evolve quickly, which makes risk assessment harder. More than 80 percent of confirmed breaches in the finance industry is originated from "web applications" according to a recent survey (Verizon 2016). This percentage was around 30 percent in 2013 (Kopp et al. 2017). This information is itself enough to estimate the magnitude of risk coming from digitalization.

Many countries do not have the architecture and standards for cyber-resilience, and/or there are gaps in the existing structures. Many cyber incidents are determined through audits. There is no definition of a cyber security workforce, but IT personnel are usually expected to serve in the cyber security workforce. Auditors, controllers within financial institutions, and regulators also serve as workforce while they conduct their routine business (BIS 2018).

Estimating the cost and likelihood of cyberattacks is difficult because cyber incidents are very new, and the transmission mechanism of incidents are not known by the experts. It is possible that risk management systems of financial companies will not be strong enough to cope with all attacks in the future. Additionally, social consequences might be worse than anticipated. Due to the strong interaction and connectivity among financial companies, cyber risk is important for the whole industry. Cyber risk can become part of the systemic risks if attacks cannot be inhibited in a short time. As a result, public cooperation of financial regulators may be needed in vast incidents (Kopp et al. 2017).

*Risk Management Principles for Cyber Security*

Many developed countries and large emerging economies have prepared their cyber security risk management programs as regulatory requirements in the finance sector (BIS 2018). There are supranational risk management programs, such as the "G7 Fundamental Elements of Cyber Security for the Financial Sector" issued by G7 (G7 2016), which defines cyber security risk management elements as follows:

Element 1—Governance: It is the board of directors'/senior management's responsibility to govern the risk management process in financial companies. The board of directors defines and facilitates duties of personnel, manages and measures performance and effectiveness of the strategy, provides adequate resources, and connects to governing authorities.

Element 2—Risk and control assessment: Companies should assess their prospective cyber risks and prioritize the important ones. When necessary, companies should connect to third parties (such as other financial parties and financial authorities). They should also set controls to protect against cyber risks, such as systems, controls, procedures, and training. Lastly, they should protect against detected cyber threats in the limits of the laws and regulations.

Element 3—Monitoring: Financial companies should systematically monitor to detect cyber risks and to evaluate the effectiveness of identified controls (such as audits, testing, exercises, and monitoring).

Element 4—Response: Companies should assess the nature, scope, and impact of a cyber-incident; minimize its impact; communicate with internal and external stakeholders; and organize joint response activities as needed.

Element 5—Recovery: Financial companies should resume their operations responsibly by allowing for continued remediation. Continued remediation includes eliminating harmful elements of the incident, restoring system and data conforming normal state, identifying and mitigating vulnerabilities, and communicating appropriately with internal and external stakeholders.

Element 6—Information sharing: Financial companies should timely share information with internal and external stakeholders about threats, vulnerabilities, incidents, and responses to enhance defense, limit damage, increase situational awareness, and broaden learning.

Element 7—Continuous learning: Financial companies should review cyber security framework and strategies regularly to follow up changes in cyber risks, re-allocate resources, identify gaps, and incorporate lessons learned from earlier incidents.

It is noteworthy to mention that only a limited number of countries have determined specific regulatory and supervisory initiatives against cyber security risks. These initiatives can be a valuable starting point to fight against cyber threats, but they do not cover all cyber security risks. Due to the constantly evolving nature of the cyber threats, the initiatives can be prescriptive and outdated very often. As a result, some regulatory agencies do not spend effort to prepare principles against cyber threats (BIS 2017).

## Conclusion

Many financial activities are effectuated through online transactions. Internet technologies are expanding in developing and developed countries (Gencer 2010; Pangaro 2018). While customers enjoy easy and fast domestic and international money transfers, online investment options, deposit and lending options, insurance, leasing, factoring, invoicing, and crowdfunding activities, the risk management challenges of financial companies increase.

Digitalization in finance does not affect core risk management principles and practices; however, it exacerbates mainly operational and reputational risks. Risk managers must enlarge the scope of their operational understanding and risk measures. Contagion risks further exacerbate these challenges.

The most important risks are related to e-financing/e-banking activities. Financial companies must adopt innovations in a short time frame, which is too fast to understand all the risks about the process. Digitalization means that the entire financial architecture is open and vulnerable to outside attacks. The risk management systems reduce the risk of fraud and human error, but they also make the financial company totally dependent on the computerized system. Furthermore, the complexity of operational and security issues makes the risk management more difficult. Sometimes, financial companies cannot undertake these burdens alone and they choose to collaborate with new technology companies. These collaborations may in turn extend the definition of existing risks on the financial companies. Finally, consumer privacy and identity-theft issues lead to an increase of management efforts in security controls, authentication, and authorization. The recommended risk management principles pave the way for financial companies to set up a well-functioning risk management effort against e-financing risks.

Another important new dimension of risk comes from the outsourcing activities of financial companies. Financial companies often need to collaborate with new technology companies, or FinTechs, to outsource high-tech services, which are far more costly if generated in-house. Unregulated and technologically savvy FinTechs provide innovative and user-friendly services; however, working with FinTechs poses additional challenges for finance companies. These risks range from strategic and operational risks to country and contractual risks. Mainly, financial companies must ensure that the outsourced operations comply with financial regulations, protect the privacy of customers, and provide high-quality service to customers. Risk management principles for outsourcing help financial companies plan for an effective risk management process.

Another emerging risk for financial companies is cyber security. Ranging from various service areas in finance, cyber-threats usually target consumer privacy, money extortions from customer accounts or in-transfers, and interruptions in normal business of finance companies. Risk management activities recommended for cyber-resilience mostly coincide with risk management activities for e-financing and outsourcing. As a result, many developed and developing countries have issued their regulatory requirements to combat cyber risks. The "G7 Fundamental Elements of Cyber Security for the Financial Sector" can help financial companies to prepare a risk management plan against cyber-threat risks.

Digital innovations mostly increase operational risks. Customer privacy, reputation, strategic consistency with the outsourcing service providers, compliance with regulations, and business continuity are among the new topics that risk managers must handle. A difficulty of the new technology is that neither risk managers, senior managers nor the board of directors in financial companies are technology experts. Risk management and control departments must now hire technology savvy IT graduates to address operational risks.

The business continuity management and risk management principles for the digital era suggest more flexibility in operations and a holistic risk management approach, which summon an "enterprise risk management" approach fed with "real options" to suggest flexible processes and capacity, diversification in suppliers, outsourcing of providers and distribution networks, and risk pooling of customers and investment assets for financial companies (Sheffi 2015). Enterprise risk management focuses on the risk management of a company first, and then run risk silo management tools to have an integrated view toward risks. Business continuity management guidelines incorporate real options and enterprise risk management, offering financial companies more space to move in case a disruption occurs in the operations. Overall, this is an exciting time for financial firms as real challenges await with immense opportunities and rewards for those who can deal with them.

## References

Alt, R., Beck, R., & Smiths, M. T. (2018). FinTech and the transformation of the financial industry. *Electronic Markets, 28*, 235–243.

Arner, D. W., Barberis, J., & Buckley, R. P. (2016). The evolution of FinTech: A new post-crisis paradigm? *Georgetown Journal of International Law, 47*(4), 371 413.

Arumugam, M., & Cusick, K. (2008). *General insurance 2020: Insurance for the individual* (Institute of Actuaries of Australia 16th General Insurance Seminar). Coolum Australia.

Barber, B. M., & Odean, T. (2001). The internet and the investor. *Journal of Economic Perspectives, 15*(1), 41–54.

Barber, B. M., & Odean, T. (2002). Online investors: Do the slow die first? *Review of Financial Studies, 15*(2), 455–487.

Bascand, G. (2014). Innovation and risk management – Insights from executive management at Statistics New Zealand and the Reserve Bank of New Zealand. Retrieved from https://www.bis.org/review/r140711b.htm.

Baur, D. G., Cahill, D., Godfrey, K., & Liu, Z. (2017). *Bitcoin time-of-day, day-of-week, and month-of-year effects in returns and trading volume.* (SSRN Working Paper).

Beck, H. (2001). Banking is essential, banks are not: The future of financial intermediation in the age of the internet. *Netnomics, 3*(1), 7–22.

BIS-Bank for International Settlements. (2003a). *Management and supervision of cross-border electronic banking activities.* (Basel Committee on Banking Supervision).

BIS-Bank for International Settlements. (2003b). *Risk management principles for electronic banking.* (Basel Committee on Banking Supervision).

BIS-Bank for International Settlements. (2005). *Outsourcing in financial services.* The Joint Forum: Basel Committee on Banking Supervision.

BIS-Bank for International Settlements. (2006). *High level principles for business continuity.* (Basel Committee on Banking Supervision, The Joint Forum).

BIS-Bank for International Settlements. (2018). *Cyber-resilience: Range of practices.* (Basel Committee on Banking Supervision).

Bouri, E., Molnar, P., Azzi, G., Roubaud, D., & Hagfors, L. I. (2017). On the hedge and safe haven properties of bitcoin: Is it really more than a diversifier? *Finance Research Letters, 20*, 192–198.

Bradford, T., & Keeton, W. R. (2012). New person-to-person payment methods: Have checks met their match? Agricultural and business conditions, tenth federal reserve district. *Economic Review – Federal Reserve Bank of Kansas City*, 41–77.

Brandl, B., & Hornuf, L. (2017). *Where did FinTechs come from, and where do they go? The transformation of the financial industry in Germany after digitalization* (SSRN Working Paper).

Brennen, J. S., & Kreiss, D. (2016). Digitalization. In K. B. Jensen, E. W. Rothenbuhler, J. D. Pooley, & R. T. Craig (Eds.), *The international encyclopedia of communication theory and philosophy*. Wiley Blackwell-ICA International Encyclopedias of Communication.

Christoffersen, P. F. (2012). *Elements of financial risk management* (2nd ed.). Academic Press. MA, Elsevier Inc.

Cisco. (2019). *What is cyber security?* Retrieved June 15, 2019, from https://www.cisco.com/c/en/us/products/security/what-is-cybersecurity.html.

Contini, D., Crowe, M., Meritt, C., & Richard, O. (2011). *Mobile payments in the United States: Mapping out the road ahead* (Boston FED Report).

Deloitte. (2017). The future of risk in financial services. Retrieved from https://www2.deloitte.com/global/en/pages/financial-services/articles/gx-future-risk-in-financial-services.html.

DFS-Digital Financial Services. (2016). *Basic Terminology* (Guideline Note, No: 9). Retrieved from https://www.afi-global.org/sites/default/files/publications/2016-08/Guideline%20Note-19%20DFS-Terminology.pdf.

Doering, P., Neumann, S., & Paul, S. (2015). *A primer on social trading networks-Institutional aspects and empirical evidence* (SSRN Working paper).

Ebringer, T., Thorne, P., & Zheng, Y. (2000). Parasitic authentication to protect your e-wallet. *Computer, 33*(10), 54–60.

ECB – European Central Bank. (2012). *Virtual currency schemes*. Frankfurt.

Ely, B. (n.d.) *Financial regulation*. Library of Economics and Liberty. Retrieved from https://www.econlib.org/library/Enc/FinancialRegulation.html.

FATF-Financial Action Task Force. (2014). *Virtual currencies key definitions and potential AML/CFT risks* (FATF Report).

Finextra. (2015). *Half of the world's banks set to fall by the digital wayside-BBVA*. Retrieved from https://www.finextra.com/news/fullstory.aspx?newsitemid=26965.

Franke, R. H. (1987). Technological revolution and productivity decline: Computer introduction in the financial industry. *Technological Forecasting and Social Change, 31*(2), 143–154.

Freixas, X., & Rochet, J. C. (2008). *Microeconomics of banking*. London: MIT Press.

G7. (2016). *G-7 Fundamental elements for effective assessment of cybersecurity in the financial sector*. G7/8 Finance Meetings, Washington, DC.

Gangwal, S. (2016). Analyzing the effects of adding bitcoin to portfolio. *International Journal of Economics and Management Engineering, 10*(10), 3519–3532.

Gencer, M. (2010). The mobile money movement: Catalyst to jump-start emerging markets. *Innovations, 6*(1), 101–117.

Gimpel, H., Rau, D., & Rollinger, M. (2018). Understanding FinTech start-ups-A taxonomy of consumer- oriented service offerings. *Electronic Markets, 28*, 245–264.

Gomber, P., Koch, J. A., & Siering, M. (2017). Digital finance and FinTech: Current research and future research directions. *Journal of Business Economics, 87*, 537–580.

Hull, J. (2015). *Risk management and financial institutions* (4th ed.). Chichester, UK: John Wiley & Sons.

Kloehn, L., & Hornuf, L. (2012). Crowdinvesting in Deutschland: Markt, Rechtslage und Regulierungsperspektiven. *Zeitschrift fuer Bankrecht und Bankwirtschaft, 24*(4), 237–320.

Kopp, E., Kaffenberger, L., & Wilson, C. (2017). *Cyber risk, market failures and financial stability.* IMF Working Paper, WP/17/185.

Mead, W. (2016). Banking and the E-Book moment. In S. Chishti & J. Barberis (Eds.), *The fintech book : The financial technology handbook for investors, entrepreneurs and visionaries.* Chichester: Wiley & Sons.

Menat, R. (2016). Why we are so excited about FinTech. In S. Chishti & J. Barberis (Eds.), *The fintech book : The financial technology handbook for investors, entrepreneurs and visionaries.* Chichester: Wiley & Sons.

Mensi, W., Lee, Y. J., Al-Yahyaee, K. H., Sensoy, A., & Yoone, S. M. (2019). Intraday downward/upward multifractality and long memory in bitcoin and ethereum markets: An asymmetric multifractal detrended fluctuation analysis. *Finance Research Letters, 31*, 19–25.

Merritt, C. (2010). *Mobile money transfer services: The next phase in the evolution in person-to-person payments* (Federal Reserve Bank of Atlanta, Retail Payments Risk Forum White Paper).

Merton, R. C. (1992). Financial innovation and economic performance. *Journal of Applied Corporate Finance, 4*(4), 12–22.

Millo, Y., Muniesa, F., Panourgias, N. S., & Scott, S. V. (2005). Organized detachment: Clearinghouse mechanisms in financial markets. *Information and Organization, 15*(3), 229–246.

Mishkin, F. (1992). *Anatomy of a financial crisis. Journal of Evolutionary Economics, 2*(2), 115–130.

Moenninghoff, S. C., & Wieandt, A. (2013). The Future of peer-to-peer finance. *Schmalenbachs Zeitschrift fuer Betriebswirtschaftliche Forschung, 65*(5), 466–487.

Mollick, E. (2014). The dynamics of crowdfunding: An exploratory study. *Journal of Business Venturing, 29*, 1–16.

Nakamoto, S. (2008). *Bitcoin: A peer-to-peer electronic cash system* (Bitcoin Working Paper).

Nienaber, R. (2016). Banks need to think collaboration rather than competition. In S. Chishti & J. Barberis (Eds.), *The fintech book : The financial technology handbook for investors, entrepreneurs and visionaries.* Chichester: Wiley & Sons.

Pangaro, G. (2018). *Emerging markets: The growing importance of digitalization to emerging market investors.* Baltimore, MD: T. Rowe Price Group Inc.

Proviti and North Carolina State University's ERM Initiative Survey. (2017). *Executive perspectives on top risks for 2018: Key issues being discussed in the boardroom and C-Suite.*

Scott, S. V., Van Reenen, J., & Zachariadis, M. (2017). The long-term effect of digital innovation on bank performance: An empirical study of SWIFT adoption in financial services. *Research Policy, 46*, 984–1004.

Sheffi, Y. (2015). *The power of resilience: How the best companies Manage the unexpected.* Cambridge, MA: MIT Press.

Tursoy, T. (2018). *Risk management process in banking industry* (MPRA Paper, No: 86427).

Van der Kleij, E. (2016). Tech Giants becoming non-bank banks. In S. Chishti & J. Barberis (Eds.), *The fintech book : The financial technology handbook for investors, entrepreneurs and visionaries.* Chichester: Wiley & Sons.

Van Greuning, H., & Bratanovic, S. B. (2000). *Analyzing bank risk: A framework for assessing corporate governance and financial risk management* (World Bank Report, No. 48238), Washington, DC.

Verizon. (2016). *Data breach investigations report 2016.* Retrieved from http://www.verizonenterprise.com/resources/reports/rp_DBIR_2016_Report_en_xg.pdf.

Von Solms, R., & van Niekerk, J. (2013). From information security to cyber security. *Computers&Security, 38*, 97–102.

WEF-World Economic Forum. (2018). *The global risk report 2018* (Insight Report), Geneva, Switzerland.

WEF-World Economic Forum. (n.d.). Understanding the impact of digitalization on society. Retrieved from http://reports.weforum.org/digital-transformation/understanding-the-impact-of-digitalization-on-society/.

CHAPTER 18

# Emerging Risks: Concluding Remarks

*Dieter Gramlich and Thomas Walker*

## Relevance of Emerging Risks

The contributions in this book provide evidence of the intensity and variety of changes in our ecological, societal, and technological environment and their implications for the financial sector. In addition to highlighting the potential opportunities and threats emerging risks bear for financial institutions and markets, the chapters outline the role the financial system can play in positively affecting its environment. They point to the reciprocal dependency of the different systems and the need to consider these interactions. In doing so, emerging risks appear to matter more than ever.

Emerging risks require urgent attention for two main reasons. Firstly, they already affect the financial sector and therefore require immediate action. The contributions of Q. Rayer, P. Pfleiderer, and K. Haustein as

D. Gramlich
Department of Banking, Baden-Wuerttemberg Cooperative State University, Heidenheim, Germany
e-mail: dieter.gramlich@dhbw-heidenheim.de

T. Walker (✉)
Department of Finance, John Molson School of Business, Concordia University, Montreal, Canada
e-mail: thomas.walker@concordia.ca



T. Walker et al. (eds.), *Ecological, Societal, and Technological Risks and the Financial Sector*, Palgrave Studies in Sustainable Business In Association with Future Earth, https://doi.org/10.1007/978-3-030-38858-4_18

well as M. H. B. Adzmi, H. Cai, and M. Suzuki in this volume refer to the damages natural disasters have imposed up to now and their effects on the financial assets, while M. Horn, A. Oehler, and S. Wendt as well as S. Burcu Avci address potential exposures from the implementation of new technologies in finance. These topics, in combination with recent events, show the growing relevance of emerging risks. A good example would be the hurricane season of 2019 and the devastation left behind by Dorian, which points to an increasing extremity in meteorological events.[1] Another one would be the massive cyberattack against Capital One, one of the largest credit card issuers in North America, in which hackers stole the personal information of approximately 100 million North Americans and posted it on the Internet. This event stands out due to its impact size and shows our extreme vulnerability to cyber risks (Lindsey 2019).

Secondly, as emerging risks are expected to evolve further, actions to mitigate their future effects must be taken now, or they would come too late. The need to act today is particularly sustained in the contribution from Skandier with her suggestion to establish a new green bank to provide the means for reducing the carbon bubble. The urgency of acting today is further felt as tipping points, defined as the levels of risk that, once exceeded, can make the system collapse with potentially unhealable consequences (Lenton et al. 2008), are closing in. The collapse of the housing market in the US during the subprime crisis can be considered as an example of a tipping point in the economy (Alexander 2019). Prices in the real estate market reached an exaggerated and ultimate level ("the subprime bubble"), after which a sudden and extreme correction happened. The decrease in housing prices in the US with subsequent high losses on financial assets worldwide was further fueled by the opaqueness of the market for subprime bonds and the tendency of the financial markets to overreact and panic.

As far as tipping points in our ecological system are concerned (Lenton et al. 2008), the potential breakdown of the Gulf Stream serves as a good example. Increasing greenhouse gas emissions, rising temperatures, and melting glaciers with subsequent effects on the temperature of our ocean waters, the accumulation of freshwater, and the concentration of salt can halt the driving forces of the circulation (Liu et al. 2017). In case the Gulf

[1] Hurricane Dorian particularly hit the Bahamas and is considered to be the most damaging cyclone the country has ever experienced, with winds reaching speeds of 320 km/hour (Caspani 2019).

Stream were to stop, it would be impossible to reactivate it and would have severe consequences for our climate, agriculture, and living conditions.

The potential impacts from emerging risks are exacerbated by the fact that they affect an economic and financial system that is already in transition. Limits to growth, trade conflicts, increased public debt, and the reduced effectiveness of the central banks' monetary policies make the economic system less robust and more vulnerable. The financial sector is going through a process of fundamental regulatory and technological transformation while still being affected by the consequences of the subprime and debt crises as well as by the challenges of a low interest rate policy in most countries around the world. Analyses of emerging risks in finance thus have to consider the fragilities of the financial system—as opposed to a fragile overall system—and the interactions between these fragilities. Looking at these vulnerabilities in connection with emerging risks is also referred to as a case of "double exposure" (Leichenko et al. 2010, p. 117).

The need to comply with and react to new developments in our ecological, societal, and technological environment can—and to a large extent should—be viewed from a risk management perspective. Alternatively, opportunities may arise from investments into sectors benefiting from eco-social changes and the creation of new risk management tools (Read 2016). For example, financial institutions may direct their investments to renewable energy, energy trading, emissions trading, recycling technology, and social investing. In turn, new risk management tools offered to investors and firms can serve as insurance against extreme weather damages and cyber risks. A prerequisite for this business to flourish and offer a wide-ranging set of hedging and insurance instruments is the development of expertise in the area of emerging risks. The adjustment of rating systems to a changing climate, as presented by J. Leaton in this book, the modeling of man-made disaster scenarios by M. Windirsch, and the discussion of hurricane risk landfall options (HuRLOs) by M. Boyer, M. Breton, and P. François developed in this volume point into this direction.

In addition to purely economic aspects, researchers ask about the extent to which the financial sector contributes to overall welfare and balance in society (Lietaer et al. 2012; Kirschenmann et al. 2016). Indeed, social inequalities are often attributed to the financial market as a result of business transactions, and emerging risks focus on anticipating and mitigating risks that affect society at large. Income inequality, the concentration in the distribution of wealth, the destructive power of large portfolio investments, and unsustainable practices in the long-term management of pension funds contribute to concerns about the usefulness of the financial system for society as a whole. As a result, there is an increased probability that political and regulatory authorities will intervene and control the financial markets due to their possibly detrimental implications for our society (transition risk).

Different groups of stakeholders put increasing pressure on financial institutions. Depositors in financial institutions demand compliance with their personal investment principles, and institutions must comply with responsibility principles to maintain positive relationships with their customers on the lending side. Employees are concerned about the effects of business strategies on the ecological and societal environment and critically question the strategies pursued by management. Particularly, younger employees who grew up in a more sensitive and critical environment are attuned to the sustainable dimension of their financial institution's strategies. Yet, for the financial institutions, it is very important to keep their younger workforce with up-to-date skills as part of their human resources.

## Characteristics of Emerging Risks

The characteristics of emerging risks are key to model and manage the risks (see Fig. 18.1). Ecological, societal, and technological challenges arise from outside the financial and economic spheres. Up to now, they have been barely considered and have scarcely influenced financial

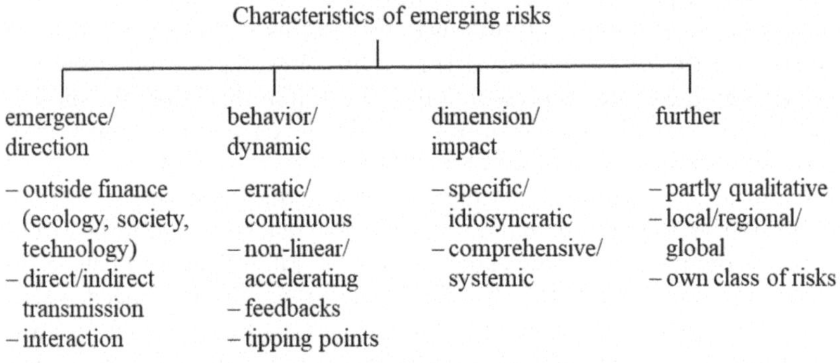


**Fig. 18.1** Characteristics of emerging risks

decision making. Particularly, because only few emerging risks directly affect the financial sector, the decision makers usually tend to ignore them in the pricing of financial assets. However, as ecological and societal challenges are expected to become more pressing in the future, and as it becomes evident that the allocation of capital plays a crucial role in both the buildup and mitigation of emerging risks, it will be crucial to fully include the changes in the external ecological, societal, and technological systems into financial decision making.

Most of the current work on upcoming challenges for the financial system pertains to climate risk and its main driver, the emissions of greenhouse gas (ECB 2019). Climate risk is a major part of emerging risks as it includes a broad range of severe short-term and long-term effects. These include individual factors such as the effects of extreme weather and extreme violence, and those from continuous trends such as the gradual rise in temperatures and the increase of cyber risks.

In addition to its direct effects, climate change has an influence on other emerging risk dimensions and relates reciprocally to them: as shown by the contribution of B. Condon and T. Sinha to this book, rising temperatures and droughts negatively affect agriculture and reduce the income of farmers who then decide to migrate. Moreover, migration can lead to increased urbanization and related social constraints as well as to the unavailability of resources in migration areas such as land and water. Urban concentration has a further impact on urban microclimates and feeds back on the climate in general. The widespread impacts of climate change may justify concentrating actions on climate change-related problems. However, if policies and regulations focus on climate risks in isolation, there is a chance that other emerging risks as well as their interconnectivity with climate change are overlooked.

When the interactions between emerging risks are not considered, the respective policies may even conflict with each other. For example, imposing the need to insulate houses and use renewable energy as part of a climate policy may increase the cost of living and fuel social inequalities as the poor would be more affected than the rich. C. Cucuzzella and J. Owen refer in this book to an inverting effect of a recent housing policy in Montreal: the need to incorporate requirements mandated by a socially oriented policy in house construction made the real estate business less attractive and decreased the supply of living spaces.

Research in this topic should also consider that the financial system is not homogeneous and static. Rather, it is composed of different types of institutions with different patterns of susceptibility to changes in the ecology, society, and technology. Usually, emerging risks such as hurricanes, flooding, migration, or violence do not directly affect banks and investment funds. Rather, companies, households, and governments are exposed to these risks and because the customers of banks or investment funds hold their assets, the financial institutions are affected indirectly via the claims of these customers (Battiston et al. 2017). Their portfolios are mainly exposed to the shrinking creditworthiness of companies and sovereigns due to lacking sustainability considerations. In cases where the infrastructure of banks and investment funds, particularly the IT system, are directly damaged by disasters, these institutions also suffer from higher operational risks. Similarly, higher temperatures and extreme weather conditions can affect the healthiness and productivity of employees.

Furthermore, insurance companies—as another major player in the financial markets—are susceptible to an increase in natural and man-made disasters (Hagendorff et al. 2015). Insurance companies, notably property and casualty insurers, offer protection against natural and technological hazards and are thus directly exposed to emerging risks. In addition, the interconnected relationships between financial institutions, for example via reciprocal stake holdings, leads to a further complexity in the relationship pattern.

Emerging risks are difficult to manage as they display a dynamic and changing behavior over time. As has been mentioned, emerging risks may be associated with erratic and short-term volatile behavior on one hand, and long-term trends on the other hand (ECB 2019). Q. Rayer, P. Pfleiderer, and K. Haustein indicate in this book that the intensity of single events is increasing. The problem with this more extreme behavior as well as gradually ascending trends is that they may exceed a critical threshold at which point the system collapses with almost irreparable consequences (Gramlich and Oet 2018). The impacts of emerging risks are both accelerating and self-feeding: as mentioned by Q. Rayer, P. Pfleiderer, and K. Haustein as well as B. Condon and T. Sinha, rising temperatures and the associated melting of glaciers and the defrosting of the Canadian and Russian tundra releases carbon dioxide and methane, which add to the existing greenhouse gas emissions and result in an accelerated momentum.

Because of the multifold and partially indirect association between emerging risks and the financial sector, the structure and dynamic of transmission processes are difficult to assess. Emerging risks may affect the system via their material effects on infrastructure and well-being (physical risks), via administrative measures taken by governments and regulators to mitigate them (transition risks), or manifest as a changed perceptions and valuations by individuals toward products and companies (behavioral risk). Particularly, as the analysis by R. Bopp in this book shows, if financial institutions display a gap between their pretended and realized behavior toward sustainability, they are exposed to a reputational risk and may jeopardize their license to operate. In order to model and manage the opportunities and threats from emerging risks, these characteristics must be respected accordingly.

## Approaches to Modeling and Management

Approaches to modeling and managing the opportunities and threats from emerging risks are grounded on a new, appropriate framework. Particularly, the framework addresses the objectives and elements to be considered (Lagoarde-Segot and Paranque 2018). In it, non-financial targets complement financial targets, and factors emanating from the outer financial system, that is, ecological, societal, and technological factors, add to purely financial elements. The principle of "thinking sustainability first" (HLEG 2018, p. 61) constitutes a new paradigm for the financial markets and should become a standard for "business-as-usual" (GoC 2019, p. IV). In their contribution to this book, S. Kibsey, S. D. Kibsey, A. Addas, and C. Krosinsky set the stage for the changing instruments in management: new information tools include a taxonomy for sustainable policies and products while management tools comprise forward-looking scenarios, a recognition by managers of their fiduciary duty, and knowledgeable middlepersons to act upon and make enlightened decisions (see Fig. 18.2).

It is generally stated and concluded by several contributions to this book that—although the need to incorporate emerging risks into the modeling and management of financial institutions is highly acknowledged—research in this area is still developing (NGFS 2018, p. 3). Overall, the specific inclusion of the financial sector in the comprehensive relationship between ecology, society, and technology has only recently attracted attention (Rezende de Carvalho Ferreia et al. 2016, p. 113). Parallel to the development of research on emerging risks in finance in academia and in practice, governmental authorities have started initiatives to promote sustainable finance. Their efforts to build a stable financial system foster the transformation of the macroeconomy into a sustainable economy, that is, an economy that is balanced in terms of the current outcomes from

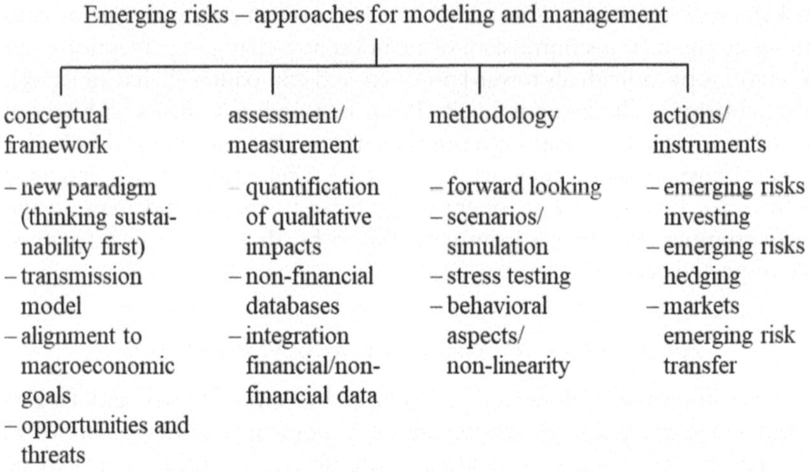


**Fig. 18.2** Emerging risks—approaches for modeling and management

economic activity and their future consequences for ecology and society (Gramlich 2014).

Governments and central banks around the world have recognized that climate change is one of the most urgent emerging risks (Batten et al. 2018; ECB 2019). In order to address this challenge, the political and monetary authorities have established different expert groups and working agendas (Alexander 2019). They define priorities for the assessment and handling of both opportunities and threats from emerging risks.

The European Union (EU) has launched the High-Level Expert Group on Sustainable Finance (HLEG), which aims to direct the financial sector toward supporting a sustainable economy (HLEG 2018). They have developed a set of recommendations to direct the financial sector toward supporting a sustainable economy. The working program includes a classification and labelling for green finance products, that is, products that comply with sustainable finance goals (HLEG 2018). Similarly, the Global Alliance for Banking on Values (GABV) is developing metrics for the quantification of sustainability factors (GABV 2017).

The G20 countries have established a study group to explore the relevance of environmental factors for green finance and the risk-return management in finance (NGFS 2018). The Network for Greening the Financial System (NGFS), which is composed of 16 central banks and supervisory authorities worldwide, has recently expressed the mandate of central banks to incorporate climate change into monetary policy and announced a related working agenda for 2019 (NGFS 2018, p. 10).

The Bank of England (BoE) is the first central bank to publish work on the consequences of climate change for monetary policy (Batten et al. 2018; Scott et al. 2017). The contribution by S. Batten, R. Sowerbutts, and M. Tanaka to this book highlights that rising food prices and macroeconomic downturns from climate change may affect inflation and money supply. In its recent *Financial Stability Review*, the European Central Bank (ECB 2019) noted that it will strengthen its activities to better assess the impact of climate change on the financial system. A major goal is to get evidence of the transmission structure and the ways factors affect financial institutions. In 2018, the government of Canada appointed the Expert Panel on Sustainable Finance (GoC 2019). The mission of the panel is to develop standards for the Canadian financial system to secure a sustainable economic future, particularly by linking funds to climate objectives.

Research centers at universities have been established to foster the idea of sustainable finance. The Centre for Sustainable Finance within the Cambridge Institute for Sustainable Leadership (CISL) has published reports about the fact that the regulatory banking framework Basel III ignores risks stemming from environmental challenges (CISL 2014) and about the inclusion of environmental factors into the risk management of financial institutions (CISL 2016). Similarly, the University of Oxford's Sustainable Finance Programme focuses on environment-related risks and opportunities in finance. Moreover, the University Alliance, founded in 2017, targets international cooperation in the field of sustainable finance.

Although various institutions and initiatives have established different priorities to protect themselves against the threats of emerging risks and to benefit from their opportunities, the principles defined for modeling and management are similar. Among others, these include:

- Approaches should be based on adequate data that allow for a quantification of the interactions between emerging risks and finance and to develop projections for future scenarios. Databases that offer the required data already and include, for example, the information provided by the Intergovernmental Panel on Climate Change (IPCC) or the World Resources Institute. Alternatively, specific databases are to be developed as, for example, the Canadian Centre for Climate Information and Analytics (GoC 2019).

- Models and practices should take on a forward-looking perspective and incorporate uncertainty rather than past experiences in future decision-making processes (Gillingham et al. 2015; ECB 2019). For instance, scenarios should include the financial system's future susceptibility to changing conditions in the environment (Ramirez et al. 2017), particularly to increasing temperatures, extreme weather events, and water scarcity.
- Non-linear modeling techniques such as simulations, stress tests, and feedback analyses need to be further developed and employed. When properly applied, they will provide a range of possible outcomes for the future rather than univariate results (Gramlich 2018; NGFS 2018). At the same time, they must comply with the need of being reproducible (Gan and Valdez 2018).
- Analyses should consider behavioral aspects: financial markets do not always act rationally. Rather, they tend to exaggerate both and overreact to positive and negative news with abrupt and intensive adjustments (CISL 2015). Agent-based modeling approaches (Thober et al. 2018) may help explain the behavioral characteristics of interactions and the effects of emerging risks.
- Knowledge and skills for the people involved in sustainable finance and emerging risks have to be developed and sharpened. This includes the education of present and future employees (today's students).
- With a special focus on banks, regulators and supervisors must incorporate ecological risks when assessing banks' capital requirements (Alexander 2019).

## The Next Steps

Emerging risks comprise more than the risks associated with climate change. In addition to climate risks and ecological challenges such as the scarcity of resources, they incorporate developments in society and technology with the potential to disrupt the financial system on one hand and providing new business opportunities on the other. However, as there are no known patterns from the past that provide any insights into how to deal with these challenges and as there is urgency to do this quickly, substantial efforts are needed to address these developments.

The number of research projects that focus on sustainable finance has considerably increased recently and addresses various aspects of green investments and green finance as well as regulatory and central bank challenges from an environmental and social perspective. At this time, relevant approaches are still at an early stage and necessitate further development. Whereas the current focus is on climate finance and green finance, additional work is needed to explore the nexus of sustainability and finance from an integrated risk-return perspective. The main directions suggested here are:

- The development of a basic conceptual framework, as it is currently missing, that is, an architectural concept of the functional relationships and transmission patterns within the ecology-society-economy-finance nexus.
- A quantification of ecological, social, and technological aspects which will serve as a basis for the assessment and management of emerging risks.
- Researchers and policymakers must further investigate the sensitivity of financial institutions, sectors, and regions with respect to socio-ecological changes and business models. With respect to the possible interactions between climate factors and financial performance, potential approaches have to account for indirect effects on one hand, that is, the effects from climate change on the real economy (production, consumption) and from there on the portfolio of financial institutions and, on the other hand, for the direct effect climate change has on operational risks (NGFS 2018, p. 5; Schoenmaker and van Tilburg 2016, p. 331).
- Analyses must account for the dynamics inherent in emerging risks, such as the changing and non-linear connectivity between financial assets, institutions, and markets. Whereas current dependencies between financial parameters—measured via stock prices, default rates, and risk premiums—are mainly driven by purely economic factors such as competition, interest rates, and costs, the new linkages are further explained by the vulnerability of the system to emerging risks.
- Emerging risks have a systemic dimension. In addition to the effects on single institutions, analyses must consider the effects of common exposures on the stability of the financial system as a whole.
- There is a need for appropriate methodological and alternative data-based approaches which entail a forward-looking, mid- and long-

term perspective capturing the effects from upcoming changes in ecology and society on the financial system as well as potential non-linear feedbacks.
- Finally, appropriate databases should be developed.

We hope that this book inspires further discourse among academics, practitioners, and regulators, and that it provides food for thought on many pressing issues that stand to affect our financial system and society as a whole.

## References


Alexander, K. (2019). *Principles of bank regulation*. Cambridge: Cambridge University Press.

Batten, S., Sowerbutts, R., & Tanaka, M. (2018). Climate change: What implications for central banks and financial regulators? In B. Caldecott (Ed.), *Stranded assets and the environment* (pp. 250–281). Abingdon.

Battiston, S., Mandel, A., Monasterolo, I., Schütze, F., & Visentin, G. (2017). A climate stress-test of the financial system. *Nature Climate Change, 7*(4), 283–288.

Caspani, M. (2019, September 10). Dorian's death toll in Bahamas rises to 50: Official. *Reuters*. Retrieved from https://www.reuters.com/article/us-storm-dorian/dorians-death-toll-in-bahamas-rises-to-50-official-idUSKCN1VV2A1.

CISL – Cambridge Institute for Sustainability Leadership. (2014). *Stability and sustainability in banking reform: Are environmental risks missing in Basel III?* Cambridge.

CISL – Cambridge Institute for Sustainability Leadership. (2015). *Unhedgeable risk: How climate change sentiment impacts investment*. Cambridge.

CISL – Cambridge Institute for Sustainability Leadership. (2016). *Environmental risk analysis by financial institutions – A review of global practice*. Cambridge.

ECB – European Central Bank. (2019). Special features – Climate change and financial stability. In: Financial Stability Review, May, 120–133.

GABV – Global Alliance for Banking on Values. (2017). Real economy – real returns: The business case for values based banking, Zeist.

Gan, G., & Valdez, E. A. (2018). Nested stochastic valuation of large variable annuity portfolios: Monte Carlo simulation and synthetic datasets. *Data, 3*(3), 1–21.

Gillingham, K., Nordhaus, W., Anthoff, D., Blanford, G., Bosetti, V., Christensen, P., McJeon, H., Reilly, J., & Sztorc, P. (2015). *Modeling uncertainty in climate change: A multi-model comparison*. Cowles Foundation Discussion Paper, No. 2022, New Haven, CT.

GoC – Government of Canada. (2019). Final report of the expert panel on sustainable finance, Gatineau.
Gramlich, D. (2014). Sustainability, financial markets and systemic risk. In J. Hawley, A. Hoepner, K. Johnson, J. Sandberg, & E. Waitzer (Eds.), *Handbook of institutional investment and fiduciary duty* (pp. 222–238). Cambridge University Press.
Gramlich, D. (2018). Sustainability stress testing the financial system. In T. Walker, S. D. Kibsey, & R. Crichton (Eds.), *Designing a sustainable financial system: Development goals and socio-ecological responsibility* (pp. 173–197). Palgrave Macmillan.
Gramlich, D., & Oet, M. (2018). Systemic financial feedbacks – Conceptual framework and modelling implications. *Systems Research and Behavioral Science, 35*(1), 22–38.
Hagendorff, B., Hagendorff, J., & Keasey, K. (2015). The impact of mega-catastrophes on insurers: An exposure-based analysis of the U.S. homeowners' insurance market. *Risk Analysis: An Official Publication of the Society for Risk Analysis, 35*(1), 157–173.
HLEG – EU High-Level Expert Group on Sustainable Finance. (2018). Financing a sustainable European economy: Final Report 2018 by the High-Level Expert Group on Sustainable Finance – Secretariat provided by the European Commission.
Kirschenmann, K., Malinen, T., & Nyberg, H. (2016). The risk of financial crises: Is there a role for income inequality? *Journal of International Money and Finance, 68*, 161–180.
Lagoarde-Segot, T., & Paranque, B. (2018). Finance and sustainability: From ideology to utopia. *International Review of Financial Analysis, 55*, 80–92.
Leichenko, R. M., O'Brien, K. L., & Solecki, W. D. (2010). Climate change and the global financial crisis: A case of double exposure. *Annals of the Association of American Geographers, 100*(4), 963–972.
Lenton, T. M., Held, H., Kriegler, E., Hall, J. W., Lucht, W., Rahmstorf, S., & Schellnhuber, H. J. (2008). Tipping elements in the Earth's climate system. *PNAS, 105*(6), 1786–1793.
Lietaer, B., Arnsperger, C., Goerner, S., Brunnhuber, S. (2012). Money and sustainability: The missing link. *A report from the Club of Rome (EU Chapter) to Finance Watch and the World Business Academy.* Triarchy Press.
Lindsey, N. (2019, August 15). What happens next after the massive Capital One data breach. *CPO Magazine*. Retrieved from https://www.cpomagazine.com/cyber-security/what-happens-next-after-the-massive-capital-one-data-breach/.
Liu, W., Xie, S.-P., Liu, Z., & Zhu, J. (2017). Overlooked possibility of a collapsed Atlantic meridional overturning circulation in warming climate. *Science Advances, 3*(1), 1–7.

NGFS – Central Banks and Supervisors Network for Greening the Financial System. (2018). NGFS First Progress Report, Paris.

Ramirez, L., Thomä, J., Brunke, J., Röttmer, N., Duran, M., Weber, C., Dupré, S., Granzow, M., & Fulton, M. (2017). The transition Risk-O-Meter. Reference scenarios for financial analysis, Paris.

Read, C. (2016). Environmental challenges and financial market opportunities. In G. N. Gregoriou & V. Ramiah (Eds.), *Handbook of environmental and sustainable finance* (pp. 293–305). Amsterdam: Academic Press.

Rezende de Carvalho Ferreia, M. C., Sobreiro, A. V., Kimura, H., & Luiz de Moraes Barboza, F. (2016). A systematic review of the literature about finance and sustainability. *Journal of Sustainable Finance & Investment, 6*(2), 112–147.

Schoenmaker, D., & van Tilburg, R. (2016). What role for financial supervisors in addressing environmental risks? *Comparative Economic Studies, 58*(3), 317–334.

Scott, M., van Huizen, J., & Jung, C. (2017). The Bank of England's response to climate change. *Bank of England Quarterly Bulletin, 2017*(Q2), 98–109.

Thober, J., Schwarz, N., & Hermans, K. (2018). Agent-based modeling of environment-migration linkages: A review. *Ecology and Society 23*(2): Art. No. 41. https://doi.org/10.5751/ES-10200-230241.

# Index[1]



[1] Note: Page numbers followed by 'n' refer to notes.



T. Walker et al. (eds.), *Ecological, Societal, and Technological Risks and the Financial Sector*, Palgrave Studies in Sustainable Business In Association with Future Earth, https://doi.org/10.1007/978-3-030-38858-4

The manufacturer's authorised representative in the EU is Springer Nature Customer Service Centre GmbH, Europaplatz 3, 69115 Heidelberg, Germany. If you have any concerns regarding our products, please contact ProductSafety@springernature.com

Printed and bound by CPI Group (UK) Ltd, Croydon, CR0 4YY
30/09/2026
02225644-0015